Comedia Series • No – 26

TEACHING THE MEDIA

By Len Masterman

Comedia Publishing Group
9 Poland Street, London W1V 3DG   Tel: 01-439 2059

Comedia Publishing Group was set up to investigate and monitor the media in Britain and abroad. The aim of the project is to provide basic information, investigate problem areas, and to share the experiences of those working in the field, while encouraging debate about the future development of the media. The opinions expressed in the books in the Comedia series are those of the authors, and do not necessarily reflect the views of Comedia. For a list of other Comedia titles see page 342.

First published in 1985 by Comedia Publishing Group
9 Poland Street, London W1 3DG.

© In all editorial matter Comedia Publishing Group and the editors
© In all contributions copyright the author

ISBN 0906 890 527 Paperback
ISBN 0906 890 535 Hardback

Cover Design by Nigel Cook

Typeset by Photosetting, 6 Foundry House, Stars Lane, Yeovil, Somerset BA20 1NL. Tel: Yeovil (0935) 23684

Printed in Great Britain by Unwin Brothers Ltd., The Gresham Press, Old Woking, Surrey

Trade Distribution by Comedia

To the memories of
Tim ('Tad') Masterman
and John Daniels

Acknowledgements

This book has grown out of literally hundreds of discussions, dialogues and conversations which I have enjoyed in the recent past with friends, students and colleagues throughout Britain and abroad. Since there is scarcely an idea in the book which is not in some senses collaborative, it is important to begin with an acknowledgement to media educators everywhere, a great many of whom are working indefatigably and often at great personal sacrifice, to establish this important area of the curriculum. If this book has any strengths, they are reflections of the work of an important and growing movement. Its weaknesses and omissions, of which there are many, are my own. Special thanks, however, are due to Dave Morley for his perceptive comments, general support and great tolerance in accepting yet *another* delay in the receipt of this manuscript.

Special thanks also to

- Paul and Lindah Kiddey, constant sources of inspiration and help.

- David Jackson, Mike Hamlin, David Light, Malcolm Stanton and Roy Goddard – members of the Nottingham Politics and English Groups and talented and committed colleagues from whom I continue to learn.

- Dr Herbert Marchl and Dr Breda Pavlic of UNESCO, and Maitland Stobart of The Council of Europe for providing me with the opportunities to work with so many distinguished international colleagues.

- Gill Corban and Michael Stearn of Balmain for their generous hospitality and for introducing me to the ATOM network.

- To all of my Australian colleagues whose enthusiasm re-kindled my own. Special thanks to Jan Smith, Robert Newton, Liz Jones, John Martin, Barrie McMahon, Robyn Quin and Peter Greenaway.

- Neil Campbell and Martyn Youngs. The sections on game shows (Chapter Seven) and Geography (Chapter Eight) owe a great deal to their original work.

- Alan Jenkins and Harry Tolley for their updates on developments in Geography.

- Philip Simpson, David Lusted and Cary Bazalgette of the British Film Institute Education Department and James Learmonth, HMI. All have laboured long and hard in the cause of media education in England and Wales, and current developments in the subject have a general indebtedness to them.

- Robbie Robertson, Eddie Dick, Rick Instrell, Julie Watt, Liz Liddell, and many others who have played such an important part in recent developments in Scotland, from which many of us south of the border have learned a great deal.

- Terry Eagleton, Terry Hawkes, Colin McCabe, John Good, Tony Davies, Brian Doyle and Francis Mulhern: leaders of a series of seminars held in Nottingham on *Ideology and English Teaching*, which greatly clarified many of my own ideas.

- and Val Cook, Nigel Cook, Graham Murdock, Liz Curtis, Ros Cross, Phil Wardman, Martin McLoone (and all at Donney and Nesbitt's), Kevin Williams, Jill Vincent, Chris Camp, Audrey Eaton, Suzanne Gillespie, Jane Hawkins, Peter Groves and Val Layton.

Some apologies are also due, particularly to Professor Miguel Torres of Valparaiso, and many others to whose generous invitations I was unable to respond whilst engaged on this book.

Finally, writing is, at the best of times, an unsocial activity. This book was written in the holidays, at weekends and during the evenings of a heavy working year. It could not have been completed without the assistance, tolerance, love and support of an exceptional woman, whose social life I curtailed and whose routines I disrupted. In return she offered original ideas (many of which are included in this book), perceptive comments on the manuscripts, and unfailing encouragement. Thanks, Paula.

The courtesy of the following is also acknowledged for permission to reproduce copyright material:

The Observer for reproduction of their property page; Michael Simons and Cary Bazalgette with Simon Clemens and Andrew Bethell for *Teachers' Protest* photographs; James Curran, Jean Seaton and Methuen Ltd. for Press Conglomerates table (Appendix B); Lindah Kiddey and Blue Bell Apparel Ltd. for Press Release, photograph and press cuttings; Stuart Hood and Pluto Press for extracts from *On Television*; Liz Curtis and Pluto Press for extracts from *Ireland: the Propaganda War*; Ian Baker, Dr Patricia Edgar and Macmillan Ltd., Melbourne, for extracts from *The News in Focus*; David Jackson and Marisa Horsford for extracts from *Poems*, and for contact sheet of Marisa's photographs; *The Age* for photograph of Malcolm Fraser at the Glendi festival; the *Newark Advertiser* for photograph of children's party.

Contents

Introduction   xii

1. Why?   1

Media saturation   3
Media influence   3
The manufacture and management of information   8
Media Education and democracy   11
The increasing importance of visual communication and
information   13
Educating for the future   14
The growing privatisation of information   15

2. How?   18

A theoretical framework for media education   20
Core concepts   23
A distinctive mode of enquiry: towards critical autonomy   24
Practical work   26
Media pedagogy   27

3. How not to...   38

The media as agents of cultural decline: the legacy of
Leavis & Thompson   38
The media as popular art forms   49
The media as aids to learning and disseminators of
knowledge and experience   62
The media as agents of communication   65

4. Determinants   71

Introduction   71
Media determinants and pedagogic problems: the case of
The Companies You Keep   72
Media determinants: Some general resources   78
    General reference works   78
    Trade publications   79
    Free resource material   80
Media determinants   82
    Owners and controlling companies   82

Media institutions   86
The state and the law   88
Media self-regulation and control   96
Economic determinants   102
Advertisers   106
Audiences   114
Media personnel   115
Sources   117

5.   Rhetoric   127

Selection   129
The rhetoric of the image   140
Image and text   146
The effect of camera and crew   156
Set-ups   159
Film and sound editing   164
Interpretative frameworks   165
Visual codings   172
Narrative   175

6.   Ideology   187

Defining ideology   187
Ideology in the classroom   198

7.   Audience   215

Introduction   215
Problematising audiences: Morley, Hobson and Smythe 217
Audience positioning   229
Subjectivity   236
Pleasure   237

8.   Futures   241

Introduction   241
Media Education across the curriculum   242
    Geography   243
    Science   251
    English   254
    History   256
Holistic approaches to Media Education   260
    Interaction between educators and parents   260
    Interaction between media teachers and media per-
    sonnel   262

Interaction in the training of teachers and media
  personnel   266
Media Centres   267

Notes   269

Select annotated bibliography   285

Appendices
  A. Resources for Media Education
       Bibliographical, research and reference resources   322
     Simulations   324
     Photoplay materials   326
     Teaching packs   326
     Teacher training resource   328
     Regional resource banks   329
     Regional networks, groups and contacts   329
     Journals and magazines   332
     Organisations with an interest in Media Education   336
  B. British press conglomerates   337
  C. UNESCO Declaration on Media Education: The
     Grunwald Declaration   340

Introduction

This book is organised around a number of simple questions. They are questions to which all teachers, from primary to post-school, will need to have answers if they are to teach about the media effectively. *Why* teach about the media? (Chapter One). *How* can we best go about it? What kind of conceptual framework will help us make sense of the field? (Chapter Two). Upon what kind of *assumptions* has media education been based in the past, and why has it been less than conspicuously successful? (Chapter Three).

Chapters Four to Seven are the core of the book and describe in some detail how the conceptual framework outlined in Chapter Two might be developed in the classroom. Chapter Four asks why media texts are as they are and looks at a number of important interacting determinants of media texts. This is a lengthy chapter, much of which is intended to be a handy reference guide. Since it has been necessary to cover a great deal of ground, to provide resumés of a large number of arguments, and to pack in a good deal of information, first-time readers are advised to skim this chapter judiciously wherever they feel it to be necessary.

Chapter Five asks how the media achieve their effects, and explores their wide range of rhetorical strategies. Chapter Six tackles the thorny question of how to teach about ideology, whilst Chapter Seven examines an area traditionally neglected by media education, that of the complex interactions which exist between texts and audiences. Finally, Chapter Eight asks how media education might best be developed as a lifelong, school and community-based process.

Teachers coming to this book in the expectation that it will primarily offer them a series of lesson plans, ideas on what to do on Monday morning, descriptions of the minutiae of classroom organisation, or even a linear developmental model for media education, may be disappointed. There *are*, I hope, in these pages, enough concrete suggestions and ideas for innovative classroom practice to satisfy the most pragmatic media teacher. But *Teaching the Media* is not *Son of Teaching about Television*. It attempts to do something quite different and, in the long term, I hope, more important. It seeks to move towards the delineation of a number of *general principles* for teaching across the media, principles which, it is hoped, may have general application to the teaching of any age range and which I have illustrated with a range of practical classroom examples and suggestions. It seeks, that is, to convey an under-understanding of the processes and principles of media education which will free teachers of dependency upon this or that piece of material or series of exercises, and enable them to work inde-pendently and confidently in setting up their own media education programmes. These programmes will be designed, in their turn, to promote independent judgements upon the media by students and pupils.

This way of thinking and writing about media education, a way which seeks to encourage the *transfer* of critical reading abilities across a divergent range of media experiences by identifying key principles, concepts and areas of continuity, breaks with a rather long tradition in media education (to which I have myself contributed), in which the uniqueness of each medium is taken to be the 'obvious' starting point for thinking about the subject. The effect of this has been to fragment the subject at the very point at which it is vital to establish its coherence. As a result, this book enjoys the dubious and somewhat unusual distinction of being 'about' the media whilst saying very little about the distinctive nature of TV, radio or the press. Most scandalously of all, perhaps, it has little to say about the cinema.

Now film has traditionally (and institutionally) held a position of pre-eminence within the study of popular culture in Britain. The work of The British Film Institute (BFI) and the Society for Education in Film and Television (SEFT), in particular, has been of immense importance in establishing this particular configuration. Both institutions, too, have played an important part in encouraging the development of television education, yet without ever quite managing to quell the impression that television is, for them, a Cinderella area, ultimately of less importance than film. Other media have suffered from systematic lack of attention. Radio has been a long-neglected field. And where are the insitutions which are promoting an active and critical press education? As to advertising, its structural impact upon virtually every aspect of contemporary media does not appear to have made any discernible impression upon courses in universities, colleges or schools. Such important fields as public relations and telecommunications are suffering a similar neglect.

So in this book I have found it necessary to re-shuffle some well-established priorities within media education and, in that re-ordering, film has come out close to the bottom of the pack. This is less, I hope, a denigration of the possibilities of using film within media education, than an acknowledgement that teachers are already quite well catered for in this area by existing arrangements (the publication of David Lusted's splendidly comprehensive *Guide to Film Studies in Secondary and Further Education*, BFI, 1983, indicates just how voluminous the literature and available resource material is). It is, too, a reflection of my own predilections. For, having used a great deal of film in my English teaching in the 1960s and early 1970s, particularly with low-stream kids to whom print was synonymous with failure, I have found myself developing, over the years, quite low tolerance thresholds for the elitism of much film culture and criticism. And I have allowed myself to be increasingly guided in my teaching by the dominant media experiences of pupils and students, by my own assessment of the comparative significance and ideological importance of different media, and by my own conviction that if a critical education is going to be of any value at all, then it will need to be firmly grounded in the life-experiences of each learner.

On all of these counts the primacy of television seems to me to be unchallenged, with the press, radio and cinema lagging some way behind. That primacy is reflected in the emphasis given to television in the pages which follow. But it is an emphasis which is itself strictly subordinate to the need to establish critical approaches which students can apply to *any* media text. As to advertising, PR and the new technology, their importance within media education derives from their structural influence upon *all* of the media.

Finally, on a personal note, one of the most rewarding outcomes of my earlier book, *Teaching about Television*, was the number of readers who took the trouble to write to me offering comments and criticisms, and letting me know about their own work. Those who were kind enough to do that have increased my own understanding of many of the issues raised by teaching about the media, and have taught me a great deal about developments throughout Britain and, indeed, across the world. Many have become firm friends. Any comments upon the text which follows will, therefore, be most warmly welcomed.

Len Masterman, Nottingham
August, 1985

Chapter 1

Why?

The question 'Why teach the media?' is the proper starting point for this book, since it is a question which those who are either new to the field, or simply sceptical about its possibilities or value in the school curriculum will need to have answered to their satisfaction if they are to proceed any further. Yet it is also a question which more experienced media teachers must constantly ask of themselves, and continue to answer in ways which evolve with developments in the media, if their teaching is to maintain its relevance, direction and sense of urgency.

There is no once-and-for-all set of answers to the question 'Why teach the media?' Yet the need for each of us to produce clear and intelligible answers is paramount, not simply because those answers will need to inform every aspect of our work, but also because, if we are convinced of the importance and necessity of media education, then we shall need to be not simply teachers of, but *advocates for* our subject, *advancing* its cause whenever we can within our own institutions, amongst parents and with colleagues and policy makers. Our reasoning will need to be *compelling* and *persuasive*, as well as plain and intelligible.

It is a sad fact, however, that rationales of media education have rarely managed to match the pace and sophistication of developments in the media themselves. As communication systems and information flows become increasingly central components of social, economic and political activity at all levels, media education remains marginal within educational systems everywhere. The media themselves are constantly changing, expanding and developing, frequently in the direction of an increasingly sophisticated management of their audiences, but sometimes in ways which open out more democratic possibilities. Education needs to be equally flexible and open to change. For the creation of a public opinion which counts because it is well-informed on media issues is a matter of urgent necessity if these possibilities are to be realised. One of the major themes of this book is that this task can only be successfully carried out if our traditional conceptions of education are considerably expanded to include the work of many groups and agencies who have a legitimate stake in the development of media literacy. It is a task for broadcasters, for parents, for community and special interest groups, for political activists, and for *all* who are involved in education – adult educators, teacher-trainers, teachers of all subjects at all levels – and not simply one which can be carried out by a small band of media 'specialists'.

In opening up greater possibilities for wider institutional and community involvement in media education, those of us in formal educational institutions will need to recognize that we are primarily learners tapping into a pool of experience and expertise much richer and wider than our own and that the possible rationales for media education will be as varied and wide-ranging as the interests of those who participate in it.

From some of these rationales we will learn a lot; others we may wish to challenge. But in order to do either effectively we will need to be certain of our own ground. So I offer here seven of my own reasons for arguing that media education be given the most urgent priority:

1. The high rate of media consumption and *the saturation of contemporary societies by the media*.

2. The ideological importance of the media, and *their influence as consciousness industries*.

3. The growth in the *management and manufacture of information*, and its dissemination by the media.

4. The increasing *penetration of media into our central democratic processes*.

5. The increasing *importance of visual communication and information* in all areas.

6. The importance of *educating students to meet the demands of the future*.

7. The fast-growing national and international pressures to *privatise information*.

Each of these trends and tendencies demands a commensurate expansion in critical consciousness, and the coherent development of educational programmes which will encourage critical autonomy. The above list, however, is simply my own – partial, incomplete and reflecting my own priorities. It is offered as a starting point for readers to delete, augment or amend as they think appropriate. And that process of revising, amending and updating our thinking is one in which we will all need to be continuously involved, ensuring as best we can that our teaching develops in step with changes both in the media and in society.

1. Media saturation

In the mid-1970s it was estimated[1] that children between the ages of 5 and 14 were spending 44% more time watching television than they were in lessons in school. More significant even than that striking percentage, however, are the figures for the consumption of all the major media in Britain today. Jeremy Tunstall has recently estimated, for example, that the average British adult spends *75 hours every week* with television, radio, newspapers and magazines.[2] This figure not only indicates the extent to which the experience of most of us is saturated by the media, no matter how resistant we take ourselves to be to their influence, it also draws attention to the complexity with which the media interact with one another and integrate themselves into the pattern of our daily lives.

We considerably under-estimate the impact of the media if we consider only those occasions on which we give them our fullest attention. For there are many occasions when we engage with media as a *secondary* activity, when we have the radio or television on whilst doing something else. Indeed, there are even *tertiary* uses of the media, when a radio or television set may be on in an empty room, perhaps being listened to with half an ear by someone who is engaged in washing the dishes whilst holding a conversation. But the real significance of these different uses of the media is that they are frequently integrated not simply with other activities but with one another. It is quite possible for us to clock up three hours of media consumption over breakfast, for example, if we engage with three different media in primary, secondary and tertiary ways. As I sip my early morning tea, for example, I may be primarily engaged in reading the newspaper, have the radio on in the background, and be tuned to one of the Breakfast Television shows in the next room in order to check the time on the screen clock. And if I listen to the car radio on my way to work (or read a newspaper in the train) and look at a magazine over lunch, I can quite comfortably have registered four or five 'media hours' of consumption before participating in an afternoon seminar on the regrettable fact that children watch so much television.

2. Media influence

Of course it is not simply the time we spend engaged with the media which makes them significant. The media are important shapers of our perceptions and ideas. They are Consciousness Industries which provide not simply information about the world, but ways of seeing and understanding it. Stuart Hall:

'As social groups and classes live... increasingly fragmented and sectionally differentiated lives, the mass media are more and more responsible (a) for providing the basis on which groups and classes construct an 'image' of the lives, meanings, practices and values of *other* groups and classes; (b) for providing the images, representations and ideas around which the social totality, composed of all these separate and fragmented pieces can be coherently grasped as a *whole*. This is the first of the great cultural functions of the modern media: the provision and the selective construction of social knowledge.'[3]

The notion of the media as Consciousness Industries calls into question the common belief that the media's prime functions are to provide news, information or entertainment for their audiences. It also goes beyond the view that the media exist to promote or sell products. As Australian critic Humphrey McQueen has said:

'To make sense of... media... it is essential to get the relationship between the media and advertising the right way round: commercial mass media are not news and features backed up by advertising; on the contrary, *the commercial mass media are advertisements which carry news, features and entertainment in order to capture audiences for the advertisers*... It is a complete mistake to analyse the relationship between media and advertising by supposing that the media's prime function is to sell advertised products to audiences. On the contrary, the media's job is to sell audiences to advertisers.'[4]

The idea that the media are Consciousness Industries takes us further than this, however, for it suggests that the principal product of the media is not the audience, but particular kinds of audience *consciousness*, as Canadian economist Dallas Smythe has suggested:

'The prime item on the agenda of Consciousness Industry is producing *people*... who are ready to support a particular policy, rather than some other policy, be it buying brand X rather than brand Y of automobile, or "supporting" one or another political candidate... or supporting Israel or the Arabs in their long struggle in the Middle East.'[5]

Smythe argues that historically the mass media were 'beckoned into existence' in the last quarter of the nineteenth century by the possibilities which they opened out both to advertisers and society's moral and political guardians for the creation of particular kinds of audience consciousness.

As we shall see in Chapter Seven, there are a number of problems implicit in this view of the media. But the general argument remains a powerful one: 'Seizure of radio and television stations, the telecommunications net and mass production newspapers is an immediate imperative in every *coup* or revolution. Symbolically and practically, this act sums up the role of information in maintaining or overthrowing a social system. In a fundamental sense, control over the means of informing people is the basis of political power – whether those means be the mass media of communication, informal political education, or the barrel of a gun. As Alfred Sauvy put it, the power to build television stations is like the medieval power to build castles along the Rhine.'[6]

We shall examine in Chapter Five the range of techniques employed by the media in producing particular kinds of consciousness. Here it is enough to stress that the very act of selection itself marks out some events, issues and explanations as being more important and significant than others. The media tell us what is important and what is trivial by what they take note of and what they ignore, by what is amplified and what is muted or omitted. 'What is noted,' Roland Barthes observed, 'is by definition notable.'[7] 'What is *omitted*,' Smythe noted, 'will hardly shape the strategic level of policy determination for that Society.'[8] Hall concludes:

'The line ... between *preferred* and *excluded* explanations and rationales, between permitted and deviant behaviours, between the "meaningless" and "meaningful", between the incorporated practices, meanings and values and the oppositional ones is ceaselessly drawn and re-drawn, defended and negotiated: indeed, the "site and stake" of struggle.'[9]

It needs to be insisted at this point that there is nothing inherently sinister about these processes of selection, agenda-setting and interpretation. Any medium, however organised and financed, will *inevitably* be involved in such activities. The problems arise when this work takes place behind the backs of the audience. If broadcasters could only bring themselves to be more open about the problematic nature of 'objectivity', then much of the power and many of the problems associated with the media would begin to wither away. But concepts of impartiality and objectivity are, of course, central to the philosophy of broadcasting institutions in Britain. Broadcasters frequently go out of their way to assure us that their function is to 'reflect' the world as it 'really' exists:

'Good evening. Ever since the Prime Minister launched his Great Education Debate a few months ago with his controversial remarks about standards in our Secondary Schools, the arguments have rumbled on about exactly what is taught and how. Tonight in _Panorama_ we won't be dealing with the arguments or with the experts. Instead we want to show what school can be like for millions of children and their teachers. Are these really the best days of our children's lives? The school we've been to is an ordinary comprehensive school in outer London ... This isn't a conventional _Panorama_ report. There's no reporter and no commentary. It offers instead a fly-on-the-wall view of life in one school today.'

David Dimbleby's introduction to Angela Pope's film of that 'ordinary' London Comprehensive School, _The Best Days?_ assures us that the film is somehow _not produced_. And much of what we see and hear on television and radio appears so seamlessly authentic that the claims of the media to be 'windows on the world' do have considerable plausibility. Indeed, a major problem facing those who wish to develop the study of the media in schools is that one of their fundamental assumptions – that the media are signifying practices or symbolic systems which need to be actively read – flies in the face of many people's common-sensed understanding of the media as largely unproblematic purveyors of experience.

   Paradoxically, however, this is precisely the reason why the media are of such enormous ideological importance, and why media education is such an urgent necessity. For those who control and work in the media do not simply have the power to set agendas, provide explanations and construct their own versions of events. They have the much more significant power to project these things as natural and authentic – simply part of the way things are.

   Barthes coined the influential notion of _myth_[10] to describe these examples of 'the falsely obvious', those decorative displays of 'What-goes-without-saying' which are the stock-in-trade of the media. Ultimately the mythologising propensities of the media, and 'the ideological abuse which ... is hidden there' are not merely a matter of academic, pedagogic or theoretical interest. They can be, quite literally, matters of life and death. Media education, I would argue, is _that_ important.

   The Falklands conflict provides a classic illustration of this, principally because of the brevity of the time-scale involved. The situation did not permit a lengthy cold-war build-up of ideological hostility, for example. Rather, in a matter of weeks, it was necessary to persuade many decent and thoughtful people that it was worth giving up their lives (or at least that it was worth others giving up *their* lives) for the future of some small islands of whose very existence they had been blissfully unaware only weeks previously. Indeed, even when the Task Force sailed, while 70% approved of its being sent, 60% of the British people opposed the taking of military action to end the conflict.[11] The figures began to change significantly only after Britain captured South Georgia.

Clearly an enormous amount of ideological work was necessary to achieve these movements of public opinion. In the early days, no doubt, some patriotic support could be generated by cashing in on that deep well of residual nationalism actively fostered by international sporting events and royal occasions in more innocent times, and actively encouraged by the media's coverage of such events. But a whole battery of news management techniques, not excluding lies, suppression and misinformation, was necessary in order to persuade the public of the rightness of the Government's cause.[12]

Living through the Falklands conflict was, for me, a dramatic confirmation of the need to develop a widespread critical understanding of the media, not simply in schools, but at all levels of society. It is an aim worthy of our enthusiasm and dedication as teachers, for it would represent a distinct step towards the kind of lifelong educational enterprise envisaged by the UNESCO publication, *Learning to Be*, and designed to truly enfranchise the citizens of every state:

'Education . . . should contribute to a project which is very typical of our time, that of replacing a mechanical, administrative type of authority by a lively democratic process of decision making . . . The citizen's job is no longer to delegate his power but to wield it at all levels of society and stages of life . . . The development of democracy is required for peace. It encourages tolerance, friendship and co-operation between nations . . . in the complicated and complex play of politics and diplomacy, the attitudes of the peoples concerned weigh more than might appear, particularly when they have a realistic and unsentimental idea of peace. When State authorities have to deal with majorities of really adult citizens or with powerful active minorities, they cannot sweep the people they govern into whatever dangerous designs they may have devised as easily as when they are handling malleable, ill-informed populations who have been tricked out of their real interests.'[13]

3. The manufacture and management of information

In his study of media treatment of the Falklands crisis, Robert Harris draws the following conclusion:

'The episodes which caused the most disquiet . . . were not necessarily unique to the Falklands crisis. The instinctive secrecy of the military and the Civil Service; the prostitution and hysteria of sections of the press; the lies, the misinformation, the manipulation of public opinion by the authorities; the political intimidation of broadcasters; the ready connivance of the media at their own distortion . . . all these occur as much in normal peace time in Britain as in war.'[14]

The manufacture of information is one of the few growth industries in Britain today. Multi-national corporations, government agencies and departments, the political parties, the armed services, and even quite small institutions like locally-based companies and Universities now have their own permanent public relations departments. The Government Information Service contains some 1,200 civil servants, and each Whitehall department has its own P.R. team, some (Defence and Environment, for example) around 100 strong.[15] In Northern Ireland, the army employed more than 40 press officers, and were able to offer journalists a 24-hour service in the mid-1970s.[16] Even Buckingham Palace has a press office of seven people.[17] The Government itself possesses a battery of techniques for ensuring that the public hear what their rulers consider appropriate and desirable. In particular, the Lobby system, through which some political journalists (the Lobby) receive unattributable briefings from ministers, has become a conduit for official information, a means of disseminating government propaganda under the cloak of impartial journalism.

Meanwhile, much information which it is in the public's interest to know is suppressed by a veritable web of secrecy and legislation which is deliberately general and wide-ranging, in particular the Official Secrets Act, the Prevention of Terrorism Act, D Notices, and the Law of Libel. Cockerell, Hennessy and Walker have drawn attention to the historical parallels which exist between the extension of the franchise and the need to control public opinion:

'There is a curious coincidence between the Lobby's birth in the 1880s and the birth of the first legal moves to control how much the public knew about what what was happening within Government and Whitehall: in 1889, only five years after the Lobby was born, the first

Official Secrets Act was placed on the Statute book. The paradox was that as Britain was moving towards becoming a democracy – by extending the vote to men of all classes (women still had forty years to wait) – mechanisms were being created to frustrate popular participation in government and to control, channel and even manufacture the political news.'[18]

The Media Studies movement itself has not been too humble to attract the interest of broadcasting institutions of whom it has often been critical. The BBC and the Independent Television Companies Association (ITCA), for example, have helped finance a chair in Media Studies at Stirling University, and its first incumbent, Alistair Hetherington, has already produced research indicating that in the coal dispute of 1984–5 'the main television news channels have done their best to present a fair, balanced and accurate picture.'[19] The BBC, along with a number of newspapers, is also beginning to take an interest in the media education movement in schools. Any genuine desire by media institutions to co-operate with schools will be generally welcomed by media teachers, for the media themselves possess reserves of expertise and resources which would be invaluable to schools. What must be kept absolutely clear, however, is the fact that the objectives of media education are demystificatory and critical. The lines between public education and public relations must be rigidly drawn.

* * *

It is worth recalling that the public relations industry, historically, has always developed out of essentially defensive positions. The industry originated in the USA at the beginning of this century as a direct result of press attacks on big business. Attempts at state and national regulation of corporate enterprises ('trust busting') forced companies to re-think their previous attitude of secrecy and aloofness from the press, and in 1902 the President of Standard Oil could say 'We've changed our policy. We are giving out information.'[20] It was not until the 1930s that the trend developed towards permanent and specialised public relations departments within business in the USA, and during this time the first developments in Britain began to take place.

The Institute of Public Relations, PR's professional association, was founded in 1948 and today has 2,400 members both in Britain and overseas. The growth of this new industry (largely but not entirely devoted to the manufacture of information) obviously has important implications for the ways in which public opinion is formed, and consent engineered in our society, but so far it has drawn little in the way of response from educational institutions (apart from those offering qualifications in the area).

Media education ought to constitute one such critical response since much PR material finds its way directly into the media in the form of news and features on a scale unguessed at by most of the public (see Chapter Four). This is why the media can all too frequently be considered less as bastions of untrammelled expression essential to the preservation of democratic freedoms than as weapons used in the service of particular interests. What public relations machinery seeks is not simply the expression of the ideas and viewpoints of established institutions, but 'a differential advantage in their circulation and distribution.'[21]

This situation has led to some writers arguing that we *all* need to learn much more about how to use the media effectively for our own purposes, and that trade unionists, community activists and others who feel that they get a raw deal from the media need to work much harder in cultivating sympathetic media contacts, putting out media releases, holding press conferences and the like.[22] There is obviously a good deal of sense in this, and any media education course which is designed to encourage action and change will wish to involve its students in this kind of interaction with local and national media. Indeed, media education students could well give their own institutions a lead in this direction. For most schools and colleges make no attempt to liaise in a positive way with the media, to feed them stories of their successes and accomplishments, and to make routine contact with individual journalists. One reason why news stories about schools are frequently unfavourable is that they tend to come to journalists' attention only when there is a problem – when parents complain or pupils misbehave, for example. And the source of such stories is not generally the school itself, but those who have grievances against it.

Is there an inconsistency in the argument here? How can it be reasonable for schools to practise media manipulation, but unfair when big business does the same thing? If there are dangers in propaganda being passed off as innocent news stories, does it matter very much in moral terms who is producing the propaganda? Isn't criticism of the big organisations simply sour grapes? Maybe. But however assiduous individuals and small groups may be in cultivating their use of the media, the imbalance between them and the big battalions will remain. Even organisations which we may think of as large and powerful, such as trade unions, do not have the same kind of resources available to them as their opponents, as Jeremy Tunstall has pointed out:

'Both the civil service machine and the business/management machine have greater legitimacy; they are regarded as the "natural" source of routine news by relevant specialist journalists; they have flotillas of public relations men who pump out good news, while still being conscious of the art (almost unknown in trade union circles) of sometimes staying silent.

Both big business and big government also have advertising and can – if they choose – buy themselves large amounts of publicity. Trade unions do not have such resources.'[23]

For organisations used to media hostility, then, using the media constructively can be legitimately seen as a way of at least beginning to counteract the dominance of big government and big business. But it is no more than a beginning. Inequalities of access, of resources and of distribution and circulation remain.

To be really successful, however, the PR game demands and feeds upon public ignorance. And it is between the providers and consumers of information that the *greatest* inequalities lie. Media education represents perhaps one of the best hopes that society has of countering the most blatant duplicities of the public relations industry, of encouraging more demanding standards from journalists, of producing more discerning, sceptical and knowledgeable audiences, and of clarifying the rules for manipulating the media for everyone so that we can all play the game if we so wish – though never, of course, on equal terms. Media education, then, is one of the few instruments which teachers and students possess for beginning to challenge the great inequalities in knowledge and power which exist between those who manufacture information in their own interests and those who consume it innocently as news or entertainment.

4. Media education and democracy

Media education is also a matter of some urgency since the media have now penetrated to the heart of our democratic processes. General elections long ago ceased to be 'external' events which the media happened to cover. They have become, rather, essentially *media events* with itineraries, speeches, debates, walkabouts and the like planned with media priorities and deadlines very much in mind. Anyone who has canvassed door-to-door during a general election will testify to the importance of television, in particular, in determining the decisions of 'floating' voters. Television, too, encourages voters to make choices not on the basis of the suitability of the local candidates for whom they will vote, but on the qualities of the party leaders. The American trend of presenting politics as a matter of personalities and images, rather than issues is gaining ground in Britain. In the 1979 election there were 'only' seven full-length interviews with party leaders on British television. In the 1983 election there were 16. News programmes also emphasized the activities of the party leaders and covered the election in the manner of a presidential campaign.[24]

It is no exaggeration to say that party leaders are now packaged and presented to us as though they were packets of soap or cornflakes. As a recent study of government manipulation of the news media has demonstrated, the 'Director of Marketing' of the Conservative Party, a former executive of the company which makes Mars Bars, sees little difference in principle between marketing a chocolate bar and promoting the qualities of a political party. In addition, Mrs. Thatcher employs the services of a playwright (Sir Ronald Miller) to compose her speeches, a media guru (Gordon Reece), who 'produced' such stars as Bruce Forsyth and Eamonn Andrews, to coach her through her television appearances, and a press secretary (Bernard Ingham) who is not above bullying – with some success – senior executives of the BBC.[25] This is to say nothing of the activities of the advertising agency, Saatchi and Saatchi, who have planned the Conservative Party's last two successful election campaigns.

The Left, too, in spite of general hostility to PR and advertising as tools of capitalism, is becoming more convinced of the importance of using these weapons for their own purposes, rather than allowing their uncontested monopoly by the Right. The Greater London Council's advertising campaign *Say No To No Say*, the planning of the Labour Party's 1983 general election campaign and party political broadcasts by the advertising agency Wright and Partners, and the manicuring of Labour Party leader, Neil Kinnock's image since the disastrous election defeat of 1983 are all indications that the Left is becoming increasingly convinced of the necessity of actively promoting not only policies, but personalities and images through the media.[26]

Once again the educational system lags well behind these contemporary developments. The burgeoning Political Education movement in schools is to be welcomed. But the movement's journal, *Teaching Politics*, has not carried a single article in its 13-year history on the impact of television upon British politics, and only one on the role of the press.

Research by Jane Wills on the way television is used within political education classes revealed that whilst teachers encouraged students to be critical of the issues and events depicted, the processes of depiction themselves were regarded as unproblematic. Of the 12

teachers she surveyed who were using television wit
education teaching, 'only one. felt the need to
students the constructed nature of what they see on
mitigate their undifferentiated faith in the med
majority of young adults rate television as being thei
source of political information.[28] In a world in which images are fast
becoming of greater significance than policies, in which slogans often
count for more than rational argument, and in which we will all make
some of our most important democratic decisions on the basis of
media evidence, media education is both essential to the exercising of
our democratic rights and a necessary safeguard against the worst
excesses of media manipulation for political purposes.

In this section I have looked at the importance of media education
for 'democracy' only in the most limited sense of that word, that is in
relation to the processes of understanding *explicitly* political
information, and of exercising one's voting rights once every five
years. As I have already suggested, however, media education
is also an essential step in the long march towards a truly
participatory democracy, and the democratisation of our institutions. Widespread media literacy is essential if all citizens are to
wield power, make rational decisions, become effective change-
agents, and have an active involvement with the media. It is in this
much wider sense of 'education for democracy' that media education
can play the most significant role of all.

5. The increasing importance of visual communication and information

Schools continue to be dominated by print. To have difficulties in
decoding print is, in school terms, to be a failure. Outside of school
the most influential and widely disseminated modes of communication are visual. As we have seen, television is probably the
most important source of political information in our society and it is
also regarded by most people as the most reliable source of news,
perhaps because of its ability to present a visual record of events.[29]
Even print itself is coming to be regarded as a visual medium. Layout,
design and typography are widely understood to be a significant part
of the total communication process, whilst even the term 'print-
media' is frequently a misnomer, since in most texts print is rarely
unaccompanied by visual images.

Schools, sooner or later, will have to recognise the importance of
developing in their pupils the ability to examine visual images
critically. Indeed, the increasing use of video-tape material in the

..ng of history, geography, science and the humanities will mean
. the ability to assess visual evidence will be a cross-curricula skill
which will need to inform teaching and learning in all subjects. There
are strong arguments, then, for urging the development of media
education in schools, not only as a specialist area in its own right, but
across the curriculum as a necessary adjunct to literacy in the
teaching of all subjects. This aspect of media education will be
considered in greater detail in Chapter Eight.

6. Educating for the future

It was in 1963 that the Newsom Report drew attention to the
importance of developing media education programmes in schools.
Since that time *a whole generation* of pupils has passed through our
schools, of whom few have received even rudimentary guidance on
the ways in which the media construct their meanings. The major
cultural and political changes produced by the media over the past 20
years have made little impression on our schools, and the gap
between the practices and priorities of most classrooms and the situations which pupils face in the world outside is now more dangerously
wide than it has ever been. Yet it was still possible, in 1984, for Her
Majesty's Inspectorate to publish a discussion document designed to
influence the future of English teaching,[30] which made little or no
reference to computers, structural unemployment, multi-ethnic
questions or the mass media. At the very moment when the energies
and enthusiasms of teachers need to be mobilised to face the very real
challenges of the future, some influential HMI are encouraging a
retreat to the imagined standards of the past.

Every child in school today will spend most of her adult life as a
citizen in the 21st century. We do not need to go back but to go
forward to basics,[31] to developing those aptitudes and abilities which
everyone will need if they are to be adequately educated for life in the
next century. At present our schools largely continue to produce
pupils who are likely to carry with them for the rest of their lives either
a quite unwarranted faith in the integrity of media images and
representations, or an equally dangerous, undifferentiated scepticism
which sees the media as sources of all evil.[32] The loss to our society in
terms of its democratic health is incalculable. So, too, is the loss to the
media themselves, particularly to those many responsible journalists
and broadcasters who see themselves as primarily serving the public
interest, and who need a well-informed and knowledgeably critical
audience, as much as that audience needs them.

7. The growing privatisation of information

As we move into the post-industrial Information Society, in which information is fast becoming the core component of advanced economies, so an education which cannot begin to grapple with the implications of developments in communications technology – electronic publishing, multi-channelled satellite broadcasting, interactive cable systems, television data systems, and the everyday use of video-cassette and disc materials – can hardly be said to be an adequate education at all. Integral to many of these developments is the growing privatisation of information and leisure services of which the sale of British Telecom, the 'de-regulation' of broadcasting, the pressure upon the BBC to take advertising, the commercial sponsorship of sport and the arts, and the development of commercial rather than community cable services are all recent manifestations. Teachers often appear indifferent to such developments. They ought not to be. For, sooner rather than later, they will themselves be directly affected by them – perhaps most cataclysmically of all. The truth is that the turning of information into a commodity and the growth of transnational corporative data systems threaten the very future of all public information systems, not least the education system itself.

The imperatives of the new information order stand in stark contrast to the values of our public educational institutions, based as they are on the philosophy that information should be:

(a) freely available to those who need it or can use it (rather than to those who can afford to pay for it);

(b) openly accessible to all (rather than highly controlled);

(c) generally available as a public service (rather than restricted at the discretion of the large institutions who produce or buy it);

(d) distributed through educational institutions which are accountable to the public (rather than institutions which are accountable to the market place).[33]

Crucially, when information becomes a commodity, as Herbert Schiller has pointed out, 'The role and character of information itself' begins to change.[34]

'When this occurs, not only do those with the ability to pay gain advantaged access, but eventually – and, ultimately most importantly – they become the arbiters of what kind of information shall be produced and what is made available. The market unsentimentally yet inexorably confers this authority on those with the fatter bank accounts.'[35]

The production of *socially* useful information is undermined by the production of *profitable* information, and the philosophy that information is inherently social and public begins to wither away. Schiller:

'What is now underway . . . is a vast extension in cultural control and domination, to say nothing of economic and political mastery. Here we are concerned with the effort to structure a new global system of authority on the basis of information control, of an order hitherto unimaginable. What has been a substantial influence, resting on familiar media flows – news, TV programmes, films, books, magazines – *is being extended to include the entire flow of information*, corporate data streams in particular.'[36] (original emphasis)

In Britain, the straws are already blowing ominously in the wind. Lord Gowrie, Minster for the Arts, attacks the notion of a free library loan system. The BBC may soon be compelled to take revenue from advertising. Wealthy overseas students find it easier to gain access to our Universities than either students from poorer overseas countries or well-qualified domestic students. Shirley Williams, the SDP President, warns that teachers could soon be made obsolete, and the public education system by-passed by private companies (IBM, Westinghouse, Texas Instruments) producing packaged and cheaply available computerized learning programmes.[37]

Certainly, given the vast amount of public expenditure on teachers' salaries, education must soon be ripe for privatisation unless teachers can argue convincingly that they are involved in something rather more important than the transmission of information – a task which a computerised system of education could perform at a fraction of the current cost. What the transnational computer companies will *never* produce, however, is *an expansion in critical consciousness* to match the expansion in information and communications technology. Only a fully autonomous public educational system will be able to do that. But if it fails to respond to that challenge, why should it not go to the wall?

At the moment, as I have argued, it shows little sign of providing such a response. That is why media teachers can justifiably see themselves in the very vanguard of their profession. They can play a leading role in shaping a public consciousness capable of articulating the public interest and of urging popular control of information and of information-generating institutions, particularly in the educational sphere. They can do this by encouraging discussion, participation in, and critical judgement of, these issues by their students. If they fail to take up this challenge, then the future is bleak indeed. For if they will not do it, who else will?

* * *

To be convinced of the importance of and need for media education is one thing. To develop a successful media education practice is quite another. There would, no doubt, be many who would be willing to put their weight behind the media education movement, were it not for the fact that much of what passes for media studies is unimpressively fragmented and heterogeneous. *Can* the media be studied and taught in a way which is as systematic, as intellectually rigorous and as conceptually coherent as more established subjects? It is to this question that we must now turn.

Chapter 2

How?

The halting progress made by media education over the past 50 years has not been entirely due to teacher indifference or pupil resistance. The formidable intellectual and pedagogic problems facing teachers with an interest in the field have perhaps been equally important. The major problem can be simply stated: how is it possible to make any conceptual sense of a field which covers such a wide range and diversity of forms, practices and products?

At an in-service course on media education which I recently attended, films, television, radio, pop music, advertising, youth culture, newspapers and magazines were all discussed, and felt to be legitimate parts of the field. Recently, too, I encountered a student working on a media studies project who was looking at the development of tee-shirts as communication media, an interesting example of the apparently limitless possibilities for proliferation in the field.

The problem isn't simply that 'the media', on examination, look less like a coherent field of study than a convenient catch-all category into which any form of communication can, with sufficient ingenuity, be bundled. It is also that each medium can itself serve a dizzying multiplicity of functions. Television, for example, serves the role of cinema, newspaper, sports arena, theatre, music hall, concert hall, and magazine all rolled into one. It is no simple task to make intellectual sense of a single medium, let alone each of the others, and their complex inter-relationships.

In schools the most common 'solution' to this problem has actually been no solution at all. It has been to teach the subject as nothing more than the aggregated sum of its discrete parts. So in a one-year course, half a term might be spent on film, half a term on TV, a few weeks on advertising, a little time on newspapers, and so on. This valiant attempt by conscientious teachers to aim for a comprehensive survey of the media and to 'cover' as many different content areas as possible produced, in practice, obvious weaknesses in the constitution of the subject, and formidable obstacles to its further development, as I noted in the mid-1970s:

'What would a half-term component in television or music look like? Could it be anything but superficial? And if so, is it worth doing at all?

What would give coherence to the course's constituent particular mode of enquiry? The examination of important media concepts? Or what? And what would be the subject-matter under scrutiny – which of the many aspects of each of the media? What would be the status of this content? Would its acquisition be a desirable end in itself, or a means of understanding general principles? Is there an essential body of knowledge or information? If so, what is it? And embracing all of these questions: what would constitute student learning? The acquisition of particular unnamed abilities, attitudes, information, techniques, methodologies or what? These are basic questions to which teachers will need to have answers before they can begin to set up coherent courses in media studies. They are questions which when raised at all have been answered with a resounding silence.'[1]

Rather than attempting to penetrate the media studies thicket, my own solution in the early 1970s was to circumvent it by attempting to make sense of one medium only, television. Strenuously though I argued for this approach at the time, detaching one medium from the rest could never be anything more than a short-term holding operation. For there *were* compelling reasons for studying the media together. Their connections, through their structures of ownership and control, both with one another and with a vast range of service and consumer industries; their common conventions and signifying practices, and their overlapping content; and, not least, their common function as consciousness industries, and their mutually reinforcing influence upon their audiences, made it somewhat perverse to isolate each medium from the rest. In fact, the importance of thinking of the media systemically, and of clarifying their common functions and practices, as well as their important differences, had never really been in doubt. The problem was always one of providing this way of understanding the media with a clarity and conceptual coherence that would serve as a basis for a workable media education curriculum.

The solution to that problem has emerged slowly. As media teachers began to meet and discuss their work, continuities and correspondences began to emerge out of the most diverse practices and contexts. So it is, perhaps, possible now to map out some of the ways in which the media might be (and indeed are being) studied in a more disciplined way. In the next section of this chapter, I will argue that media education possesses:

1. *a theoretical framework* which can enable teachers and students to make coherent sense of this diverse field;

and principles, which are, in Jerome Bruner's
ation 'as simple as they are powerful' and 'may be
ody at any age in some form;'[2]

c mode of enquiry or method of investigation.

these features offer distinctive ways of making sense
of the field across an often bewildering variety and range of available
subject material. Finally, I will argue that media education should
involve a different way of working with pupils and students. Like the
discipline of media education itself, media pedagogy is a distinctive
practice.

1. A theoretical framework for media education

Media education has a first principle which I saw illustrated with
beautiful simplicity many years ago by a Nottingham art teacher,
Fred Bazler. Fred held up to a class of eight-year-olds a painting of a
horse and asked them what it was. When the kids answered, 'A
horse,' Fred simply said it wasn't.[3] This caused some confusion, but
after a little prompting the children began to understand the
distinction between a horse and its representation in a painting, and
to articulate this distinction in further discussion of the painting.

The lesson was not intended to be an introduction to the media,
but it could well have served that purpose. For the distinction which
was being made between representation and reality, between an
image and its referent, between signifier and signified, is a
fundamental one within media education. The first principle of media
education from which all else flows, and to which teachers and
students will continually return is *that the media are symbolic (or sign)
systems which need to be actively **read**, and not unproblematic, self-
explanatory reflections of external reality*. Another way of stating this
principle is to say that television, newspapers, films, radio,
advertisements and magazines are *produced*. The media, that is, are
actively involved in processes of *constructing* or *representing* 'reality'
rather than simply transmitting or reflecting it. (Whilst some have
argued that the media *manufacture* their products in much the same
way as any factory might, some important limitations do need to be
placed on the notion of media manufacture, as I shall suggest in
Chapter Eight.)

It is this bedrock assumption which enables us to link and make
conceptual sense of the diverse range of signifying practices employed
by each medium. The very notion of media education itself is derived

from this principle. If there were no distinction to be made between representation and reality, if the media really were 'windows on the world', then media study would be as purposeless as studying panes of glass. This view of the media would allow us to examine only the diverse areas of experience covered by the media – sport, theatre, news or current affairs, for example – rather than the media themselves. Media education *necessarily* assumes that these experiences are reconstructed, represented (re-presented), packaged and shaped in identifiable and characteristic forms by media institutions, media technologies and the practices of media professionals.

Furthermore, it may be said that the ideological power of the media is roughly proportional to the apparent *naturalness* of their representations, the ideological potency of a medium arising principally from the power of those controlling and working in it to pass off as real, true, universal and necessary what are *inevitably* selective and value-laden constructions within which are inscribed particular interests, ideologies and ways of making sense (discourses).

If media products are constructions, then at least four general areas immediately, and with some degree of logic, suggest themselves for further investigation:

(i) *the sources, origins and determinants of media constructions:*
The question of 'Who constructs?', whilst important in opening out for scrutiny the interests inscribed within any text is, nevertheless, also seriously misleading. It tends to personalise the complex processes of industrial production and also implies that texts may be 'explained' in terms of the power and control exercised by a few individuals. As we shall see, it is necessary to understand the determinants of media texts as a much more complex web of often conflicting interests and pressures, some of which will be examined in Chapter Four.

(ii) *the dominant techniques and codings employed by the media to convince us of the truth of their representations:*
This very broad area of media rhetoric will be considered in Chapter Five.

(iii) *the nature of the 'reality' constructed by the media; the values implicit in media representations:*
This, the ideological role of the media, will be examined in Chapter Six.

(iv) *the ways in which media constructions are read or received by their audiences:* (Chapter Seven).

There are at least two important additions which need to be made to this general model as it stands. It is necessary to understand both media texts, and this way of conceptualising them, dialectically, as being always in a process of movement and change. First of all, media texts themselves need to be comprehended in their *physical* movement, as objects which are produced, distributed, exchanged and consumed. Yet even this is to misread the real processes of media production. For what the media produce are not primarily texts, but audiences (and audience consciousnesses) which are segmented and sold to advertisers. Moreover, this process of audience production is itself simply a small, though necessary, part of the larger cycle of capitalist production, distribution, exchange and consumption:

'In economic terms there are three types of commodities: primary commodities (e.g., wheat), intermediate products (e.g., flour), and end products (e.g., bread). In economic terms, the audiences of the mass media are intermediate products. Like other factors of production, they are consumed in producing, i.e., selling, the end product; their production and use by the advertiser is a marketing cost. The end product of the giant corporations in the consumer goods and services sector is those consumer goods and services. The audiences produced by the mass media are only part of the means to the sale of that end product.'[4]

Audiences may be an intermediate product, but there is an important sense in which audiences and audience consciousness are *indeed* end products. Dallas Smythe:

'At the larger, systemic level, people, working via audiences to market goods and services to themselves, and their consciousness ultimately are the *systemic* end product: *they* are produced by the system ready to buy consumer goods and to pay taxes and to work in their alienating jobs in order to continue buying tomorrow.'[5]

The media's crucial role is a *reproductive* one. The media is producing particular kinds of audiences and audience consciousness reproduce the conditions which enable further economic production to take place.

Secondly, the separating out of the four elements of the model which I have proposed, whilst convenient for the purposes of further analysis and discussion, is seriously misleading unless each 'area' is understood as influencing, permeating and interacting dialectically with every other in a way that makes it difficult, finally, to conceptualise them as 'separate' areas at all. So questions of audience cannot be limited to what is postulated as a final point on a supposedly linear process of communication. Audiences are present as important textual determinants from the very beginning, and influence every part of the production and communication cycles. Similarly, questions of ideology cannot be confined to the analysis of the content of media texts. Owners, media professionals, advertisers, audiences and even media forms and conventions, all perform their own ideological operations upon and within texts, and questions of ideology permeate every area of the conceptual model, which I have proposed.

Whilst the theoretical framework which I have suggested does not provide any kind of adequate account of the processes of media production, it may, for the time being, serve the purposes of media education. This is because it is a model which *centres media texts* and the complex questions they raise, in a way which perhaps adequately reflects the priorities and concerns of teachers and students. In other words, the emphasis placed within the theoretical framework on the key areas for investigation which arise out of a media text are intended to make the processes of textual investigation within the classroom more systematic and rigorous, and to lead students and teachers alike to an examination of a wider range of extra-textual influences. Both media teachers and students, however, do need to be sensitive to the danger that detailed attention to media texts alone, whilst pedagogically appropriate, may produce a less than adequate account of the processes of media production, or of the complex ways in which the media are related to other societal institutions.

2. Core concepts

Media teachers should attempt to make a list of the principal concepts which they wish their students to understand, for it is these concepts which can provide the subject with its continuity and coherence across a wide range of media texts and issues. Here is my own list. It is by no means comprehensive but may be a useful starting point for teachers compiling their own list of key concepts:

ideology	non-verbal communication
genre	anchorage
rhetoric	preferred meaning
realism	denotation and connotation
naturalism	discourse
construction	deconstruction
selection	audience positioning

myth	audience segmentation
distribution	narrative structure
mediation	pleasure
representation	sign/signification (and perhaps signifier and signified)
subjectivity	sources
code/encoding/ decoding	participation/access/control

Of course, these concepts vary enormously in complexity. Some (*selection*, for example, or *construction*) can be taught to everyone, from the youngest primary school children to adults. They can be deepened year by year in a spiral curriculum of the kind suggested by Bruner. Others are much more difficult to grasp. Here the art of the media teacher lies in breaking down their conceptual complexity to simpler, yet intellectually respectable forms, which can be understood by the group or class concerned. In Chapter Six I suggest a number of ways in which this might be attempted with the concept of ideology.

Developing a conceptual understanding of the media will involve both *critical reception of* and *active production through* the media (see pages 25 and 26). At all ages it will develop through the choice of content material appropriate to and of interest to the student group concerned. It should go without saying that these concepts should be made explicit, in an appropriate form, to pupils and students, and not simply exist within the heads of teachers.

3. A distinctive mode of enquiry: towards critical autonomy

It is scarcely possible to define an appropriate mode of enquiry for media education until we answer the question 'Appropriate for what?'. What precisely are we trying to achieve with our pupils or students in a media education course? I would wish to argue that one of the primary objectives of media education should not be to produce in pupils the ability to reproduce faithfully ideas, critical insights or information supplied by the teacher. Nor should it involve simply encouraging the students' own critical insights within the classroom, important though this may be. The really important and difficult task of the media teacher is to develop in pupils enough self-confidence and critical maturity to be able to apply critical judgements to media texts *which they will encounter in the future*. The acid test of any media education programme is the extent to which pupils are critical in their own use and understanding of the media *when the teacher is not there.* The primary objective is not simply critical awareness and understanding, it is critical *autonomy.*

It is very important, then, that media education

(i)   does not degenerate into the stultifying and laborious accumulation of facts, ideas and information about the media

(ii) should not consist of dehumanising exercises or 'busy work' on the media, designed primarily to keep students occupied

(iii) should not involve the dutiful reproduction by students of the teacher's ideas.

I would want to argue that the most satisfactory media education syllabuses will not be *essentialist* in terms of their content. Students may be freed, that is, of the oppressive load of content which *must* be covered. Syllabuses should seek, rather, to define the processes and principles which will enable students to stand as quickly as possible on their own two critical feet. Course content, teaching methodology and questions of evaluation will need to be thought through in the light of this priority. Content, in particular, needs to be thought of, not as an end in itself, but as a means to developing critical autonomy, and not submerging it. A good deal of the content of an effective media course, then, will not be predictable. The teacher will generally find it a considerable advantage to maintain maximum flexibility, to be opportunistic, and not to plan too far ahead. The students' own interests and preferences ought certainly to be given due weight, as should programmes, articles and issues which emerge as matters of topical concern amongst the group. The attractiveness and immediacy of this kind of content ought to be a powerful motivating factor within media education, and continuing dialogue and negotiation between teacher and students about course content will be necessary in order to guarantee this.

    The critical act within media education should look three ways. First of all, it should pay the closest attention to a particular text or issue. Though media education attempts to develop *general* critical abilities and an understanding of general principles, they must always be grounded in 'local analysis' (to borrow a phase from Leavis). Secondly, the development of a critical consciousness will be dependent on occasions upon the provision of relevant information from outside of the text. Access to such information and an ability to find one's way around it will need to be built into any media education course. The provision of information should always be judged by its relevance to the development of critical abilities.

Thirdly, the act of criticism must look *beyond* the particularity of a specific text or issue towards those general principles which seem to have relevance to the analysis of similar texts and issues. It must work, that is, for critical transfer to new situations. That is the foundation upon which critical autonomy will be built. The objective is close to that outlined by Leavis in his essay on *How to teach Reading*: 'The aim here is to insist on the essentials, the equipment and the training that will enable the student to look after himself.'[6] I shall be parting company with Leavis, however, by arguing that within media education the aim of critical reading should not be primarily evaluative, but *investigative*. Since this challenges the basis upon which media education has been taught since the 1930s, the case will need to be argued in some detail, and I shall consider this issue in the next chapter.

4. Practical work

Practical work in a variety of forms will be an important, indeed an essential, component of any worthwhile course in media education. If students are to understand media texts as constructions, then it will obviously be helpful if they have first-hand experience of the construction process *from the inside*. Teachers, too, need to involve themselves in this kind of work at their own level of sophistication.

Some 'caveats' on practical work are necessary, however. Practical activity does not, in itself, constitute media education. In particular, the commonly-expressed belief that, through practical work, students will *automatically* acquire critical abilities and begin to de-mystify the media needs to be challenged. Rather, the link between practical work and analytical activities *needs to be consciously forged by the teacher*. It must be worked for. It cannot be assumed. Indeed, there is an obvious sense in which the production of cheaply-made student radio, television or newspapers may actively *increase* media mystification, when beginners compare their own halting efforts with the polished products of media professionals. The role of the teacher is of crucial importance in establishing that one of the primary aims of practical work is to subject professional media practices to critical scrutiny, rather than to emulate them.

There is an attendant danger in practical work to which all media educators need to be alert. It is what I will call *the technicist trap*: a reductive process through which media education and the practice of media criticism come to be seen as a series of purely technical operations. A heightened awareness of the technicist trap is necessary because the high degree of expertise and training in the arts of audio-visual production possessed by some media educators has, as its obverse, a tentativeness – a lack of confidence emanating from a lack of training – which is felt by many media educators when they engage their students in the crucial activity of critical analysis.

We can avoid the technicist trap if we remember two of the basic principles of media education. First of all, communication forms are not 'innocent', and transparent carriers of meaning. They are impregnated with values and actively shape the messages they communicate. Secondly, practical work is not an end in itself, but a necessary means to developing an autonomous critical understanding of the media.

Without this informing purpose, practical work becomes, in its most vestigial forms, mere 'busy work' and, in its more advanced manifestations, a form of *cultural reproduction* in which dominant practices become naturalised. Cultural reproduction is a poor aim for media education. It is uncritical; it enslaves rather than liberates; it freezes the impulses towards action and change; it produces deference and conformity.

Re-affirming the primacy of cultural criticism over cultural reproduction can help us re-assess priorities for practical work. It may well be that the most significant forms of practical activity will not necessarily be those which call for the most elaborate and prestigious equipment, nor those which take the form of extensive and time-consuming projects. Rather, they may be much less ambitious workshop activities, simulations and code-breaking exercises which can be woven into the fabric of a critical media education.[7]

5. Media pedagogy

The possibilities which media education can open up to pupils in terms of their understanding of and possible intervention in an important area of their experience, will quickly be extinguished if the introduction of the subject is not accompanied by major pedagogic transformations. For media education offers the possibility, not simply of a change of labels on the timetable, but of new ways of working. Indeed, I will argue that teaching effectively about the media *demands* non-hierarchical teaching modes and a methodology which will promote reflection and critical thinking whilst being as lively, democratic, group-focused and action-orientated as the teacher can make it.

It is only fair to point out, however, that there has recently been some criticism of 'progressive' teaching approaches to media education, and it will be necessary to consider some of these arguments. This section, then, will attempt to

a) argue for the importance of non-hierarchical teaching approaches to media education,

b) urge the importance of the processes of dialogue, reflection and action within media education,

c) discuss some recent critiques of progressivist practices in media education.

a) Non-hierarchical teaching

The reasons for adopting non-hierarchical teaching modes within media education may be quickly summarised:

(i) If one of the major objectives of media education is the development of critical autonomy, then any pedagogy which makes students dependent upon the teacher will be counter-productive. We need to develop approaches in which student confidence can be nurtured through group dialogue, and in which students can make their own judgements, develop the ability to analyse those judgements, and so take on responsibility for their own learning and thinking as quickly as possible. The teacher has an important role here, for critical thinking will not simply blossom from thin air. The teacher's task is to help everyone concerned make problematic what they think they know, and to develop the ability to question underlying assumptions. In this situation it should be clear that the simple regurgitation by students of teacher judgements emphatically will not do. I see very little justification at any educational level for what is, in many secondary schools, the almost universal practice of dictating notes, no matter how important the information within them is deemed to be. For what is always communicated by such a practice is the information that knowledge can be successfully *imprinted* via a hierarchical mode of transmission.

What students do need, of course, are reference skills which will enable them to find information for themselves from original sources. The provision of a wide range of source and reference material has rarely been raised as an important area for development within media education, but if the teacher can build up a bank of basic reference materials, then she will find that the apparent need to deposit information upon students will disappear. Accordingly, a good deal of attention is paid in this book to the provision of reference material for students (see

Chapter Four and Appendix A), and the development of critical skills in handling information. Students need to go to this material in order to solve or clarify particular problems, however. The process suggested on page 26 in which students move from the study of particular issues or texts to an understanding of general principles, should encourage students to go to reference material with particular questions in mind. Further, detailed work on sources (see pages 117ff) will enable students to weigh information carefully in the light of the interests of those who provide it. Given these two preconditions, the danger that reference material will simply replace the teacher as an unproblematic fount of information and wisdom, and the controller of the group's thinking, will be greatly diminished. It should, instead, develop the students' autonomy, their ability to learn how to learn.

(ii) A major task of the media teacher and her students is to tap as fully as possible the perceptions and insights of the group. The reasons for this are simple. The group will have a wider range of perceptions, experiences and cultural reference points at its disposal than any teacher could have. Therefore, as co-operative investigators, group members can share a much more varied range of meanings and responses, and have the potential, from a wider range of reference points, to render textual meanings at all levels of analysis more problematic. Media teachers generally understand this very well from their experience of investigating with a group a particular film or television programme, a process which, even with quite young primary school children, is generally a mutually illuminating experience.

Someone, of course, has to set this process in motion, and the initial responsibility must lie with the teacher to be as lively and inventive as possible in opening up communication within the group. As the group moves on from denotative investigation to an exploration of the text's deeper connotative and ideological meanings (see Chapter Six), the teacher, at first at least, may again need to take a lead. But it is not a lead in which she stands in front of her class as an accredited expert, but one in which her perceptions and interpretations are as open to investigation and change as everyone else's. The practice of media education, then, is one in which all participants share what they think and question why they think as they do. It is a process of group enquiry. The moment it ceases to be that it will become the site of either student resistance or, even worse, of student submission to the authority of the teacher.

(iii) The nature of the media themselves encourage non-hierarchical teaching modes. Not only, at their best, do they spread information and knowledge *laterally*, speaking across rather than down to their audiences. They also generally speak with the same voice to an audience divided by class, race, gender, and so on. In media lessons, teacher and students alike are equally and equal objects of address. Breaking with this equality by establishing a more hierarchical mode can have unfortunate consequences. It is likely to be seen by students (though it would never be expressed in these terms) as a form of cultural expropriation through which their own cultural forms and pleasures (especially in the areas of music and entertainment) become subjected to mediation by teachers and in danger of being wrested from students altogether. Notwithstanding the necessity of problematising the out-of-school media pleasures of both students and teacher alike, if media education is ever seen as a mechanism through which educational institutions recuperate students' media tastes, relaying them back to students via the sensibility of the teacher, then it will again become the site of considerable student resistance.

(iv) Recent research on media audiences (see Chapter Seven) has shown that meanings are produced not by texts themselves but by the interaction of texts and audiences. This has important implications, not simply for the analysis of television texts, but for pedagogic practices within every classroom. Certainly, within media education, if the full implications of work on the significance of audience responses has been fully grasped, it is scarcely possible to pursue a pedagogy within which students are treated as the recipients of pre-ordained information and ideas, rather than as active makers of meaning in their own right.

(v) Finally, a pedagogy which is concerned to de-naturalise media texts and to ask in whose interests they are produced, by what processes and with what results, can hardly avoid raising precisely those questions in relation to the school curriculum itself and the ways in which it is transmitted. This is particularly so as school curricula and teaching methodologies are, as Ferguson and Alvarado have argued, generally formulated not as discourses, as ways of conceptualising experience, but as forms of *realism* whose

'main components are a respect for empirical data (the facts) coupled with a common sense which in a particularly British way

trusts itself to be beyond serious reproach. The most intellectually pernicious forms of such a realism manifest
themselves in the practices of the teacher whose Anglo-centric
world view is presented to pupils as the way things *are*. Or the
realist lecturer who stands above and beyond material reality in
order to pass judgement on the foibles and biases of the
unworthy... This is the realism of which we write and it assumes
a straight correlation between the 'real' and the bourgeois-liberal
English vision.'[8]

Media teaching – every bit as much as media texts – needs to be
problematised and opened up to investigation within the classroom.
The methodology as well as the content of media education needs to
be the subject of dialogue and collaborative investigation between
teacher and taught.

b) Dialogue – Reflection – Action

The transformation of relations opened up by media education
entails much more than a movement towards 'progressive' methodologies, however. Methodologies, whether traditional or progressive, are always, for better or worse, influenced at the point of
reception by the bedrock assumptions and attitudes of the teacher. As
we shall see, it is possible for progressive methodologies to serve
manipulative purposes, or to treat 'experience', whether the students'
or the teacher's, as unproblematic. So it is necessary to make clearer
some of the assumptions and beliefs about human potential and
learning upon which the pedagogy already outlined is based. For
what I am concerned with here is what I will call, for want of a better
term, a *philosophical approach* to learning, rather than simply a
pedagogic *method*, less a series of techniques which teachers can try
out on Monday morning, than some guiding principles to a complex
process which challenges many of our most common-sensed
approaches to teaching and learning.

This approach follows closely that practised by Brazilian
educator, Paulo Freire, who argued for a pedagogy which would
liberate rather than oppress or domesticate.[9] His approach rests
firmly on a belief in our human potential to reflect critically upon our
experience, to discover what, within our own and others' experiences,
oppresses and limits our thinking and our actions, and finally to act in
order to transform those debilitating factors in the interests of all
human beings and of the ecological systems of which we are a part.

First and foremost, Freire *trusts* the potentiality and inclination of human beings to move in these directions. Secondly, he also recognises that most of what passes for education militates against this movement for liberation. Changing the status quo demands an acknowledgement that education is never neutral, but always political, and has the potentiality to be either liberating or domesticating. Every teacher needs to reassess her practice in the light of this. Next, it is necessary to problematise 'objective knowledge'. How and why has this information been selected? By whom and in whose interests? Against what and whom is this knowledge directed?[10] De-mystifying the world, seeing it not as a 'given' to be accepted, but as something to be critically worked on, to be shaped and changed by human agency, is a necessary pre-condition for a liberating educational praxis. It is necessary, too, to 'take as a point of reference the concrete reality of the learners and their own experience in this reality,'[11] and to abandon narrative and hierarchical modes of transmission, which turn learners into the passive and alienated receivers of others' 'knowledge'. As teachers we need to work hard to eradicate whatever is oppressive and dehumanising in ourselves and in our treatment of others. That means opening up our *own* experience and conduct, and not only that of our students, to critical scrutiny through group dialogue, and bringing into question traditional structural relationships within education: the relationship of teacher to student, of student to student, and of both teacher and students to knowledge itself.

Dialogue – reflection – action: the component parts of Freire's formula for a liberating education are all to be understood dialectically. Dialogue is both the basis of reflection and action, and the site to which they return for continuing regeneration. Dialogue – an approach I think demanded by media education – needs to be differentiated from discussion, a distinction which may serve to reinforce that already made between an 'approach' and a method.

Discussion, whilst far preferable to teacher-dominated discourses, and having some potential to transform consciousness, often falls short of this. At its most limited, dominated and controlled by the teacher, it can be merely a manipulative mechanism for enabling her to pass on information already in her possession, a scarcely disguised form of 'banking' education.[12]

In another limited form it becomes a substitute for action, an end in itself in which there is probably much to be said for both sides, and the group must finally agree to disagree. A close variation might seek to establish consensus, in the belief that 'the truth' probably lies somewhere between the various 'extremes' which have been articulated (a model which owes not a little to media paradigms of discussion). Both forms are essentially celebrations of individualism and pluralism, and of the tolerant, liberal and open atmosphere in which these symbiotic ideologies can flourish, rather than ways of creating knowledge through the attainment of more complex understandings, and of developing strategies for action. Discussion too frequently leaves things as it finds them. It *can* change individuals, but as a method it is ideally suited to the purposes of those who seek, consciously or unconsciously, to manipulate students. Worse still, it can function as a safety-valve which conveys to the participants the illusion of action, whilst the problems under discussion remain unaltered.

Dialogue, on the other hand, involves a genuine sharing of power – even if differential power relationships exist outside of the dialogue. Participants need to maintain an attitude of reflective self-criticism upon their thinking and actions within the dialogue in order to eradicate manipulation. Dialogue involves listening carefully and responding directly to what has just been said. It is genuinely a *group* process (rather than something which is engaged in by a number of discrete individuals) in which members recognise the power which can be generated through co-operative learning, group action and reflection, and are prepared to work through the group in order to maximise their own effectiveness.

Through dialogue it is possible to develop *dialectical thinking*,[13] which recognises the internal contradictions and tensions which exist within the group and within each individual, and which understands that such contradictions are inherent in all situations and issues which the group explores. Dialogue does not attempt to *dissolve* contradictions into consensus, but actively *seeks contradictions out* as the motivating power for change. Dialogue seeks to understand phenomena, including the group's own activities, not as static and 'knowable', but always in their processes of change and development. Whereas discussion frequently does little more than re-cycle pre-existing ideas and knowledge, dialogue aims to generate new and more complex forms of understanding.

Finally, dialogue is orientated towards action. Using and intervening in the media are important parts of any media education course, but action is more likely to be successful if it is undertaken by a group than by individuals, and if it is based upon a dialectical analysis of the situation in which it is proposed to intervene.

Because group processes are likely to be central to any worthwhile form of media education, it is important that 'discussion' – so long accepted by many excellent teachers as being intrinsically valuable – should be problematised, so that through the practice of as many teachers as possible it can begin to evolve into something potentially more liberating and powerful.

(c) Critiques of progressivism

There has recently been much lively debate on media pedagogy, and teaching approaches of the kind advocated in this book have been labelled 'progressive' and attacked under that banner.[14] One of the difficulties of this kind of criticism is that it has tended to ignore the diversity of educational philosophies and pedagogic practices which have been given this label. For whilst it is evident that some 'progressivist' approaches may lack intellectual rigour, treat a child's experience as unproblematic, or lack any clear political perspectives (three of the most common criticisms of progressivism), it is equally clear that others do not. Critics of progressivism have paid too little attention to the very real divergencies which exist between different progressive traditions, and too often rest their cases upon individual and frequently anecdotal examples of 'progressive' teaching, which few practitioners of any persuasion would wish to defend.

Many left-wing critics of progressivism have been influenced by selective renderings of the ideas of the Italian Marxist, Antonio Gramsci, who in the 1920s and 1930s advocated conservative curricula and teaching methods in order to prepare working-class children for an adult life in which they would struggle for socialism.[15] Gramsci argued that it was necessary for children to acquire at school the cultural baggage, the skills and the disciplined attitudes towards thinking and working which would enable them to become, as adults, effective change-agents in their society. Gramsci's criticisms were aimed at the progressive educational reforms of Mussolini's Minister of Education, Gentile, which were, in their turn, reactions against the sterile and formal instruction of traditional Italian common school education. This has led a number of writers to point to possible connections between progressive education (with its supposed denigration of knowledge, and privileging of spontaneity and experience) and an intellectual climate inimical to democracy, and favourable to the development of Fascism.[16]

Gramsci's critique of progressivism struck a chord in the 1970s with a number of radical British educators, who argued that working-class, and particularly black, children were being sacrificed on the altar of liberal middle-class progressivism by being denied the opportunity to acquire basic skills and the discipline of hard work which they would need to be effective participants in their own culture.[17] Maureen Stone, for example, has argued passionately that black children are all too frequently victims of 'free and easy' pedagogies and need to receive their fair share of more formal and academic work. Her position is unwittingly close to some progressivist stances. For she rests much of her case upon the success of formal voluntary classes organized for West Indian children outside of school hours. A. S. Neil would have approved. For the voluntary nature of the activities transforms the traditional power relations which exist in schools from the very outset. The students are willingly learning because they do not have to be there. They are in control of the situation and may walk out of the door at any time. That is a position which many progressivists would be willing to endorse. For its consequence, surely, is not that drawn by Maureen Stone – that students should receive more prescriptive work in schools – but that they should be allowed to exercise a greater degree of choice and control over their work, and that knowledge which *they* believe will be 'really useful' should be readily available to them when they require it.

Gramsci's work has not simply been used to buttress arguments for more formal schooling, however. It has also influenced those progressivist pedagogies which have acknowledged the significance of bourgeois hegemony, both within and outside of educational processes. Indeed, how is it possible to render hegemonic 'common-sense', problematic if the traditional organisation of the curriculum, and hierarchical teacher-student relations, remain unquestioned? It is, surely, only by problematising through dialogue all of these common-sense practices and assumptions in which teachers and students are alike enmeshed, that they will be able to break with dominant ideologies.

The most damning charge to be levelled against critiques of progressivism, however, is that they are based on very curious assumptions about the problems which presently beset British schools. For there is a large element of fantasy in a view of our schools as cells of progressivist philosophy and practice, dangerously child-centred, with little curriculum structure and with laissez-faire attitudes to work and discipline. It is a seriously distorted perspective which actually seems to owe more to tabloid journalism than to a close acquaintanceship with real classrooms. Sadly, the reality which emerges from the recent HMI Surveys of Primary and Secondary Schools is that they are pretty much the same as they have always been – obdurately conservative, doggedly unimaginative, and placing the highest value upon conformity. The 'basics' are not being ignored. Quite the contrary. They are being taught with a high degree of conscientiousness and intensity. That, indeed, is a major part of the problem. Even in primary schools, the Inspectors noted, 'about three quarters of the teachers employed a mainly didactic approach, while less than one in twenty relied mainly on an exploratory approach.'[18] As for secondary schools,

'over nearly 400 schools, the lasting impression was of a general uniformity of demand . . . the pattern most frequently found could be described as essentially one of "notes" and "essays" interspersed with the practice of answering examination questions alongside the drills of exercises and tests.

This pattern did not make it easy for pupils to feel that their individual reactions were valued or that their variations of information or opinion were welcome. Their files at times demonstrated the imprinting of a standard language, arising from teacher or text-book ... [In most subjects] there was a strong tendency towards extended expositions and the substantial making of notes ... Teachers justified these ways of working on the grounds that they felt constrained to impart as much information as they could in the limited time available ... There were many examples of lengthy monologues without pause for questions ...' etc., etc.[19]

These are some of the realities of life in our classrooms and it is desperately important that we begin to address them, rather than the pseudo-problems identified by right-wing politicians and the tabloids, and taken up by some on the left. Our formal system of education produces massive casualties, particularly amongst those millions of children who leave school each year believing themselves to be failures. In virtually every streamed school in the land, the lower streams soon begin to cause major problems quite predictably wreaking their vengeance in every way possible on the system which has failed them. In these situations, and as a last resort, what sometimes look like more 'open' approaches are tried, in a vain attempt to retrieve the irretrievable. One suspects that it is such initiatives as these, generally low status, unambitious and frequently manipulative activities carried out by inexperienced members of staff, which have attracted the attention of critics of progressivism. But children attending such classes are not the victims of progressivism at all. They are, rather the tragic casualties of an overwhelmingly formal system that has failed to meet their needs and does not care about (let alone build upon) their experiences.

If HMI's description makes anything clear, it is that we are in desperate need of participatory and liberating pedagogies, which will encourage teacher-student dialogue and hand over much more responsibility for their own learning to students. Solutions which ignore the complexities of teaching and learning processes and simplistically advocate a return to banking education, with socialist rather than bourgeois currency, do nothing to transform social relations in accordance with human need. Rather, they simply replace one form of authoritarianism with another. What is missing here is any understanding of the hidden curriculum of schooling and of the ways in which the most effective learning is transmitted through unquestioned *social* relations and practices. Critics of progressivism should recognise that it is in the total *experience* of schooling that its ideological effectiveness lies, and not simply in the transmission of this or that subject content. Of course, progressive pedagogies should have a hard, critical edge and not simply be, in Giroux's words, 'a pot-pourri of encounter group happenings and process-bound inter-personal activities designed to enrich our existential selves with moments of collective warmth and cheery solidarity.'[20] But any pedagogy that fails to recognise the extent to which patterns of domination and subordination are deeply embedded within all of our social and pedagogic practices and, indeed, within all of our perceptions of ourselves and others, will scarcely begin to touch the systemic oppression which operates within most classrooms. Nor will any pedagogy which treats learning undialectically and objectifies both knowledge and students. However radical the content, if education remains a banking operation in which the relationships between teacher and student, and the relationship of both parties to knowledge, remain unproblematised, then it will simply reinforce existing patterns of domination.

Here we can all learn from the women's movement, which has recognised that dehumanising factors in society are not only located in class relationships, and that access to facilities and knowledge needs to be complemented by new, non-patriarchal forms of working and learning together in order to achieve liberation. The best of progressive pedagogy shares this recognition. The attempt to 'imprint' ideas, whether reactionary or socialist, is not education but propaganda. If we encourage this form of 'learning' in schools, then our students will be vulnerable to other forms of manipulation for ever more. It is upon the ability of students leaving our educational institutions to think critically and make their own rational decisions that the future of our society depends. Media education, both in its conceptual orientation, and in its development of more genuinely liberating pedagogic strategies, can make an important contribution to those ends.[21]

Chapter 3

How not to . . .

To see the media as symbolic systems or signifying practices which deal in representations rather than reflections of reality, is to understand the necessity for 'reading' the media rather than passively accepting them as substitutes for experience. It is to recognise, as we have seen, that the ideological power of the media resides in their plausability, and in the ability of media owners, controllers, and workers to pass off as 'real' or 'natural' what are *inevitably* partial and selective constructions of the world. It needs to be stressed, however, that this way of seeing the media, though in my view the most illuminating, is not the only one on offer. The quotations interspersed throughout this chapter are a reminder of how widespread, persistent and powerful other ways of perceiving the media are. They are taken from a variety of official, academic and popular sources, and will need to be actively challenged by media teachers since they will inform the thinking of many teachers and students on the media, and will almost certainly shape the active practices of much media use in schools, quite outside of media studies lessons. This chapter, then, will present critiques of four influential ways of thinking about the media, together with a description of their origins and development:

(i)   the media as agents of cultural decline

(ii) the media as popular art forms

(iii) the media as aids to learning, and disseminators of knowledge and experience.

(iv) the media as agents of communication.

(i) The media as agents of cultural decline: the legacy of Leavis and Thompson

Media education in Britain can really be said to have begun with the publication in 1933 of F. R. Leavis and Denys Thompson's little book *Culture and Environment*.[1] The book was a clarion call to resistance against the influence of 'civilisation', of which one of the most corrupting manifestations was the mass-media. In one sense *Culture and Environment* can be seen as simply another contribution to the long history of 'respectable fears' about the moral corruption of working people through their predilection for debased amusements. Geoffrey Pearson has entertainingly catalogued this lineage which

'reaches back, via the accusations against the Hollywood "talkies" and the earliest silent movies, through and beyond the Music Halls at the turn of the century when directly similar complaints were voiced, towards the cheap theatres and penny-gaffs of early Victorian England... and then back towards the eighteenth century's disapproval of popular amusements such as fairs, interludes, public shows and minor theatres.'[2]

Leavis and Thompson's achievement was to harness this long-standing preoccupation with the social and moral decline of English society into a campaigning educational politics which was, though subject to some significant modifications, so successful that it was to maintain a hegemony over the ways in which educationalists and other responsible members of society conceptualised the media for over 30 years. Its influence remains strong today, amongst English teachers in particular, and it continues to lend some legitimacy to frequent moral panics about the media by those to whom Leavis may be no more than a name, and Thompson scarcely even that.

Culture and Environment begins:

'Many teachers of English who have become interested in the possibilities of training taste and sensibility must have been troubled by accompanying doubts. What effect can such training have against the multitudinous counterinfluences – films, newspapers, advertising – indeed the whole world outside the classroom? Yet the very conditions that make literary education look so desperate are those which make it more important than ever before; for in a world of this kind – and a world that changes so rapidly – it is on literary tradition that the office of maintaining continuity must rest.'[3]

What Leavis and Thompson offered to English teachers was a missionary position: a positive and heroic role as bastions of cultural values in a world of change, change that had destroyed 'organic' rural communities and had replaced them with mass production, standardisation and a levelling down in cultural and material life:

'Those who in school are offered (perhaps) the beginnings of education in taste are exposed, out of school, to the competing exploitation of the cheapest emotional responses; films, newspapers, publicity in all its forms, commercially-catered fiction – all offer satisfaction at the lowest level, and inculcate the choosing of the most immediate pleasures, got with the least effort. The school-training of literary taste does indeed look a forlorn enterprise. Yet if one is to believe in education at all one must believe that something worth doing can be done. And if one is to believe in anything one must believe in education. The moral for the educator is to be more ambitious: the training of literary taste must be supplemented by something more. And there has been enough successful experimenting to show that more might be done, and that it is worth doing. In the attempting the many intelligent men and women who every year go into schools might find assurance of vocation. Certainly there is a function awaiting them that might command enthusiasm. The instinct towards health – the instinct of self-preservation – that we must believe to be in the human spirit will take effect through them or not at all.

In a world of depressed and cynical aimlessness there is for them work that, aiming at considerable and considered ends, will yield enough in immediate effect to make whole-hearted devotion posssible ... we are committed to more consciousness; that way, if any, lies salvation. We cannot, as we might in a healthy state of culture, leave the citizen to be formed unconsciously by his environment; if anything like a worthy idea of satisfactory living is to be saved, he must be trained to discriminate and to resist.'[4]

It would be difficult to over-estimate the influence of that call to moral and cultural resistance amongst succeeding generations of English teachers, to say nothing of the prevailing religiosity of tone. Yet, from the perspective of today's media teacher, *Culture and Environment* also offered a more positive legacy. For the book was the first to make the discussion of media texts in the classroom an acceptable and intellectually respectable activity for teachers. The many examples, for analysis and discussion, of extracts from newspapers, magazines and advertisements which crowded the pages of *Culture and Environment* were eventually to pave the way for later and more progressive work by teachers who were much more sympathetic to the media experiences of their students than Leavis and Thompson had been. *Culture and Environment* for its part left little space for responses other than the authors' own:

'Some advertisers aim at creating the illusion of "personal" relations between themselves and their prospective customers. Give examples. When were you last taken in?'

'"Clean cut executive type", "good mixer", "representative man", "short-haired executive", "regular guy" (Americanism). Why do we wince at the mentality that uses this idiom?'

'"I would admit that it is better to read a thriller than not to read at all" (Harold Nicholson). What is there to be said against this view?'[5]

Leavis and Thompson's view of education as a process of inoculation against an anti-cultural environment, a machine-produced media 'culture', was to be so influential that it found echoes in two major educational reports, Spens and Crowther (see p. 42), which spanned a gap of over 20 years; and it still has some influence in the work of such writers as David Holbrook and Peter Abbs (see p. 42), as well as the practice of many English teachers. However, there is now, amongst many media teachers, such a reflex dismissal of Leavisite approaches to media study that some re-assessment of Leavis and Thompson's contribution to media education is long overdue. The almost exclusive emphasis upon the influence of Leavis himself, for example, may be somewhat misplaced. For there is certainly a case for arguing that Denys Thompson's impact upon schools was just as, if not more, important.

'Thompsonism'[6]

A former student of Leavis's, Denys Thompson became an English teacher at Gresham's, a minor public school in Norfolk, whilst still co-editor of *Scrutiny*, the literary quarterly associated with the Leavises, in the 1930s. In the 1940s Thompson was appointed to the headship of Yeovil School. He left *Scrutiny* in order to edit *English in Schools* – later to become *The Use of English* – which, under his editorship, was to become one of the most important influences upon the development of English teaching during the 1950s and 1960s. *The Use of English* generated a number of regional Readers' Groups, and in 1963 Thompson played an important role in the foundation of NATE (The National Association for the Teaching of English). He it was who convened a meeting, consisting largely of *Use of English* group secretaries, to set up an executive committee and plan the Association's inaugural conference. Over a period of 40 years Thompson has written and edited school text-books and anthologies, and contributed a regular supply of reviews, articles and editorials to educational journals, all proselytising and expanding upon the views outlined in *Culture and Environment*.

Certainly it would be an advantage if all our children could learn the same English speech ... Teachers are everywhere tackling this problem, though they are not to be envied their struggle against the natural conservatism of childhood allied to the popularisation of the infectious accents of Hollywood. The pervading influences of the hoarding, the cinema, and a large section of the public press, are (in this respect as in others) subtly corrupting the taste and habits of the rising generation.

(Report on Secondary Education, *Spens Report, 1938*)

Just because they (the mass media) are so powerful, they need to be treated with the discrimination that only education can give. There is undoubtedly a duty on those who wield such great power to use it responsibly. That is a matter for the whole community, and not especially for educationalists. There is also in our view a duty on those who are charged with the responsibility for education to see that teenagers, who are at the most insecure and suggestible stage of their lives, are not suddenly exposed to the full force of the 'mass media' without some counter-balancing assistance.

(15–18, *The Crowther Report, 1959, Vol. 1, Para. 66*)

... the cultural processes engendered by the consumer society ... can be pinpointed quite simply: there are large and accruing profits to be made from a vast populace rendered intellectually gullible and emotionally indolent. Cliché, sentiment, glossy patter, stereotyped images, instant jingles round the clock, are easy to manufacture, easy to slot to each other, and providing that within the populace there are no sensitive feelings for aesthetic shape and personal truth, easy to distribute not only across 'the provinces', but around the world. There is nothing, for example, easier than to slot dead clichés together making them sound warm and intimate to lazy half-illiterate readers ... We need to know whether television, by providing so much detail and that so constantly, effaces imagination and, in so doing, develops a deep passivity of mind, an unwillingness to grapple with life, an inability to initiate events. We need to know whether the casual stance adopted by the intelligent young today derives from a profound sense of cultural relativity fostered by the arbitrary flow of the serious and the trivial, the real and the unreal, which marks television entertainment, magazines, newspapers and radio alike.

Peter Abbs, 'Mass Culture and Mimesis', *Tract No. 22*
(*undated circa 1980*)

When, as a direct result of the important NUT conference on *Popular Culture and Personal Responsibility* in 1960, Penguin books published their influential collection of essays, *Discrimination and Popular Culture*, it was Thompson who was entrusted with the editorship and who provided a focusing introduction, which whilst acknowledging some possibility of the media's having a more positive role within society ('They could keep to the fore matters of public concern – art, education, aid to needy countries, the regeneration of towns.') still reinforced the main themes of *Culture and Environment*:

'Though not all teachers are willing and equipped to give their pupils lessons in discrimination, schools can still pursue one central purpose, and many of them do, supremely well. That is, to bring their pupils into as much contact as possible with the first-rate in art, literature, and music, all widely conceived. The aim is to provide children with standards... against which the offerings of the mass media will appear cut down to size.'[7]

Thompson's has been an enormously influential life's work, the significance of which needs to be recognised and reflected upon by all media educators. For though Leavis showed the kind of sustained interest in educational practice which few of his detractors amongst today's cultural theorists can match, it was Thompson who made, over two generations, the practical connections between Leavisism and schooling, and who helped provide the educational infra-structure through which Leavisism could become (and remain still) such an important influence in schools and universities.

The lessons of 'Thompsonism' should not be lost on media educators. The dislocation of media theory from educational practice in Britain over the past 15 years has been a disabling one. Publications like *Screen* and *Screen Education*, both of which began life as classroom-orientated periodicals, ceased to have any wide-spread influence in or upon schools once they became stalking grounds for the high theorists, whilst at an International Television Studies Conference held in London in 1984, a conference dominated by academics from tertiary institutions, not one of the papers given was devoted to educational issues. The result of this debilitating fissure is that media education practice is now less developed throughout the educational system of England and Wales than it is in those countries (e.g., Australia, Scotland and most European countries) where teachers have had the confidence to organise themselves, publish their own periodicals, run conferences, develop their own regional networks and confront academics with the challenge of working collaboratively with them in producing 'really useful knowledge', rather than immersing themselves in what many teachers see as elitist, formalist, and largely unintelligible debates amongst themselves.

Elitism

One of the most frequently cited criticisms of Leavisism in relation to media education lies in its alleged elitism. Keith Windschuttle's characterisation of Leavisism is only the most recent example of the kind of knee-jerking response all too common amongst media educators:

'The "Leavisite" or Cambridge University school of English criticism, which dominated university teaching of literature ... in the 1960s, despaired of the popular culture of the twentieth century which impoverished the spirit by cultivating "passive diversion". It was necessary for an intellectual elite of literacy critics to preserve the traditions of Dante, Shakespeare and Donne and to recognise their successors. Only this way would the "consciousness of the race" be preserved from the contaminations of the new mass culture ... The "high culture" approach is inadequate for television ... its critique is grounded in the value system of the pre-industrial aristocracy and is a defence of that class's cultural dominance against the "philistine masses" who had been raised to prominence through the capitalist cultural market. It is not only elitist, but a hopelessly anachronistic position to take.'[8]

The charge is ironic. For *Scrutiny* was a direct social as well as intellectual challenge to the classically-educated scholar-gentlemen who had traditionally held prominent positions in the ancient universities, but whose social and intellectual positions were directly threatened by the re-drawing of the social composition of the intelligentsia, and of university students in the aftermath of the Great War. As Q. D. Leavis expressed it, in one particularly excoriating attack upon Professor G. S. Gordon, Professor of Poetry at Oxford,

'This "mode of life" has a vested interest in the profession of letters identical with its economic interests. A life devoted to the humanities means not following a vocation but taking up the genteelest profit-making pursuit, one which conveys a high caste on its members; literary appreciation must obey the same laws as other expressions of social superiority. The Discipline of Letters is seen to be simply the rules of the academic English club.'[9]

The *Scrutiny* group were, on the other hand, middle-class, provincial, from diverse intellectual backgrounds, and they valued, above all, the 'critical function'. For much of the 1930s they were ostracised by Faculties of English. Whereas Professor Gordon could assert in an inaugural lecture to the University of Oxford in 1923 that the idea that English should replace Classics as a field of serious academic study was 'an affront to life,'[10] Leavis, speaking of his work which took place *outside* of the Cambridge Faculty in the 1930s, could say that 'What governed our thinking and engaged our sense of urgency was the inclusive, the underlying and overriding, preoccupation: the preoccupation with the critical function as it was performed, or not performed, for our civilisation, our time, and us.'[11] Terry Eagleton's summary on the movement is apposite:

'In fashioning English into a serious discipline, these men and women blasted apart the assumptions of the pre-war upper-class generation. No subsequent movement within English studies has come near to recapturing the courage and radicalism of their stand. In the early 1920s it was desperately unclear why English was worth studying at all; by the early 1930s it had become a question of why it was worth wasting your time on anything else. English was not only a subject worth studying, but *the* supremely civilizing pursuit, the spiritual essence of the social formation.'[12]

Yet Eagleton, too, argues that 'the *Scrutiny* case was inescapably elitist... radical in respect of the literary-academic Establishment, coterie-minded with regard to the mass of the people.'[13] How just is this conclusion in relation to *Culture and Environment*?

The verdict needs some qualification. The main burden of the book's attack is, after all, against the *producers* of 'mass culture', rather than its consumers. And where sentimental and insincere writing finds a response it is as likely to be found amongst the middle-classes as anywhere else. The 'educated' minority who can keep alive literary tradition 'are not to be identified with any social class.'[14] They are, however, distinctly a minority. It is important to register that for Leavis and Thompson, minoritarianism was an *inevitable* result of working against the grain of industrial society, rather than a specifically anti-working-class elitism. As Mulhern has elaborated:

'It would be difficult to understand *Scrutiny*'s campaigning passion if Leavis's minoritarianism were interpreted as a full-blown self-regarding arrogant elitism. It was never that. Leavis and the Leavisites were all in favour of making the minority as large as possible. They remained minoritarians simply on the principle that, if you set your face against civilisation, you can never win a majority in your favour.'[15]

The tendency of media educators and others to collapse Leavis and Thompson's minoritarianism into a 'full-blown elitism' has played its part in preventing a more balanced re-assessment of *Culture and Environment*, a re-assessment which would involve a recognition of the radical aspects of the whole *Scrutiny* project, from which media educators may still learn: its anti-utilitarian spirit; its emphasis upon critical reading; its anti-capitalism and rejection of market values; its challenging of cultural and social orthodoxies, and its pugnacious educational politics and rejection of a notion of education designed to reproduce the prevailing order. (The purpose of education, argued Thompson, 'should be to turn out "misfits", not spare parts.'[16]). As we shall see, the charge of elitism might more accurately be brought against Leavisite critics who sought to transfer Leavis's criteria of literary value to popular cultural products in a way that Leavis and Thompson themselves never attempted.

The repression of politics

One of the most curious characteristics of *Culture and Environment*, as of the whole *Scrutiny* project, for the modern reader, is the absence of an explicit politics. This is curious, because the period in which it was written, the early thirties, was one of great political, social and intellectual fluidity. It was a period which confirmed the final decline of the Liberals and the establishment of the Labour Party as a major force in British politics. It was a period which confirmed, too, post-war changes in the social composition of intellectual workers, of which the *Scrutiny* group themselves were a part.[17] In staking out a ground for literary culture as the supreme repository of moral and spiritual values, above and beyond politics, Leavisism was bringing to completion an extended project within 'English' which was to be its most crippling legacy to media education. In order to unpack this legacy and to understand its extraordinary potency within English culture it is necessary to explore its antecedents.

Leavism was in fact the most striking and explicit re-emergence of a strand of 19th century social thinking which had periodically surfaced within English culture during the previous 60 years, Arnoldianism. Arnold's analysis of the political, social, and cultural crises besetting Victorian society, his critique of comfortable aristocratic 'barbarians', middle-class philistines, and a 'raw and half-developed' working-class,[18] his attacks on industrialism, and above all his placing of culture above and beyond the interests of classes, made a formidable weapon in the hands of the petit-bourgeois British intelligentsia of the 1930s.

For Arnold himself 'culture', with literature as its centre-point, was necessary as a specifically ideological bulwark against working-class political activism, and the crisis of culture provoked by the possibility of an extension of the franchise in the 1860s. *Culture and Anarchy*, Arnold's key work, was, specifically, a response to the 1866 suffrage demonstrations in Hyde Park organised by the Reform League, and the 'breakdown' of law-and-order occasioned by the demonstrators inflicting damage upon some railings. This was the 'anarchy' against which Arnold proposed his elaborate theory of Culture:

'[Culture] does not try to teach down to the level of inferior classes, it does not try to win them for this or that sect of its own, with ready-made judgements and watchwords. It seeks to do away with classes; to make the best that has been thought and known in the world current everywhere; to make all men live in an atmosphere of sweetness and light... the men of culture are the true apostles of equality.'[19]

What Culture offers is not simply 'sweetness and light', humane values, right reason and 'our best selves', as desirable ends in themselves, however, but as principles of *authority*:

'So whatever brings risk of tumult and disorder, multitudinous processions in the streets of our crowded towns, multitudinous meetings in their public places and parks – demonstrations perfectly unnecessary in the present course of our affairs – our best self, or right reason, plainly enjoins us to set our faces against. It enjoins us to encourage and uphold the occupants of the executive power, wherever they may be, in firmly prohibiting them.'[20]

The importance of 'English' in domesticating the working-classes both by initiating them into the national culture, and by transmitting to them moral values, led to its increasing institutionalisation as an academic subject. Beginning in the late 19th century as the 'poor man's classics'[21] the subject was soon to become, in the 20th century, central to the formation of a humanistic national education system which was seen specifically as a counterbalance to the threat of social disruption, which the collapse of liberalism, the decline of religion, and above all the spectre of Bolshevism, seemed to presage at the end of the Great War. One of the most influential documents of the time, the Newbolt Report on the *Teaching of English in England* (1921), dealt quite specifically with the question:

'We were told that the working-classes, especially those belonging to
organised labour movements, were antagonistic to, and contemptuous of, literature ... Literature ... as a subject of instruction is
suspect as an attempt to "side-track the working-class movement."
We regard the prevalence of such opinions as a serious matter, not
merely because it means the alienation of an important section of the
population from the "comfort" and "mirthe" of literature, but
chiefly because it points to a morbid condition of the body politic
which if not taken in hand may be followed by lamentable
consequences. For if literature be, as we believe, an embodiment of
the best thoughts of the best minds ... fellowship which "binds
together by passion and knowledge the vast empire of human society,
as it is spread over the whole earth, and over all time" then the nation
of which a considerable portion rejects this means of grace and
despises this great spiritual influence, must assuredly be heading to
disaster.'[22]

One witness to the Newbolt Committee gave the following analysis:

'The attitudes of the workers towards English and artistic studies is a
threefold one. One school, the oldest, will frankly deny the value of
English or of any education whatsoever; a second, the product of a
later decade, wants to know what value such studies have in the
understanding of life, in making the world around seem clearer; the
third and youngest school frankly denies the possibility of any good.
They see education mainly as something to equip them to fight their
capitalistic enemies. In the words of one young worker: "Yes, what
you say is all right – but will that sort of stuff bring us more bread and
cheese?" '[23]

It was George Sampson, himself a member of the Newbolt
Committee, who made the point more explictly than anyone in a
book springing directly out of Newbolt, *English for the English*:

'Deny to the working-class children any common share in the
immaterial, and presently they will grow into the men who demand
with menaces a communism of the material.'[24]

The main effect, then, of the re-emergence of Arnoldianism in the
1930s as a contender for intellectual hegemony, has been described by
Francis Mulhern, as

'a *depreciation*, a *repression*, and at the limit, *a categorical dissolution of politics as such* ... This discourse has done much to shape, and still sustains, England's cultivated, politically philistine intelligentsia; it is reproduced daily, with countless particular inflections, by the entire national educational system; it is a key element in the "cultural formula" of bourgeois Britain, part of an ensemble of cultural *domination*' [author's italics].[25]

This 'repression of politics' is media education's most debilitating inheritance from Leavisism. As Mulhern suggests, it remains today in our culture in the categorical distinctions often made between politics and education, or politics and literature. In spiriting politics away from the processes of signification Leavisian discourse forestalled, for 40 years, ideological investigations of the media, and of their function as consciousness industries. What it put in their place was a theory of literary value, and in particular an emphasis upon the importance of critical *discrimination*, ('the sense that this is worth more than that') as a way of keeping alive 'the consciousness of the race',[26] which persists as an underpinning concept in many discussions about the media down to the present day. Indeed, as we shall see, the short history of media education in Britain is, to some extent, simply an account of the changing meanings of the concept of discrimination, a concept inflected and stretched finally to breaking point, by attempts to apply it to the media.

(ii) The media as popular art forms

For all its hostility to the mass media, *Culture and Environment* was of crucial significance in making respectable the analysis of media texts in the classroom. It was a movement which was to be irreversible, opening the way in the late 1950s and the 1960s to the classroom use of advertisements, newspapers, comics, women's magazines, popular fiction, film, and television, particularly by English teachers. The increasing use of popular texts was paralleled during the 1960s by a significant movement away from Leavis and Thompson's position. For a new generation of teachers actually *liked* popular cultural forms, could see value in them, and were unwilling to discuss them as *inevitably* corrupting influences. They remained 'Leavisite', however, in their strong sense of moral purpose and their continued attachment to the notion of discrimination. Discrimination, however, now became something to be exercised not *against* the media, but *within* them.

1960 represents a crucial watershed. It was the year of an important and impressively well-attended national conference organised by the National Union of Teachers on *Popular Culture and Personal Responsibility*, at which the tensions between old and new attitudes were clearly discernible.[27] The quotations from Horace King, and Jack Longland, Director of Education for Derbyshire (see below) demonstrate the extent to which the old fears remained. Indeed, they had been fanned by the early inanities of commercial television, which had begun in 1955. As Peter Black wrote:

'Until ITV arrived the public had never seen . . . anyone earn a pound note for correctly distinguishing his left foot from his right, or a wife win a refrigerator for whitewashing her husband in thirty seconds, starting from Now.'[28]

ITV was seen as posing a threat to European civilisation as we knew it, perhaps less because its offerings were so tawdry, than because they were so popular. After early uncertainties, ITV's share of the audience increased dramatically. By 1957 it was 75% of those who could receive both channels.[29] The switch over from BBC to ITV was reaching 'epidemic proportions'.[30] By 1959 the ITV companies were beginning to make spectacular profits for their investors. They were, as Roy Thomson put it, 'a licence to print money.'

The hoses of mass suggestion are played alike on teachers as on the parents whose children they teach, so we must not be surprised if those china alsatians are to be seen in the windows of some teachers' homes as well, and not all of them read The Guardian *and* The Observer.

The day-school child continually has to jump within a space of hours from Abraham Lincoln to Roy Rogers, from exercises in critical discrimination to advertisement hoardings which, if they preach anything, preach that there is no such thing; from the Sermon on the Mount to Cross Bencher in the Sunday Express; *from the study and the imitation of greatness to the complacency of Richard Hoggart's little man who, in the popular press, in advertisements or on the telly – those moronic quizzes – is made to feel big because everything is scaled down to his measure; so that in the end we are encouraging a sense not of the dignity of each person but of a new aristocracy, the monstrous regiment of the most flat-faced.*

Jack Longland, Director of Education, Derbyshire

We inherit from our ancestors a European culture which was the gift of creative artists on the one hand and creative thinkers on the other. The schools, Churches and every kind of definite cultural organisation do what they can to pass on this tremendous gift from the past, to defend it against onslaughts. And on the other hand we have, if you like, commercial culture, which seems to threaten the very existence of the most precious things in the culture we seek to preserve.   Dr. H. King, M.P.

I feel this Conference has rather tended to think in terms of defending children against exploitation by the mass media, and one might be forgiven for wondering whether the Home Secretary yesterday morning saw the Conference as a means of reducing juvenile crime ... If I were asked to sum up in one sentence the purpose of education in film and television, I would simply say it is to help children to enjoy to the full all that is best in film and television.   Tony Higgins, teacher

Where education is concerned, it seems to me we are confronted with a number of problems, and the main one is that we are not yet quite sure what it is we would be trying to do if we tried to help children discriminate as regards mass media. What I tried to do was work for a very sharp critical response to the media themselves, increasing critical, discriminating sense of what was good and what was bad, and at the same time tried to encourage them to seek not popular versus high culture but a general extension of quality over the whole field.   Stuart Hall

(Popular Culture and Personal Responsibility, *NUT, 1960 (Verbatim Report of the Conference), pp. 26–7, 50, 104, 327–8)*

What the NUT Conference provided, then, was a platform for 'responsible' middle-class opinion to express its concern at the tide of commercialism and infantilism which seemed already well on the way to engulfing the nation. It was a concern which was to receive its fullest articulation some two years later in the Pilkington Report,[31] which, though rejected by the government of the day, was to some degree instrumental in ensuring that the worst fears of the NUT conference were not realized.[32]

Yet at the conference the anxious sirens of the day could not quite drown out the whisper of the future. A practising teacher, Tony Higgins, and Stuart Hall both pointed to more optimistic areas for growth in media study (see page 51), whilst Raymond Williams, in a compelling contribution, managed simultaneously to contextualise the current hysteria (with a historical survey of bourgeois attitudes to the media), to question some of the conference's prevailing assumptions (by looking critically at the paternalism of the BBC) and to urge that some consideration be given to *structural* solutions to the problems raised by the media ('I will have no more blaming the young... and no more blaming the parents and no more nagging, until we are prepared as a society to do something radical about the institutions.')[33]

It was the impulse towards more cautious discriminations *within* the media that were to provide the most immediate growth points from the conference, however. Indeed, one of the most important documents to emerge from the conference was not the official record of its proceedings, but the highly influential Penguin book, *Discrimination and Popular Culture*, published in 1964, in which 'serious' attempts were made to arrive at evaluative criteria for different aspects of popular culture.

This movement had received its official imprimatur with the publication of the Newsom Report in 1963. In words directly echoing Crowther, the report spoke of the need for schools to provide a 'counterbalancing assistance' to the mass media and of the necessity of discrimination:

'We need to train children to look critically and discriminate between what is good and bad in what they see. They must learn to realise that many makers of films and of television programmes present false or distorted views of people, relationships, and experience in general, besides producing much trivial and worthless stuff made according to stock patterns.

By presenting examples of films selected for the integrity of their treatment of human values, and the craftsmanship with which they were made, alongside others of mixed or poor quality, we cannot only build up a way of evaluating but also lead the pupils to an understanding of film as a unique and potentially valuable art form in its own right as capable of communicating depth of experience as any other art form.'[34]

I have noted elsewhere[35] that whilst Newsom was of great importance in encouraging the serious study of film in schools and colleges, its effect upon the serious study of other media was, unintentionally, almost entirely negative. For whilst, in the above quotation, both film and television are condemned for presenting 'false or distorted views', television mysteriously disappears when examples of integrity and craftsmanship are mentioned. The report recommends that film and television studies might develop as the study of art-forms comparable with literature, music and painting but such an approach clearly has its limitations when applied to television as the report implicitly recognises. As for other media, the report stresses the importance of critical work on popular magazines, newspapers and advertising, but makes no explicit links between the study of those media and film and television. Newsom, then, strengthened the position of film studies within education, at the comparative expense of other media (television in particular) which were more potent influences upon students' lives, and at the expense, too, of any exploration of the important inter-connections between different media.

The most impressive articulation of the general movement to sift the media for newer art forms came in the following year with the publication of Hall and Whannel's *The Popular Arts*, which contained many fine analyses of popular genres and artists. In their introduction, Hall and Whannel expressed what was to become the conventional wisdom among media teachers for the remainder of the 1960s:

'In terms of actual quality . . . the struggle between what is good and worthwhile and what is shoddy and debased is not a struggle against the modern forms of communication but a conflict within these media.'[36]

The book encouraged teachers to seek a kind of high culture within and even between the mass media. Ironically, however, in *The Popular Arts*, really popular films tended to be treated as works to be discriminated *against*. John Ford, for example, was judged not to be a major director since 'he does not bring to the cinema the cultural equipment of a Bergman or a Bunuel.'[37] Hawks' *To Have and Have Not* and *The Big Sleep* are not serious films, 'but their style rescues them from banality.'[38] Cinematic art resides not in the popular cinema at all, but in intellectual foreign-language films. Hawks and Ford are suspect *because* they are popular, and because they work within popular genres. On the other hand, 'no one has to be defended against de Sica, Bergman or Antonioni,' and 'we can understand the claims of Renoir, Bunuel, Kurosawa and Antonioni to this area of "high culture".'[39] Hardly surprisingly, Hall and Whannel could find little evidence of popular art within television. Treating the medium as a crude and inferior form of cinema, they compare *Coronation*

Street unfavourably with the documentaries of Dennis Mitchell,[40] whilst of popular series only *Z-Cars* and *Steptoe and Son* receive even qualified endorsement.[41]

The evaluation of newer media forms by what were actually quite traditional aesthetic criteria too often meant that 'discrimination' could be simply equated with a preference for the rather *serious* media tastes of middle-class teachers rather than the genuinely *popular* tastes of their pupils: *Panorama*, *The Guardian* and films shown in film societies, good; *Opportunity Knocks*, *The Daily Mirror* and *Carry On*... films, bad.

This approach to teaching about the media not only raised formidable pedagogic difficulties in the classroom, it also carried with it quite unacknowledged class-based notions of aesthetic taste. Richard Hoggart, writing some years earlier, had put his finger on the problem, observing the tendency to carry

'into new and confused areas of cultural activity, the old, comfortable grading by height of brow... reinforced by an implied social or educational grading... "Mass culture" is that enjoyed by the 80 percent who have not been to a grammar school... The crucial distinctions today are not those between the *News of the World* and *The Observer*, between the Third Programme and the Light Programme... between the Top Ten and a celebrity concert... The distinctions we should be making are those between the *News of the World* and the *Sunday Pictorial*, between "skiffle" and the Top Ten; and, for "highbrows", between *The Observer* and *The Sunday Times*. This is to make distinctions... which require an active discrimination, not the application of a fixed "brow" or educational scale.'[42]

Of all the shifting notions of media discrimination which we have so far charted, Hoggart's is clearly the most advanced, and the most sympathetic and relevant to the media experiences of working-class pupils. In the classroom, however, even this version of discriminatory teaching was likely to create problems, as we shall see.

The most forthright criticism of the popular arts movement, however, came from the guardians of more traditional cultural standards. Reviewing Hall and Whannel's book in *The Use of English*, David Holbrook delivered a comprehensive attack upon the authors'

'struggle for merits in the world of deliberate devaluation. They can only stand and watch and hope to applaud what is good among "pop". Yet they are, in fact, by their neutrality, helping to hold the ring for the exploiters – as the happy reception of their book by the Sunday papers showed.'[43] (See also pp. 56 and 57.)

It is worth emphasizing, too, that in spite of the theoretical progress made by the popular arts movement in the 1960s, more conservative views still carried considerable weight within schools. A survey of the ways in which the mass media were being used in secondary schools in the late 1960s revealed that 80% of grammar schools, 42% of comprehensives, and 36% of secondary moderns still managed to exclude them altogether,[44] whilst of those English teachers who did teach about the media, 36% did so in order to provide pupils with a defence against them.[45]

More serious in the long term, however, was the lack of progress made by practitioners of the popular arts movement in the classroom. Two brave attempts to apply this approach illustrate the problems. Nicholas Tucker's *Understanding the Mass Media* (1966) and Brian Firth's *Mass Media in the Classroom* (1968) were positive and sympathetic attempts to develop critical discrimination amongst pupils, by working with, rather than against, pupil tastes. Both writers experienced real difficulty, however, in making clear *how* television, newspapers, magazines and the like were to be judged. And neither book considered the even more substantial problem of how evaluative criteria might be applied *across* the media. Indeed, there is little attempt to develop cross-media insights and generalisations in either work. Media study is seen as being inevitably fragmented, its only unity emanating from a general desire to encourage discrimination. Tucker and Firth were hardly to be blamed if they did not possess the critical tools to accomplish their task. But it meant that, at best, both writers could offer little more than the hope that standards of discrimination might emerge reasonably clearly from observation and discussion. At its worst the study of the media simply ran the danger of descending into vaguely interesting discussions, measuring exercises and 'busy' work which lacked any incisive direction, dangers which continue to haunt the subject down to the present day.

Both books also made clear the implicit logic of the Newsom Report's position: film is *different* from other media. It is unquestionably a popular art form:

'The approach to the film will inevitably differ from that to the other media discussed . . . Film is going to be presented in the school rather in the way that literature is: the emphasis will be on an openness to the medium, rather than on building defences.'[46]

'It is important for the teacher to establish the point that films matter.'[47]

REVIEW OF HALL AND WHANNEL'S
THE POPULAR ARTS

There is little point in discriminating, as Hall and Whannel do, between pop and pop: Marilyn Monroe chosen as better than Brigitte Bardot, because Marilyn is an image of 'sexual vitality', holding something of herself back, while Bardot 'gives herself' to every man in the theatre. Neither are really women to us: at a deep level what needs to be discussed is the nature of phantasy objects and their effect on our capacity for object-relationship: that is, relation to others and the world. Raymond Chandler they choose as better than Mickey Spillane because he shows by his ironic asides that he knows what he is doing. I see no value in such 'discrimination': if we are to have muck, let's have outright, sheer muck, rather than muck that pretends, by snobbery or irony, to be superior. This is to falsify the false. Let's not prefer Steptoe and Son to Coronation Street because it is written in the idiom of some new smart-alick 'realism', really no more than brash journalistic vulgarity: 'No-one is going to get me drunk on a half-pint of cider take me up an alley and do me . . .' This is Steptoe's son's protest to his father: 'We can feel something indestructible between them' say Hall and Whannel, with craven deference. All I can feel is that such vulgarity, with all its destructive ugliness, must at first have been an offence in the ordinary decent home, of whatever class. Only by the acceptance induced by persistent promotion by a monster industry, and by the apologias of sociologists, have such offences to human nature become acceptable, as part of the new 'pop' world . . . I could not quite get what was wrong with Hall and Whannel's book, until I recently went to Italy. There were magnificent cities, speaking of a time when human expression in art and The City were manifestations of a whole civilisation. Yet in the shell of this former splendour, at the corners the blousons noirs sat revving their motor-cycles with the silencers removed, and parties of Americanised students ranged round in an aimless and jeering way: Rave, Elvis, Paris Match and Les Beatles have helped to establish loutish habits everywhere in Europe. In the peasant household one was still met with an ancient, proud courtesy: in the town markets there was a rich working-class vitality. On the main roads one returned to the loutishness, and, in the gathering-places, to the offensive meaninglessness, the reduction of life, of the transistor, the demonstrative sex-cults, of

> *the raucous mob. And in the centre of Florence the most
> prominent culture was the James Bond film. 'Pop' is a plague, not
> a development at all: it's a cultural decadence complementary to
> the duplicity in the American use of the word 'defence' to describe
> Napalm bombing.*
>
> *Coming home, I saw what was wrong. The trouble was that
> such studies as this are simply not written from any concept of
> what Man might be, of what civilisation could be. They have no
> sense of the astronomical distance between the manhood of
> Michelangelo's David, or the womanhood of Botticelli's Venus,
> and the grunting animals to which the Parneses* would seek to
> reduce our sensitive aspiring children. Hall and Whannel simply
> have no perception of the sincere and beautiful, nor sufficient
> anger with the mean and false. Yet their book is quite useful – as
> useful as sociology without a sense of values and relevance can
> ever be.*
>
> (David Holbrook, "*Quite Useful Neutrals*", The Use of English,
> *Spring, 1966*)

The fruits of Newsom are also harvested in Tucker's and Firth's
treatment of television. Both teach about the medium defensively;
both are hamstrung by adopting 'aesthetic' criteria for evaluating the
medium; both derive their criteria from film theory. Tucker, for
instance, advocates the study of television techniques and posits the
centrality of the television director: 'In every way he is the key figure,
and pupils will do well to know some of the directors' names and the
sort of work they produce.'[48] The sentiment finds its echo in Firth:
'... one could hardly discuss *The Monkees* without pointing out the
debt of that series to the Beatles' films made by Richard Lester.'[49]
Most television material, not susceptible to this kind of analysis, can
be dismissed in one word at the very moment it is being observed:
'Television programmes are not entirely made up of dramatic serials,
plays and old films, and some notice might be taken of other standard
time-killers – quizzes, "pop" programmes and comedies, for
example.'[50] Worse, discussion is advocated, in which conclusions, in
Leavis and Thompson style, are already cut and dried:

*A reference to Larry Parnes, a pop promoter in the 1960s.

'Quizzes are often very popular, and the reason must be that there is often a very large money prize at stake. The difference between a quiz and a give-away show can at this point be made clear. Is it skill that enables the contestants to win or merely luck? Is it interesting to watch because it tests the audience's knowledge as well, and tries to bring viewers into the programme or is it because we see people tormented and often humiliated by their desire to get their hands on a big prize? Does the question-master ask his questions directly, or does he coax, hint and generally become the most important part of the show? Some of these programmes are mildly entertaining and occasionally instructive, but for the most part "they are good for killing time, for those who like their time dead." '[51]

The popular arts movement, then, had a number of important consequences, none foreseeable by those who initiated the movement. First of all it led to the increasing exclusivity and, in many instances, the ultimate separation of film – the one medium to have any serious credentials as art – from the study of other media. It thus encouraged the establishment of specialist courses in film at a number of universities, colleges and schools, ironically, at a time when film-going probably had fewer claims to being considered a genuinely popular pursuit than at any other time in its history. Secondly, it unwittingly contributed to the scandalous neglect of television and press studies which was to continue throughout our educational system from almost an entire generation after Newsom. Thirdly, the movement produced no coherent philosophy for understanding or studying the media. It produced few recorded examples of classroom practice, and little in the way of an effective tradition. It is a measure of the movement's failure that in the 17 years since the publication of Firth's book, no other full-length classroom-orientated book on media education has been published in Britain. The popular arts movement led media education into a wilderness, from which it has only, in the last few years, begun to emerge.

Against discrimination

As I have suggested, the short history of Media Education in Britain can be seen, to a large extent, as a history of the changing inflections of the concept of 'discrimination', a concept which, in spite of the changing attitudes and sympathies of those who have espoused it, has maintained its centrality as a key objective in the study of the media with remarkable persistence. The principal arguments against discriminatory approaches to teaching the media may be briefly summarised:

1. It is impossible to examine the short history of Media Education without recognising it as an essentially *middle-class, defensive and deeply paternalistic movement,* unjustifiably confident in the assertion of its own standards and judgements, and largely contemptuous of, and bent upon 'improving' the tastes of students.

As a result, *discriminatory approaches to the media have been essentially negative exercises*, which have singularly failed to mobilise the energies and enthusiasms of large numbers of teachers and students. As we have seen, in spite of holding a dominant theoretical position for around 50 years, there is little documented evidence that discriminatory approaches have generated very much in the way of successful Media Education practice.

2. *Very little theoretical work has been done to establish widely agreed criteria for evaluating the media.* This may be because of the implicit recognition that such criteria are chimerical. It has, therefore, been difficult for anyone – students, teachers or media critics and 'experts' – to make evaluative judgements about the media with anything other than a wholly unfounded confidence or spurious authority. Without the existence of some kind of *authority structure*, either within the subject content itself or in the critical approaches adopted to it, media education has not easily been able to survive in most British classrooms.

3. Added to the problem of deciding what, precisely, constituted good television or bad journalism were *doubts about the appropriateness of applying aesthetic criteria at all* to much media output (e.g., news, photo-journalism, advertisements, etc.).

4. Though discriminatory approaches centred the value question – the key issue was always 'Precisely how good *is* this particular text?' – these approaches actually posited *a naively transcendental notion of value*. Value (or the lack of it) was held to inhere timelessly within the text itself, awaiting discovery by the careful, but ideologically innocent reader, and validated not by an explicit theory, but by appeals to an educated consensus (see 6 below). What remained unquestioned in this approach were *the social and ideological bases of particular interpretations and judgements* and the assumptions and criteria underpinning assertions of value. Always left hanging unanswered were the questions, 'Value for whom?' and 'Value for what strategic purposes?'

5. In focusing so sharply upon value questions, discriminatory approaches tended to pay particularly close attention to the analysis

of media texts. This was both the strength of the movement, and a source of weakness. In their neglect of the contexts within which texts are produced, distributed and consumed, *discriminatory approaches could shed little light on the nature of the media as consciousness industries*. They did produce, however, a sensitivity in analysing the moment-by-moment nuances of a text, which sociological analyses of the media were quite unable to match.

6. There were insurmountable difficulties, from the late 1960s onwards, in making discriminatory approaches to media teaching work in most classrooms. In particular, it was the widespread introduction of comprehensive education which had, by the early 1970s, sounded the death-knell of Leavisism within most schools. To see why this was so, we need to go back to 1937.

In that year, Leavis was challenged by Rene Wellek in the pages of *Scrutiny* to make his assumptions more explicit, to defend them more systematically and 'to become conscious that large ethical, philosophical and ... aesthetic *choices* are involved.'[52] Leavis refused the challenge. He was not a philosopher, but a literary critic, he argued, and to respond fully to poetry was 'incompatible with the judicial, one-eye-on-the-standard approach suggested by Dr. Wellek's phrase: "your 'norm' with which you measure every poet."' His criticism was for 'readers of poetry as such. I hoped by putting in front of them in a criticism that should be kept as close to the concrete as possible my own developed "coherence of response", to get them to agree ... that the map, the essential order of English poetry seen as a whole did, when they interrogated their experiences, look like that to them also.'[53]

Leavis's ultimate appeal was not to a general consensus but to a literary one ('readers of poetry'). His famous question, 'This is so, is it not?' was addressed to readers engaged in 'the common pursuit of true judgement'. Leavis's aesthetic could only be validated, tautologically, by those who were already in broad agreement with it: 'What *Scrutiny*'s audience did not know already,' as Mulhern has pointed out, 'it could not be told.'[54]

Now, it was possible to teach literature in universities, and (as the pages of Thompson's journal for English teachers, *The Use of English*, made clear) in predominantly white, middle-class, single-sex public schools and selective grammar schools on the basis of some kind of consensus of shared values and assumptions. But within the multi-ethnic, predominantly working-class, mixed-ability comprehensive school classroom, Leavisism began to fall apart. For there, basic reading difficulties were turning one child in every five into a 'slow learner' and linking print indissolubly with failure. There, there were no comfortable closed circles of agreed meaning or if there were they were far from congruent with Leavisite sympathies. And there the minoritarianism of Leavisism – the anti-democratic spirit of a project which left, *by definition*, the responses of majorities out of the account – was finally understood by many teachers to be not only unworkable, but unworthy.

At this point I must pause to acknowledge the protests of many teachers and parents. Are we to be denied our right and duty to help our students distinguish the creative from the meretricious, the worthwhile from the third-rate in the media? Is even *The Sun* to escape scot-free? Are we sacrificing too much in a dangerous slide into relativism? Some sacrifice certainly is involved (not least to our egos as teachers) if we are deprived of the opportunity of demonstrating precisely why this newspaper is so contemptible or that television programme so valuable. Yet I am only suggesting a deferred and modified gratification. I am not arguing that the value question should be disposed of entirely. It simply needs to be moved from centre-stage in order to facilitate our chief objective: increasing our students' *understanding* of the media – of how and in whose interests they work, how they are organised, how they produce meaning, how they go about the business of representing 'reality', and of how those representations are understood by those who receive them. And that word 'understanding', with its emphasis upon the development of a critical intelligence in relation to the media, will need to be given a centrality previously accorded to the concept of discrimination.

The value question will not simply lie down, however. Questions of value *will* inevitably be raised in relation to the media. They should be deferred until the process of investigation is complete, however, and then considered by the student group in all of their variety and complexity. What range of cultural and sub-cultural evaluations (including those of the teacher) are being brought into play within the group? What problems, issues, inconsistencies and incompatibilities are raised by these evaluations? How have they been *produced*? To what uses is the text being put? What purposes are we asking it to serve for us? And can we analyse our own responses, not monolithically ('Great!', 'Crap!', 'Rubbish!', etc.), but dialectically, noting how our pleasures, gratifications, boredoms and frustrations change from moment to moment as we produce meaning from the text?

From Leavis we should, I think, hold on to the importance of critical reading, but as a process which needs to be informed by an understanding of a far wider range of contextual factors than Leavis ever concerned himself with. With the advent of sociological approaches to the media, and the development of the new 'disciplines' of Communication and Cultural Studies, close textual analysis has, over the past decade, been in danger of falling into disuse. It remains a centrally important critical activity in media education, however, and a compelling reason for urging English teachers in particular to put media education once again firmly upon their agendas. They will need to learn the lessons of the past, however. The media are too complex and important to be recuperable to this or that discipline. Media teachers need to be able and confident enough to step outside of their own specialist disciplines, taking from them whatever is appropriate and discarding what is not. And they need to be intellectually curious enough to explore the contributions which disciplines other than their own can make. That is the challenge of media education. It is one important and worthy enough to be taken up by every teacher who wishes to meet rather than retreat from the challenges of both the present and the future.

(iii) The media as aids to learning and disseminators of knowledge and experience

It is now necessary to consider briefly two inter-connected views of the media whose common assumption may have the widest general currency of all. Both are based on the idea that the media offer a relatively unhampered passage to experience. This assumption has been routinely written off by media educators for so long, that there is a danger of our forgetting not simply how 'common-sensed' this view is (see page 64), but how powerfully it is institutionalised and resourced within education, and how assiduously promoted by broadcasters (page 6).

The first of these views sees the media as 'aids' to learning. To be effective, it is argued, teachers need to possess enough technological mastery to 'match' teaching and learning methods to the appropriate technology. Educational technologists are available in many large educational institutions to give material support both to teaching staff, and to this view of the media and they, in turn, are backed up in many countries in the world by well-established professional networks, publications and organisations, all promulgating, with greater efficiency and at far greater expense than the media education movement can muster, principles which are the very antithesis of our own. For the use of media technology as a servicing agent is not simply linked to a mythical view of the media as neutral transmitters of ideas and information, but also to the rigid and (for media educators) damaging distinction between the educational uses of media and their prolific, informal, 'non-educational' use. This dichotomy is, in turn, linked to a further and equally misleading distinction between the media's function in providing experience 'in the raw' (in factual programmes, or sometimes even in 'realistic' plays and soap operas. See p. 64), and their entertainment function (in 'escapist' programmes and features which are deemed to have little connection with reality). Again, these distinctions are frequently endorsed by broadcasters and journalists whenever educationalists or academics attempt to take the popular media seriously (see pp. 64–5).

These distinctions between the educational and non-educational uses of media, between the media's 'reality' and 'escapist' functions, are actually challenged by the second view of the media which I wish to consider in this section. Whilst still remaining within the 'media-as-aids-to-learning' paradigm, this approach recognises the danger-ously wide gap which can exist between what is often the hermetically sealed world of the classroom and the environment, rich in educational possibilities, to which pupils are exposed out of it. It attempts to close this gap by making practical links between schools and out-of-school educational influences, amongst them the media. In the words of a UNESCO paper the teacher should possess

'The ability to create, coordinate and manage learning situations which do not originate and do not terminate exclusively inside the school premises, but which draw upon all kinds of contribution, stimulation and information deriving from an extremely varied and diversified cultural and technological environment.'[55]

Two features of this call for the integration of the mass-media (amongst other influences) into the teaching of all subjects are worth noting. First of all, it places emphasis upon the primacy of *pupils'* experiences of the media, and upon the implications of these experiences for formal learning. As we shall see (Chapter Eight) this is an important argument which can be used progressively to develop Media Literacy programmes across the school curriculum. Secondly, and more questionably, by linking the mass media with other influences upon the child (family, community, peer group, etc.), by conceptualising the media as simply a part of the 'environment' in which we all live, a view of the media, not as symbolic systems, but as unproblematic sources of 'experience' is being suggested (a view given some support by the *Bullock Report* of 1975, which advocated both the extension of media 'appreciation' and the increasing use of television as a source of vivid experiences). No doubt the teacher who can switch easily from a television extract to a text-book, or from an

'The difficulty about soap operas is that ... you don't have a story it's just circular it goes round and round and round. You have people, real people, and I didn't like any of them.'
(Brian Thompson, travel writer, discussing Brookside *on* Did you See...? *BBC2, 15.4.84)*

TV AM Interview with Caroline Kennedy, a student who is writing a thesis on the representation of social issues in Dallas

Anne Diamond	*But they're not really the social issues that affect you and me, are they? I mean we don't live in a great South Fork ranch, do we, with loads of money and oil spouting out all over the place?*
Caroline Kennedy	*Admittedly the material setting and situations of* Dallas *are different to the lives you and I would lead, but certainly the social issues are very relevant. I mean there are marriage problems in it, abortion has been mentioned, euthanasia, contraception – social issues that are very pertinent to a lot of people in Western society today.*
Anne Diamond	*But it is unreal isn't it? And their handling of it is unreal.*
Caroline Kennedy	*I don't think so ... once people get over the luxurious settings, they get involved with the characters ... they'll discuss those people's personal problems with their neighbours, friends and families once the episode of* Dallas *is over.*
Anne Diamond	*So in studying this ... what have you had to do, just stay glued to the television all the time?*
Caroline Kennedy	*Well, no, half of my thesis is about the theoretical basis that justifies a study of a melodramatic serial, i.e.* Dallas*, the reappraisal of the 50s melodramas and*

	films, and a re-appraisal of the serial Coronation Street – the naturalistic serial. So half of the thesis involves the theoretical justification. Now the other half is divided into a visual analysis of Dallas...
Anne Diamond	*Gosh! Visual interpretation and things like that. It all sounds very grand, but listen, you haven't answered the major question, which is 'Who killed Bobby?'*
Caroline Kennedy	*I haven't a clue who killed Bobby, and I don't think any of the characters know either, no more than they knew when JR got shot.*
Anne Diamond	*Caroline Kennedy, that is obviously the fact you must know in order to finish your thesis, but we're all going to have to wait aren't we?*
Caroline Kennedy	*Oh, absolutely.*
Anne Diamond	*Thanks very much. How amazing! Fancy doing a thesis on Dallas! Right, let's go on to our own soap character of the day, which is...*

LP to a newspaper article, who uses the media creatively as alternative sources of information, will provide a livelier and more interesting classroom environment for her students. But if these sources of information are not subjected to the kind of critical scrutiny advocated by media teachers, then an entirely mystificatory view of the media, and of knowledge, will have been smuggled in under the guise of educational progressivism and relevance.

(iv) The media as agents of communication

Of less historic influence and significance than the models discussed so far in this chapter, communication models of media

> *One of the most powerful sources of vivid experience is the general output programmes of television, particularly documentaries and drama. Many teachers are already basing a good deal of classroom work on such programmes. In some primary schools they use after-school programmes as a stimulus for talking and writing, and assemble collections of books to exploit the interest the programmes arouse. In secondary schools the practice is more widespread, and we met teachers who brought the experience of the television screen into the classroom, preparing for evening programmes and following them up the next day. Some classes were reading the texts of television plays with enjoyment and others were writing scenes for themselves. In a few schools we came across serious study of the medium of television itself. We were impressed by such work as we did see, but are concerned that a decade after the publication of the Newsom Report there is still little evidence of the kind of study it recommended: 'We should wish to add a strong claim for the study of film and television in their own right.' We believe that in relation to English there is a case for the view that a school should use it not as an aid but as a disseminator of experience. In this spirit we recommend an extension of this work. Although there is unquestioned value in developing a critical approach to television, as to listening and reading, we would place the emphasis on extending and deepening the pupils' appreciation.*
>
> *(The Bullock Report;* A Language for Life, *1975, ch. 22, para. 14)*

study are becoming of increasing importance in both tertiary and secondary educational sectors. Degree courses in Communication Studies are now widespread, and it is also possible to sit Advanced GCE papers in the subject.[56] From 1976–80 The Schools' Council funded a Communication and Social Skills project designed to define the contribution that practical work by 11–16-year-olds, using television, film and tape-slide, might make to the teaching of communication and social skills.[57] More recently, 'the new vocationalism', the government's answer to teenage unemployment, has encouraged in its lavishly-funded TVEI (Technical and Vocational Education Initiative) and CPVE (Certificate of Pre-Vocational Education) schemes, the development of depoliticised and technicised communications, and social and life-skills courses. Whilst some enterprising media teachers have used these schemes as ways of developing their students' critical consciousness, and whilst there are certainly in-service opportunities for working in these areas with teachers who are new to media education, it remains a matter of conjecture as to how long the Manpower Services Commission will allow this oasis of critical education to survive in the prevailing desert of know-thy-place technicism. I have already outlined some of the problems of what I have called the 'technicist trap' (Chapter Two), but nowhere are these problems more evident than when communications are placed at the service not of the development of a critical consciousness, but of the needs of industry. The warning signs were there in 1977 when the Associated Examining Board issued its notes of guidance to Communications teachers:

'The subject is an aid ... in industry, to the conveying of information in a wide variety of forms. A student who has successfully completed a Communications Studies course at "A" level is bound to be better equipped in his [sic] approach to the writing of letters, handbooks, manuals and other documents...'[58]

It is the domesticating and enslaving, rather than the liberating potentialities of 'communications' which are now being given full reign in TVEI and CPVE schemes, and even within Advanced level communications courses with their demands for regurgitative and reproductive skills, rather than critical abilities.

Here, however, I wish to summarise some of the principal difficulties involved in studying the media as component parts of a wider study of communications:

1. The first problem concerns the very concept of Communication itself. For if there are problems in studying the media in a disciplined way, what is one to say of a concept which can be used to designate everything from a private conversation to the building of a motorway, from *Coronation Street* to a crease in your trousers, from satellites to school magazines? The freedoms which many teachers enjoy in teaching under such a pluralistic umbrella are probably more than counterbalanced by the confusion over, and lack of discipline in, what is actually taught and how.

2. But the attempt to constitute Communication Studies *as a discipline* raises severe problems. For this notion is premised not simply on the unlikely idea that a telephone conversation, a haircut and *Dallas* can be drawn together within one area of study, but also that it will be *profitable* and *illuminating* to do so. It is premised, in other words, on the notion that there are

abstract *theories of communication* which are worth studying in their own right, outside of the contexts within which actual communications take place, and that these theories can demonstrate to us the underlying connections between apparently widely divergent practices and processes.

This raises an immediate problem for media teachers. For the attempts, in establishing the discipline of Communication, to draw out what are taken to be deep structural connections between media communications and, say, inter-personal communications mask the very characteristics of the media which make their study a matter of such urgency: their one-way structure; the gross inequalities between those who manufacture information and those who consume it; their function as consciousness *industries*; the complexity of the contexts within which they produce their texts, and their audiences produce meaning, etc. What are crucial about the media are not the similarities which they share with inter-personal forms of communication, but their *differences*.

3. The third thing which needs to be noted about the field of communication study is that whilst it has frequently been associated with 'value-free' empirical research (content analyses, 'effects' research, etc.), it has generally been used and developed to serve the interests of those who are in control of communications processes. The goal of much communication theory – 'effective communication' – has either been to ensure the delivery of particular desired outcomes in the audience (the purchase of a particular product, or support for a political party, for example) or to investigate whether the media were responsible for violent or anti-social behaviour. In all of these cases the key objective has not been to increase our understanding of the complexity of the media, but to increase the ability of those who control the media (either politically, commercially or professionally) to manipulate and affect the *audience*. Communications research has generally taken for granted, and sought to make more effective, a top-down, one-way, essentially undemocratic model of media communication.

4. Even in its own terms, empirical communications research has rarely produced important findings. This is because the attempt to separate communications from the social, historical, legal and economic contexts in which they are produced, circulated, transmitted and consumed, is doomed to failure. Effects studies, for example, are frequently based on simplistic linear hyper-

dermic models of communication which all too often serve the reactionary purpose of scapegoating the media in order to distract attention away from more deeply rooted social injustices. Such studies may hypothesise, for example, that urban riots or violence are the result of watching particular television programmes. But it is notoriously difficult to distinguish between the effects of the media and those of other socialising influences. And if we *really* wished to get to the roots or urban riots or violence, then we would have to study such phenomena in all of their social complexity, and look at such factors as the frustrations engendered by social injustices, unemployment, poor housing, overcrowding, poverty, the aggressive and competitive nature of society, and so on. Now the relationship between all of these factors and the media will be extremely complex, but we might at least hypothesise that the displays of conspicuous consumption in advertisements and television programmes might themselves be a general source of considerable frustration (that, indeed, may be their purpose), which may be particularly acute if they are received within a context of unemployment or social deprivation. In order to make these uncomfortable structural connections between social violence and television, however, we need to have moved considerably beyond the kind of simplistic communications model in which individuals are hypothesised as committing acts of looting or violence because they have seen them on television.[59]

5. Empirical content analyses also have severe limitations. At one level it is useful to know, say, the precise number of blacks or the elderly who appear on current affairs television, but it is also obvious that, again, we need to *interpret the contexts* within which they appear to make any sense of what is at stake in representations of these or other groups.

6. Finally, as Bonney and Wilson have suggested, 'communication' is not simply an idea or a concept:

'It is in process of becoming a profession, with the establishment of communication associations. It is also institutionalised by virtue of the establishment of communication courses and the associated development of a communication literature. It is, in fact, an ideology. In particular, it is a kind of empiricist ideology, in which the so-called act, or process, of communication is represented, not only in the abstract, but through the various practices associated with the establishment of courses, associations and a body of canonical literature, as separable from the social contexts in which the relevant activities occur. . . .

To push to the background the social, political, economic or cultural context in which media texts are produced, distributed and consumed – to treat it as external to the meaning and impact of those texts – is tacitly to endorse or legitimize it, to treat it as if it were simply there, a timeless, unproblematic fact of nature like the oceans or land formations which constitute the fixed background against which communications technologies – cables, satellite, micro-wave transmitters, and so on – are developed, installed and operated.'[60]

This book, by contrast, will attempt to give full weight to the contexts in which media texts are produced, circulated and consumed and it is to a consideration of the first of these areas, the contexts of media production, that we must now turn.

Chapter 4

Determinants

Introduction

This chapter attempts to explore some of the ways in which students might be encouraged to understand why our media and the texts they produce are the way that they are. It attempts, that is, to unpick some of the main structural determinants of the media and to suggest some ways in which students might be made more aware of the legal, economic and institutional frameworks within which media texts are produced. The chapter necessarily contains a great deal of information and discusses a large number of interlocking issues in an attempt to provide a general map of the relevant terrain. But it is less important for students to grapple with large amounts of information *than to grasp the inter-related nature of the complex web of influences at play within any media text* and to be able to weigh a number of different factors in the balance in assessing texts.

To be specific. It is perhaps less important for students to immerse themselves in the details of, for example, who precisely owns which media institutions (though some students may wish to do this within project work) than to possess

(a) an understanding of the general significance of overall patterns of media ownership and control within the context of

(b) an awareness of other important sources of power and influence within the media.

What is important, in other words, is for any pupil or student to know enough about, say, the Official Secrets Act, the influence of sources, the structural influence of advertising upon the media, the law of libel, the growth of public relations, institutional self-censorship *and* general patterns of ownership and control to be able to recognise them in play within a particular text. It is the tensions and contradictions which exist *between* and *within* each of these sources of influence and power which need to be engaged with.

What the teacher will require above all are a wide range of resources at her disposal (many of which may be currently somewhat unfamiliar to her), an ability to seize upon events of current importance in order to give her work vitality and relevance, and a willingness to work, not through mechanical exercises, but via media texts and media issues of importance and concern to her pupils. None of the areas covered in this chapter should be worked upon for its own sake. Rather, the various topics discussed in this chapter ought ideally to be introduced whenever they seem most relevant in illuminating matters or texts of topical interest and importance to the group.

It is in this light that the information and ideas in the remainder of this chapter will need to be considered. What is offered here is a general map of terrain so far largely uncharted by media teachers. It includes general summaries of a large number of issues and arguments, and a consideration of strategies for dealing with them in the classroom. But it is an important qualification that the information and reference material provided here should not be misconstrued as offering any encouragement to the development of a largely factually-orientated media studies curriculum.

The teacher's task is formidable. The model suggested here is more complex than those generally advocated within media education. Yet there is little evidence that even a single source of influence and power, that of media ownership for example, has ever been taught really effectively within schools.[1] There is little point in suggesting new and more complex analyses of media determinants if the problems of communicating these to school students remain as intractable as they have proved to be in the past. For this reason the chapter begins by examining a recent resource for teaching about media industries, the British Film Institute's booklet, *The Companies You Keep*. An analysis of the pedagogic problems raised by this booklet will be followed by a number of teaching guidelines for working with students and pupils on topics which appear to require the handling of formidable quantities of information. This will be followed by an attempt to identify and make sense of a number of structurally interwoven factors which act as powerful determinants of media texts.

1. Media determinants and pedagogic problems: the case of *The Companies You Keep*

Perhaps the clearest way of illustrating some of the difficulties which face teachers who wish to teach about media determinants is to examine a recently published resource on 'the leisure, entertainment and advertising industries and the pictures they produce,' the booklet *The Companies You Keep*, produced by the British Film Institute as part of its admirable *Selling Pictures* project materials.[2]

Let me say from the outset that *The Companies You Keep* is easily the most imaginative attempt so far to make questions of media ownership and industry accessible to secondary school pupils. The layout is appealing, methods of presentation are original (it includes a 100-year comic-strip history of Thorn/EMI) and stylistically the booklet makes a real attempt to communicate with its pupil audience directly, adopting a vocabulary and tone which is accessible and explanatory without being patronising.

The booklet begins by asking some key questions:

'How can it affect someone's decision to buy or not to buy *Honey* if they know that the publisher of the magazine, IPC, is part of Reed International which also owns Reed Building Products, which makes lavatory bowls and shower fittings?

Or how much more or less is someone going to enjoy watching their video of *The Deerhunter* if they know that the film was produced by EMI, put on video by Thorn EMI and possibly played back on a JVC machine (imported by Thorn EMI) which they have hired from Radio Rentals (owned by Thorn EMI) and seen advertised on Thames Television (half owned by Thorn EMI)? *The quick answer is not a lot.*'[3] (Emphasis added)

The questions raised here are, of course, crucial. They concern the *relationship* between patterns of ownership and control and the media products that most of us consume quite innocently without asking too many questions about their provenance. The problem is that the influence of owners and controllers may frequently be long-term, diffuse and indirect and may, indeed, be actively contested by other important sources of power and influence of the kind which will be discussed later in this chapter. For teacher and student alike this translates itself into the very tangible classroom problem of demonstrating that particular patterns of ownership actually make a difference. How, precisely, can we detect the hand of Reed International in *Honey* or of EMI in *The Deerhunter*? This is not simply a knotty intellectual problem but, crucially, a motivational one. For if we cannot demonstrate direct connections and influences between media conglomerates and media texts, then what reason do students have for mastering the formidable bodies of information they are often asked to acquire if they are to make sense of the media as industries? Even with students whose motivation may be generally good, we are inviting problems if we ask them to acquire, at considerable effort, tools for which we have not yet found any effective use.

The authors of *The Companies You Keep* are caught, as we all are, in the central paradox which bedevils this area of media studies. On the one hand they wish to draw attention, quite properly, to the significance of power relations, of economics, of interlocking business interests, and of the overriding importance of the profit motive within the cultural industries. On the other, these are *structural* influences whose effects are frequently covert and widely diffused, so that the authors are not able, to their own satisfaction, to draw direct and specific connections between them and the media texts we consume.

In addition, whilst many of us are convinced that the question, 'Who owns and controls the media?' *is* of crucial long-term importance, we know that there are some senses, at least, in which this question may not matter very much at all. To the readers of, say, *The Observer*, or *The Mirror*, and perhaps to some of the journalists who work on those papers, the changes produced by a change of ownership may be less striking than the extent to which things continue as they did before. In taking over a newspaper a conglomerate is also taking over a pre-existing relationship with that segment of the market which is served by the paper. The very nature of *The Observer* and *The Mirror* themselves – the functions they perform, the readerships they serve, their characteristic styles and tones, their dependence upon particular advertisers – are constraints within which *any* owners will have to work. In this sense their room for manoeuvre may be rather more limited than is popularly supposed.

Similarly, when we compare, say, *World in Action* with *Panorama*, ITN with BBC News, the output of Channel 4 with that of BBC 2, or Thames' *The English Programme* with any series for schools produced by the BBC, then we have to revise any simplistic notion we may have that commercial ownership of the media inevitably involves the cynical manipulation of audiences, that public service broadcasting is untainted by commercial considerations, or that media institutions necessarily exercise tight control over every aspect of their corporate enterprises. We have to recognise, as always, that the media are sites for struggle between conflicting interests, and that ownership/management power is not abolute, monolithic or uncontested.

Yet if Rupert Murdoch could not turn *The Times* into a scandal sheet even if he wished, he was able, after the resignation of an independently-minded editor, to install senior staff of his own choosing, and generally keep quite tight control over editorial policy. And though the effect of all this may not be immediately evident to the newspaper's readers, the issues which such a situation raises are of the greatest significance: issues of journalistic and editorial freedom;

of increasing concentration of ownership and lack of diversity in the press; and of whether it is desirable within a democracy to regard the media and the dissemination of information as an extension of property rights.

To return to *The Companies You Keep*. It begins by outlining some of the characteristics of the capitalist system and noting the tendency of *conglomerates* to *diversify* and *consolidate*. Again, it is stressed that, 'We're asking you to think about the relation between the system as we've described it . . . and the pictures that you see every day.'[4] There follows a history of Thorn/EMI and three pages devoted to diagramatic illustrations of some of the interlocking corporate interests of three major conglomerates, the Imperial Group, Reed International and Granada. As I have suggested, the writers and graphic designers have worked hard to make a good deal of information palatable, but even so the vast majority of 14–16-year-olds will find this pretty hard going.

But any student who has worked her way through this formidable body of information is entitled to expect some pay-off for the effort involved. The second half of the booklet, however, is devoted without forewarning to advertising. None of the companies discussed in the first part is mentioned again as we are taken through the work of an advertising agency. I should stress that this section is also well written and designed. Although brief, it contains some of the best material currently available for students on advertising.

The problem with *The Companies You Keep* is that whilst each of its sections has value in its own right, the booklet as a whole makes little conceptual sense. The second section might have been expected to examine some of the media texts produced by one of the conglomerates analysed in section 1. However, the admittedly formidable task of drawing out connections between these companies and their media products is abandoned. Instead, we are taken into the world of advertising and look at the work of advertising agencies in relation to two specific campaigns. But the relationship between company and text *in advertising* is not at all problematic. It is scarcely a secret that advertising images are produced by big business in order to serve their direct interests. Students don't need a history of Thorn/EMI under their belts to understand that. The advertising material indeed provides a critique of the earlier section, for its strength lies in the rare emphasis which it places upon the work of agencies, the role of market research and the precise identification of target audiences. There is even reference to the bad feelings and tensions which often exist within agencies between the creative team and the account director. The approach here rests upon a model in which widely divergent interests are recognised as being in play within a text, and undermines the implicit model of the first section, in which sole emphasis is placed upon information about large conglomerates.

What pedagogic conclusions may be drawn from our analysis of *The Companies You Keep*? Like *The Companies You Keep*, this chapter will contain a good deal of factual information on the media. It should be evident from our analysis, however, that *how* such material is introduced into the classroom is likely to be at least as important as *what* should be introduced. Two pedagogic principles may be suggested:

(a) *Any attempt to deposit large amounts of information upon students, however mature and sophisticated they may be, is likely to be counter-productive in terms of their general motivation and the amount which they are able to remember and use.* Such teaching would make media education virtually indistinguishable, from the students' point of view, from any other area of the curriculum and would be likely to produce in students the kind of alienated and instrumental view of learning which this kind of teaching encourages. There is already some evidence that A-level Communication Studies is frequently taught in this kind of factually-orientated way, with emphasis upon the history, sociology and psychology of communication, and that what is being neglected is an area of central importance within media education, the development of critical reading skills. Media teachers, particularly those teaching within a context of public examinations, need to be aware of the dangers here and begin to work out strategies for resisting this depressing trend.

(b) *It is less important for students to remember information than to know where to find it, and to be able to use it.* Students may not need to learn many facts in media education but they do need to have access to a far wider range of information resources than has normally been thought necessary, and they do need to acquire the reference skills which will enable them to find their way around it. Information must earn its corn, however. To be worth acquiring it must serve demonstrably useful purposes. Within media education it is likely to be most valuable

(i) *in providing illuminative background to a topic of current concern.* Good media teaching is often opportunistic, seizing on and deepening understanding of issues and concerns of topical importance. Teachers and pupils alike will need to have essential data to hand if this kind of teaching is to be effective, however. It is too demanding and time-consuming for the teacher to have to hunt around or send away for relevant documentation each time she needs it. With a little foresight the kind of material which will be most useful can easily be predicted. If the teacher can provide basic background data on a topical issue, then she will find that there will be no shortage of stimulating material and more detailed information provided by the media themselves for the group to work with. In the week in which this is being written there has been a prosecution under Section Two of the Official Secrets Act (the Ponting Case), a judgement on a libel suit against a newspaper, a ruling of contempt against a television programme, the citing by the media of statistics from an interested source (the Coal Board) as facts, the 'planting' of questions by Conservative MPs to the Home Secretary in the House of Commons and arguments about whether the BBC should accept advertising. Any of these issues will be of interest to a media studies group. The teacher's task is to provide, on these kinds of issues, the kind of back-up documentation which will help to clarify the basic principles at stake. Thereafter the teacher and her group can swim with the tide, utilising for their own purposes all of the time, money and energy which the media expend in covering these issues. By providing a few basic resources of her own, the teacher can thus fully utilise the far richer resources available to her through the media.

(ii) *in illuminating the nature of particular media texts.* If students are to begin to unravel the significant structural determinants of a particular text, it is evident that they will need to have access to a wide-ranging resource and information bank. They may need to find out something about the institution which is producing the text, the number and nature of the text's audience, the legislative and regulatory constraints within which it has been produced, the economic determinants of its format, the nature and cost of the advertising material which it attracts, the significance of its positioning in the schedules, and so forth.[5] There is no intrinsic reason why secondary school pupils cannot be encouraged to examine such areas as these at their own level of understanding. The provision of an adequate information base will be essential to this task, however, and the next section of this chapter will examine a wide range of reference and information resources which are currently available – many of them at little or no cost. Pupils should, of course, be encouraged to go this information with particular questions in mind, actively using, rather than passively receiving it.

2. Media determinants: some general resources

The following determinants of media texts will be considered in the remainder of this chapter. The list is not intended to be exhaustive but a first attempt to indicate some of the power bases out of which media texts are produced. Media teachers should amend or augment the list as they think necessary.

Ownership and control

Media institutions

The State and the Law

Self-regulation by the media

Economic determinants

Advertisers

Audiences

Media Personnel

Media Sources

Before going on to consider each of these areas in detail, it is necessary to provide some guidance on some of the resources available for studying media determinants:

(a) General reference works

General reference texts which cover a number of these areas include:

The Media in Britain[6] by Jeremy Tunstall. A very useful source of basic information on most of the issues raised in this chapter. Much less good in its treatment of issues and arguments, however.

The Press, Radio and Television[7] eds. Morley and Whitaker. Not a reference book but the best general introductory survey of media institutional structures, media control and legal constraints.

The BBC Annual Report and Handbook and the IBA's *Television and Radio*,[8] both annual publications, contain much valuable factual information on the broadcasting institutions amongst a good deal of promotional material.

The Future of Broadcasting,[9] the Annan Report, contains a great deal of explanatory background material on most of the major *issues* in broadcasting. It is a somewhat formidable tome for students to work with but teachers will find it very useful and might well guide students to specific sections. The same can be said for the last *Royal Commission on the Press, 1974–7*[10] though much of the factual information from both reports is now out-of-date.

British Broadcasting and *The British Press since the War*, both edited by A. Smith,[11] contain valuable source materials and documentation, the first relating to broadcasting (Acts of Parliament, codes of practice and key statements by broadcasters and politicians), the second on the Press (finance and ownership in Fleet Street, the Press and the Law, etc.).

Benn's Press Directory[12] contains details of publishing houses and their holdings, and details of newspaper and magazine circulations.

Much of this reference material is rather expensive to acquire, particularly in the current economic climate, but it is worth purchasing piece-by-piece through the school library if possible. Many media teachers will already possess some of this material for their own use. My own practice is to make this available for use by students or, failing this, at least to ensure that a local library possesses most of the above titles for easy access by the teacher or any of the group.

(b) Trade Publications

The most up-to-date information (and gossip) on the media is to be found in trade journals such as *Broadcast*, *Campaign*, *Media World*, *UK Press Gazette*, *Marketing* and *Marketing Week*,[13] all lively and stimulating publications which too few media teachers, let alone students, ever have the opportunity to see. These publications are even more expensive to subscribe to than the reference works described earlier. However, there is hope. It is a simple matter to ask local advertising agencies, public relations companies, the advertising sections of large companies or media institutions, who will subscribe of these journals, to pass on old copies. *The waste paper bins of these institutions tend to be crammed full of materials which would make invaluable resources for media studies groups.* Media teachers should think very carefully about ways of cultivating contacts within the media and advertising industries. Not only is such liaison between media teachers and media professionals likely to result in a more well-informed media education for our students, as I shall argue in

Chapter Eight, but such contacts can easily open out to media teachers access not only to the kind of trade journals described above, but also to only slightly dated copies of expensive reference materials, such as *BRAD* (British Rate and Data) and *JICNARS*[14] (Joint Industry Committee for National Readership Surveys).

BRAD is a comprehensive monthly directory of advertising rates for all press publications and commercial broadcasting organisations. It also includes up-to-date circulation figures for newspapers and magazines and is an invaluable source for work on media economics and advertising.

JICNARS contains statistical analyses for advertisers of the readership profiles of large numbers of newspapers and magazines.

(c) Free resource material

Best of all, a good deal of *free* reference material is available.

The IBA, for example, has a large number of free publications available on request to the Information Office, IBA, 70 Brompton Road, London SW3 1EY. They include:

The IBA Code of Advertising Standards and Practice,

Airwaves (the IBA's quarterly journal of opinion),

Paying for Independent Broadcasting,

Advertising on Independent Broadcasting,

TV Regions and Companies

The IBA also publishes jointly with the BBC the free booklet *The Portrayal of Violence on Television: BBC and IBA Guidelines*. Full details of all IBA free publications are available from the IBA, or from the IBA annual handbook, *Television and Radio*.

The Advertising Association publishes a series of excellent student 'briefs', which are regularly up-dated, on

The Advertising Business

The Advertising Media,

The Advertising Agency,

Advertising on Television,

The Regulation of Advertising,

Facts and Figures on Advertising.

These are available from the Public Affairs Department, The Advertising Association, Abford House, 15 Wilton Road, London SW1V 1NJ.

Not free, but very cheap (£1.50) is a glossy student resource book (for 14–16-year-olds), *Finding Out... About Advertising* which has been produced for the Advertising Association by Hobson's Limited, the publishing arm of the Careers Research and Advisory Centre (CRAC).[15]

The Advertising Standards Authority (ASA), the industry's own regulatory body which exerts voluntary controls on all non-broadcast advertising (the IBA controls broadcast ads.), also has a list of very useful free publications and video cassettes.[16] Of particular interest are the free abridged version of the ASA's *Code of Advertising Practice* and its monthly *Case Reports* on current complaints. The ASA, like the IBA, will also consider sympathetically invitations to speakers to come into schools. For a small charge (£1.00), a project kit for 8–14-year-olds on what to look out for in advertising is also available.

The Independent Television Companies also supply a good deal of free material. It is valuable for media teachers to collect as much of this as possible from the ITV company serving their area, for though most of it is promotional material, it will contain helpful information and give some insight into the public image of the company – how it sees and projects itself and what it regards as its strengths (and, by omission, its weaknesses). Most valuable of all are the slim *Marketing Yearbooks* that some ITV companies distribute to prospective advertisers. They contain information on the area covered by the company, detailed profiles of the population it serves (their income, leisure activities, ownership of durables, grocery expenditure, etc.) and details of the retail infrastructure of the region.

It is worth 'phoning or writing to the Sales Director of your local ITV company and asking for copies of the current rate card, and any marketing material, including *The Marketing Year Book*, if one is available. On the whole, the companies are somewhat reluctant to distribute such material to non-advertisers, but a persuasive description of your media studies course might well do the trick. Failing this, local advertisers or agencies ought to be able to supply such material at little inconvenience to themselves. Finally, *Viewpoint*,[17] the free monthly magazine of the ITV companies, is available to schools free of charge and contains a good deal of up-to-date information, revealing articles on major issues facing ITV and inside stories on TV advertising campaigns.

As with the trade journals mentioned earlier, it is very important for pupils and students to have access to this kind of material. It will give them a new and completely different perspective on the media and help them to understand that there are considerable differences between the way in which a media company addresses its audiences and the way it speaks to its prospective advertisers. Pupils quickly understand that their 'natural' way of relating to the media is only half of the story and that the relationship which the media set up with their audiences is often a mystificatory one, which disguises the fact that it is the audiences themselves which are the prime commodities which are being bought and sold by the media. No such squeamishness inhibits the trade's own literature, and the frank discussion in trade journals and literature of the audience as a commercial commodity will prove to be a valuable eye-opener on the nature of media industries to most students.

Much of the free material mentioned here is, of course, either public-relations material or not intended to be seen by media audiences at all. It goes without saying that none of it should be accepted at its face value. Rather, it should be scrutinised in relation to the interests and purposes of those who produce it. With this essential proviso, however, much of this material can serve the purposes of media education groups better than a good deal of specifically educational material which is currently available for teachers. It can also yield insights into the media industries which are far removed from the material's original purposes.

Finally, free material is also available from two other media organisations, *The Broadcasting Complaints Commission*, which issues a free leaflet outlining its function and procedures, and *The Broadcasters' Audience Research Board* (BARB), which issues regular reports on current measurements of TV viewing figures.[18]

3. Media determinants

(a) Owners and controlling companies

As I have already suggested, it is often difficult to pin down the precise influence which individual owners and controlling companies have upon the media, since a great deal of that influence is likely to be covert, indirect, structural and long-term. Generalisations are difficult to make, too, since proprietorial styles vary a good deal between different individuals and companies. Indeed, there are sometimes even fierce disagreements about the same proprietor. I have met journalists who have worked for Rupert Murdoch and who have argued that he exerted not the slightest influence upon their work. (How could he, they argue, given his interest in some 80 other newspapers around the world, to say nothing of his television, cable and satellite investments, and his interests in a host of other industries from airlines to book publishing, from oil to films.)[19] Other journalists have felt compelled to resign in protest at the direction in which Murdoch was taking their newspaper. On the one hand, we have Tony Benn's view that

'in general the media proprietors and top-level directorate find it easy to impose their will on the outlets in print, radio or TV which they own or control.'[20]

On the other, there is John Whale's claim that

'Where it [proprietorial influence] survives at all, it must still defer to the influence of readers . . . The broad shape and nature of the press is ultimately determined by no one but its readers.'[21]

Clearly this is an area in which there is a good deal of conflicting argument and evidence. What general principles might be considered by pupils and students in thinking about questions of media ownership and control?

(i) First and foremost, as I have already argued, it is important for students to recognise that proprietorial influence is only one factor (albeit, frequently a highly significant one) in a complex mesh of influences which operate upon the media, some of which will be explored in the remainder of this chapter.

(ii) Secondly, however, there is, within the newspaper industry in particular, an undeniable *concentration of ownership*, and of the power and influence which that bestows, in a few hands. Four large companies, News Corporation, Pergamon Press, Associated Newspapers Holdings, and Fleet Holdings produce almost 90% of all national daily and Sunday newspapers sold in the UK.[22] And the newspaper industry is dominated by powerful and authoritarian figures such as Rupert Murdoch, Robert Maxwell, Tiny Rowlands, and Viscount Rothermere.[23] This is almost certainly an important factor in the pronounced right-wing skew of the political affiliations of British newspapers with *The Express*, *Mail*, *Star*, *Telegraph*, *Times* and *Sun* all espousing right-wing positions, and only *The Guardian* (Liberal/centrist) and *The Mirror* (right-wing Labour) reflecting centre or slightly left of centre positions. One of the major arguments against the concentration of press ownership, then, lies in *the lack of diversity of the British press* and in its failure to reflect the full spectrum of views current within British politics and society at the present time.

(iii) Concentration of ownership might not constitute such a problem if there were any regulatory body to ensure reasonable standards of accuracy and fairness in newspaper reporting. Unfortunately there are none (see p. 100 below for comment on The Press Council). As a result, individual proprietors and their editors can, if they choose, exercise the considerable power they possess in quite unscrupulous ways and this has almost certainly contributed to the low standard of journalism – the invasions of privacy, the personal vendettas and the slanted and opinionated reporting of what are supposedly news stories – which marks our popular national press and makes it such a matter of concern. Of course, there are other contributory factors, as we shall see (the apparent popularity of much gutter journalism with readers; the prohibitively high costs of bringing a libel suit; the lack of any statutory right to reply, etc.), and students will need to assess for themselves in the light of the other influences discussed in this chapter the precise impact of ownership concentration upon the quality of our press.

(iv) Before moving on from considerations of ownership concentration, we should briefly note the argument that control of large corporations has effectively passed from owners into the hands of professional managers who alone have the kind of expertise necessary to run complex corporative business enterprises. 'Control of the modern corporation,' it is argued, has become 'progressively divorced from ownership.' Against this Murdock and Golding argue that 'there are strong indications that the age of the owner-entrepreneur is by no means entirely over, even among the conglomerates where ... the separation of control from ownership should be at its most advanced.'[24] Certainly within the newspaper industry Rupert Murdoch of News International continues to have a considerable personal influence, Robert Maxwell, chairman of Pergamon has himself scarcely been out of the headlines since taking over The Mirror Group of newspapers, whilst Victor Matthews voiced the opinion in 1977, when his company Trafalgar House purchased Express Newspapers, that 'the Editors will have complete freedom as long as they agree with the policy I have laid down.'[25] Meanwhile, as Murdock and Golding note

'in a significant number of the leading multi-media conglomerates, the founding family and/or its descendants retain a significant and often controlling share-holding, and in a number of instances they also occupy key executive and managerial positions which give them a significant degree of control ... '[26]

Notable examples include Pearson Longman, the Thomson Organisation, and the Granada Group.

(v) Alongside the concentration of media ownership should be noted the increased *diversification* of media corporations into other industries and areas of activity. 'Diversification... represents a cushion against downswings in the profitability of particular sectors. It is a practical expression of the old adage that it is best not to put all your eggs in one basket.'[27] (See Appendix B for listings of the principal interests of the main media conglomerates.) It should also be noted, however, that this development has produced conglomerates with interests *across* the media (see Appendix B). These developments have had a number of important consequences. For, in the words of Australian critic Humphrey McQueen, 'It is often said that the media are on the side of big business. This is not so. The media *are* big business.'[28] The media, that is, are not isolated phenomena dispassionately observing and reflecting the society upon which they report and comment. They are, rather, thoroughly integrated at a corporate level with a vast range of service and consumer industries. It is this fact which makes it of some importance that the media should be considered *as a whole* (rather than in isolation from one another), gives some substance to the idea that the media serve important economic and ideological roles within the processes of capitalist production in general, and makes it unsurprising that, on the whole, the values and assumptions of media texts are not greatly at variance with those of the capitalist system.

Resources
The best resources for checking on the current state of media ownership are the annual reports of the major media conglomerates. These are freely available from the following addresses:

News International plc, PO Box 7, Grays Inn Road, London WC1X 8EZ (01-837-1234).

Associated Newspapers Holdings plc, Carmelite House, Carmelite Street, London EC4Y 0JA (01-353-6000).

Lonrho plc, Cheapside House, 138 Cheapside, London EC2V 6BL (01-606-9898).

Pearson plc, Millbank Tower, Millbank, London SW1P 4QZ (01-828-9020).

Thorn/EMI plc, Thorn EMI House, Upper St. Martin's Lane, London WC2H 9ED (01-836-2444).

Trafalgar House plc, 1 Berkeley Street, London W1X 6NN (01-499-9020).

Reed International plc, Reed House, 83 Piccadilly, London W1A 1EJ (01-499-4020).

International Thomson Organisation Ltd., Thomson House, PO Box 4YG, 4 Stratford Place, London W1A 4YG (01-629-8111).

Who Owns Whom is a useful general guide to media ownership, whilst the annual reports of the Press Council, *The Press and The People* contain detailed appendices on the national and regional newspaper industries.[29] Each issue also contains an independent examination of the structure of a leading British newspaper organisation.

Studies of individual media magnates can make interesting topics for project work. Two readable and accessible sources are Hugh Cudlipp's historical mini-studies of Hearst, Northcliffe, Rothermere, Luce and Beaverbrook, *The Prerogative of the Harlot*[30] and Michael Leapman's recent biography of Rupert Murdoch, *Barefaced Cheek*.[31]

(b) Media institutions

It is of obvious value for students to have some knowledge, however vestigial, of the institutional sources of media texts. A fundamental distinction between *public service* and *commercial* media institutions will need to be made from the outset, but this key distinction is not an unproblematic one. For example, the distinctions made over 20 years ago by Raymond Williams between *authoritarian*, *paternalistic*, *commercial* and *democratic* communications organisations cut across simple public service/commercial polarities and have a good deal of relevance to today's discussions on the future of broadcasting institutions.[32] In thinking about media institutions, some attention will need to be paid to

(i) a possible range of models for public service broadcasting (paternalistic, representative, democratic),

(ii) the characteristics and limitations of the BBC's interpretation of the concept of public service,[33]

(iii) the extent to which commercial broadcasting does or can be made to serve the public. (See, for example, the philosophy, organisation and programming of Channel 4), and

(iv) the increasing privatisation of information, the push towards a market economy in broadcasting and in the development of communications technology, and the threats to the future of public service broadcasting that this implies (see Chapter One).

Can significant structural differences between media institutions be approached through the study of media texts? Ed Buscombe has suggested one very concrete example of how this might be done in his analysis of the small but important differences which exist between BBC and ITV link persons and continuity announcers:

'The announcers of the BBC are heard but never seen ... The BBC's disembodied voice is, one might say, representative of a culture which puts its faith in the word. Television, we are often told, is a visual medium, but when the BBC wishes to address us directly it does so by means of the word alone. This is the voice of authority, speaking in the tones of Standard English which signal not only a particular cultural authority, but also a particular class, that class which has appropriated to itself the right to define what is true culture, what is best, and the best for us. In these tones we hear the authentic note of the public service ethos, secure in a belief in its own virtue and necessity ... By contrast, ITV addresses us personally, in the flesh. Instead of the austerity of the word we are given the warm humanity of real people. And instead of the impersonal righteousness of public service we are seduced by the smile of consumer capitalism. ITV, after all, must sell us something if it is to live. Some *thing*. Its best chance is to lead us to those things through people. And the people it shows are just like ourselves. Whereas the BBC claims to speak for all by speaking in the tones of the class that represents the Good of the Nation, ITV speaks in the popular idiom. Its regional structure, not a single metropolitan body, but a loose federation of 15 locally-based companies, permits that its accents are those of its supposed roots in the places where real people live. And its representatives are "personalities", known to millions, identified by name. BBC announcers are never identified.'[34]

Pupils will already have some ideas about the public image of their regional commercial television company, from a familiarity with its output. An examination of, say, a regional news programme, together with the company's own publicity material (see Resources section above) will reveal how it attempts to convey its particular 'regionalness' and how far it seeks to reflect the diversity of its area. Are there any examples of 'community involvement' by the company, and if so, how far are these principally PR exercises? And why should the company bother to try and convince us that it has a genuine involvement in its region? More formally, Hood, and Morley and Whitaker[35] have provided succinct general outlines of the major, constitutional, organisational and financial differences between the BBC and the IBA/ITV/ILR. More up-to-date information and specific details are available in the annual BBC and IBA Handbooks.

It is important that media studies teachers should make themselves as familiar as possible with the 'philosophies' and practices of particular media institutions, since they will be able to pass on many helpful ideas to pupils incidentally and anecdotally. Tom Burns' study of *The BBC*[36] remains the most detailed sociological study of the Corporation, whilst the British Film Institute has produced an excellent dossier on Granada Television, *Granada: The First 25 Years*.[37]

(c) The state and the law

The principal obstacles to press freedom lie, in the words of barrister Geoffrey Robertson, 'not in prejudiced proprietors, circulation crazed editors or incompetent journalists, but in a web of vague legal doctrines which catch facts and opinions essential for informed scrutiny of social power.'[38] Censorship in the British media is rarely official, direct or heavy-handed. Indeed, it is frequently not thought of or described as 'censorship' at all. This is because there are real and proper divergencies of interest within democratic societies between the media and the state. Part of the very legitimacy of democratic governments rests upon their support of 'free' media, that is media which are not, in an obvious way, part of the ideological apparatus of the state, but possess plausible claims to be independent of government and acting in the public interest. The relationship of the state to the media, therefore, is one in which the independence of the medium is, for the most part, *formally* observed, whilst being undermined by

(i)   direct legal controls which are deemed to be in the national interest,

(ii) indirect forms of media *self-control* which are provoked by the threat or fear of legal sanctions,

(iii) the possibility of direct state control during periods of armed conflict,

(iv) the constitutional constraints operating upon media institutions, and

(v) the voluntary self-censorship and control exercised by the broadcasting institutions (apart from those provoked by the threat of legal sanctions).

The first four areas will be considered in this section, and the fifth in the next section of this chapter.

Some knowledge by students of the legal constraints upon the media is desirable for two reasons. First of all, they will scarcely be able to make informed judgements about texts if they do not understand the formal limitations within which they are produced. Secondly, the law as it now stands frequently works against the public's right to know, stifles public debate, and provides a cloak of secrecy behind which civil servants, big business, and those who hold public office, can all hide. It is a matter of great urgency that this situation should be improved and changed but this can only be achieved through the growth of an informed public opinion on these issues. Media education could play an important role in contributing to this kind of public awareness, but it can only do so if media teachers are prepared to keep themselves informed of current debates and developments in this area, and work through them with their students.

It is not an easy task. Any attempt to teach about what are inevitably somewhat tangled and difficult legal issues in a formal way is likely to be found tedious in the extreme by both pupils and teachers alike. As with the questions of ownership and control, the objective should be to sensitise pupils and students to some of the *general* constraints within which media texts are produced, so that these may be brought to bear, whenever relevant, upon the elucidation of particular texts. Again, the discussion of these issues, whether general or in depth, will need to be provoked by and linked to the study of specific issues, and cases of topical interest. To facilitate this work, this section presents a brief background guide to some of the most important legal and self-imposed institutional constraints upon media texts.

(i) Legal controls

The major legal constraints upon British journalists and broadcasters are the Official Secrets Act, the Prevention of Terrorism Act, and the laws of Libel and Contempt.

The Official Secrets Act. The Act prohibits the unauthorised passing on of information by anyone holding an office under the crown (from a postman to a civil servant, a soldier to a government Minister) and all public servants are required to sign it. The present Act went through all of its stages in the House of Commons in 1911 in just 35 minutes. It was presented to the Commons as an anti-spying measure, at the height of an anti-German spy scare, but the Act provided the government with the opportunity to tighten up what they considered to be two defects of the earlier Official Secrets Act of 1889. That Act had placed the onus *upon the prosecution* to prove that disclosure of information was against the public interest. It also failed to catch the *receivers* of leaks. Section One of the 1911 Act prohibited the passing of any information which might indirectly assist an enemy for the purpose of prejudicing the interests of the State. Section Two – the notorious catch-all section which has brought the Act into such disrepute – was so framed that it covered the unauthorised passing on *and* publication of *any* information acquired by a civil servant in the course of her work, whether or not it was prejudicial to state security. Technically it made the disclosure by any civil servant of the colour of her office wall or the texture of the office's lavatory paper a criminal offence. It is this section of the Act which is largely responsible both for the secrecy which makes reliable information so difficult for the media to extract from the government and civil service, and for the inhibitions which the media have in publishing whatever information they do gather.

In the past few years there have been a number of particularly controversial prosecutions brought under the Official Secrets Act, which relate either directly or indirectly to questions of media freedom. In the so-called ABC case, two investigative journalists, Duncan Campbell and Crispin Aubrey, were prosecuted under Section One for publishing information on Signals Intelligence which monitors foreign communications. Most of the information was available from other published sources. Campbell and Aubrey were acquitted, but the inhibiting effect upon future investigative journalism of a case in which the accused faced the possibility of a 14-year prison sentence, was considerable.

In 1984 a young civil servant, Sarah Tisdall, was imprisoned for six months under Section Two for leaking to *The Guardian* a confidential memorandum written by the Secretary of State for Defence, Michael Heseltine, to Prime Minister, Margaret Thatcher, about how the publicity surrounding the arrival of cruise missiles could be handled in order to put the government in the best possible light. The information Sarah Tisdall released was of no military value or use to a hostile power. It was classified as secret *in order that the details could be kept from the British public*. Sarah Tisdall explained her own motivation in a *World in Action* interview:

'Well I felt it was immoral and that the Secretary of State for Defence who was accountable to Parliament had decided he was not going to be accountable to Parliament on that particular day that the cruise missiles arrived. He was going to wait until after they were here and at the end of his allotted question time tell the House that they were here and then get up and leave before the Opposition had time to react in the House, and go off to Greenham to have his photograph taken.

Interviewer: He was going to evade proper Parliamentary scrutiny?

Sarah Tisdall: Yes, he was.'[39]

The conduct of the government, the judiciary and *The Guardian* in the Tisdall case was deplorable. The newspaper took advantage of the information by publishing it, but failed to protect its source and handed over the confidential memorandum to the police. The Government did not take on *The Guardian*, which was equally guilty of an offence under Section Two, but chose to prosecute as a criminal a young woman who had done nothing more than cause the government some embarrassment. Finally, the judge's sentence of six months' imprisonment was generally condemned as a savage reprisal for the leak. Labour MP Robin Cook, writing in *The Times*, summed up the fundamental hyprocisy of the Tisdall case:

'Every week ministers release information of the kind that has put her in prison. The distinction is that when they do it they are briefing the lobby but when she did it she was leaking.'[40]

Finally, the extraordinary case in 1985 of Clive Ponting, the civil servant who was faced with a crisis of conscience when his Minister, Michael Heseltine, knowingly lied to parliament about the sinking of the Argentinian cruiser the *General Belgrano* during the Falklands conflict, brought the most widespread criticism of Section Two of all. Ponting leaked information about the *Belgrano* to Labour MP Tam Dalyell and was prosecuted under Section Two. Having been guided by the judge that under the law Ponting had no defence – that the 'interests of the state' were synonymous with the interests of the government of the day – the jury nevertheless acquitted Ponting. The implications of this momentous decision will probably not be clear for some time yet, but some reform of Section Two of the Official Secrets Act now seems certain. The day may even be a little closer when Section Two will be scrapped altogether, and a Freedom of Information Bill enshrining the public's right to know will be put on to the statute books.[41]

The Prevention of Terrorism Act. The current threatened use of the Prevention of Terrorism Act to censor news from the North of Ireland exemplifies once more the paradox that it is not so much 'terrorists' but the British public who are conceived of as a problem for those in government. Following the Carrickmore affair,[42] broadcasters, who in their professional capacity have *any kind of contact at all* with the IRA or INLA, risk prosecutrion under the Prevention of Terrorism Act, and the broadcasting organisations have reviewed their internal 'guidelines' (i.e. explicit instructions) accordingly.

The belief of the government that to report on the IRA is somehow to assist it, deserves some critical scrutiny and discussion by students. Simon Hoggart's argument is worth considering: Is it likely that the public on seeing a 'terrorist' would be 'dumbly converted to his cause? ... But suppose they were. Suppose, faced with David O'Connell or the Derry terrorist, they decided that the Republican cause was just and fair. Should the BBC suppress the case for the convenience of the Government?'[43] As Liz Curtis has suggested

'There is no tangible threat to national security involved in reporting the words or deeds of "terrorists". So why does the public not "need to know"? The missing unspoken link in [the] argument ... is the authoritarian conception that the public itself presents a problem. The public's response to information about "terrorists" will not necessarily suit the authorities. Publicity alone will get the "terrorists" nowhere: it is the public reaction that matters. So "society" has to be protected from itself.'[44]

The censorship of news from the North of Ireland is thus now even more severe than in 1971 when Jonathan Dimbleby pointed out the difficulties facing journalists who wished to increase the British public's understanding of events in the province:

'The censorship and restrictions now imposed on reporters and editors make it practically impossible for them to ask the question "why?" Why do the Catholics now laugh openly when a British soldier is shot down and killed, when a year ago they would offer the army cups of tea? Why do the Catholics refuse to condemn the bombings and the shootings? Why do they still succour the IRA ... ? What influence today does the Civil Rights Movement have? Or the SDLP? The answers to such questions are fundamental to understanding the problem, crucial to any judgement of British policy, yet they cannot be asked by BBC employees: quite simply the management of the BBC has decided that it does not want such questions raised. Its reporters and editors stand transfixed – censored – in a maze of insuperable restrictions.'[45]

Libel. The law of libel acts as a further disincentive to investigative reporting of the powerful and influential. A libel writ can be issued in order to discourage the publication of a story, or to achieve redress for one already published. Since it is an option open only to the wealthy in society, however (being an extremely expensive under-taking for which legal aid is not available), the law tends to discourage newspapers from investigative reporting upon the activities of wealthy targets, and leaves unpunished personal attacks on those who do not have the means to take the newspaper to court.[46]

Contempt. The law of contempt prevents newspapers from publishing anything which might prejudice a fair trial. There is obvious sense in this. 'Trial by the media' has evident dangers. However, the law of contempt is frequently used to prevent the legitimate publication and discussion of important issues which are *sub-judice*. As Whitaker has suggested, governments may 'defuse a public outcry by appointing a tribunal which will deliberate for months and restrict discussion until after the initial fuss has died down... If Richard Nixon had been president of Britain... he could have kept the Watergate scandal hushed up for years by "inquiries" and minor court cases.'[47] Less hypothetically, *The Sunday Times* was prevented from giving details of the thalidomide scandal because writs against Distillers, the manufacturer of thalidomide, took years to settle. Robertson's verdict on the doctrine of contempt is that whilst there is justification for curbing press comment in criminal trials, in which a jury might be influenced by what was read, 'there can be no justification for prohibition of public debate on issues arising in civil cases which are tried by judges alone – persons supposed to have sufficient fortitude to decide cases on the evidence heard in their court, not outside on Fleet Street.'[48]

The kind of legal restrictions upon reporting outlined here actively nurture the obsession with secrecy of those in power in Britain :

'Secrecy is built into the calcium of every British policy-maker's bones. It is the very essence of his – or her – concept of good governance. As a result the policy-maker wants to control official information – and to that end there is a cornucopia of statutes, codes and conventions.'[49]

Cockerell, Hennessy and Walker have argued that the present government under Mrs Thatcher represents the culmination of a hundred years of political news management, and that secrecy and restrictions upon information have been every bit as important a part of its armoury as active propaganda:

'No precedessor of Mrs. Thatcher at Number Ten has been so conscious of image and its construction. She has brought in a breed of advertising agent and public relations executive not seen before in British politics. She has become presidential in her use of American techniques of presentation and news management. Yet the successful sale of Mrs Thatcher and her brand of Toryism has been possible only in a context: our unique culture of confidentiality, the uninformed deference of the electorate, the ease with which the public attention can be diverted from real but half-hidden issues of state, the privacy afforded the decision-takers for their vital deliberations about our lives and interests. Secrecy and propaganda are reverse sides of the same coin.'[50]

As I have already suggested, consideration of the legal constraints upon the media should be linked to the discussion of particular cases of topical interest wherever possible. But some work on legal constraints may also be introduced within news simulations – an important part of every media teacher's repertoire – through the introduction into selection or in-tray exercises of stories which may be libellous or contravene the Official Secrets Act, The Prevention of Terrorism Act or the law of Contempt.

(ii) Self-censorship provoked by fears of legal sanctions
The British media, hedged around by these repressive legal frameworks, practise extensive self-censorship in order to steer clear of legal complications:

'The routine newspaper response has been to employ teams of lawyers to sanitise its papers before publication, degutting public interest stories which might provoke court reprisals. Press lawyers are inevitably more repressive than press laws, because they will always err on the safe side where they cannot be proved wrong. The lawyer's advice creates a broad penumbra of constraint, confining the investigative journalist not merely to the letter of the law but to an outer rim bounded by the mere possibility of legal action.'[51]

(iii) State control in times of crisis
It should be observed that there *are* occasions when the state

intervenes *directly* in the media, and broadcasting in particular. These are during periods of armed conflict. As Schlesinger, Murdock and Elliott point out:

'It is important to distinguish what has happened during a total war (World War II), limited engagements (the Suez Crisis, the Falklands adventure), and a counter-insurgency campaign within the national territory (Northern Ireland). Each of these has occupied a distinct position on the sliding scale of state control.'[52]

In general terms, all students should understand that during a period of total war the state exercises strict control over the transmission of news and information, and can do so 'without thereby risking the legitimacy of the system because in national emergencies security prevails over free expression.'[53] In more limited engagements (e.g., the Falklands campaign), the ground between state control and media freedom is more fiercely contested (see pp. 191ff).

In the case of the reporting of political violence in peace-time, state control is much weaker, yet 'it is in the interest of the state to suggest that "the war against terrorism" is *like* a real war and that therefore, extra "responsibility", "self-restraint" and understanding are needed from the media to assist in the state's struggles to preserve order.'[54] So the threat of full legal sanctions can be employed whenever necessary, but control more frequently takes the form of 'responsible' self-regulation by the media and gentlemen's agreements between high-ranking representatives of the state and the media, as we shall see.

(iv) Constitutional constraints on media institutions

In considering the legal frameworks within which the media operate, students should have the opportunity, at some stage, of examining the constitutional differences between the BBC and IBA. Stuart Hood has noted the important distinction between the generally permissive nature of the BBC's Charter and the more restrictive nature of the Television Act of 1954 which set up the Independent Television Authority. In general terms very few restrictive injunctions occur in the BBC Charter. For example,

'The BBC has never been required or directed in any Charter or Licence to observe impartiality. What has happened is that the Postmaster-General has *desired* [my emphasis] the Corporation "as in the past" to refrain from broadcasting any expression of its own opinion on current affairs or on matters of public policy. The situation is therefore based on trust – on the belief, to quote the White

Paper on Broadcasting Policy published in 1946, "that the Corporation would ensure that such subjects would be treated with complete impartiality."[55]

As we shall see, the BBC repaid this trust by instituting a voluntary system of corporate controls which ensured that only those of acceptable background and views would exercise responsibility and power within broadcasting.

Commercial television was treated very differently. The Independent Television Authority (later the Independent Broadcasting Authority) was constituted to select and appoint the commercial television companies, supervise the programme planning, control the advertising and transmit the programmes. The ITA's watchdog role was made explicit in a series of duties laid upon it which included ensuring the provision of accurate and impartial news, a reasonable proportion of regional programmes and 'a high standard of quality' – duties which were 'assumed to be part of (the BBC's) unwritten ethical code.'[56] (Fuller details of the duties of the IBA and of the BBC's Charter are available from the IBA and BBC annual handbooks.)

(d) Media self-regulation and control

In this section I shall consider (i) some of the voluntary mechanisms of control adopted by media institutions, (ii) some of the ways in which media institutions exercise social control of their employees, and (iii) the work of self-regulatory bodies such as the Press Council and the Advertising Standards Authority.

(i) Voluntary controls

Voluntary censorship and self-regulation occur within the media via a whole range of guidelines and practices. *D Notices*, for example, constitute a voluntary system of censorship whereby senior representatives of the media agree not to carry stories on sensitive defence issues.[57] The BBC and IBA have internal regulatory codes on such topics as violence, and standards of taste and decency, and the IBA also has a code of Advertising Standards and Practice. Both the BBC and IBA also produce internal guidelines for production staff, the BBC's *News and Current Affairs Index*, and the IBA's *Television Programme Guidelines*, which deal with sensitive areas such as the reporting of the North of Ireland. The BBC also diffuses 'guidance' via its Director News and Current Affairs Committee (DNCA), which meets weekly and, in Antony Easthope's words,
'discusses news matters in a general and academic tone – how the

Metropolitan police or the CIA feel about recent coverage, who is given a "hard" interview (Benn), and who is given a "soft" one (Hattersley). The minutes find their way into the news studios throughout the Corporation. They rarely order or prohibit, but they make perfectly clear to any ambitious reporter what the current "line" is to be.'[58]

Because its minutes are internal BBC documents with restricted circulation, 'the effect of DNCA on news is hardly ever mentioned in the press',[59] but recent research by the Glasgow Media Group has very astutely shown how important DNCA was in controlling reporting of the Falklands conflict, for example.[60]

In addition to formal and informal institutional guidelines, mention should also be made, under 'voluntary controls', of gentlemen's agreements, between, say, the police or the army and the media, in which the parameters within which the media will work in any *future* crisis are worked out in a 'civilised' way.[61] Closely connected with these kinds of agreements are what Schlesinger *et al.* term 'Seminar and discussion country': extended talking-shops between senior media personnel and senior civil servants, ministers and academic specialists, from which the public are excluded. 'Such encounters are seen as a constructive way of keeping lines open, and despite real differences of view, regular consultation on neutral ground is thought to help resolve emergencies when they arise, because the people concerned will know one another.'[62]

(ii) Social control mechanisms
Any consideration of the routine constraints upon what gets broadcast and printed in the media will need to take into account some of the mechanisms through which the media exert social control over their employees and, ultimately, over their audiences. Among these may be mentioned:

The hierarchical and paternalistic nature of the BBC and IBA. The Chair of each body is appointed by the Government. BBC Governors and IBA members, who in terms of the law *are* the BBC and the IBA, are appointed from the ranks of 'the great and the good'. As Hood, who spent many years working in the upper-echelons of the BBC and ITV has explained:

'They are people who move freely in the upper reaches of our society; they have frequently been members of the civil service or have dealt with government departments at a high level; they come from the schools and universities from which our politicians, our administrators, judges, clergymen and service officers are still predominantly drawn; they belong to the same clubs as prominent businessmen, civil servants, retired colonial administrators. It is not difficult to imagine the kind of opinions they hear and share, the kind of comments they are likely to hear passed on programmes, on the political situation, on the role of television, on youth, on the feminist movement, or on the activities of the left ... If their function is seen as being antennae which transmit the opinions of the public ... then they are highly unrepresentative of the population even if they are well-informed on the views of the establishment. The intelligence they gather from their various contacts permits them to make "correct" decisions – decisions which do not run counter to the views and requirements of the centres of power in our society.'[63]

Both the BBC and IBA have National Councils and networks of regional and local advisory committees, as well as specialist advisory committees in areas such as education. The Annan Committee noted that 'the function of the advisory bodies is not to represent consumers but to tell the Broadcasting Authorities their own personal reactions to programmes as people who keep in touch with what others think ... Lord Aldington (Chairman of the BBC's General Advisory Council) also told us, in a revealing aside, that the BBC picked the kind of people with whom they could get on ... Few of those who gave evidence loved these bodies ... Many thought them unrepresentative ... Certainly they cannot be regarded as part of the mechanism through which broadcasters are made accountable to the public: they are appointed by, and operate through, the BBC and the IBA.'[64]

The BBC and IBA are, then, hierarchical, undemocratic institutions which promote in their employees a greater sensitivity to the needs and pressures of those *above* them in the hierarchy than of those below. Were the Governors and the committees serving each institution to be elected, or to consist of representatives (or delegates) of different interest groups within society, and their proceedings made public, then this might at least begin to open up institutions which are supposed to be serving the public interest to some kind of democratic accountability, and make them rather more responsive to public criticism than they are at present.[65]

The social backgrounds of media professionals. Most of those who hold positions of authority in broadcasting are white, male and middle-class. Institutional screening and selection procedures for appointments and promotions ensure that this imbalance is perpetuated. On these processes Hood, again speaking from first-hand experience, is devastating and worth quoting at length:

'The process of selection is at its most formal in the BBC, which at an early stage adopted an appointment procedure similar to that of the Civil Service – indeed at one time BBC appointment boards included a representative of the Civil Service Commissioners, whose function was to see that roughly the same "standards" as those of the Civil Service were maintained: that is to say, that the same type of person was recruited with the same educational background and the same class and social outlook. (His main way of establishing the candidate's *bona fides* was to ask detailed questions about the public school the candidate had attended, about what games he had played and what the name of his house-master had been.)... As for the appointments board itself, it is a test of the candidates' self-confidence, of their ability to verbalise, to "field" awkward questions – the cricketing metaphor is typical and significant – to present themselves well... There was a further criterion which in some cases eliminated candidates who are otherwise seen as being bright and eligible. That criterion is expressed in the question "Will they make good BBC material?" – that is to say, do they give indications of being prepared to undergo the process of institutionalisation, of moulding into a "BBC man or woman" who will understand what is required of them at all points in their careers... Once the board has made its choice, successful candidates are subjected to a further filtering process – vetting by the security services of the State, which also report on performers employed by the BBC. At this point those who have been politically active on the left can expect to be turned down.'[66]

On promotions, Antony Easthope has expressed the situation succinctly:

'No-one gets promoted unless they happen to have the right views – which they will then put forward quite sincerely in *Sixty Minutes* and *Newsnight*.'[67]

Conformity to institutional norms. Within the BBC 'referral upwards' is a well-established philosophy, in which difficult decisions are referred to one's superior(s) in the institutional hierarchy. Referral upwards, in practice, results in a great deal of self-censorship, as Anthony Smith has explained:

'There is seldom any doubt about what the man above you thinks on any important issue. You can therefore avoid referring upwards by deciding in a way which you know he would approve of.'[68]

Journalists need to engage in similar forms of self-censorship in order to get their material accepted, as a reporter covering the North of Ireland for a British daily paper explained to Eamonn McCann:

'You must remember that every journalist wants what he writes to appear, and in practice all journalists know pretty well what their paper's line is, what is expected of them. There is a fair amount of self-censorship. This happens without thinking. No journalist I have met writes what he knows will be cut. What would be the point? If he has a story which he knows will cause controversy back at the newsdesk he will water it down to make it acceptable.'[69]

Those practices which are most effective and efficient in enabling journalists to produce, not what they think, but what their newspapers want, quickly become internalised as part of a reporter's professional ideology.

(iii) Self-regulatory bodies

Occupying ground between internal and external controls are two self-regulatory watchdog bodies set up by different arms of the media to police their own practices and deal with external complaints from members of the public: The Press Council and the Advertising Standards Authority. The Press Council has been widely criticised for its general ineffectiveness in controlling journalistic excesses and defending decent journalistic standards. Dominated by the interests of the newspaper industry itself, the Council is a watchdog with no teeth and is, indeed, often freely and vigorously attacked by many of the newspapers whose practices it condemns. Newspapers have no legal obligation to publish or take notice of the Press Council's findings, and Geoffrey Robertson's recent study of the Council demonstrates that even members of the public who make successful complaints are frustrated by the slowness of its procedures.[70] The Council's annual report, *The Press and the People*, is a valuable resource for media teachers and students, however. It contains details of the Council's adjudications (easily adaptable for use as classroom simulations) and invaluable statistical and informational appendices on the press in Britain.[71] Again, it is somewhat slow in production. The 1981–2 report, for example, did not appear until 1985.

The Advertising Standards Authority is a more enlightened body. Like the Press Council, it is meant to indicate to those outside of the industry that external interference in its affairs is unnecessary because of its self-imposed disciplinary procedures. The Authority's Chairperson and a majority of its Council members are independent of the advertising industry, and the Authority actively seeks out and encourages complaints through advertising its services. It publishes a monthly report of its adjudications, as well as a good deal of educational material for schools. The ASA's judgements are confined to abuses perpetuated by specific advertisements. The ASA does not, of course, offer any systemic criticism of advertising, and media teachers using ASA materials will need to work at a much deeper level than the Authority itself suggests. In its self-regulatory role the Authority has definite teeth. Advertisers, agencies and the media have agreed to observe its code of practice in the spirit as well as in the letter, and newspapers and magazines have agreed not to run advertisements which contravene the code. The ASA, it should be noted, does not deal with television and radio advertising, which are the responsibility of the IBA.

Finally, since 1981, the BBC and IBA's internal complaints review procedures have been replaced by an external body, The Broadcasting Complaints Commission, which was set up as a result of the Broadcasting Act of 1980. The Commission keeps a low profile, has a limited remit and is not particularly active. It upholds very few complaints. In 1984/5, for example, though it received 218 complaints, the Commission adjudged that only 33 of these fell within its jurisdiction. Of these 33 cases, only 15 were adjudicated upon during the year. And of those 15 cases, only 10 were finally upheld, hardly an encouraging sign that broadcasting is becoming more democratically accountable.[72] Details of the Commission are available from 20 Albert Embankment, London SE1.

'What can we do about it?' students frequently ask, after having examined some of the questions raised so far in this chapter (the legal restrictions upon media freedom, the undemocratic nature of media institutions, the impotence of attempts to check the worst excesses of the media, etc.). One answer is for the group or the school to join the Campaign for Press and Broadcasting Freedom which has an interest in all of these issues. The Campaign has the long-term objective of working towards Freedom of Information legislation, and one of its immediate objectives is to achieve the right of reply for those who are misrepresented by the media. The Campaign's regular bulletin, *Free Press*, carries up-to-date information on media freedom and the activities of the Campaign and is an excellent resource for students. The Campaign will also be helpful in providing speakers for schools on the issues discussed in this section, and in suggesting strategies for group action. Joining the Campaign is an excellent way of keeping abreast of these issues and of making contact with sympathetic journalists, broadcasters and others who are interested in issues of media freedom. The involvement of media teachers and students will, in turn, broaden the scope of the movement, whose most active members, at the moment, tend to come from the media professions. Special membership concessions are available for educational institutions. Details from the Campaign for Press and Broadcasting Freedom, 9 Poland Street, London W1 3DG.

(e) Economic Determinants

One of the most important functions of media teaching is continually to bring economic questions to the surface during the analysis of media texts. This is necessary since real economic relations are subjected to so much mystification within capitalism, and hard economic facts are so rarely available for open inspection that there is always a danger of forgetting that many of the questions of the kind discussed in this book – questions of audience, of institutional self-regulation, of the importance of news sources, or of media genres and conventions, for example – are really, at heart, economic issues.

In my own teaching I have found it easiest to raise questions of media economics when a journalist or broadcaster has been able to join us to talk about a newspaper or programme upon which she or he has worked. A local journalist, for example, was able to talk very easily about how the evening paper we were looking at was shaped less by events than by economics. How quotations were largely manufactured because there was not enough time to check them for accuracy. How articles were cut short in mid-sentence in order to make way for an advertisement. How more news appeared on a Thursday and Friday because there was more advertising on the days when many readers were paid. How photographs should try to include as many people (preferably children) as possible in order to increase sales (see p. 103). How feature articles were simply hooks to attract specialist advertising (see p. 110). How a journalist covering a football game can produce as many as five reports under different names for different newspapers. How stories requiring little work are always likely to get into the paper (hence the reliance upon routine sources, press releases and lightly disguised PR material).

Economic determinants in broadcasting work in ways which are only slightly more complicated. Commercial broadcasting companies must do more than show a profit. They must also satisfy the IBA. For its part the BBC, though a public service organisation, needs to maintain general audience parity with the commercial sector in order to justify its licence fee. Market values are therefore of great importance in understanding British broadcasting, and are likely to become even more influential in the foreseeable future. Further, because the BBC has to request increases in its licence fee from the government, it needs to tread rather more warily in its relationship with government in times of economic stringency than it did during

*The 'kid appeal' of many local newspaper photographs has economic
determinants. This picture could sell up to 200 extra copies of the paper to
parents, grandparents, aunts and uncles.*

more prosperous days. For example, the satire boom of the 60s in
which politicians of the day were held up to national ridicule may, in
part, have been encouraged by the increase in the sale of TV sets in the
early 1960s, which gave the BBC an increasing income from licence
fees, and provided an independence from government much greater
than it enjoys today.

Even programmes which are not necessarily profitable but which
are prestigious and receive critical acclaim can be thought of, as
Graham Murdock has suggested, as a form of 'invisible earnings',
since they are 'central to the companies' presentation of themselves as
supporters of cultural diversity and excellence. This in turn helps to
reinforce their claims to a public service role.'[73] This is why one of the
most expensive forms of television – the one-off play – manages to
survive. But there is increasing pressure on it. Fewer plays are
produced each year as costs rise and it becomes increasingly
attractive for the companies to produce cheaper programmes which
will attract larger domestic audiences and find readier markets
abroad.

It is important, then, for students to have some general sense of programme economics and to understand, to take some obvious examples, that phone-ins and disc programmes on radio, and game shows, old films, and soap operas on television, are so prevalent because they frequently combine high audience ratings with low production costs. To pupils this is not always evident. Game shows look expensive, for example, and give an impression of generosity and lavishness. But the knowledge that the most expensive single item on a game show is probably the star host's fee soon alters pupils' perspectives. And by using the company's advertising rate-card (available from BRAD (see p. 80) or direct from the company) it is a simple matter to make a general estimate of the show's profitability. Looking at game shows with this kind of information to hand allows pupils to see through the mystificatory pseudo-relationships set up by the show, and uncover the real economic relationships which exist between contestants, host and television company.

One aspect of television to which I try to pay specific attention in considering programme economics is the *set* in which the show takes place, since this significant production cost has received little critical attention. In one of the few detailed studies available on how a television series is made, Alvarado and Buscombe note that for the Thames' series, *Hazell*, 'about half of all above the line costs goes on sets and props.'[74] In this situation genres which require only one set (e.g., game shows), or which use a few sets *ad infinitum* (soap operas) have a considerable economic advantage over forms such as the single play, in which many sets may be used only once. Similarly, sitcoms set within specific and confined locations such as a prison (*Porridge*), a hospital (*Only When I Larf*) or a building site (*Auf Wiedersehen Pet*) have a headstart over those which require a variety of locations. Some series, *Crown Court* for example, or *Village Hall*, consist of separate 'playlets' whose common characteristic is that they take place within the same set, whilst it is the particularity of their settings which frequently give series and soap operas their titles: *Coronation Street*, *Crossroads*, *Brookside*, *St. Elsewhere*, *Fantasy Island*, etc.

In some programmes there is a striking contrast between the lavish location shots of the title sequence, and the production values of the programme itself. The glossy packaging diverts attention from the cheaply-produced content. The title sequence of an American series such as *Dallas*, for example, with its split screens, its projection of its cast as stars, its helicopter shots and its colourful location shots gives the impression that we are about to see a no-expenses-spared, multi-million dollar movie. None of the promises of the title sequence are delivered by the programme itself, which is made according to factory principles and consists largely of close-ups and two-shots in a few interior sets. That title sequence, however (and perhaps the life-styles of its characters), seems to cast a halo of 'expensiveness' around the whole production, since many students do believe *Dallas* to be as lavishly produced as a block-buster movie.

Apart from the importance of sets there are other ways in which economics determine what we may think of as purely 'aesthetic' structures. The narrative structures of American television pro-grammes differ in quite obvious ways from those of their British counterparts, for example. Pre-title sequences hook us straight into the action, and minor cliff-hangers or small puzzles must punctuate the narrative in order to carry viewers across more frequent commercial breaks. Similarly, ITV and BBC sitcoms obey different narrative logics, the former falling easily into two parts, each with its own distinctive structure and climax, the latter having more continuous and unilinear narratives. Even the well-established structures and laws of games bend to the logic of media economics. Australian cricket, formerly an eight-ball over game, now has six-ball overs to accommodate more commercial breaks, whilst in the USA, in order to make soccer more attractive to television viewers, the game's administrators prohibited draws, amended the off-side law and even flirted with enlarging the goals.

Pupils should understand a little about the commercial at-tractiveness of imported American material. However lavish Ameri-can programmes may look, they are comparatively cheap for British television companies to buy. Successful American programmes having already made profits in their own domestic market can be sold abroad for a fraction of their original cost. Buying American material is, for British companies, considerably cheaper than producing equivalent programmes of their own. Snoddy[75] calculated in February 1985 that for the BBC the average cost per hour for drama was £215,000, for light entertainment £95,000, and for documentaries £60,000. Compare this with the $60,000 per episode which Thames paid in January 1985 for the American series, *Dallas*, a price which was considerably more than the BBC was prepared to pay. Costs for a good American series would normally run from around £30,000 per hour downwards.

The IBA has a quota restriction of 14% for non-British made material on television, largely to guard against an over-reliance upon American material, and the BBC operate 'a similar but vaguer control'.[76] No such restrictions face companies providing television material via satellite and cable, however, and so far the indications are that they will be heavily reliant on cheap American imported material to fill up their schedules. The early schedules of Rupert

Murdoch's satellite network, SKY, which covers a good deal of Europe, for example, consist principally of music and action programmes (in order to cater for its large non-English-speaking audiences) with a heavy reliance on cheap and dated American series such as *Charlie's Angels* and *Fantasy Island*.

The growing importance of international markets for media products[77] has had material effects upon our own domestic production. It may be of ominous significance for the future of our television comedy that one of the most profitable British exports of all has been *The Benny Hill Show*. An American commentator writing for an audience of British broadcasters on how to target material for the American market, has suggested:

'Benny Hill works because his humour is so visual, like Charlie Chaplin or Laurel and Hardy, plus it is a bit bawdy, a visual kick for Americans since our situation comedies tend to talk about rather than show sexual innuendos. Many British comedians and situation comedy shows, albeit funny in the U.K., have failed to make an impact in the U.S. because the humour is verbal, the situations are "British", and even the names are not "American" names. Robin of *Robin's Nest* became Jack in the American adaptation *Three's Company*. Colloquialisms do not readily translate, even if in the same language.'[78]

Visual and voyeuristic comedies; sitcoms from which localised and topical references have been rigorously excluded; costume dramas which are identifiably and archetypally 'British' (*The Six Wives of Henry VIII*; *Edward and Mrs. Simpson*; *Nicholas Nickleby*), and series which emphasise action or spectacle, and are conceived, planned, financed and executed as international products from the start (*Dempsey and Makepiece*) – these are the kind of media products which, stimulated by the prospects of international profits, may be expected to develop apace.[79]

(f) Advertisers

Conventional approaches to teaching about advertising (e.g., through the study of particular advertisements, or even the study of specific advertising campaigns), whilst of considerable value, scarcely begin to touch upon either the ways in which advertising operates as a deep structural determinant of media texts, or upon the permeating influence of advertising upon virtually every aspect of the media. It is important for media teachers to move beyond the traditional position of considering advertising as a separate or discrete sphere, with quite distinct boundaries which mark it off from television programmes or newspaper articles, and to begin to see media content and advertising as inextricably bound together. Some of the ways in which adertisers act as determinants of media texts may be briefly suggested:

(i) At the very simplest level it should be noted that many companies and advertising agencies now spend a great deal of time producing, not advertisements, but *advertorials*, i.e., thinly disguised advertising copy, much of which will find its way into the media in the form of news stories. Since these stories keep the manufacturer's name in the public eye without incurring advertising costs, many companies now spend much time and ingenuity in planting them. Press releases from commercial companies will frequently be reproduced by the press, with little or no alteration, as news stories, particularly if they are linked to 'pseudo-events'[80] which have been manufactured by the advertisers to catch the media's eye. (See pp. 108 and 109).

(ii) A perusal of any free 'newspaper' or Advertiser will reveal some obvious ways in which feature articles are written purely in order to encourage specific advertisers to buy space around the article. This is not simply a characteristic of free newspapers, however, but is practised most extensively by 'quality' newspapers such as *The Sunday Times* and *Observer*. In the illustration on p. 110, for example, the article on property acts as a hook to direct readers to the property advertisements which take up most of the page. The close association of advertisements with particular features of the kind exemplified here demonstrates how advertisements actively distort news values.[81] It leads to the proliferation of consumer-orientated features, and self-evidently discourages critical writing, and the provision of impartial information to readers.

(iii) Advertisements are more than simply significant determinants of individual stories, however. They have an important influence upon the *very structure of newspapers* themselves, and upon the ways in which they package and organise the world on which they report. Many newspapers – again the 'posh' Sundays are a good example – are now structured into sections on Business, The Arts, Leisure and Travel, Property, etc., each of which is accompanied by specialist advertising. When one looks through these papers noting the ways in which feature material and advertisements are packaged together, their messages mutually reinforcing one another, it becomes difficult to take them seriously as *newspapers*. Rather, their structure, in James

Public relations handouts . . .

EN'S WEAR

SOHO SQUARE
ONDON W1

ISSUE DATED

... not every day that a 1984 version of a Greek winged messenger with wings on her heels and clad in a micro-toga congratulates you winning a prize in a competition. But that's who delivered the st prize of a fortnight for two in Greece and £500 spending money Wrangler's Olympic Competition to winner Dave Ainsworth of mford on Monday. The presentation was made in the Wrangler partment of Debenhams in Romford.

FASHION WEEKLY

161, FLEET STREET,
LONDON, E.C.4

ISSUE DATED 22 NOV 1984

awards

Top prize-winner Dave Ainsworth (centre) with Greek goddess Lee Hutley, Debenhams' general manager Rod Grant (left) and Wrangler's major accounts manager Kevin Dooley (right).

● David Ainsworth, 36, of Romford won an Olympic Holiday for two and £500 spending money in the Wrangler Olympics competition. Thousands of people entered the contest and Wrangler arranged a 'surprise' messenger in the form of a Greek goddess to make the presentation ceremony a memorable occasion.

BARKING & DAGENHAM POST

DAGENHAM
ESSEX

ISSUE DATED 21 NOV 1984

Lucky Dave wins *another holiday*

LUCKY Dave Ainsworth got a kiss and a cuddle from a 'Greecegram' girl last week when he won an Olympic Holiday competition run by Wrangler Jeans.

Ford worker Dave, 36, of Barnstaple Road, Romford won a holiday

for two in Greece with £500 spending money.

He entered the competition through Wrangler's department in Debenhams, Romford. Dave is a competition addict and this is the fourth holiday he has won in two years.

BARKING & DAGENHAM ADVERTISER

182 HIGH STREET NORTH
LONDON E6

ISSUE DATED

HAVERING POST

EEK ENDING NOVEMBER 17, 1984

All Greek to Dave

Dave Ainsworth got a nd a cuddle from a egram' girl last week e won an Olympic Holpetition run by Wrang-

, 36, of Barnstaple Harold Hill, has won a for two in Greece with pending money.

ntered the competition Wrangler's depart-Debenhams, Romford, possibly matched up tures of six celebrities joke Olympic events.

FOURTH

is a competition addict is the fourth holiday won in two years. He is quoist on who his lucky ion will be.

liday tickets were pres Dave, an Administra-n Fords, by General Rod Grant (left) and Dooley of Wrangler. was congratulated Greecegram girl, comth mini toga.

The man who can't stop winning

MEET Dave Ainsworth, the man who has developed the knack of winning free holidays.

He said he has won so many that he can't fit in his latest prize until 1986.

Mr. Ainsworth, a Ford office administrator of

Barnstaple Road, Harold Hill, has just won another holiday — in Greece. And when he went to Debenham's store in Romford to collect his

prize he found a scantily-clad Greek winged messenger to greet him.

After receiving the prize — a fortnight for two, plus £500 spending

money, he said: "I just can't seem to stop.

"Two years ago I won a competition which took me to the World Cup finals in Spain. I go back to Spain this weekend after winning a golfing holiday.

"I also have to fit in a £600 holiday."

Mr. Ainsworth won his latest prize by devising a "witty Olympic event." He dreamed up a contest with Sir Robin Day, as the gold medalist.

November 1984 Debenhams News

Debenhams Diary

Wrangling a trip to sunny Greece

IT WAS a rather glamorous surprise telegram in the shape of Greek goddess Lee Hutley, who presented customer Dave Ainsworth with his prize of a Greek holiday for two and £500 worth of spending money at Debenhams, Romford.

In a competition organised nationally by Wrangler — which attracted thousands of entries — Dave had to choose a suitable candidate from six famous people, including John McEnroe and Jane Fonda, and match them with an unusual Olympic sporting event before completing a tie-breaker.

Dave, 36, lives in Romford and works as an administrator at Ford Motors. He will be taking his holiday next year.

From left to right are: Rod Grant, GM special projects; Lee Hutley, Dave Ainsworth, winner and Kevin Dooley, major accounts manager, Wrangler.

.... reproduced as news stories.

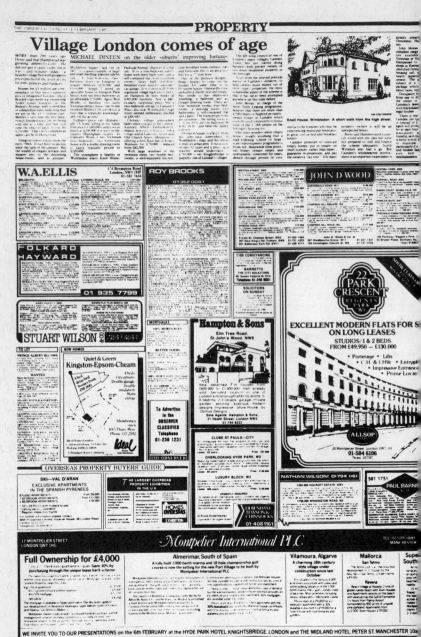

Articles act as 'hooks' to direct readers to ads, and deliver them to advertisers.

Curran's words, 'organises readers into market lots, packaged in suitable editorial material for sale to advertisers.'[82]

(iv) Advertising's influence goes much deeper than shaping the structure of individual newspapers, however. It determines which (and what kind of) newspapers will and will not be available to the public. It shapes the structure, that is, of the whole newspaper industry. The classic statement of the advertisers' position was put in the 1920s in a practical handbook for advertisers:

'You cannot afford to place your advertisements in a paper which is read by the down-at-heels who buy it to scan the "Situations Vacant" column.'[83]

Obviously, to advertisers, the well-heeled are a far more attractive proposition than the poor, and as Curran has emphasised

'These inequalitites are reproduced in the market structure of the press. For how advertisers spend their money decisively influences what publications are available on the market... The effect of advertising finance is thus to distort the structure of the press in a way that reflects and also reproduces inequalities in society.'[84]

A prime example of this was the closing down of *The Daily Herald* in the 1960s, though its readership of 4.7 million was almost double that of *The Times*, *The Financial Times* and *The Guardian* combined. The *Herald's* circulation was falling, it is true, but the paper really ran into trouble because its readership profile (largely working-class, with more male than female and more elderly than young readers) possessed little appeal to advertisers compared with the much smaller, middle-class readership of the 'quality' newspapers. As Curran has argued, the loss of the *Daily Herald*, *News Chronicle* and *Sunday Citizen* in the 1960s, all left-of-centre newspapers which were deserted by advertisers, has been an important influence on the right-wing skew of the British press described earlier in this chapter.[85]

(v) As the paymasters of commercial television, advertisers obviously act as a powerful pressure group upon the television companies. In the constant interchange of ideas and opinions which take place between advertisers and media people about media programming, the criticisms and suggestions of advertisers are taken very seriously indeed. The months before the launching of TV AM in February 1983, for example, were a very anxious time for the new company, since its future hinged entirely on whether advertisers would or would not support its show, *Good Morning, Britain*. Accordingly it launched a campaign to woo advertisers (Peter Jay, TV AM's first chairperson, addressed them as 'you, the most important of all of our customers')[86] and deployed its galaxy of tele-stars (Anna Ford, Angela Rippon, Michael Parkinson, David Frost, etc.) as guarantors to advertisers of the show's probable success. This period saw a constant flow of 'helpful' comment and advice from advertisers about the new programme, and appeals by the show's stars to the advertisers. Here is Michael Parkinson talking about us, his audience, in a way which kids and students invariably find quite distasteful:

'Whether you sell shower attachments, toilet paper, toothpaste, hairdryers, razor-blades, corn-plasters or cosmetics, toasters or kettles, porridge, waffles or cornflakes, orange-juice, tea, or coffee, the chances are that our audience will be using them, spraying them, shaving with them, brushing with them, eating them, drinking them or running out of them around the time they're watching our programme.'[87]

The advertisers failed to get wholeheartedly behind the show, however, many expressing a concern that it was going rather too up-market for their liking (a reversal, this, of the trend we observed with newspapers. For the principal television advertisers are the manufacturers of foodstuffs and domestic products whose target audience is the 'mass', rather than the specialised, market). The sharp about-turn in the 'philosophy' of TV AM within the first few months of transmission, from its 'mission to explain' to its descent to Roland Rat, showbiz gossip, and other trivia, owed not a little to pressure from advertisers, and their reluctance to support the show through its early teething troubles.

The origins of Breakfast Television in Britain, incidentally, demonstrate very well the ways in which an avowedly public-service organisation like the BBC can be driven by commercial imperatives to compete with commercial television and can even directly contribute to a lowering of the standards which a commercial station has set itself in the quality of the information it intends to provide. For the BBC pre-empted TV AM's launch with its own show, *Breakfast Time*, which offered little original reporting or features but a diet of cosy chat, interviews with entertainers and such 'features' as horoscopes. Notwithstanding TV AM's own management problems, the BBC's endeavours in this field have certainly made a significant contribution to a situation in which early morning television in Britain is now governed entirely by the narrowest economic factors. Breakfast TV now consists of two more-or-less identically trivial shows which are of very little significance and which seem to please few apart from the advertisers.

(vi) The easy co-mingling and association of advertising and non-advertising material is a feature of the media which is becoming of increasing importance. A great deal of the avowedly non-commercial content of the media is devoted to the endorsement of particular products, even within public service broadcasting. Writers, film stars, academics and musicians appear on chat shows and magazine programmes in order to plug their products. Specialist programmes can endorse everything from books to fertilisers, whilst shows like *Top of the Pops* and *The Tube* not only explicitly advertise records and use the recording companies' own promotional pop videos, but also act as a showcase for the latest fashions and styles.

Indeed, products and companies which are *excluded* from television advertising frequently find their way onto the screens during the programmes themselves through their sponsorship of sporting and cultural events. Sponsorship, like advertising itself, creates a characteristic 'skew' in the fields in which it operates, providing lavish rewards for the top stars in those sports or activities which have wide media coverage or which are already popular , but providing little support either for important grass-roots actitivities, or less glamorous and prestigious fields of endeavour.

Any consideration of the inter-penetration of advertising and non-advertising material will also need to recognise that television advertisements themselves frequently contain the most interesting visual *content* provided by the medium. They are, of course, far more carefully and expensively produced than the programmes themselves and are frequently more experimental, imaginative and witty than the material which surrounds them. They provide in concentrated form, as Smythe has suggested, the qualities which are spread more thinly throughout the programmes themselves.[88]

(vii) Finally, in assessing the importance of advertising as a determinant of media content, it should be noted that even when not endorsing particular products, the media frequently provide an *ambience* sympathetic to advertisers and consumerism, whether it be in the lavish life-styles of *Dallas* or *Dynasty*, the fascination with new gadgets of *Tomorrow's World*, or the elevation of consumer goods to the status of icons in game shows such as *The Price is Right*. It was the *ambience* of *Good Morning, Britain* which Anna Ford was seeking to convey to advertisers when she described it as 'an alive, funny and original show set in pleasant and friendly surroundings.'[89]

Conclusion

Even this brief survey of some of the ways in which advertising acts as an important determinant of media texts will be enough to reveal the extent to which conventional approaches to teaching advertising lag way behind the current practices of the industry itself. Educationally we need nothing less than a complete re-orientation of our understanding of advertising and its relationship with contemporary media if we wish to understand either phenomenon. I have tried to show some of the ways in which that re-orientation might begin. Much detailed work needs to be done, however, if we are to challenge the belief successfully disseminated by many advertisers that 'in general advertising influence is negligible, and even where it is not ... it is harmless.'[90]

(g) Audiences

There is a view of the media which asserts that *decisive* power within them is exerted by audiences through their active choice of some media texts rather than others. This, the theory of *consumer sovereignty*, proposes that 'the broad nature of the press is ultimately determined by no-one but its readers.' John Whale, a proponent of this view, argues that 'the press is thus predominantly conservative in tone because its readers are.'[91] Owners of newspapers, according to Whale, have little power, and are as likely as not to sustain heavy financial losses. Yet, strangely, 'businessmen and business organisations still seem to like owning newspapers.' Why? Because 'the spirit of public service never wholly dies ... Where it [proprietorial influence] survives at all, it must still defer to the influence of readers ... It is therefore the readers, in the end, who are figures of power.'[92]

As we have seen, however, it is not audiences, but *the willingness of advertisers to purchase access to them* which is the crucial factor in determining 'the broad nature' of the press. Small audiences which are attractive to advertisers are of greater significance than much larger audiences with lower socio-economic profiles. But do not audiences exert a genuine power through their media choices? If audiences choose not to watch a television programme, or buy a newspaper or magazine, is it likely to survive? As we shall see in Chapter Seven, there is indeed a power possessed by audiences. The problem is that whilst audiences possess power, there are no mechanisms through which they are able to exercise it. Indeed, as we shall see, media organisations dispossess audiences of their power in order to sell it to advertisers.

It is evident, however, that most media texts take account of and may be influenced in their content and rhetorical modes by the audience to whom they are addressed. Questions of audience – however imprecisely formulated – are clearly frequently influential determinants of media texts. It is worth stressing, however, that a text's 'inscribed' audience is an abstraction. Real men, women and children have little *direct* influence upon media texts and it is not even strictly accurate to say that popular media texts 'give people what they want'. For there is no mechanism for finding out what this might be outside of the texts they consume. We cannot say what unsatisfied needs exist since they can only be summoned into existence by new texts.

Audiences, then, whilst often having an important influence, do not exert direct *power* in relation to media texts. Any text must address its intended audience in a language and tone with which it will feel comfortable, and must, to some degree, speak to its audience's interests. But the audiences addressed by the media are themselves selected on the basis of their importance either to advertisers or media institutions. Audience influence is thus differential and mediated. And some very large media audiences appear to have very little influence at all.[93] (See pp. 221 and 222.)

(h) Media personnel

In placing emphasis upon some of the major structural determinants of media texts this chapter breaks with a long tradition of media education which has been concerned to draw attention to the dominant role of particular *individuals* (and in particular producers, directors, writers and stars) within the processes of media production. Any consideration of the legal, institutional and socio-economic constraints upon media products leads, inevitably, to a recognition of the limitations within which most media professionals are compelled to work. It is no denigration of the struggles of individuals within the media to suggest that in the future any understanding of their work will need to be premissed on a rather greater recognition of the structures within which they operate than we have acknowledged in the past and rather less of an appreciation of the personal and creative qualities which they bring to their work. For what remains remarkable about most media texts is the extent to which they remain identifiably the products of their institutions rather than of the individuals who have produced them. Traditional critiques of the media have always acknowledged this. Indeed, the notion of the auteur – one of media education's most durable concepts – designated precisely those individuals who were able to transcend the institutional frameworks or generic formulae within which they worked.

I am not arguing here that the work of individual writers, directors, producers, stars, or technicians for that matter, is of little significance, but suggesting that a dominant emphasis upon authorship promotes, in Graham Murdock's words, 'a systematic mis-recognition of the actual processes of production,'[94] and of the nature of the media as industries. For many of the people involved in media production have little or no say in the planning of their work and have, in Stuart Hood's words, 'as little real influence on the end product as they would have on an assembly line. Film crews, for instance, will find themselves scheduled to shoot material for a programme about which they know little and about which they have not been consulted. The result is that they often have scant interest in what they produce . . . The result is a state of alienation – a situation in which the worker is divorced from the products of his or her own skills.'[95] In addition, industrial planning favours homogenised media – classically, in television, series and soap operas which are standardised products, and make standardised demands upon personnel – rather than products which are different, experimental or cannot be accommodated within conventional production techniques.

Notions of authorship continue to have a remarkable resilience, however. As recently as 1981 it was possible for a study of *British Television Drama*[96] to be published which consisted of critical studies of the work of such writers as Jim Allen, Trevor Griffiths and Alan Plater, but did not even raise as problematic the economic, ideological and institutional constraints within which television drama is produced. There is, too, an ironic contradiction in the attempt to recuperate a great deal of work which is specifically socialist and which represents experience from a collectivist and working-class perspective to a project which is defined by categories ('creativity', 'authorship', etc.) which are thoroughly individualistic and bourgeois. If students are to *understand* the media then it may be more important for them to pay attention to the institutional struggles of these worker writers than to pay homage to their work. And most of these writers would certainly agree that it is more important to enjoy, understand and act upon their work and the ideological issues it raises than to celebrate their own special 'talents'.

(i) Sources

'There is no single or simple explanation of news' concluded Herbert Gans in his detailed study of American television and magazine newsrooms, 'but if a handful of explanatory factors had to be singled out, I suggest that of all the considerations, those governing the choice of sources are of prime significance.'[97] Chibnall, in demonstrating how news about law-and-order frequently reproduces the definitions and interpretations provided by police and army sources, suggested that the techniques of news sources in controlling and managing information were 'the most significant and yet under-researched influence on media representations and accounts.'[98] Gans concurs:

'My observations on source power suggest that the study of sources deserves far more attention from news researchers than it has so far obtained... Above all, researchers should determine what groups create or become sources and with what agendas; what interests they pursue in seeking access to the news and in refusing it. Parallel studies should be made of groups that cannot get into the news and why this is so.'[99]

As media teachers we have been similarly neglectful of the crucial influence of sources. This is hardly surprising, however, when one considers the indifference frequently displayed by the media to examining critically the interests of their sources of information. Consider, for example, the following radio interview, an eye-witness account of an episode in an industrial dispute:

Interviewee: A rather large picket arrived, up to, I think, getting on for 1,000 people by about 10 o'clock last night. They then threw bricks against the walls, etc. We then tried to get our first van out at 2.30 this morning, which was forced back by the pickets, who then started throwing bottles and rocks and all the rest. And they in fact knocked down a side wall which crushed a policeman who was underneath it.

The van had then to come back in. Two hours later when more police reinforcements had arrived, we managed to get two vans out loaded with newspapers.

Sir Robin Day: Were there enough police in the end?

Interviewee: I can't answer that because I don't know how many police you need per man in this sort of situation. But it would seem to me that the crowd did overwhelm the police.

Sir Robin Day: And about how many police were there when reinforcements arrived in all, roughly?

Interviewee: I think we ended up with around 250 to 300.

Sir Robin Day: Was there fighting or was there just scuffling or what?

Interviewee: There was fighting. I could see one man butting a policeman. And there were other people who seemed to hit the policemen and then vanish back into the crowd, and I felt quite sorry for them really because the police were there, really taking the brunt of what seems to me to be just a sort of mob rule, that's the only way I can describe it.

Sir Robin Day: They were hitting the policeman where? On his body? His face?

Interviewee: On his body, on his chest, on his face. It looked like they were bundling them and kneeing them at the same time.

Sir Robin Day: They weren't using instruments or bottles? They were using their fists.

Interviewee: I saw bottles hurtling towards the van and over the heads of the policemen, but I didn't see a bottle go into the group of policemen at all.

Sir Robin Day: For the benefit of listeners who may have lost sight of the essential issue behind all this trouble, what is the issue at the heart of this dispute in your view? . . .
(The World at One, 23.11.83)

The interviewee was Eddie Shah, chairman of the newspaper group in dispute with the National Graphical Association. Throughout the interview he was treated as a reliable eye-witness to the events he described and at no point was attention drawn to the possible partiality of his account. Sir Robin Day's questions merely sought to clarify details, and to offer Shah the opportunity to elaborate his story unhindered. Finally Shah was offered an open invitation to sum up 'the essential issue ... at the heart of this dispute.'

By way of contrast, here is an eye-witness account of another picket-line confrontation, this time by a trade-unionist:

Nick Ross: Mr. Taylor, how on earth do you explain what happened at Orgreave today?

Jack Taylor: Well, I think you should be asking that question to police, not just asking it to me. They were in a position today where we saw scenes that we ... well, I thought we'd never see them in Britain. We had people on horses, policemen, riding into crowds of miners with batons swinging. We had policemen with dogs, we had policemen by the thousand there. It's O.K. you saying to me how can I explain it. I'll tell you what, everyone seems to assume that it was equal. What we had was miners in tee shirts and jeans and running pumps. And we had police in shin-guards with riot shields, with long staves, attacking working people.

Nick Ross: Mr. Taylor, can I just get this right for people who saw the news footage earlier? Your interpretation of what happened is that 5,000 miners, striking miners, were peacefully picketing. The police then stormed the picketing miners.

Jack Taylor: Today there we had a situation where policemen were really *beating* miners. Now if they believe they can beat us into submission as well as starve us into submission, they don't understand us.

Nick Ross: Well, some people, Mr. Taylor, will certainly agree with what you say. I suspect that the vast majority will be *astonished* at hearing your account, particularly since there are so many reports from independent witnesses. I've got one here, for example, from a garage owner nearby who says that the pickets smashed his doors, took three of his cars and set them alight – so many independent people are saying that it was pickets who were running amok, not the police.

Jack Taylor: I'll tell you what, I was there. I was there, and I can tell you what I saw. I saw policemen ... in fact I were chased along a road three hundred yards myself and the problem is if you were the back one you got a beating. I were pulled by the hair to the ground, and if you want witnesses I can bring you witnesses to say that was right. Now if you are telling me that this is the sort of country that you and me are looking forward to for the rest of us lives, I'll tell you what we want to have a re-look.

Nick Ross: ... In our Westminster studio is Eldon Griffiths, Tory MP, who is Parliamentary Spokesman for the Police Federation. You heard that Mr. Griffiths – what is your assessment of what happened today?

Eldon Griffiths: I think you used the right word and you said it was astonishing that Mr. Taylor should paint a picture of the police attacking the pickets...

(Sixty Minutes, 18.6.84)

Here we have a very different story. Taylor, though the only eye-witness available, is not asked to give an account of what happened (though he does all the same). He has been invited to the studio in order *to be called to account*, to justify his members' actions to the nation. ('How on earth do you explain what happened at Orgreave today?') In spite of the vividness of his account (an account which had actually been corroborated some minutes earlier by ITN news footage and which was to turn out to be far closer to the truth about the events at Orgreave than the BBC's own news footage), Taylor's story is given no credence by Ross, who dismisses it as astonishing. Ross's invitation to Griffiths, who was never closer than 150 miles from the events is, by contrast, notably open and generous ('What is your assessment of what happened today?') in the manner of the treatment of Shah in the earlier interview.[100]

 The different status accorded to Shah's and Taylor's eye-witness accounts is revealing. It demonstrates very clearly the willingness of the media to pass on as 'facts' information provided by official sources (the army, the police, the government, large companies, i.e., employers) and their general distrust of accounts from other sources such as members of the public, workers, or even trade union officials. As Brian Whitaker has suggested,

'What an examination of published stories and their sources reveals is that news – certainly the serious news – is mainly a one-way traffic: "Them" telling "us" what they want us to know. Any senior politician, company, trade union leader, "personality", or even a bishop can get their message over to the masses simply by issuing a statement, giving an interview or holding a Press conference. The Press, being "objective", faithfully reproduces the message, even if it is a pack of lies, or just plain daft. What matters is that we pay attention to the right people.'[101]

The phenomenon is world-wide. Here is Ian Baker, an Australian journalist:

'The main danger for society ... is that the media as we know it ... is very much an establishment captive. It is open only to the powerful, to those in authority, and to the educated articulate minority as a means of communicating views. And worse, it is susceptible to sophisticated manipulation by public relations agents.'[102]

In Northern Ireland Liz Curtis has shown how

'For the first few years of the conflict, the army and police were the sole source of information on day-to-day violence. Assisted by the fact that the British editors expected reporters to give the authorities' line but not to seek out opposing versions, the army was able to get across its version of incidents virtually unchallenged.'[103]

The sources of the most systematic news and information manipulation in Britain, however, are the Government and civil service, and it is important that students have some knowledge of the mechanisms through which the state manages information. All media teachers will find Cockerell, Hennessy and Walker's *Sources close to the Prime Minister* an invaluable guide to this area, and in particular to the system of Lobby journalism, the Whitehall news machine, the work of the Prime Minister's Press Secretary, and the general strategies adopted by the political parties during an election campaign. I have made a good deal of reference to some of these issues elsewhere in this book, but here I would like to turn to three questions to which we will need to have some answers if we are to work with students of this aspect of the media. First of all, *why* are the media so uncritically accepting of information from accredited sources? Secondly, what is the *effect* of such practices? Do they matter? And, finally, how can both we, as teachers, and our students, begin to treat media sources more critically in the classroom?

Why, then, are the media so dependent upon, and so uncritical of, information from official and institutionalised sources? The answer is simple. Such sources, although they may frequently use the media for their own purposes, are still nevertheless the repositories of the most authoritative information which is routinely available. On many occasions, without their co-operation, journalists might have no story at all. And to be on especially favourable terms with one's sources can be a considerable advantage in that especially juicy stories may be placed exclusively in one's lap. Journalists need their sources just as much as sources need the media, and the problems facing journalists who are sceptical of their sources is formidable. A number of writers have described in detail the techniques of 'freezing-out', 'black-balling', 'harassment' and 'repression' used by sources to enforce conformity upon journalists who produce unfavourable stories.[104] So it pays to be on good terms with one's sources, and many journalists socialise and feel a strong sense of identification and empathy with the motives and objectives of those about whom they write.

It also makes sound economic sense to use material which is freely available, can be attributed to an authoritative source, does not have to be chased, and has been produced with generous resources. In this situation, as Whitaker has pointed out,

'Unorganised people hardly get a look in. The reason is that ordinary people are difficult, expensive and inefficient sources ... The Press are protected when dealing with organisations because representatives who speak to the Press are under the discipline of the body that employs or appoints them. Individuals are responsible to no-one ... Some newspapers take this even further and refuse to trust the observations of their own reporters. Staff of the *Liverpool Daily Post* and *Echo*, for example, are urged not to estimate the numbers of people in demonstrations themselves, but to get a figure from a 'reliable source' (i.e., the police) ... We have already seen how, in Northern Ireland, it pays to go along with the army's version of events. Even if that version is wildly wrong, it's still safe to print. The army is backed by the Government and you can't play safer than that.'[105]

Does it matter that journalists are often so close to their sources? Isn't the odd piece of media manipulation by a source a reasonable price for journalists (and us) to pay for receiving what is generally authoritative information? And we should not forget, of course, that journalists, far from being uncritical dupes, are frequently sceptical by nature and often possess a good deal of cynicism about the information which they are asked to process. Most journalists would bridle at the suggestion that they are simple conduits for PR material, and any obvious attempts by an institution to burnish its own image in a story will simply be edited out. There is a great deal of promotional material, let us not forget, which *does not* find its way into the media.

The real problem, however, is that simply by reproducing what they consider to be the most accurate and authoritative information available, journalists may be colluding with the agenda set by their sources and underwriting the values implicit in the information they provide. The result of what Stuart Hall *et al.* have called the

'systematically structured *over-accessing* to the media of those in powerful and privileged institutional positions... is that their "spokesmen" become... the *primary definers* of topics. The media... do not simply "create" the news; nor do they simply transmit the ideology of the "ruling class" in a conspiratorial fashion. Indeed... the media are frequently not the "primary definers" of news events at all; but their structured relationship to power has the effect of making them play a crucial but secondary role in *reproducing* the definitions of those who have privileged access, as of right, to the media as "accredited sources". From this point of view the media stand in a position of structured subordination to the primary definers.'[106]

The reliance of journalists upon accredited sources of information is important, then, because even when the system is operated with complete integrity – when sources do not obviously attempt to manipulate the media, and when journalists are both critical of and conscientious in their handling of the information they receive from their sources – the crucial powers of agenda-setting and primary definition remain with the sources, and form the common-sensed parameters within which journalists are expected to work.

How can critical work on media sources be encouraged in the classroom? The first point to make is that the assessment of any kind of media information in the light of the interests of those who produce it is such a basic aptitude within any media literacy programme that it should be used as a matter of reflex in the study of any media text and should, indeed, be developed across the curriculum, since it is the basis of critical thinking in all subjects. The question 'Who says so? And why?', then, should be asked as a matter of routine within media education. But what problems arise when students attempt to seek answers to those questions?

One of the most immediate and formidable is that frequently there *is* no obviously named source. When a politician is interviewed on television we can easily relate what she says to the interests she represents. But how can we do this with a newspaper story which is simply *there*, coming, apparently, from nowhere? Here students need to develop the skills of digging out the sources from stories by recognising significant code words ('an official spokesperson said that...', 'sources close to the Prime Minister suggest...'), and developing an understanding both of the sources monitored routinely by journalists, and of the kind of organisations which issue press releases and hold press conferences. Brian Whitaker has very usefully cited 19 of the most common sources relied upon by newspapers. Using this master-list, students should be able to go through a page or two of a newspaper and accurately assign each story to its appropriate source.

'Sources monitored routinely

1. Parliament

2. Councils

3. Police (and the army in Northern Ireland)

4. Other emergency services

5. Courts (including inquests and tribunals)

6. Royalty

7. "Diary" events (e.g., annual events like Ascot or conferences known about in advance)

8. Airports

9. Other news media

Organisations issuing statements and holding press conferences

10. Government departments

11. Local authority departments

12. Public services (transport authorities, electricity boards, etc.)

13. Companies

14. Trade unions

15. Non-commercial organisations (pressure groups, charities, etc.)

16. Political parties

17. Army, Navy, Air Force

Individuals making statements, seeking publicity, etc.

18. Prominent people (e.g., Bishops and film stars)

19. Members of the public.'[107]

Having assigned stories to their sources, students should be able to look at the balance which exists between stories derived from routine sources, special press statements and press conferences, and individuals.

Attention to the influence of sources also raises a crucial question to which the media teacher will continually return: that of structured *absences*. For one of the most important, yet frequently un-recognised, sources of distortion in the media (and, indeed, in the teaching of all school subjects) lies in the sheer *availability* of dominant views. Media teachers need actively to consider and, wherever possible, to present to their pupils, those images which are *not* readily available, those interests which have been filtered out, those voices which are not easily heard, which tell different stories, offer alternative explanations, and *crack the unanimity* of the subjects they raise.

For this reason it is important for media teachers to seek out and collect alternative sources of information and images in teaching about any topic. There exists, throughout Britain, an independent film and video network (see p. 323), which is a useful source of material offering different perspectives and alternative modes of presentation and distribution from mainstream broadcasting. Information about what is both available and likely to be relevant to your needs can be obtained from the Film Officer of your local Regional Arts Association, or from local independent film and video workshops themselves. The magazine *Camerawork* (see p. 333) offers critiques of dominant photographic practices and is an excellent source of alternative images, whilst alternative newspapers and magazines should also be routinely perused for both their stories and images. These tend to be available *en masse* in many alternative bookshops.

* * *

This chapter has attempted to provide some answers to the question of why media texts are the way that they are, and to break new ground by suggesting ways in which students might weigh in the balance a large number of often conflicting influences which bear upon the production of media texts. As I have suggested, it is, perhaps, more important for students

a) to have a general familiarity with the structure of the major arguments in this area,

b) to know their way around the range of information resources available, and

c) to have some grasp of the complexity and inter-dependency of the influences at play *as a whole*, than to

a) become immersed in the study of any one influence, or to see a single influence in isolation from others, or

b) acquire and regurgitate large amounts of information which may quickly become out-of-date.

So much, then, for the determinants of media texts. We must turn now to a consideration of those texts themselves. *How* are they produced? (By what methods, and employing what kind of rhetorical devices?) And *what* precisely do they signify? It is to an examination of these two fundamental questions that we must turn in the next two chapters.

Chapter 5

Rhetoric

The processes of media production are, for the most part, actively concealed from the public. Media professionals frequently assert that they are simply reflecting the world as they find it, a claim which is given a good deal of authenticity by the dominant conventions of illusionism and realism employed by the media.[1] This claim is, however, an ideological one. It is a claim to an authority and power, a bid for uncritical audience assent, which is entirely mystificatory. Simply to pose questions about the precise ways in which media texts have been constructed is to undermine this authority and to see texts as the products of specific human choices and practices. To draw attention not simply to what a text says but to how it is organised, the effects it achieves and how it produces them, is to take an important step from subservience to a text to critical liberation from it.

A critical understanding of media, then, will involve a reversal of the process through which a medium selects and edits material into a polished, continuous and seamless flow. It will involve, that is, the *deconstruction* of texts by breaking through their surface to reveal the rhetorical techniques through which meanings are produced. The project is analogous to that undertaken in the theatre by Brecht, and in the cinema by Godard. Substitute 'media' for 'theatre' in the following quotation from Terry Eagleton (which outlines Brecht's critique of bourgeois theatre) and it becomes possible to see how 'deconstruction' can lead beyond an impressionistic viewing of television programmes, and reading of newspapers and, indeed, become part of a more totally liberating curriculum for schools:

'Bourgeois theatre, Brecht argues, is based on "illusionism": it takes for granted the assumption that the dramatic performance should directly reproduce the world. Its aim is to draw an audience, by the power of this illusion of reality, into an empathy with the performance, to take it as real and feel enthralled by it. The audience in bourgeois theatre is the passive consumer of a finished, unchangeable art-object offered to them as "real". The play does not stimulate them to think constructively of how it is presenting its characters and events, or how they might have been different. Because the dramatic illusion is a seamless whole which conceals the fact that it is constructed, it prevents an audience from reflecting critically on both the mode of representation and the actions represented.

Brecht recognised that this aesthetic reflected an ideological belief that the world was fixed, given and unchangeable, and that the function of the theatre was to provide escapist entertainment for men trapped in that assumption. Against this, he posits the view that reality is a changing, discontinuous process produced by men and so transformable by them.'[2]

But however much we may be sucked into the illusion of a particular film or play, we are always finally aware that we are watching representations – performances which have been scripted, rehearsed and acted – and not reality. This is far from the case with much television and many newspaper stories, however, where even the most alert critic constantly needs to be on her guard against the apparent authenticity of what is seen or read. The necessity for deconstruction in television and newspaper analysis, then, is even more imperative than it is in the theatre or the cinema.

How does one begin this process? In the remainder of this chapter a number of techniques will be considered which are commonly used by the media to construct meaning. What these practices have in common is that they are operations performed by the media, which take place, as it were, behind the backs of the audience. There is nothing necessarily sinister about these practices. Many of them, indeed, are an *inevitable* part of making meaning in any form. Some difficulties arise, however, when television professionals are less than honest and open about the techniques they are using and wish to claim rather more for their work than they are entitled to. But the greatest problem lies in the extent to which many users of the media remain innocent of the influence of such techniques in their consumption of the media. Whilst a little more honesty by media professionals would be welcome, the major task remains an educational one, that of raising audience consciousness of the media's routine rhetorical practices. Knowledge of the following rhetorical techniques might help students of all ages to become much more critically aware of how the media make meaning, and could perhaps form the basis of media literacy programmes within the teaching of all subjects:

1. Selection

2. Exploiting the ambiguity of visual evidence (*The Rhetoric of the Image*)

3. Combining image and linguistic text

4. Suppressing the existence or effect of camera, crew and reporter

5. Set-ups

6. Film and sound editing

7. Interpretative Frameworks

8. Visual Coding

9. Narrative.

1. Selection

All media texts are the outcome of a multitude of choices, many of which are made so naturally and spontaneously that they are sometimes hardly recognised, even by those who make them, as active choices at all. If we can recognise, with American critic David Altheide, that 'almost anything could be said about any event,'[3] then we should ask of any media text why that event or occasion was selected, why this or that way of treating it was chosen, and whose interests are served by amplifying, through reportage, its significance. Are there any events which have not been covered which might have provided a different perspective? What is of the utmost importance here, and constitutes a significant early step towards media literacy, is the insight that the act of selection is itself *evaluative*. The media mark particular people and events as more significant than others simply by reporting them. For 'what is noted', to repeat an earlier observation of Barthes, 'is by definition notable.[4] The media, therefore, carry out what is perhaps their most important ideological role through a process which is generally regarded as being ideologically innocent, the process of reporting 'the facts'.

'Selection', then, is a concept of central importance within Media Education. It can be introduced as early as the Infant School (six- and seven-year-old children in Nottingham schools have worked effectively on telling a story by selecting photographs from a larger pack) and taught in increasingly sophisticated forms thereafter (through the use of simulations such as *Teachers' Protest* or *Radio Covingham*, for example – see Appendix A). But this kind of work is essentially the same as that undertaken by sub-editors, publicists and media consultants the world over. Here is how one of the public relations team who burnished Richard Nixon's image during the 1968 Presidential Election, television expert, Gene Jones, used to work:

'Gene Jones would start work at five o'clock in the morning. Laying coffee and doughnuts on his desk, he would spread a hundred or so pictures on the floor, taken from boxes into which his staff already had filed them. The boxes had labels like VIETNAM... DEMO-CRATIC CONVENTION... POVERTY: HARLEM, CITY SLUMS, GHETTOS... FACES: HAPPY AMERICAN PEOPLE AT WORK AND LEISURE...

He would select a category to fit the first line of whatever script he happened to be working with that day. The script would contain the words of Richard Nixon. Often they would be exactly the words he had used in the acceptance speech, but re-recorded in a hotel room somewhere so the tone would be better suited to commercial use.

Jones would select the most appropriate of the pictures and then arrange and rearrange, as in a game of solitaire. When he had the effect he thought he wanted he would work with a stopwatch and red pencil, marking each picture on the back to indicate what sort of angle and distance the movie camera should shoot from and how long it should linger on each still. "The secret is in juxtaposition," Jones said, "the relationships, the arrangement. After twenty-five years, the other things – the framing and the panning, are easy."

Everyone was excited about the technique and the way it could be used to make people feel that Richard Nixon belonged in the White House.'[5]

Another simple and cheap classroom resource for selection work is a photographic contact sheet, containing images of the same people or events. Any keen amateur or professional photographer can easily provide contact sheets for classroom use. An example of how a contact sheet can be used as the basis for simulation work is provided on page 133. Here pupils have to choose, from 30 photographs, one which would be appropriate as a cover photograph for a book of poems written by the girl on the photographs, 10-year-old Marisa Horsford. Some of Marisa's poems, which were recently published by a Nottingham community-based publishing group,[6] are reproduced on page 132. Group discussion of these images raised such important questions as the widely divergent impressions which can be conveyed of the same person through the selection of different images; the power of those who have the authority to select such images; the dominant visual stereotypes of black children and adolescents in Britain, and whether one should reinforce or challenge them, and the ways in which commercial considerations encourage the circulation of some images rather than others.

Some primary school teachers have had a great deal of success in adapting for younger children selectivity simulations originally intended for older students.[7] *Front Page*, *Radio Covingham*, *Television News*, *Choosing the News* and *Teachers' Protest*[8] all require students to produce their own front page, radio, or television programme by selecting, rejecting or modifying basic source material. Even if the material itself is not suitable for use with a particular class, it is important for media teachers to be familiar with this kind of material, and with the basic simulation models which are currently available so that they can begin to produce simulations appropriate to their own classes, in however rudimentary a form. It should be said that simulations do inevitably carry with them the danger that students may unquestioningly reproduce dominant media forms and conventions, but as students become more adept at simulations the teacher can deliberately introduce elements which break established media codes: having television news shot entirely in close-up, for example, or dispensing with news-readers and allowing reporters to link as well as report their stories.

Another frequent problem with simulations is that pupils may not give enough consideration to the reasons *why* they choose particular stories or images. If selections are made on the spur of the moment, or without any reflection, then much of the value of this kind of activity is lost. With primary school children, for example, it may be necessary to give a good deal of practice in deciding whether stories are important or not, by asking the children to place them into one of three categories: Important/Unimportant/Don't Know:

e.g., Mr Aslin (their headmaster) drove home after shool yesterday.

Mr Aslin drove home from school yesterday and had an accident and is now in hospital.

The Queen drove through Nottingham yesterday.

The Queen drove through Nottingham last year, had an accident and spent some time in hospital, etc.

Of course it is not possible to evaluate these stories outside of the context in which they are likely to be used. Pupils need to be asked if such stories are important within particular contexts (for inclusion in a class newspaper, or a national TV news programme, for example) and quickly discover that value is not inherent within a story, but relates to its usefulness for particular purposes. In working on news simulations with primary and lower secondary school pupils it is often helpful to have groups evaluate each individual story from the perspective of its usefulness to a particular context (daily paper; weekly TV programme, etc.), consigning it to one of three boxes – Accept, Reject or Hold, as it comes in.

THE RICH ONES

The luggage
    is being packed
Into the chauffeur
    driven Rolls Royce.

As the poor ones pass them
    they turn away
      because they can't
    stand the sight of them.

    The poor
      ones don't take
any notice.

MOTHERS IN THE STREET

Two completely different women

Are walking down the street.
    Then they get closer
    and finally they meet.

Both babies
    start to cry and in
    their minds

they have the same thoughts

But their mothers can't understand.

GETTING ON
WITH GROWN
UPS

It all depends
    what mood they're in.

If they're in a
    good mood you get on well.

If they're in a
    bad mood they say get to bed
    or something
      like that.

    That's how
    I get on with
      grown ups.

YOU'RE
NOT GETTING IN YOUR
LINES PROPERLY

You're still not
    getting in your lines
    properly.
      You should
      be able
      to get
    in your lines
without your teachers
telling
you.
    Especially you
      Fourth Years
      I hope
      this
    will
be
the
last
    time
      for
        moaning
    now.

WE ARE
NEVER RIGHT

When you're a child
    you're
    never
    right.

But they're wrong because
    I
    proved
    it
    that
    sometimes
    we are
    right.

They don't know
    every
    thing
    you know.

Which photograph would be most suitable as a cover for Marisa's volume of poetry?

CONSTRUCTING IMAGES OF SCHOOL

SEQUENCE ONE   *SEQUENCE TWO*

P.T.O.

(An exercise for eight-year-olds)

P.T.O.

These final two images in both sequences (see previous pages). How far are our interpretations of them determined by the images which precede them?

More advanced work on selection will recognise that, in Claud Cockburn's words, 'all stories are written backwards – they are supposed to begin with the facts and develop from there, but in reality they begin with a journalist's point of view, a conception, and it is the point of view from which the facts are subsequently organised.'[9]

Even this may be a somewhat optimistic view, for as we have seen (Chapter Four), both the 'facts' of the case and the angle from which they are reported, are frequently set not by journalists at all, but by news sources. The conclusions of Altheide's research on American television news that most stories are

'already pretty well set before they leave the station ... The story is simply the ... medium through which a definition of an event – the angle – is presented.'[10]

need to be modified slightly to take into account the influence of sources upon reporters' definitions of events. Nevertheless, it remains important that pupils should have ample opportunity to select material from tightly defined angles. The two sequences of images on pp. 134–6 were selected from a set of thirty images by eight-year-old pupils from two pre-determined angles to give quite different impressions of their school, and they succeed in doing that even though the two final images are the same in each sequence. What each sequence does here is to provide a context which narrows down the range of meanings which we can give to the final two images, and produce two diametrically opposed readings of them.

This kind of exercise leads naturally into work which explores the ambiguity of visual images and the functions of context and commentary in anchoring particular meanings to them (see Sections 2 and 3 below). It remains important, however, before going on to more complex work, to give due weight to the crucial significance of selection, and the criteria for making it which permeate every aspect of media production. Everything we see in the media, however seemingly natural, is the end product of innumerable filtering processes, and frequently implicit human choices. Our first task in looking critically at the media is to bring such choices to the surface, to recognise them, that is, *as* choices.

Apart from the kind of important general questions (see p. 129 above) which can be raised with the youngest pupils, a more systematic way of revealing the range of choices available within the media to more mature secondary school students is to draw attention to the distinction between *syntagmic* and *paradigmatic* relations. Every media text is a syntagm, a combination of discrete units which makes up a signifying whole. A sentence, a newspaper story, an advertisement or a television programme, are all syntagms, combinations of functionally different signs which interact with one another to produce meaning. The opening of a television news programme might consist, for example, of a medium close-up shot of a white, middle-aged, male newsreader who is sitting behind a desk in a brightly lit studio and looking directly at camera. He is wearing a smart dark suit, and a blue tie. Syntagmically this might be expressed as:

Medium close-up shot/of white/middle-aged/male/newsreader,/ who is sitting/behind/a desk/and looking/directly/at/camera/. He/is wearing/a smart/dark/suit/and a blue/tie.

Each unit of the syntagm has been selected from the wide range of functionally similar signs which exist within that unit. That is, as well as having an interactive syntagmic relationship with functionally different signs, each unit has a differential paradigmatic relationship with functionally similar signs: e.g.,

BIG CLOSE-UP	YELLOW	VERY OLD	REPORTER
CLOSE-UP	BROWN	ELDERLY	EXPORT
MEDIUM CLOSE-UP SHOT	**OF WHITE**	**MIDDLE-AGED**	**NEWSREADER**
MEDIUM SHOT	BLACK	YOUNG	INTERVIEWER
LONG SHOT		CHILD	ENTERTAINER
VERY LONG SHOT		BABY	MEMBER OF THE PUBLIC

STANDING	UNDER	A CHAIR	GLANCING	ABOVE
BENDING	ON	A TABLE	SQUINTING	BEHIND
WHO IS SITTING	**BEHIND**	**A DESK**	**AND LOOKING**	**DIRECTLY AT CAMERA**
KNEELING	INSIDE	A COFFEE TABLE	STARING	BELOW
SQUATTING	IN FRONT OF		IGNORING	TO THE SIDE OF

Any secondary school pupil who is studying a foreign language will understand the concept of the paradigm quite easily, and attention to paradigmatic relations in analysing media texts can increase awareness of the range of choices available to media producers, and effectively de-naturalise the text. Replacing just one paradigmatic unit with another will help focus attention on the precise function of that unit within the syntagm. Replacing 'medium close shot' with 'big close-up' in the above syntagm, for example, demonstrates that the way in which newsreaders are normally shot is not natural, but an active choice, which produces a particular ideological effect (that of 'respectful distance'). A big close-up could have one of two possible effects, depending upon the demeanour of the newsreader. It could either invite us to distrust the newsreader by closely scrutinising his facial movements, or (if the newsreader were assertive) dominate us by the size and power of his image. For a surrealistically de-naturalising effect, try combining one randomly chosen element in each paradigm to form a completely new syntagm. Are the results actually as outrageous as they at first seem to be? Or is television simply locked in to a very narrow range of conventions and possibilities?

An American former advertising executive, Jerry Mander, has suggested another simple way of illustrating the multiplicity of choices made within any media text. His Technical Events Test, though set within a simplistic television-as-drug view of the medium, does draw attention to the range of technical choices constantly being made within television production:

'Put on your television set and simply count the number of times there is a cut, a zoom, a superimposition, a voice-over, the appearance of words on the screen – a technical event of some kind.

You will find it goes something like this. You are looking at a face speaking. Just as you are becoming accustomed to it, there's a cut to another face (technical event). Then the camera might slowly draw back to take in some aspect of a wider scene (technical event). Then the action suddenly shifts outdoors to the street (technical event). Intercut with these scenes might be some other parallel line of the story. It may be a series of images of some-one in a car racing to meet the people on that street we have just visited (technical event). The music rises (technical event). And so on.

Each technical event – each alteration of what would be natural imagery – is intended to keep your attention from waning as it might otherwise. The effect is to lure your attention forward like a mechanical rabbit teasing a greyhound. Each time you are about to relax your attention, another technical event keeps you attached.

When you try the Technical Events Test on a few thirty- or sixty-second television commercials you will find that advertising has roughly twice the technical action of the already hyped-up programs that the ads interrupt. On the average, a thirty-second commercial will have from ten to fifteen technical events. There is almost never a six-second period without a technical event. What's more, the technical events in advertising have much more dimension than those in the programming. In addition to the camera zooms, pans, rolls and cuts, they are far more likely to have words flashing on and off the screen, songs going on and off, cartoon characters doing bizarre things, voice-overs, shots from helicopters and so on.

The Technical Events Test is extremely subversive to television. This is one reason I have asked you to do it. As people become aware of the degree to which technique, rather than anything intrinsically interesting, keeps them fixed to the screen, withdrawal from addiction and immersion can begin. I have seen this happen with my own children. Once I had put them to the task of counting and timing these technical events, their absorption was never the same.'[11]

I would prefer to put the matter differently. Recognition of the *inevitably* selective nature of media texts actively subverts the media's spurious claim to present events 'exactly as they happen'. Students frequently respond to their heightened consciousness of media selectivity with a quite unjustifiable sense of outrage. Broadcasters and journalists need to recognise that this is frequently the result of their mystification of their own working practices, their claims to an objectivity which they can never possess, and their denial of their own mediating function. But criticisms by students or anyone else which assume that the media can ever give us a picture of the world 'as it really is', miss the mark. As Enzensberger pointed out many years ago, 'There is no such thing as unmanipulated writing, film, or broadcasting.'[12] Our democracy would be a great deal healthier if media professionals openly acknowledged that, if the public understood it, and if we all acted upon it. At a stroke this would reduce the power of the media to project their representations as objective evidence, produce less mystificatory and more illuminating journalism, and give audiences a more realistic understanding of the media's capabilities and limitations.

2. The rhetoric of the image

Another early step towards media literacy lies in the ability to recognise some of the problems of assessing visual evidence. Television, for example, is considered by most people to be the most reliable source of information available to them, perhaps, as Tunstall has suggested, because 'TV news is much more cautious – it has a legal requirement to be neutral', whilst 'the popular press deliberately surrenders "reliability" in search of excitement',[13] but no doubt also because television deals primarily in visual images which appear to be open, transparent and authentic, and which establish a consciousness of what Barthes called the subject's 'having-been-there'.[14] They present us, that is, with evidence which appears compelling, and which we can, to a large extent, judge for ourselves. How well-founded is our trust in the authenticity of this evidence?

We might begin by accepting what media teachers rarely acknowledge: that most of us most of the time implicitly trust much of the visual evidence presented to us by the media. We should go further and say that this trust is generally justified. After all, if I watch a footballer scoring a goal or a horse winning a race on television, I do not assume that these events have been constructed for my benefit by television companies. I can be reasonably sure that they did actually take place and – with some important qualifications – in the ways in which I observed them on television. John Berger:

'Cameras are boxes for transporting appearances. The principle by which cameras work has not changed since their invention. Light, from the object photographed, passes through a hole and falls on to a photographic plate or film. The latter, because of its chemical preparation, preserves these traces of light. From these traces, through other slightly more complicated chemical processes, prints are made. Technically, by the standards of our century, it is a simple process. Just as the historically comparable invention of the printing press was, in its time, simple. What is still not so simple is to grasp the nature of the appearances which the camera transports... The material relation between the image and what it represents (between the marks on the printing paper and the tree these marks represent) is an immediate and unconstructed one. And is indeed like a *trace*... Photographs do not translate from appearances. They quote from them.'[15]

Photography, in Frank Webster's words (following Walter Benjamin), 'represented a process of *mechanical* reproduction wherein it appeared that the observer was himself removed from the scene. Machines recorded the world in such a way that the person pressing the shutter appeared scarcely involved. There was no obvious subject intercepting between an audience and pictures of reality.'[16]

Visual images, then, are highly *authentic*. Those people and that event, presenting themselves to the camera, were, irrefutably, *there*. And we know that with greater certainty than we would from a written or an eye-witness account. Many media teachers are so used to thinking of the media as being entirely the *manufacturers* of the events they portray, that it is necessary to stress that the media's claims to be windows upon or mirrors of experience does have *some*, albeit limited, basis in fact. Acknowledging this could have two important effects. It might begin to make dialogue possible between teachers and media practitioners, who too often seem to be locked into entirely incompatible ways of conceptualising the media. Secondly, it might counteract an all-too-common tendency to make the media the scapegoat for all of society's ills. For if the news is entirely manufactured by the media, who else can be held responsible for its representations?

When the media do seem to line up consistently against popular movements, such as CND or the labour movement, it is understandable that those who care about the democratic health of their country should wish to give little credence to media representations. But they should recognise that this is a game at which two can play. For example, during television coverage of the Orgreave picket line in the 1984–5 coal dispute, ITN showed some disturbing footage of violence on the picket line, including one sequence in which a policeman repeatedly used his baton on an unarmed picket who had fallen to the ground. Two points are worth making about these shots. First of all, someone at ITN at least had the courage and honesty to show this sequence. (The BBC, in its coverage, suppressed any evidence of police violence in both its film and commentary.[17]) But, secondly, it is also clear that ITN shot the sequence by acccident. For instead of closing in and getting a closer view of this dramatic incident, the camera, in a remarkable movement, *pans away from it*, as though the crew were embarrassed by the explicitness of what they were shooting.

Still, the sequence *was* shown by ITN and it became the major story on the following day. It is worth drawing attention, however, to some of the reactions provoked by this direct evidence of police violence. On the next day's edition of *The World at One*, Sir Robin Day managed to cast some doubt on the evidence by speaking of 'Some particularly disturbing shots which *seemed* to show one policeman striking a picket several times across the head with a truncheon' (original emphasis). In the same programme the Assistant Chief Constable of South Yorkshire argued that we did not see the context within which the policeman was moved to beat the unarmed miner across the skull. ('The television cameras didn't show what happened before and what happened after. Maybe the man (the miner) had in his hand some offensive weapon. He may have been carrying a knife. He may have been carrying anything at all which could have caused injury to that officer.') Some months later, when film-maker Ken Loach included the sequence in his film of the dispute and dubbed on sound of the truncheon hitting the miner's skull, the Chief Constable of Northumbria actually thought it worthwhile to go on *Right to Reply* to *complain about the dubbing*.

Now neither the irony nor the absurdity of these appeals to the constructed nature of the image should be lost on us as media teachers. For, in many situations, as I shall demonstrate later in this chapter, we would wish our students to attend to precisely this kind of detail. But to show undue concern about the lack of contextualisation or the use of a sound effect in a film in which a defenceless man (whomever he may be) is beaten up before our eyes, is to lose all sense of human values. I am not arguing here that media manipulation is defensible in a cause to which I subscribe, but reprehensible in one to which I am opposed, though that is probably the most common response of all to the media today. Nor do I believe that deliberate attempts to deceive an audience are ever justified, even in the cause of the oppressed. But these arguments do need to be placed in the context of the fact that all media inevitably manipulate. What is important, as I have continually stressed, is that audiences recognise this and assess for themselves, in so far as they are able, the evidence before them in the full light of this understanding. The aim of this book is to develop in children and students the abilities necessary to make this kind of difficult judgement. But the employment of this or that technique does not of itself necessarily either invalidate or confirm the truth of particular claims made through the media.

A great deal of weight, then, deserves to be attached to the authenticity of visual images but that, as I have suggested, is only a part of the argument. As we have seen, questions of selection – which images have wide circulation, and which never get shown – are of paramount importance. And any visual image is necessarily seen from *some* point of view – both physically and ideologically. But apart from these important qualifications, there are frequently difficulties in establishing precisely what visual images *mean*.

Consider the final two photographs on page 136. What sense do we make of these images? How do we understand them? Are the boys in the first photograph studying hard or just bored? Is the second photograph a scene of playground violence or one of innocent sport? Clearly in *interpreting* visual images we are moving away from the firm ground of their authenticity towards areas of ambiguity and doubt.

What are the sources of this doubt? There are two. First of all, visual images are *polysemic*. In them so many contending sign-systems jostle for our attention that their possible meanings multiply before our eyes as we slowly take in more of their details. We need to narrow our focus, concentrate on some details to the exclusion of others, in order to make specific sense of images. But there is nothing within the image itself which will reveal to us what is or is not of significance. Secondly, media images have been frequently wrenched from a context that would help us make sense of them. 'An instant photographed' as Berger has said, 'can only acquire meaning insofar as the viewer can read into it a duration extending beyond itself. When we find a photograph meaningful, we are lending it a past and a future ... Discontinuity always produces ambiguity.' As we have seen, by placing the final two photographs in different contexts, primary school children were able to produce two diametrically opposed readings of each image, and to understand the conclusion of Berger that photographs are 'irrefutable as evidence, but weak in meaning.'[18]

They do not appear so in the media. There, they are continually used to authenticate a particular point of view. This is achieved through *anchoring* (the term is Barthes'[19]) or pinning down one *preferred meaning* from the many which are potentially available. Anchorage can be performed by a caption or commentary, but anchorage is also possible without language. It can be achieved, as we have seen, by contextualising the image within a series of other images, the very seriality of the images narrowing down the range of possible interpretations available for each individual shot.

So vital is it for pupils to grasp the curious reversal through which ambiguous visual images, containing many possible free-floating meanings, can come to *legitimate* particular interpretations, that we need to slow the process down still further. When television reporters and newspaper sub-editors provide a commentary or a caption to an image, or place an image in a particular context, they *impose* meaning upon it. To television viewers or newspaper readers, however, commentary or caption is rarely experienced as imposition. Quite the reverse. The caption or commentary, we are assured, has plausibility because *there* is the visual evidence which supports it. Anchorage does more than impose meaning, however. It simultaneously *suppresses*, and makes less easily available to the viewer, the image's alternative and perhaps contradictory meanings, rather in the manner of those Gestalt images in which we can see either a vase or two silhouetted profiles, but never both simultaneously. Finally, further anchorage is supplied by the wider context within which images are placed. The same image may produce very different readings if it is placed on page three of *The Sun*, in a photographic exhibition in an art gallery, or in a Channel Four programme on pornography.

More detailed work on the relationship between visual images and linguistic texts will be considered in the next section of this chapter. Here it is necessary to mention briefly a number of other issues which arise in assessing visual evidence in the classroom:

a) Single visual images are frequently assumed to be the simplest starting point for studying the media, and the study of 'the image' is often the first element of many school media courses. In my own experience, before image-study can be successfully undertaken with students of any age, it is necessary to do a good deal of preliminary work on the *constituents* of images – the non-verbal communication patterns which need to be interpreted in order to make sense of images.[20]

b) Next, image-analysis may be of limited value in helping students to assess problems of visual evidence if it is based upon the analysis of formally composed images from advertisements and magazines (the Sunday colour supplements seem to be particularly popular sources of material for many teachers). Such images, frequently having been produced with a precise purpose in mind, too often lack the polysemic richness of genuine photographs which demand and repay close investigation. Second-hand book shops tend to be more fruitful hunting-grounds, where collections of old magazines and illustrated books containing historically interesting visual material can often be picked up extremely cheaply.

c) As always, questions of selection are of prime importance in assessing visual images. Attention should be drawn to the unseen presence in any photograph, that of the photographer who has chosen that moment, that angle, that film, and, as likely as not, has arranged that composition (see Section 5 below) to convey not 'the truth' but her version of what is significant. 'Photography', in Szarkowski's words, 'is a system of visual editing. At bottom it is a matter of surrounding with a frame a portion of one's cone of vision ... it is a matter of choosing from among given possibilities, but ... the number of possibilities is not finite but infinite.'[21] A Nottingham primary school teacher, Chris Shaw, adapting (and improving) an idea from Golay[22] has had some of her class enact a dramatic sequence of events, which the rest of the class observed through the view finders of their cameras. The beauty of this exercise is that without requiring expensive equipment (old broken cameras will do) it provides realistic insights into the selectivity of the camera and throws up many conflicting interpretations of a straightforward sequence of events.

d) Perhaps the most important level of activity and analysis in considering visual evidence lies in the domain of picture editing – most important since a photographic print will represent for most pupils a *finished* product, rather than the raw material for further work. A picture editor can enlarge, select, suppress, crop, distort and juxtapose images to suggest his own preferred meanings, which may be quite independent of the photographer's. Mark Godfrey, a photographer covering the Vietnam war, could say:

'I would send my film in . . . and a picture editor in Saigon would pick the frame he felt dramatic enough to transmit. Often I was horrified to find that the photographs made high drama out of field situations which were boring and tedious.'[23]

Studying picture editing, unfortunately, suffers from the same problem as studying news broadcasts: scrutiny of either press photographs or televised news cannot easily reveal the selective practices which result in one version of reality being presented rather than another. The essential ingredients for the study of such practices lie on the cutting-room floor. Simulation, however, can enable pupils to practise techniques of picture editing themselves. Selection and editing exercises distributed by the Society for Education in Film and Television have been available for use by schools for some time now (e.g., *The Market*, *The Visit*, *Teachers' Protest*, etc. See Appendix A), but more recent material allows scope for creative cropping and layout exercises, in which pictures need to be selected, cropped and organised in order to present a particular point of view. Andrew Bethell's *Eyeopeners Two*[24] contains simple examples of what might be done in the classroom whilst Bethell and Simons' newspaper simulation, *Choosing the News*,[25] requires pupils to select and crop photographs in designing the front page of a newspaper. Finally, Harold Evans's magnificent collection of images in his study of photojournalism, *Pictures on a Page*, contains material which can easily be adapted for classroom exercises in cropping and layout.[26] The advantage of using this material is that students can compare their efforts with the results achieved by professional picture editors.

3. Image and text

We have already examined some of the reasons why it is possible for words, in Harold Evans's phrase, to 'turn images on their heads':

'The photograph of a couple locked in embrace may be captioned Love or it may be captioned Rape. Time and again in war both sides have used one and the same photograph to attribute crimes to the enemy.'[27]

An important analytical skill which needs to be developed throughout any media literacy programme, then, is the ability to 'shred' images from their commentaries or captions, to remain cognisant, that is, of the full range of meanings implicit in visual images in spite of the tendency of the accompanying commentary to 'close' on a particular preferred meaning. This section examines a number of ways in which this ability might be developed.

I have suggested elsewhere a range of simple games and activities designed to introduce students to this area of study,[28] and clearly introductory work on commentary can evolve naturally out of the kind of selection exercises described on pp. 129–137 above. Here is a more advanced exercise undertaken by 16-year-old students using the simulation *Teachers' Protest* (see Appendix A). The normal way of playing this simulation is to ask students to select particular images to support a pre-determined angle. In this version, news teams were given *precisely the same set of images*, and asked to interpret them from different points of view (see pp. 148ff).

In some pieces of film or television there may be alarming discrepancies between the commentary and the images on the screen. Examples are surprisingly common once you begin to look for them, and they make excellent material for classroom use. Here is the commentary from an early live television programme, *Saturday Night Out*, originally transmitted in 1956 but recently re-shown by the BBC in a compilation programme *We Bring You Live Pictures*.[29] The makers of the programme had been given an old train which they planned to blow up and de-rail as a live spectacle for viewers at home. The commentator is Bob Danvers-Walker:

'Now here, in a sense, is the spot marked X, where the accident will happen, where demolition charges have been laid.

The train wreckers are behind the crest, with two men with automatic weapons giving covering fire.

Now where is the train?

It's not the cold that's making me tremble it's the excitement here. It's terrific.

Now out of that belt of timber in the background comes engine No. 30740 and three coaches belting down the track to meet their end in a *mighty* crash over the embankment.

Commentary 1   *Commentary 2*

Violence
erupted in
the streets
of London
today as
teachers
demon-
strated in
protest at
the govern-
ment's new
pay offer.

Solidarity
was the
name of the
game in
London
today as
teachers
staged the
biggest
protest in
their history
against the
govern-
ment's pay
increase of
only 2%.

The turn-out
was
disappoint-
ing but
violence was
provoked by
small
militant
groups who
arrived by
coach from
places many
miles away.

Teachers
came from
all over the
country in
support of
the march.

The vast
majority
were
socialist
sympath-
isers tho'
members of
the public
ignored
their
propaganda.

Many young
teachers,
reported to
be living
below the
poverty line,
still
managed a
smile as the
march took
on a
carnival
atmosphere . . .

Commentary 1

Commentary 2

Slogans
attacking
the Prime
Minister
were later
used as
weapons
against the
police,

enlivened by
the presence
of many
brightly
coloured
placards.
The march —

Militants
shouted at
the police
and incited
the crowd

Well
organised
and peaceful —

And as
emotions
began to get
out of
hand...

allowed
teachers to
put their
case.

Commentary 1   *Commentary 2*

The police showed their contempt for the marchers. There was little support from members of the public particu- larly . . .

and even won sympathy from a friendly 'bobby'

Parents who found their hands unexpected- ly full as children had the day off school. In some areas vandalism was reported as children roamed the streets

As well as from parents, brought along by their children to support the teachers.

Nearly 200 tons travelling at 45 miles an hour and unmanned.

They've lashed the whistle down.

They've lashed the whistle down and you'll hear her coming down there.

Down she comes closing the gap to where the Royal Engineer Sappers have laid their trap.

See that smoke? Here she comes!

A line to be *buckled* and *wrecked* by high explosives that will send her hurtling down the 30-foot slope, into a snow- and ice-covered mass.

Here she comes! Vivid realism that brings to life those dramatic stories of Special Service and commando raids of the war.

Now here is high drama in real life.

It's terrifying!

Now anything can happen in the final holocaust of twisted and torn metal.

You've never seen anything like this before on your television.

Now watch!'

The commentary's over-kill is very funny since it accompanies nothing more sensational than an antiquated train steaming along a track. The long-awaited climax is even more hilarious. There is a small bang, and the engine and front carriage leave the rails but remain upright. And there it stays, tooting its whistle. There is no carnage, no twisted and torn metal, no holocaust.

At this point the commentator clearly has a crisis of credibility on his hands. He is on air live. What is he to say next? Secondary school students produced the following solutions:

'Well, it just goes to prove the safety of British transport, and the excellence of our engineers. Instead of the mighty crash you could well have expected, this glorious piece of machinery continued safely down the bank, avoiding all harm to any possible passengers. The superiority of the British engine is made fully evident through this enthralling experiment.' *(Catherine Lodder)*

'Well, wasn't that spectacular, probably not as amazing as planned but still pretty spectacular.

You at home probably won't be able to sense the atmosphere here but I can assure you that it is *electric*!

We cannot go near the train yet as there is a high risk of it exploding. Yes, just like a time-bomb waiting to spring its fiery energy into the thick black sky.

I can see figures in the distance through the smoke. They are only visible as silhouettes against the fresh, white snow surrounding the 200-ton wreck. It appears they have fire precautions at hand. But don't worry you at home, everything is under control here. Our boys won't make a drama out of a crisis!' *(Nicola McMullan)*

There is, of course, a great deal of interest in discovering how the real commentator solved his dilemma. Here is the actual commentary:

'What a grand old lady! Still on her legs! You've got to take your hat off to her. Great Heavens! What a fantastic sight! Still blowing her whistle!

Well once again *Saturday Night Out* has shown you things happen *as* they happen, *when* they happen . . .'[30]

The cinema newsreel compilation film, *Protest for Peace*,[31] also contains striking discrepancies between its film footage and its commentary, and is a valuable reminder that media texts are collaborative projects, and frequently contain internal tensions and contradictions indicative perhaps of the differing perspectives of those who work on them. This is how the commentary on one of the extracts from the film, an account of one of the 1968 anti-Vietnam war marches through London, sets the scene:

'It started as a march through the heart of London. Most of the demonstrators were young, their intentions seemed honourable. They came from most walks of life. Vanessa Redgrave as usual was in the vanguard of the would-be peacemakers. But also there were troublemakers, people not content to just voice their disapproval of the war in Vietnam. A hard core with intentions to drag the majority of well-intentioned demonstrators down to their sickening level. And so they marched through the Sunday streets of London to Grosvenor Square and the American Embassy. Riots were being incited. At Grosvenor Square, police, warned to expect trouble, waited, their intention to keep the peace, prevent trouble. But at the head and in the midst of the advancing column the hate-makers were at work. This was how they turned a demonstration for peace into a bloody riot such as Britain has never before witnessed.'

I have frequently played the film through silently to students and asked them to provide a commentary from perspectives which are either hostile or favourably disposed towards the demonstration. But no group, no matter how hostile, has ever been able to match the virulence of that commentary, which is delivered with a stridency of tone which harks back to propaganda newsreels of the 1940s. At this point, the commentary, having established its interpretative framework, is content to lapse into silence and allow the images to speak for themselves. The images are simply accompanied by wildtrack sounds of crowds, and an insistent, ominous drumbeat. Camera-positioning, as usual is behind police lines.

But just before the end of the film some astonishingly brutal images of police kicking a demonstrator who is on the ground call into question the whole stance and tone of the commentary. Film and commentary begin to pull apart at the seams. An attempted resolution by the final piece of commentary simply emphasises the deep fissure which has opened up within the film:

'Police were injured while defending themselves and doing their duty. Only 45 demonstrators were hurt. The police have won the highest possible praise for their incredible self-control against brute force on a day when a demonstration for peace ended as a war in the heart of London.'

Protest for Peace is an extremely useful text for classroom work on media rhetoric, since its techniques are deployed so openly. That particular way of representing events belongs to another era, yet there are clear continuities with the presentation of news and documentary material on television in the 1980s. The commentaries may have become less declamatory, but many of the techniques remain remarkably intact. Television coverage of the 1984–5 coal dispute, for example, used as a matter of routine, wildtrack 'riot' sounds to cover images shot at different times and places, labelled those who were loyal to their union as 'militants' and those who disregarded union policy as 'moderates', and continually positioned cameras to encourage identification with the police or the working miners (including one infamous occasion when a camera was placed inside a car driven by a working miner's wife). The importance of teaching this aspect of visual literacy, then, should need no emphasis for there seems little doubt that these techniques – and their range is remarkably small – will continue to be used by television, not simply in Britain, but throughout the world, in times of political, industrial or social crisis, in order to engineer consent for dominant ideologies. The extent to which they will continue to be effective will depend almost entirely upon the efforts of media teachers everywhere. Ours is urgent and important work, and the sooner we tackle it, on a systematic and co-operative basis, the better.

Though I have been primarily concerned to examine the relationships between images and linguistic texts in this section, it should be said that media teachers have probably paid too little attention in the past to the significance of sound as an element which is every bit as selective and open to manipulation as the image. Indeed, it could be argued that television is itself primarily a sound medium. Television's illusionism, for example, is principally sustained by the continuity of its sound. We read into fragmented and edited film material a continuity which owes a great deal to the uninterrupted flow of sound which accompanies it. And when we 'watch' television it is rarely a continuously visual experience. We may frequently look away from the screen, involve ourselves in other actitivies, and even leave the room for short periods. We do not shut out sound quite so easily, however, and the sound-track continually alerts us to those points of maximum interest on the screen, whatever we are doing, or wherever we happen to be in the house.

There is a sense, too, in which sound is taken to be an even more significant guarantor of authentiticy than the visual image. For the idea that a *recorded* sound-track has a largely unproblematic relationship with the *original* sounds which have been recorded, has a remarkable degree of resilience even amongst film theorists. Consider, for example, the following quotations collected by Tom Levin:

'What we hear from the screen is not an image of the sound but the sound itself, which the sound camera has recorded and reproduced again ... There is no difference in dimension and reality between the original sound and the recorded and reproduced sound, as there is between real objects and their photographic images.'   *(Bela Balazs)*

'There is clearly a difference between a filmed object or action (it is a photograph of the thing or act) and a recorded musical sound. For [the latter] is the sound itself. There is no ontological difference between hearing a violin in a concert hall and hearing it on a sound track in a movie theatre.'   *(Gerald Mast)*

'In principle, nothing distinguishes a gunshot heard in a film from a gunshot heard on the street.'   *(Christian Metz)*

'In cinemas – as in the case of all talking machines – one does not hear an image of the sounds but the sounds themselves ... They are reproduced, not copied.'   *(Jean-Lous Baudry)*[32]

The unanimous rejection in these quotations of any parallel between the processes of reproducing images and sounds is a denial of the existence of an ideology of sound. So it is necessary to labour an obvious point. Sound tape can be edited, manipulated and used to re-order and distort 'reality' just as easily as film and video-tape can. Microphones, like cameras, are also necessarily *positioned* – again both physically, and ideologically. It *matters*, in radio or television coverage of a meeting, whether the microphones are placed in the body of the hall or on the platform. And if there are mikes all over the hall, then the balance between them is of the utmost significance.

I remember, a few years ago, observing the sound engineers setting up and balancing the microphones in preparation for a public debate which was being broadcast on both television and radio from Birmingham Town Hall. The engineers were quite explicit in their concern to ensure that platform speakers could easily talk over any amount of protest from the audience. Similarly in documentaries about schools it is often a simple matter to detect the intentions of the film-makers by noting, in classroom sequences, whether the dominant sounds come from the teachers or the children. Give dominance to the teacher's mike (as in the BBC's series on the public school, Radley) and you get a very different impression from the choas of sounds which results from the dominance of a mike in the middle of a classroom.

Sound, in other words, carries authority codings which are every bit as significant and powerful as those of visual images. The present government understands this very well, and certainly rather better than many film critics. For the positioning of the microphones in the House of Commons at the present time is a godsend to Labour MP Dennis Skinner, who provides a refreshingly inventive and subversive sub-text of daily quips and insults to the speeches of front bench Conservatives and SDP MPs, particularly SDP leader Dr David Owen ('Dr Death'). The government's response to the impact made upon radio by Skinner and other left-wing MPs has been to place extra microphones in the House as an 'experiment', in order to neutralise their impact.

What is interesting about the case of Dennis Skinner is that in the recordings of parliamentary proceedings we pick up, by chance, the kind of voice which is generally carefully excluded from normal broadcasting. Skinner doesn't belong to the charmed circle of those who are normally invited to participate in discussion programmes and panel shows. One of the reasons for this is that his critique of the House of Commons as a comfortable private club, and his scepticism of its adequacy as a vehicle for furthering the interests of working people brings into question the cosy and uncritical relationship which exists between parliament and the broadcasting institutions and, in particular, the general assumption of almost all political broadcasting that democracy can be equated with parliamentary representation, and the right to vote once every five years. Any *democratic* attack upon the simplistic equation of democracy and parliamentary representation inevitably draws attention to an issue upon which broadcasting institutions are conspicuously silent, the hierarchical and *undemocratic* nature of most British institutions including, of course, the BBC and the IBA themselves.

The ideology of sound, then, works in ways which parallel the ideology of the image. Of greatest significance is the primary act of selection – who gets included and excluded; which issues are discussed and which are not; which interpretations are acceptable and which beyond the pale. Then there are the multiplicity of choices involved in shaping, organising, editing and making sense out of sound material. In film and television this work is carried out quite separately from the organisation and arrangement of images, even though the two may need to be synchronised later. It is therefore as much the subject of ideological work as images are. And, as we have seen, it is inextricably bound up with questions of power, control, legitimation and authority.

Those programmes in which members of the public take part are of particular interest in this context, since they contain within them, as we have already seen, potential threats to or disruptions of established power relations. So control is kept extremely tight. Public contributions may be circumscribed (as in game shows), rehearsed and virtually scripted (as with *This Is Your Life*), or lacking in visual or auditory authority (as in *Question Time*). But one of broadcasting's most delectable pleasures, at least for me, occurs in those moments when a member of the public begins to prize loose the broadcaster's control by breaking the rules of the game. It is the moment when the smile freezes in momentary panic on Eamonn Andrews's face as someone departs from the script. Or that point in *Question Time* at which Sir Robin Day signals his alarm by shifting uneasily in his seat, before interrupting or hectoring a member of the audience who expresses a deviant opinion. But it is phone-in programmes, ('in which *you*, as members of the public can put *your* views'), which demonstrate the fullest repertoire of controls which are available to broadcasters. As always, it is the pre-programme screening procedures which are of most significance. The very concept of the

'phone-in' involves self-screening by the audience (the telephone still being a luxury beyond the means of most working-class people[33]), whilst the broadcasting institutions themselves effectively sift out 'unreasonable' callers at the switchboard. But even if a member of the public manages to overcome these obstacles (let alone the difficulty of actually getting through), she will find her voice dominated by the authority of the voices in the studio, both in terms of quality (inevitable) and volume (controlled by the producer). She is literally an outsider who can be (and frequently is) interrupted, spoken over, turned down and, if necessary, cut off without so much as a by-your-leave by those who control the proceedings in the studio.

4. The effect of camera and crew

Media images represent to us events which are played out in front of a camera. What they continually *purport* to show us, however, is that which remains tantalisingly beyond their grasp: those events which *would* have taken place if the camera had *not* been present. The camera, like the microphone, can have a whole range of effects. I was recently working with some sixth form comprehensive school students, when a television company asked for permission to come in and make a short film of our activities. The arrival of the cameras and crew was a major event. The setting up of the equipment, the conversion of the classroom into a mini-studio, and the sheer presence of so many television personnel (10 in all) all made this into a special occasion. On the day of the filming I was better prepared than usual, and chose to wear clothes which I fancied might have some visual appeal. So did the students.

The session itself was disappointing. The camera and lights were inhibiting to us all and even normally articulate students were reluctant to venture an opinion. Every time one of them spoke, every piece of available equipment was turned towards her. Had the production team been bent on making an exposé of comprehensive schools, we might all have made the tabloids the next morning. Fortunately, this was part of a programme about *interesting* developments in education, so the director intervened in order to encourage the kind of lively responses she was looking for. 'If you don't speak up and get involved,' she told the students, 'then you won't be on television.' The effect was instantaneous. The students began to go over-the-top in their attempts to upstage one another. The director did not attempt to catch much of our discussion on the wing. When someone said something of interest the director stopped the discussion, focused the camera and lights on her and asked her to repeat it. All of my contributions to the discussion were re-shot at the end, after the students had left, and cut into the final film. Nothing could have been further removed from our normal way of working.

I have spoken earlier of the authenticity of visual images. But we need to ask what precisely is being authenticated. Very often it may be nothing more than images which are specially manicured for the media themselves. In Vietnam, for example, the practice of American soldiers in cutting off the ears of dead Viet-Cong was not discovered until close to the end of the war. For obvious reasons, it was not a practice that was engaged in whenever there were cameras or even reporters present.[34] Similarly, in Britain, police are trained to exercise particular restraint whenever television cameras are around. The assumption on which television shows like *Candid Camera* and *It'll Be Alright on the Night* [sic] are based is that television cameras are *not*, for most of the time, really truthful at all. It is necessary to have special programmes in which the camera will reveal what *really* happens. They don't, of course. People in *Candid Camera* respond to situations set up by and for television. In *It'll Be Alright on the Night* we witness slips in *performances* which are taking place in front of a camera.

Newspapers, for their part, report, in the main, simply what people tell newspapers. Investigative journalists frequently need to disguise the fact that they are journalists if they wish to uncover important information. As we have seen, this is a difficult, time-consuming and expensive operation, so most newspapers dispense with it and supply instead more easily acquired information, much of which has been specifically tailored for the media.

But if the presence of the media encourages the covering up of problems and embarrassments, it also provides, for many people and institutions, as it ultimately did for my own students, opportunities to *project*. Again, Vietnam reporters observed that the presence of TV cameras caused many GIs to behave 'as if they were making *Dispatch from Da Nang* ... They were actually making war movies in their heads, doing little guts and glory leatherneck tap dances under fire, getting their pimples shot off for the networks.'[35]

Press officers dream up media campaigns designed to attract the cameras, commercial organisations support those sports and clubs which are most frequently covered by the media, to the neglect of others, and pressure groups of all kinds spawn pseudo-events[36] to catch the media's eye. Conservative critics even argue that the camera is the direct cause of a host of deeply-rooted social problems from urban riots and football hooliganism to political terrorism.[37]

Some documentary film-makers such as Roger Graef and Paul Watson, acknowledging the distorting effect of the camera, attempt to minimise it by shooting their subjects over a lengthy period of time. The camera becomes part of the furniture, it is argued, and its presence is soon forgotten or ignored. In Watson's classic series, *The Family*, in which a television crew virtually lived with the Wilkins family in their council house over a period of months, there was one revealing episode in which we followed a lengthy and involved wrangle between the Wilkins's daughter and her boyfriend about the date of their projected wedding. The scene appeared to vindicate Watson's methods. Here was a small, relatively trivial argument which was compelling viewing because it was so true to life, the kind of material rarely seen on television. The daughter wanted an early wedding; the boyfriend remained adamant that it should take place rather later. The participants' involvement in their argument seemed total. The camera was forgotten.

Later episodes revealed more details. The daughter's wish for an early marriage arose from her desire to have the event take place whilst *The Family* was still being filmed. Far from being dispassionately observed by television, the argument had been *caused* by it.

The discussion's real agenda, hidden from the audience, was not so much about dates as about whether or not the marriage should take place on television. At the very moment when the camera seemed least obtrusive, it was most decisively changing the nature of the experience it appeared to be merely recording.

The media work hard to convince us of the authenticity of their representations, yet assiduously conceal their own means of producing meaning, and the effect that they have upon the events portrayed. In seeking to represent reality, they too readily promote mystification. A deconstructionist criticism will be concerned to draw attention to precisely those elements in the processes of representation which it is the function of much media rhetoric to conceal. For this reason, attention to the effects of the means of production upon the events they portray will need to provide a recurring motif within the deconstruction of media texts or within any demystificatory account of media representations.

5. Set-ups

'Television is the only profession,' in the words of former TV producer and MP Philip Whitehead, 'in which the word cheat is an inseparable part of the vocabulary. I think it's alarming that so often, in order to preserve a smooth visual flow and in order to re-create an assumed sequence of events . . . you do dishonest things.'[38] Whitehead is discussing here, amongst other things, television's tendency to set up or rig many of the situations upon which it reports. But how sinister is this tendency, and how dishonest? Certainly a common response to the discovery that certain 'documentary' events have been staged is one of outrage, and when such an event becomes public knowledge it can create a minor scandal. So it is necessary to state from the outset that there is not necessarily anything inherently wrong in film and television directors reconstructing events and setting up situations specifically for the camera, although one would want to draw the line well before the point reached some years ago by the French television crew who provided children with stones to throw at soldiers in Northern Ireland. Apart from Enzensberger's fundamental point that 'Every use of the media presupposes manipulation,'[39] a great deal of rigging is inevitable if images and sounds of the quality which we tend to expect from television and the cinema are to be produced. Their intention is generally to clarify rather than to mislead. The major problem with this practice is a familiar one. It arises from the reluctance of broadcasting institutions to own up to their own production practices, and their tendency to posit an innocently transparent view of the media. Whitehead's charge of dishonesty should really not be applied to the practices of staging and reconstructing at all, but to the failure to acknowledge openly the prevalence of such practices.

Film-makers, in my experience, are generally very ready to make such an acknowledgement privately. They tend to have three reasons for not doing so more publicly. First of all, they frequently argue that television viewers actually understand pretty well how television is made, and recognise that film *is* film – edited, constructed and staged where necessary – and not reality. Secondly, they argue – and there is evidence here to support them – that the public is not greatly interested in how television is produced and would object to films which deconstructed themselves by drawing attention to their own methods of production. Thirdly, since many film-makers believe that their art lies precisely in their ability to conceal art and to render their techniques invisible, they are, understandably, less than enthusiastic about injunctions to expose its seams.

How valid are these arguments? The case against them – the media educator's case – hinges on the first point. How familiar *are* audiences with the conventional techniques of making film and television? In my own experience there is very little specific knowledge of such matters amongst the public at large. For example, I was recently working with a group of around 30 teachers and talking about the use of cutaways[40] in television interviews. Not one of the group either knew of the concept or had heard of the technique. Yet why should they have? They had received no media education in school or in their training as teachers. Nor had they had the opportunity of discussing the media before in any kind of educational context. They were a well-educated group who didn't even understand the ABC of a medium which is continually feeding them with ideas and information. Not that they believed very much of what they saw on television. Far from it. Like many teachers, they were actually quite sceptical about the medium. But it was a generally *uninformed* scepticism – a gut-level undifferentiated *suspicion* – which may ultimately be as inadequate and as potentially dangerous a response to the medium as an undifferentiated faith in it.

It is within this context – of a general lack of public knowledge of the mechanics of producing images – that debates about the ethics of staging need to be set. Broadcasters do have some responsibilities to their audiences which are not being met by their perpetuating illusionist and ideologically convenient myths about the media. And certainly a greater awareness by many broadcasters of the ideological significance of their own professional practices is long overdue. As I shall argue later (Chapter Eight), media education should be an important part of the training of all media personnel. But the final responsibility for ensuring that audiences understand the mechanisms through which film, television and newspapers are produced needs to be placed, not at the door of media professionals, but of teachers. In the final resort it is not the 'dishonesty' of our broadcasting system which constitutes the major problem, as Philip Whitehead alleges, but the inefficiency of our educational system.

A perusal of newspaper photographs will reveal that they, too, are, for the most part, specifically staged for the camera. Harold Evans cites two striking examples:

'There is a set of pictures of Presidents Truman and Eisenhower, meeting for a hand-over ceremony, which faithfully records their mutual animosity. One photographer finally and momentarily coaxed the smiles he had expected at the event; and that was the picture which went round the world. From the Korean war the world saw an appealing picture of an American soldier "sharing his last drops of water with a dying peasant". Bert Hardy, the famous *Picture Post* photographer, told me: "I set it up. Everybody was walking past but I had the idea and asked a GI to give the old man some water for the sake of the picture. He said he would if I was quick – and if we used my water ration." Was the photograph truth or fiction? Hardy, who won prizes for his brave photographs of the landing at Inchon under fire, can recall scores of "news" photographs he staged. His candour nibbles at the credibility of photojournalism.'[41]

A detailed case-study of photojournalistic practice has been provided by Ian Baker, himself a working journalist in Australia. Here is his account of the pictorial coverage of the visit of the then Prime Minister of Australia, Malcolm Fraser, to a Greek community festival in Melbourne:

'When Fraser arrived about 2pm there were an estimated 35,000 people packed into the Myer Bowl seating and spreading out beyond that up the hill. He was quite clearly greeted by a mixture of cheers and boos, as he entered from the stage after having been driven into a back entrance through a VIP tunnel at the rear. At least five plainclothes security men and a considerable force of uniformed police were on hand watching him. He was led off the stage to seats arranged for him. I took up a position some fifteen feet away where I could keep him in clear view throughout. With me, were my television crew, another from Channel O, several other reporters, and *The Sun* and *The Age* photographers. Apart from a brief trip up to the stage to make a short speech during the telecast segment he sat stoically in

that front row seat for most of the time he was there. I observed at one
stage that he was attempting to clap in time with the stage music and
that he was quite out of time. From my constant observation I formed
the opinion that he was uncomfortable and ill-at-ease in the situation.
I also observed that the photographers, as is usual, took frequent
shots of him in this period. As well, they took several shots of the
stage show, which featured Greek dancing (groups in colourful
costumes) and a colourful ballet segment performed by dancers from
the Australian Ballet. By contrast to his mixed reception, the former
Labor Minister Al Grassby was cheered soundly as he helped
compere proceedings, especially when he broke into bursts of Greek,
and when he joined dancers on stage at the end of the show.

As he left about 4pm Fraser was again given a mixed reception.
He was taken up the stage and down underneath it to a room where
the official organizers provided a drink and a chance for a long list of
supporters to be introduced. I, and *The Age* and *Sun* photographers
kept a few yards in front of him as he was taken through to this room.
The photographers busily snapped shots of him along the way. We
waited outside the room for a few minutes. Then, *The Age*
photographer called out Fraser's press secretary and asked him if the
PM would "be in" a shot taken with some dancers. He agreed to take
the request in to Fraser and disappeared into the room. In the
meantime, *The Age* photographer organized three young Greek
dancers in costume to be on hand in an area just near the room.
Fraser came out with the press secretary, and Mrs. Fraser and their
two girls in tow, and immediately went over to the area and said,
"What do you want me to do?" He was asked to dance in formation
with the dancers by the photographers and they snapped away while
he made an uncomfortable attempt. This of course, was going on
completely out of view of the main bulk of the crowd at the festival.
One of his children pushed through the crowd of people (about 20)
standing around the area under the stage where the pix were being
shot and called out, "Come on Dad. Dance a bit." He then smiled
and made another attempt. That is the picture that appeared on the
front page of both morning dailies the following morning ... That
completed, he moved off quickly to his car waiting in the exit
tunnel.'[42]

The views of the two photographers who were working on the
assignment are illuminating. First of all *The Age's* photographer:

'Fraser just wasn't helping. He was just sitting there straight and
fixed. You see a million pictures of him like that every day. It doesn't
show where he was. You have to show that he was at a Greek Festival,

The Age

so he has to be with Greeks... The PR was happy for me to set the picture up... If we just ran a picture of the PM sitting there people wouldn't stop and read. If we just took what was on you might as well not have any photos. I didn't even print the other pictures.

You set it up and try to get people to look at it... If I took a picture of him at a coal mine I couldn't put in a pix of him just standing there, could I? He'd have to have a hat on and be talking to miners. If he doesn't do it I'd set it up.

We create our own news a lot of the time. On general (non-sporting pictures) about 80 per cent of mine are posed.

Fraser is using the press in this case. He hasn't a great image with the Greeks. He expected the press to do something with the Greek Festival. That's the only bloody reason he was there. It doesn't bother me as long as he plays ball. If I can get him with his pants down I will. If I can get something different or dramatic I will. You have to make it more interesting than it seems. He did it because his PR told him to do it.

My professional ability is my creative ability. I think up and create pictures. I do it better than most of the others. If I hadn't set the Fraser shot up I wouldn't have had a pix. And I would be looking for a job if I kept that up.

Normally the PRs set them up. We don't have to.'

The Sun's photographer commented:

'I'd estimate that I'd set up about 85 per cent of general pix. It doesn't bother me at all.

My job is to get pictures that will sell newspapers. That's what we're all about. The executives talk in public about public responsibility but what they want from us is pictures that will catch the eye and sell the paper. If I ask you to do something for a picture and you do it, then it did happen, didn't it?'[43]

That final piece of professional casuistry ('it did happen, didn't it?') indicates the extent to which media professionals, even at their most open and honest, apparently find it necessary to cling to even the most threadbare vestiges of their professional ideology. Clearly, much remains at stake in perpetuating *some* notion of illusionism. What the case-study reveals clearly, however, is the inadequacy of interpreting photographic set-ups as some kind of media subterfuge. What is involved here is less perhaps deception than a convention which enables professionals to do their jobs routinely and effectively, which is generally carried out with the compliance of the subject being photographed, and which scarcely fools (nor is intended to fool) its audience. Does media education need to do more in the area of photojournalism than draw out what most pupils no doubt implicitly understand? That whilst the public circulation and ideological intentions of many newspaper photographs make them deserving of critical scrutiny, setting up and posing are activities which are apparently endemic to photography, and always likely to take place whenever anyone produces a camera and that, in this respect at least, newspaper images may not be markedly different from the kind of domestic photographs which we take for our own amusement and pleasure.

6. Film and sound editing

The processes of editing within broadcasting need some comment. As we have seen, Whitehead has suggested that 'it's alarming that so often, in order to preserve a smooth visual flow, and in order to reveal an assumed sequence of events . . . you do dishonest things.'[44] As with set-ups, the fictionalising of events through editing becomes less a matter of concern once it is widely understood. It is, indeed, an *inevitable* part of making films, television and radio. Encouraging students to look at so-called factual media material as fiction is not necessarily as provocative as might at first appear. Here is the distinguished Canadian verité documentary film-maker, Frederick Wiseman:

'[Documentaries] are fictional forms . . . Editing is the assessment and evaluation of individual sequences and assembling of these disparate, originally unrelated fragments, into a dramatic form. This process has an internal and external aspect: internal in the need to compress a sequence down to a usable form, external in the way individual edited sequences are joined so as to impose a thematic and dramatic unity on otherwise chaotic material.'[45]

In what senses precisely does editing fictionalise? First of all, as Wiseman suggests, the film-maker creates *new* meanings through the smooth juxtaposing of originally fragmented and unrelated images and events. The meanings of a film or a piece of radio are not implicit within the original events which they represent, but are the product of the film or radio programme itself. Secondly, to edit is to falsify the dimension of time,[46] and to create the crucial distinction between real time and film (or radio) time. The apparent continuity of film is always spurious precisely because of the compression of time. Thirdly, editing inevitably involves the processes of selection, omission and compression of a wide range of material. Fourthly, editing is carried out according to a narrative, thematic or aesthetic logic which, again, is the creation of the film-maker rather than an inherent quality of the original events (see Section 9 of this chapter). I have suggested earlier, ways of encouraging even very young pupils to manufacture their own meanings through the manipulation of visual material (pp. 132–6). The purpose of this section has been to emphasise how this kind of practical work needs to feed into the critical analysis of the editing of media texts themselves.

7. Interpretative frameworks

So far we have examined a number of the mediating processes which are an inevitable part of the construction of media 'reality'. In spite of the fact that media images are selected and edited to produce particular effects, however, the media still rarely allow us to judge the images they present on their own merits. As the audience, we are habitually nudged in the direction of this or that interpretation, pushed into simple, unproblematic positions from which the events depicted may be viewed and evaluated. As we have seen, one of the ways in which this is achieved is through the use of commentary or caption. Specific ways of seeing and interpreting particular programmes are also established in publications like *Radio Times* and *TV Times*, with their emphases upon spectacle, stars and individuals.[47] Within individual programmes, however, one of the most important ways in which events are brought out of 'the limbo of the random' and 'within the horizon of the meaningful'[48] is through the responses of the anchor-person.

Anchor-persons tell us through their control of the programme's meta-discourse – their linking, framing, commenting upon and placing of each item – how the programme's other discourses (the subjects it treats) should be read.[49] Our tendency to identify with the anchor-person has a number of sources: her position of structural dominance within the show, her direct eye-contact with us at home (see Section 8 below) and, perhaps, above all, her often long-standing familiarity to us as a person we feel we really know. The tendency of the anchor-person to provide indicators of how various items in the programme should be read may be easily illustrated. Here are introductions by different anchor-persons to three interviews. Remember, the people being interviewed have not yet had any opportunity to speak for themselves. What impressions are we given of them?

'Changing the subject completely, over the last few months quite a few musicals have come and gone on the London stage with themes so varied that it seems song-writers will try anything in their search for success. Well, yet another new formula is being tried, at Her Majesty's Theatre. It's called *Fire Angel* and it's based on the unlikely combination of a New York Mafia setting and the story of Shakespeare's *Merchant of Venice*. Well, while the Bard may be revolving in his grave, let's meet the co-writers...

(Jan Leeming: Pebble Mill at One*)*

'From the Provo on the run, repeatedly picked up by the police and the army, the face has subtly changed of the man the authorities suspect of master-minding most of the past five years' terrorism. Suspect but can't prove. The authorities simply have no evidence that will stand up in court. Now Adams assumes a studious legitimacy. But however well groomed he's become, his opponents reckon they know their man.'

(Fred Emery, Panorama. *Introduction to an interview with Sinn Fein MP Gerry Adams)*[50]

'There is no end to the questions that MPs put to Ministers. The frequent recipient of hard questions is the Foreign Secretary. The most unexpected question, surely, is one he has received from a

Birmingham MP. It's all about the clothes the Queen is wearing on her tour of the Middle East. The questioner wants Her Majesty to stop pandering to what he calls "the customs of religious bigots" by wearing long covering dresses. Now this, he claims, is insulting to the Queen's own sex. The questioner is Mr. John Lee, Handsworth's Labour MP. He talks to Peter Colbourne.'

(Tom Coyne, Midlands Today*)*

In this final extract the dissociation of the anchor-person from the views of the person he is introducing, through the familiar devices of placing certain words in inverted commas, or using such phrases as 'he calls' or 'he claims', is made explicit by the coda to this item, delivered this time by Pauline Bushnell:

'I think that people will agree that, despite the problems, the Queen is doing a great job.'

Now it may well be that MP John Lee is a quirky eccentric, that Gerry Adams, under the cloak of political respectability, remains a terrorist, or that the writers of *Fire Angels* are simply exploiting the Bard for commercial purposes. But we should, I think, be allowed to judge these things for ourselves on the evidence available, rather than having such opinions pre-packaged for us by the media.

The interpretative framework for an interview established by the anchor-person will invariably be taken up and elaborated by the interviewer who, far from being, in Sir Robin Day's phrase, 'a humble seeker after truth', will continually sign-post to us the viewers – by the general line of her/his questioning, as well as 'appropriate' reactions, interruptions and gestures – how the words of the interviewees are to be interpreted.

Here are two examples of how interviewers' questions can chime in neatly with the general line being taken by programmes on a particular issue. They are taken from the notoriously partial television coverage of the 'winter of discontent' (termed by one writer a 'winter of industrial mis-reporting') in early 1979:

'Isn't the strike by ambulancemen potentially one of the most disastrous things that could happen to society?'

(John Stapleton, Nationwide*, BBC1, January 16, 1979)*

'How do you justify putting lives at risk? If somebody dies will it be on your conscience? Is more money worth a life?'

*(*BBC News, *January 19, 1979)*[51]

It takes extremely confident and accomplished interviewees to challenge such sign-posting. One technique is to send the interview up. Here is athlete Daley Thompson doing just that on Canadian radio:

Presenter   In Edmonton, a young Englishman has won the title of the best all-round athlete in the world. His name is Daley Thompson and he won the gruelling decathlon and he won the event with the best performance since Bruce Jenner won in the Montreal Olympics two years ago. Thompson's not only any Englishman, though. He's twenty years old, bright, brash and black. Already he's being compared to Mohammed Ali as a future spokesman for blacks in England. He's talking here to Ray Martin.

Reporter: Twenty years old is very young for a sport like this. You look toward the Americans and they tend to be a few years above that.

Daley Thompson: Well, I started a few years earlier than everybody else.

Reporter: Have you thought of coming to Canada or the United States?

Daley Thompson: Er – Yes, I've thought about it a lot but I can't go because every weekend I have to do my washing and it's too far to travel.

Reporter: Further down the track, have you looked to Bruce Jenner who holds the world record? He made a lot of money out of winning that Olympic championship in seventy-six. Would you look towards that as where you're going?

Daley Thompson: I don't know – I mean – first of all I've got to win it in 'eighty or 'eighty-four or 'eighty-eight yet and I can't get into that unt il I've actually done it.'[52]

This interview is somewhat unusual in that the interviewer does not immediately pick up on either of the frameworks established by the presenter (Thompson as star athlete, or racial representative). Nor does he respond in any way, either to Thompson's answers or the light-hearted, mischievous tone in which they are delivered, presumably because that would break with the framework and tone which *he* has already attempted to set.

On occasions, challenging the media's explanatory frameworks can be part of an overt political strategy. Here are two classic examples from a master of the art, Arthur Scargill, President of the National Union of Mineworkers. Scargill is frequently accused of not answering interviewers' questions, but to see his media performances as simply evasive, is to miss their point. What Scargill challenges are the taken-for-granted assumptions on which interviewers base their questions and their view of the world. Indeed, on some occasions Scargill has even challenged the right and appropriateness of television interviewers asking particular questions at all. In the following example he manages to reverse entirely the conventional roles of interviewer and interviewee.

'Peter Snow: Why, when you said that about President Reagan and Mrs. Thatcher, didn't you attack anything about what President Andropov was doing or saying as well?

Scargill: Well, you see, have you read my full speech in Moscow?

Snow: Yes, I have.

Scargill: Have you?

Snow: Yes.

Scargill: I don't believe you, I'm sorry.

Snow: Well, what did you say...

Scargill: (interrupting) Mr. Snow, have you seen the full text, *honestly*?

Snow: Mr. Scargill, may I ask you to tell us...

Scargill: (interrupting) Tell me first of all, tell me first of all, have you seen the full text of the speech?

Snow: I have not seen any reference in that text to an attack on what President Andropov's troops are doing in Afghanistan...

Scargill: (interrupting) Mr. Snow, have you seen the full text?

Snow:	... or military government in Poland.
Scargill:	Mr. Snow, have you seen the full text? Because every other broadcaster has told me they haven't. Have you seen it, truthfully?
Snow:	Can you ... ? Can you ... ? Can you ... ? Can
Scargill:	No, I'm asking you a question. Then I'll answer your question. Have you seen the full text?
Snow:	I have not seen any *references*, any *reference* ...
Scargill:	I didn't ask you that. Have you seen the full text?
Snow:	I have not seen any reference ...
Scargill:	Have you seen the full text?
Snow:	But ... but ... you tell me, Mr. Scargill. Would you tell me ...
Scargill:	I'm asking you a question.
Snow:	Well I'm asking *you* the questions, if I may say so.
Scargill:	Not this time you're not. I'm asking you, have you seen the full text?
Snow:	To be quite honest, I have not seen the full text ... '

In this next example, far from evading the reporters' questions, Scargill answers them with scrupulous logic and considerable wit. But only after he has turned the questions on their heads, replaced the journalists' interpretative framework with his own and given their questions a meaning his interlocutors had never intended. He is being interviewed on *The World at One* during the 1984–5 miners' dispute on the day after the violence on the picket line at Orgreave in June, 1984:

| 'Interviewer 1: | Mr. Scargill a lot of the middle-aged miners, the old miners – there were a lot of young miners there yesterday (at the Orgreave picket line) – but a lot of the older ones, I was talking to them and they were really upset and disturbed by the level of violence yesterday. Do you think if these incidents carry on you will still have the support of the older men behind you? |

Scargill:	Well I also deplore the violence of the police, and I think everybody else does. It's almost terrifying in 1984 to see the level of violence perpetrated by the police on unarmed pickets. I mean let's be fair...
Interviewer 1:	But... (tries to interrupt)
Scargill:	Wait a minute. You've asked a question. You've got people down at that picket line in full riot gear, on horseback, with staves, with batons, and with police dogs facing, what? Miners in shirt sleeves, in trousers, jeans and a pair of pumps. That's what you're fighting. My God! There's no contest is there? The only thing that we've got on our side is that we're right. We're fighting for the right to a job.
Interviewer 2:	But some of the pickets were carrying bricks as well.
Scargill:	Look. The people who were down there are being battered, and all I can tell you is the condemnation that I've got is for the police who have shown, in an indiscriminate fashion, almost blind hatred towards miners on those picket lines and I think they should be condemned by anybody who believes in civil liberties.
Interviewer 3:	What do you think of the suggestion that not everybody who was involved in the violence is a member of the NUM?
Scargill:	Oh, I don't know whether they're Police Federation members or what they are. All I can tell you is that the people that I saw inflict violence down there were apparently all wearing police uniforms and riot gear.
Interviewer 3:	One of the pickets last night thought that they might have been members of the Communist Party for instance.
Scargill:	I don't think there are too many police officers in the Communist Party.
Interviewer 1:	Following your injuries, what would you say to a miner who perhaps might be considering some kind of revenge attack upon police?

Scargill:	I would say that the best way that you can support this dispute is by joining the strike if you're not already on strike. If you are on strike, not staying at home but joining the picket lines wherever they may be in order that we can bring this dispute to a swift and successful conclusion.
Interviewer 1:	But Mr. Scargill, these mass pickets aren't bringing this dispute to a conclusion. The dispute surely will only come to an end when you get round a table and talk (laughs).
Scargill:	What a stupid assertion that you make isn't it? How the hell do you know it's not making any effect? As far as we are concerned it's brought all *you* people out to this hospital this morning hasn't it? It's certainly had some effect upon *you*. And I can tell you that we shall go on arguing our case, going on to picket lines, because we are fighting to save our communities, our pits and our industry and that's a commendable fight that should be supported by everybody.'

8. Visual codings

The kind of reversals exemplified above, in which the power to define a situation is temporarily wrested away from the broadcasters, is unfortunately rare. For the most part, presenters, interviewers and anchor-persons remain firmly in control, their status as guarantors of truth reinforced, in the case of television, by the medium's dominant visual codings. For example they, like station announcers, news-readers and weather forecasters, are amongst the small band of people who are allowed to talk direct to camera. As Stuart Hood has argued:

'All these persons have one thing in common. They are there to give us information which we are asked to assume is accurate (as indeed some of it is), unbiased and authoritative (which it is less likely to be). They have authority vested in them by the television organisations and can be described in a useful phrase as "bearers of truth". But there is another and more interesting category. It includes the monarch, the prime minister, cabinet ministers when they make official broadcasts (what are called ministerial broadcasts) and the leader of the parliamentary opposition front bench, who is allowed in certain circumstances to reply to a ministerial broadcast if the broadcasting authorities judge that it was controversial. All these persons – and one or two others including the Archbishop of Canterbury as head of the Church of England – are allowed to address the television audience ("the public" or "the nation" as the broadcasters call it on such occasions) directly. They do so by reason of their constitutional or political authority. On other occasions (for instance when the Chancellor of the Exchequer is interviewed about the Budget) they are all (with the exception of the Queen) treated like ordinary people; that is to say, they are shown in profile or in such a way that their gaze is not fixed directly on the viewers but on the interviewer who is with them in the studio. In other words their statements have to pass through someone else, as it were – they have to be mediated. If they attempt to take on the role of a person of authority and address an audience directly, the director will cut away from them and go back to a shot of the interviewer ... There are, however, certain politically unimportant persons who *are* allowed to address the camera directly – people like comedians, who are the equivalent of medieval jesters and, like the jesters, they are allowed to act as if they had the same privileges as the men and women of power in our society. For that is what the full face picture means: that the man or woman on the screen has power and authority.'[53]

The whole area of visual coding deserves specific attention in any consideration of how the media construct their meanings. Authority is reinforced or undermined not simply by eye-contact patterns, but by appearance, dress and the way in which the image is framed:

'The convention is that in "factual" programmes they (subjects) should be shot from eye-level and not from above or below, since shots from either of these angles would present an image slanted in more senses than one. The other convention deals with the question of how "tight" a shot may be. Generally, important figures will be shown in medium close-up which shows them from the waist up. This may be replaced by a close-up which shows only the subject's head and shoulders. It would be very rare for a big close-up – a shot showing only the head – to be used of an important person. Just as in our normal social intercourse we observe certain conventions about how close we come to other people and how close we allow them to come to us, so when choosing their images, television cameras keep a certain distance from their subjects ... It is almost inconceivable that one should see on the television screen a big close-up of a figure of authority – of a prime minister or international statesman. The camera stands back from them. But in the case of ordinary people it is not unknown for the camera to come close in, particularly if the subject is in a state of emotional excitement, grief or joy.'[54]

Similarly, there are codes of geography within a studio which tell us who is important and who less so, or which indicate the relationship which exists between the subjects on the screen. The positioning of an interviewer between proponents of two conflicting views is a powerful visual reinforcement of the broadcaster's 'neutrality'. On the other hand, in 'chat' shows, interviewees sit together in comfortable chairs in keeping with their role as guests. The Glasgow University Media Group have drawn attention to the dominant codings in the reporting of industrial relations news:

'... all those things which enhance a speaker's status and authority are denied to the mass of working people. This means that the quiet of studios, the plain backing, the full use of names and status are often absent. The people who transcribed our material here pointed out to us that the only time they had difficulty making out what was said was in interviews with working people. Not because of "accent", but because they were often shot in group situations, outside, and thus any individual response was difficult to hear. The danger here is that news coverage is often offering up what amounts to sterotypical images of working people.'[55]

Compare this with the control which Margaret Thatcher manages to exert within interviews. Since her encounter with the spirited questioning of a viewer, Mrs Diana Gould, on the sinking of the Argentine cruiser, *The General Belgrano*, during *Nationwide* (BBC1), the Prime Minister, guided by her image builders, now scarcely ever leaves the confines of Downing Street if she is giving a television interview. Interviews with her now come across less as legitimately probing investigations of a democratic leader than as formal state occasions to which a few favoured interviewers have been given privileged access. Away from their familiar territory, surrounded by the symbols of the Prime Minister's office, and placed in the role of guests at a formal occasion, it is scarcely surprising that interviewers like Sir Robin Day, John Tusa and Brian Walden should become, in numerous indefinable ways, more deferent and subordinate than they would wish, or perhaps even realise themselves, to be. It is precisely this kind of unconscious servility which the strategy is designed to achieve, and it works exceedingly well. In terms of their tone, their social interactions and their visual codings, these interviews are very far removed from the studio grillings which other party leaders, to say nothing of lesser mortals, have to face.[56]

9. Narrative

Finally, mention must be made of one of the media's dominant techniques for shaping the events it handles: the use of narrative. The media tell stories – incessantly. In duration they may last from a few seconds (a news story or advertisement) to perhaps 25 years (*Coronation Street* began in 1960) or even several life-times (the story of the Royal Family). Raymond Williams has observed that we have become a thoroughly 'dramatised' society:

'. . . more drama is watched in a week or weekend by the majority of viewers than would have been watched in a year, or in some cases a lifetime in any previous historical period . . . The implications of this have scarcely begun to be considered . . . Whatever the social and cultural reasons may finally be, it is clear that watching dramatic simulation of a wide range of experiences is now an essential part of our modern cultural pattern.'[57]

Williams is referring here to the proliferation of dramatic fiction on television, but this is only one of a multiplicity of dramatic forms now carried by the media. As we shall see, the media's 'factual' genres also package their content as stories, giving them a dramatic shaping which may be every bit as formal as that of overtly fictional forms.

It is important for students routinely to consider media texts as narratives for three reasons. First of all, familiarity with narrative strategies and the issues raised by different narrative forms will be transferable to a wide range of media (not to mention literary) genres, and to any new media text. Secondly, because the differences between many media forms are largely explicable in terms of their different narrative structures, it is evident that students will need to grapple with issues of narrative if they are to make important basic distinctions between dominant media forms. Thirdly, and most importantly of all, narrative study raises in an unforced way, the central concern of media education: the 'constructedness' of what are frequently portrayed as natural ways of representing experience. To draw continual attention to texts as narratives is to give emphasis to precisely the kind of questions around which this book is organised: who is telling this story? (Or, more correctly, what are its determinants?) What techniques are employed in the telling? What values are implicit in the story so narrated? And to whom is the story addressed?

Some basic techniques for studying narrative may be quickly suggested. Three simple exercises which may be used to achieve increasingly sophisticated results in the classroom are those of *narrative sequencing, narrative prediction* and *narrative cloze*. *Narrative sequencing* involves the placing of narrative fragments into their correct sequence. Reference has already been made to materials which enable pupils to create their own media narratives, through the manipulation of visual images (p. 129ff), but the technique can be used upon any narrative which the teacher is able to cut up and re-arrange. It can, therefore, be employed very effectively, not only with a sequence of still images, but also a comic strip or a newspaper story. In reconstructing the correct sequence, the student brings closer to the surface her largely subconscious knowledge of and familiarity with the media's dominant narrative structures.

Narrative Cloze consists of narratives from which every fifth (or seventh, tenth, etc.) word or image has been extracted. The student must guess the missing linguistic or visual content from the context in which it appears. A rather cruder form of cloze exercise can be applied to television by playing the first and last parts of a narrative. The group must guess what happens during the missing extract. *Narrative prediction* exercises involve group prediction of how a narrative will evolve. The narrative flow is stopped by the teacher at various points so that the group can make their predictions on the basis of the evidence they have seen so far.

The advantage of all of these techniques is that they are *problem-solving exercises* which require students to pay particularly detailed attention to the text and its narrative strategies. They allow students to demonstrate competencies which many do not realise they possess, and they promote insights into some of the general principles of narrative through a close engagement with, and scrutiny of, specific plots and characters. I have demonstrated elsewhere how these techniques may be used with very simple material, such as comic strips, to promote 'tele-literacy', and an understanding of the basic elements of narrative structure.[58] Here I shall explore some of the further possibilities of narrative prediction in particular, since this is the simplest activity to organise across all of the media. (Cloze and sequencing presenting certain difficulties in relation to film and television narratives, since these media are less accessible to manipulation by the teacher.)

Playing through a piece of film or television fiction in 10-minute segments and asking the question 'What happens next?' really does help students of all ages to focus upon the *functions* of characters, and to see them as *actants*,[59] pushing the plot along and making possible different narrative strategies, rather than as 'real' people, whom we love or hate, or with whom we identify. It also clarifies, as I have suggested, the competencies which students employ in making sense of and gaining pleasure from narratives, and the complicated decoding processes which they go through in order to 'read' characters through their clothing, gestures, facial expressions and the like. Prediction exercises also draw attention to the ways in which we as viewers are offered both physical and ideological positions in relation to characters and plots (see Chapter 7), the ways, that is, in which we are invited to make judgements upon characters and events through the use of identification techniques, music, camera positioning, and so on.

Finally, prediction exercises demonstrate both the range and the limitations of most media plots, and the ways in which each successive scene narrows down the possibilities further. A key question to raise here is 'What cannot happen?' In *The Rockford Files*, which I have used both with primary school children and sixth form students, it is fairly clear that Jim Rockford cannot be killed, fail to solve the case, or act dishonourably. He is also unlikely either to settle down and get married or to renounce women entirely. Indeed, he can do nothing which will radically alter his circumstances.

Similarly, in *Auf Wiedersehen, Pet*, a comedy series about a group of British working-class men working on a building-site in Germany, 'the lads' cannot break up as a group in the first programme or all decide to come home in the second. In either *The Rockford Files* or *Auf Wiedersehen, Pet*, if any of these unlikely alternatives were to be realised, we would have an entirely new series on our hands. It is not, notice, that these alternatives, in either series, remain outside of the logic of the narratives themselves. Indeed, in both *Rockford* and *Auf Wiedersehen*, these options not only remain *possible* within each story, it is around the very possibility of their happening that the tensions and climaxes of each series are built. It is the *series format* which places so many narrative options out of court. Each programme in the two series, then, poses questions (Will Rockford be killed? Has he finally met the right woman? Will the divisions between the lads prove irrevocable? Will they resolve their problems by going back home?) to which the series formats themselves provide the answers. We apparently gain our primary pleasure from these series not from discovering *what* will happen next, but from discovering *how* their pre-ordained conclusions will be reached.

Another smashing classroom exercise is to pre-record the openings of a few television or film narratives. Three or four minutes of each will generally be sufficient. In spite of their differences, what functions do they have in common? And what techniques do they use to do their work – in setting the scene, unobtrusively filling out background information, introducing and establishing the characters, setting up some problem, disjuncture or conflict for the narrative to develop and resolve[60] – as economically as possible?

There are frequently distinctive structural differences between the openings of British and American series, the latter working much harder to hook their audience straight into the action, sometimes at great length, before the credit sequence. The credits themselves may be dropped strategically into the action over three or four minutes without lessening the narrative tension (as in *Knight Rider*), and a great many American series, with an eye on the international market, use dialogue sparingly at the beginning of the narrative. (The pilot film for the US series, *Miami Vice*, for example, opened with a five-minute pre-credit sequence which contained scarcely any dialogue at all.) Close scrutiny of narrative beginnings can make explicit, too, generic differences between series, serials, and single plays and films. It can also be used to explore gender (and other forms of) stereotyping. What roles are performed by men and women as the narrative opens? What limits are placed upon some characters and what possibilities open out for others from the very outset? It is useful here to play the beginning of a narrative and have students write or think of *alternative* story-lines which reverse expected gender roles. This sharpens perception of gender stereotyping in the original narrative when it is played through in full.[61]

The use of narrative by the media is not confined to fictional genres, however. News, current affairs, documentary and sports programmes all attempt to inform or entertain us by telling us stories and by constructing heroes, villains, conflicts, reversals and resolutions. Dramatic shaping is endemic to most television editing, and the medium is frequently involved in the production of fictional forms even when dealing with avowedly factual material. Television, for example, constructs sporting events as primarily *dramatic* occasions. The chief characters are introduced to us, their hopes and aspirations outlined, and their backgrounds sketched in with a particular emphasis upon any past triumphs, misfortunes, or ironies. Frequently, these characters will already be as familiar to us from their past appearances in other sporting dramas as characters in a soap opera. A big sporting event such as a Cup Final, an Olympic Games, or a World Cup, becomes a stage upon which a thousand mini-dramas of hopes dashed and triumphs achieved will be played out. In presenting sport as emotional drama with which we can identify, television garners huge audiences, many of whom may have only a peripheral interest in the sport itself. Constructing sport as dramatic narrative offers a *predictable* interest which real sport, with its fickleness, and frequent dullness and lack of excitement, cannot guarantee.

Of course, sporting events can frequently be extremely dramatic, but media narratives about sport, in their tendency to focus upon a few favoured stars or heroes, and to pre-package events in dramatic form, too often misrepresent the nature of the sport itself, and may even miss the most important stories. Coverage of the 1984 Olympics threw up a large number of examples. The story of British interest in the 100 metres was centred around the familiar character of Alan Wells, who was given full in-depth treatment, even though he was not running particularly well and was, in fact, eliminated in the semi-finals. Two black British athletes, ignored and unsung throughout the coverage, did reach the final, however. Mike McFarlane finished fifth and Donovan Reid seventh. But who, to this day, remembers them? In the women's track events, British silver-medallist Wendy Sly will have been relatively unknown to most viewers when she crossed the line in the 3,000 metres final. Indeed, in a radio interview the day before the race she had been very critical of the media's view of the race as a contest between Zola Budd and Mary Decker, and pointed out that there was a very strong field in the final. Ironically, the fall of Mary Decker and her after-the-race accusations of Zola Budd continued to divert the media's attention away from all of the other athletes almost as much as it had before the race.

Apart from the media's tendency seriously to mis-read the nature of sporting events by superimposing their own dramatic structure upon them,[62] one should also note that the narratising, sensationalising and personalising of sport make difficult any serious critical understanding of the structural problems and issues raised by different sports, denigrate the significance of collective or team effort within sport, and give no account of the attractions and pleasures of sport which lie quite outside of their peaks of excitement.

As we have seen, documentaries are perhaps also best analysed as fictional forms. The structure of a documentary film – the way it begins, builds interest and tension, and finally offers a resolution – has, at best, a tangential relationship with the real events it represents. The meanings a film offers through its editing and choices of shot, its balancing of episodes to produce light and shade and its observation of parallels and correspondences, are not qualities of the events themselves but are *produced* by the film-maker. As Heath and Skirrow have argued, the organisation of the television documentary is *novelistic*: 'it maps out fictions, little dramas of making sense in which the viewer as subject is carried along . . . '[63] Finally, it should be noted that a primary determinant of the narrative structure of most television documentaries is the institution of television itself, hence the continual emphasis in most documentary narratives upon the photogenic and the visually arresting, and upon material which will entertain and hold the audience.

All news, likewise, involves dramatisation – the construction and telling of 'stories'. Writing of the 'new journalism' of the late 19th century, Anthony Smith has observed

'In the newspaper office, the "story" became the basic molecular element of journalistic reality: a structured nugget of information – the basic unit through which the reader was to be presented with events. The techniques of journalism became analogous to those of fiction, and lay partly in the ability to discern those elements which could be made into a transmittable artefact. There was a convenient division into "hard" and "soft". There was the clear, underlying recognition of the audience as a market. The specialism of the journalist, and especially of the editor, lay in knowing what the market required. Reality was categorised into pages – home, over-seas, political, women's interest, sport, the City, and so on. Special new kinds of events were developed which had not previously existed in human cognition, such as, for example, the "crisis", the "horror", or the "human story". Events acquired "angles" or, rather, special elements which made them more easily communicable within certain sectors of the market... Journalism became the art of structuring reality, rather than recording it... The techniques of journalism have come to consist in skilful filling of pre-defined genres, each of which stands for a certain definition of the audience's needs.'[64]

The narrative structure of news may be analysed on two different levels. First of all, news stories may be considered in terms of their striking, dramatic, questioning or puzzling openings in which equilibrium is upset or disrupted; their development or conse-quences; and their resolution. Different newspapers adopt different narrative techniques and, as with the study of televised fiction, it is revealing to look closely at how they begin. Each newspaper tends to have its own in-house narrative formula. Students can unearth these by looking at a number of different stories from the same paper. Here are some examples of different in-house formulae for beginning the kind of story which appears on the inside papers of a number of newspapers:

a) A local paper, *The Derby Evening Telegraph*, opens its stories with a sentence which

   – is short and preferably simple

   – contains a single and often unsensational and parochial piece of information

   – contains the name of the local district in which the event took place

- carries the name of the chief character

- prefaces the character's name with a string of epithets:

e.g.:'Uttoxeter's colourful butcher, Vernon Cotterill, must leave his High Street shop following the failure of last ditch negotiations.'

'Veteran Duffield bellringer and former Parish Councillor, Mr Frederick William Stone, has died aged 92.'

b) *The Mirror's*[65] stories often open with a sentence which

- contains a description of something bizarre and eye-catching

- introduces a chief character delineated by status or profession

- describes a puzzling action which will be 'explained' in the remainder of the story:

e.g. 'A magistrate vowed yesterday not to jail petty criminals who are poor or jobless.'

'A Harley Street doctor ate his lunch while burning a tattoo off a patient's chest with a laser beam.'

c) *The Sun's* opening formula consists of

- epithets describing the chief character

- his or her name

- the puzzling or unusual *consequences* of his/her action

- when the event happened

- what caused it

- as many sexual innuendoes as possible

e.g.:'Buxon pub landlady Lily Holroyd was all blushes yesterday after serving up a saucy double at *The Cock and Crown*.'

'Dishy Dawn Johnson was stripped of a top beauty queen title yesterday after the organiser admitted she was crowned by mistake.'

d) *The Sunday Express's* openings are immediately recognisable. They

- contain the low-key inconsequential beginnings of a significant event

- take a straight chronological line
- draw us into the story by picking out everyday details with which we can identify:

e.g.:'A little black labrador, alone and forlorn on the crowded pavement, cast her appealing brown eyes at hiker, Jonathan Bridge.'

'Shopper Edwin Horlington returned to his parked car with an armful of shopping. But when he unlocked his Austin Princess . . . '

'Schoolboy Brian Hennessy hared across the sports field and hurled his javelin into the air. But a gust of wind caught it . . . '

Once pupils have the hang of these simple formulae they can try their hand at parodying them, perhaps using the same basic story.

The second level upon which news narratives may be analysed is that of the structure of the newspaper or news broadcast considered as a whole. At this macro-level, news has its own definable structure (important stories at the beginning, light relief at the end; politics at the front of a newspaper, sport at the back), its familiar characters (politicians, royalty, trade unionists, show-biz personalities, and 'ordinary' victims of tragedies or eyewitnesses to accidents), its regular story-tellers (newsreaders and featured reporters) and a range of techniques for stimulating and maintaining interest (film, graphics, short items, sensational headlines). The stories of which news tells us fall into predictable categories. Newspapers structure the world into stories about Business, Leisure, Arts, Sports, etc., not because that is how we can best understand the world, but because audiences segmented by their interest in these categories can be most easily sold to advertisers. Television, for its part, has most of its news stories falling into the pre-formulated categories of Politics, Economics, Home Affairs and Sport because both BBC and ITN have specialist correspondents in these areas. Channel Four news runs more Arts stories simply because it has an Arts Correspondent, but some areas, such as Education, are generally neglected because no-one is assigned to cover routine stories in this field.

Of course, newspapers and news broadcasts do not make much sense if judged by the standards of traditional narratives. They do not follow a linear progression. They are fragmented. They don't 'add up' or help us to interpret the world as a whole. In that sense their function is the antithisis of most narratives. But perhaps that is their point:

'Making connections between events is disallowed by the journalistic format, for the news media's unit of analysis is the news item : a self-contained particle of "reality". Possible links between items, say, one story concerning a "racial disturbance" and another of high unemployment among black youth, are not suggested.'[66]

Advertisements, too, are mini-narratives. Often the narrative form is quite explicit. What characterises advertisement narratives, however, is the fact that the disruption, loss or state of disequilibrium (loneliness, illness, fear about one's sexuality, guilt about one's family, etc.) are resolved not so much by the direct action of the protagonist but through the magical agency of a product. Advertisements are modern fairy-tales in which tired housewives can become energetic, capable and loving wives and mothers, pimply men may be transformed into heroes, and social outsiders discover plenitudes of fresh breath, companionship and attention for the price of a detergent, toothpaste or skin cream. Many advertisements are so highly compressed that they may not look like narratives at all, presenting, perhaps, instantly recognisable social situations and characters from narratives which we read at a glance. In some advertisements there may be no conflict or lack of harmony, simply abundance, the product being placed in a luxurious setting of the kind which is almost – but not quite – beyond our aspirations. Such advertisements constitute *us* as the tragic victims of our own narratives, setting up dissatisfactions with our own lives and insecurities in our own identities, but always holding within our grasp at the purchase of a product, the promise of Nirvanah, an ultimate harmony.

I have placed a good deal of emphasis so far on the mystificatory, mythologising function of narrative. As Gill Davies has pointed out:

'Fictional narrative ... is a mode constantly susceptible to transformation into myth. The creation of a narrative almost always entails the shaping of awkward materials into a smooth, closed structure. And this is the essence of myth. Like bourgeois ideology, most narrative cinema denies history, denies material reality as contradictory, and denies the fact of its own production.'[67]

This kind of critique of realist narratives owes a great deal to recent work on 'the classic realist text'. A brief résumé of some of the principal arguments at issue is necessary here since media teachers need to assess their appropriateness and relevance to their own practice. Fundamental to these arguments' relevance to the study of the media is the contention that many media narratives owe a good deal to literary antecedents, and particularly the nineteenth century realist novel. For Colin MacCabe:

'A classic realist text may be defined as one in which there is a hierarchy amongst the discourses which compose the text and this hierarchy is defined in terms of an empirical notion of truth. Perhaps the easiest way to understand this is through a reflection on the use of inverted commas within the classic realist novel. While those sections in the text which are contained in inverted commas may cause a certain difficulty for the reader – a certain confusion vis-à-vis what really is the case – this difficulty is abolished by the unspoken (or more accurately the unwritten) prose that surrounds them. In the classical realist novel the narrative prose functions as a metalanguage that can state all the truths in the object language – those words held in inverted commas – and can also explain the relation of this object language to the real.'[68]

However, this metalanguage of the narrative discourse

'does not just dispose of the other discourses, it compares them with the truth or falsity transparently available through its own operations ... The simple access to truth which is guaranteed by the meta-discourse depends on a repression of its own operations and this repression confers an imaginary unity of position on the reader from which other discourses ... can be read.'[69]

The relevance of this argument to the study of the media is plain enough. For media texts (and not simply media narratives) are also characterised by a hierarchy of discourses. As we have seen, anchor-persons and newsreaders have control of a programme's meta-language through which they can organise, place and evaluate other discourses within the programme from a perspective which itself remains entirely unquestioned. The same applies to narratives. We can look critically at the actions and words of characters in a narrative, but from a position which itself remains unchallenged because it is not acknowledged as a 'position', i.e., it represses its own mode of production. This 'position', moreover, is a *position-for-us* as audience. Realist narratives, that is, create for us an imaginary unified subjectivity from which we can make sense of the action. It is in this sense that we can speak of the media's primary product as, not news or drama, but particular kinds of consciousness (see Chapter One and Chapter Seven).

Critiques of the classic realist text do raise problems, however, particularly in the context of the classroom. They should not be collapsed into critiques of all narrative forms, for example. For story-making and telling are not irredeemably bourgeois activities but timeless, popular and pleasurable ways of making sense and sharing meaning:

'Narrative is present in every age, in every place, in every society; it begins with the very history of mankind and there nowhere is nor has been a people without narrative. All classes, all human groups, have their narratives, enjoyment of which is very often shared by men with different, even opposing cultural backgrounds. Caring nothing for the division between good and bad literature, narrative is international, transhistorical, transcultural: it is simply there like life itself.'[70]

It would be unfortunate, too, if the classroom analysis of narratives were not informed by a sympathetic understanding of the *pleasures* which they can afford, both to large majorities of students and to the teacher herself – albeit that such pleasures may need to be problematised. Critics of realist texts too often slide over the question of their popularity, however, to say nothing of the resistances which audiences frequently show to more allegedly 'progressive' and avant-garde forms. This, teachers working largely with working-class students in schools, cannot do, any more than writers and directors who produce work aimed at majorities can. Trevor Griffiths:

'I chose to work in those (realistic) modes because I have to work now. I have to work with the popular imagination which has been shaped by naturalism. I am not interested in talking to thirty-eight university graduates in a cellar in Soho. It's my guess that we still have to handle realism.'[71]

If, in her engagement with popular forms, and her acknowledgement of the pleasures which they provide, the media teacher's position has affinities with that of the playwright, in one important respect, at least, she possesses rather more power. For she is present at one of the points of *consumption* of the text and can actively encourage diverse uses or readings of it. This alone – the complex mesh of responses which emerge through dialogue – should act as a break to the esssentialism of regarding particular textual devices (or particular tests, for that matter) as, in themselves, reactionary or progressive, quite outside of the readings they produce.

* * *

I have attempted to draw attention to some of the simple ways in which questions of narrative form may be raised in the study of a wide range of media texts. If there is some danger that narratives may turn audiences into passive consumers of texts by stitching them into the unproblematic, unitary and unquestioned perspective from which the tale is told, then the *analysis* of narratives can transform readers into active interrogators of texts. It can do this by drawing attention to their modes of producing meaning, by breaking through the mystifications of 'characters' to examine the narrative functions they perform, by interrupting the narrative flow in order to show how its continuity is produced, and by clarifying some of the ways in which our consciousness may be structured by narrative forms.

The specialist study of narrative – narratology – is now a well-established field in its own right. At some stage in a media studies course it may be appropriate, particularly with more mature students, to pursue the study of narrative in rather more depth than I have been able to here. Eagleton has provided the most accessible general introduction to the importance of narrative within structuralist, post-structuralist and psycho-analytic thinking,[72] whilst analyses of the narrative conventions of different media genres have been undertaken in relation to sitcoms by Cook[73] and Lovell,[74] to soap operas by Jordan, and Paterson and Stewart,[75] to documentary by Heath and Skirrow,[76] to news stories by Bazalgette and Paterson,[77] and Langer,[78] and, more formally, to a drama series by Silverstone.[79] A bibliographical overview of film narrative has been given by Lusted,[80] whilst Neale has provided a study programme on film genre and narrative along with references to available feature films and film extracts.[81] A Sixth Form teaching pack on *Narrative* (film only) is available from The British Film Institute.[82]

Some of the general theoretical issues raised by narrative are discussed in The Open University's *Popular Culture* Course, Unit 15, *Reading and Realism*,[83] and in the course reader, *Popular Television and Film*,[84] whilst Hebdige and Hurd's article 'Reading and Realism'[85] offers an accessible critique of *Screen's* position on realism. The burgeoning of interest in narrative owes a great deal to a number of seminal texts, of which the most easily available in English are Vladimir Propp's, *The Morphology of the Folktale* (1928), Roland Barthes's *Introduction to the Structural Analysis of Narratives* (1966) and *S/Z* (1975), and Gérard Genette's *Narrative Discourse* (1972).

Chapter 6

Ideology

The concept of ideology stands like a Colossus over the field of media education. It is a centrally important and highly theorised concept, yet it is used in such a bewildering range of contexts and with such a variety of often apparently contradictory meanings that it is evident that if any progress is to be made within media education then it will be necessary for media teachers both to be as clear as possible about how they use and understand the term, and to face the formidable problems of how they can at least begin to make the concept intelligible within the classroom. This chapter is no more than an attempt to begin these tasks: to clarify very briefly some fundamental problems of definition, and to map out some ways of introducing the concept of ideology in the classroom.

A. Defining ideology

The most frequent everyday usages of 'ideology' raise an immediate problem: they appear to be directly contradictory to one another. Consider the following descriptions of two linked workshops designed to explore ideological questions in education:

'*Philosophy and ideology in education*

This introductory session begins with the assumption that philosophy has an important role to play in an understanding of key ideas and issues in education. Prominent among these issues are certain ideologies, often conflicting in nature and sometimes misleading. During this session an attempt will be made to review the techniques which philosophy uses in exposing the weaknesses and the strengths in some current ideologies.

Controversial issues in the curriculum: anti-racist teaching

This session seeks to lead on from the philosophical perspective on ideology into thinking about the ideological issues which emerge in connection with a topical "controversial" curriculum issue: "anti-racist teaching". The approach will involve examining some curriculum resources which have been developed to support anti-racist techniques in the classroom, and teasing out some of their underlying ideological themes. Anti-racist teaching, however, is chosen simply as a case study and it is hoped that discussion will eventually turn to thinking about the ideological assumptions highlighted by other "controversial" issues.'

In the first description, ideologies are, evidently, somewhat set, and inflexible beliefs against which 'philosophy', an apparently non-ideological set of beliefs and practices, may be contrasted. Philosophy, indeed, can be used to put ideologies smartly in their place. 'Philosophy' is but one of a number of counters (others in common usage are education, literature, history, sport. etc.) which are frequently employed to suggest that the institutions and practices of liberal-humanism are *not* ideological but common-sensed. There are clear links here with the common usage of ideology as *any explicitly political or propagandist set of beliefs* (e.g., Marxist or Fascist 'ideologies'), as well as with what is perhaps the dominant media use of 'ideological' as a pejorative epithet to describe what Raymond Williams has called 'any social policy which is . . . derived from social theory *in a conscious way*'.[1] (Original emphasis.)

A recent example (May, 1985) of this kind of usage can be seen in a story in which a committee of the Inner London Education Authority tried to encourage teachers to consider the political implications of organised sexist and competitive sport in schools. The popular media were unanimous in their condemnation of this move to sacrifice children's harmless and taken-for-granted pleasures (i.e., boys' football) on the altar of a political philosophy (i.e., an ideology).

In the second description, ideology is used in a way almost diametrically opposed to the first. Far from being conscious and explicit, ideologies are largely unrecognised. There are two rather different ways of expressing this idea. One is through metaphors of concealment. Ideological issues, it is said, will 'emerge'. They 'underlie' our experience, form part of our common-sensed 'assumptions' and need to be actively 'teased out'. Racist ideologies, then, can be profoundly unconscious, interred within our everyday practices, ways of thinking, and language. Making ideologies explicit is a process of consciousness *raising* (i.e., heightening our conscious awareness of the assumptions underpinning our practice). On the other hand, it is sometimes argued that ideology remains unconscious, not because it is hidden, but because it is *not*. In Stuart Hall's words, ideology should be understood 'precisely as what is most open, apparent, manifest – what "takes place on the surface and in view of all men"'. Though 'what is hidden, repressed or inflected out of sight are its real foundations. This is the source or site of its *unconsciousness* ... How can the realm in which we think, talk, reason, explain and experience ourselves – the activities of consciousness – be unconscious? We may think here of the most obvious and 'transparent' forms of consciousness which operate in our everyday experiences and ordinary language: common sense ... It is precisely its 'spontaneous' quality, its transparency, its 'naturalness', its refusal to be made to examine the premises on which it is founded, its resistance to change or to correction, its effect of instant recognition, and the closed circle in which it moves which makes common sense, at one and the same time, 'spontaneous', ideological and *unconscious*.'[2]

In order to grasp the connections between the two dominant yet apparently contradictory uses of ideology,

a)   as the explicitly political, and

b)   as the common-sensed, unconscious, and unrecognised,

as well as to understand some of its other complex usages and meanings, it is necessary to take a short detour through the historical development of the concept.

1.   Williams notes an early use of the word by Napoleon Bonaparte who opposed 'the proponents of democracy ... and attacked the principles of the Enlightenment as "ideology".' In particular, Bonaparte attributed 'all the misfortunes which have befallen our beautiful France ... to the doctrine of the ideologues ... which in a contrived manner seek to find the primary causes and on this foundation would erect the legislation of peoples, instead of adapting the laws to a knowledge of the human heart and of the lessons of history.'[3] The continuity between this usage of ideologies, as beliefs erected upon rigid and doctrinaire principles, rather than upon a more humane and flexible understanding of people and experience, and today's dominant media usage, noted above, are quite clear.

2.   There is, too, a continuity between Bonaparte's pejorative sense of ideology and Marx and Engel's later use of ideology as 'false consciousness'. False consciousness derives from the 'abstraction (of thought) ... from the real processes of history',[4] a failure to realise that the ruling ideas of an epoch 'are nothing more than the ideal expression of the dominant material relationships, the dominant material relationships grasped as ideas.'[5] Against false consciousness, however, Marx and Engels posited, not 'a knowledge of the human heart', but the 'knowledge of real

material conditions and relationships'.[6] Some simple examples of false consciousness have been provided by O'Sullivan et al:

'In the case of the ruling class . . . false consciousness occurs when that class imagines its position in society is determined by the laws of God or nature – as in the doctrine of the divine right of kings for feudal monarchs, or the doctrine of individualism and the conception of society as a social contract in bourgeois philosophy.'[7]

For subordinate classes, false consciousness occurs when they interpret their circumstances according to categories supplied by dominant groups, rather than in terms of their own class interests (e.g., when they support the freedom to choose private education or health care. Or when they allow their class interests to be reinterpreted as 'consumer interests' or 'the national interest').

3.   There is in Marx a less pejorative sense of ideology as *'the set of ideas which arise from a given set of material interests'*,[8] and Lenin speaks of socialism as 'the ideology of struggle of the proletarian class'.[9] Williams notes that there is here 'clearly no sense of illusion or false consciousness... There is now "proletarian ideology" or "bourgeois ideology" and so on, and ideology in each case is the system of ideas appropriate to that class'.[10] It also becomes possible now to speak of a 'dominant ideology', and 'subordinate ideologies'.

It is now necessary to examine why ideology continues to be a matter for investigation and concern by Marxist writers and to establish the connextions between ideology and the functions of the media in modern societies.

Following Marx's view that 'the ideas of the ruling class are in every epoch the ruling ideas', it is of some importance to understand the precise mechanisms through which this process takes place. How is it that subordinate groups, in particular, come to hold beliefs which simply guarantee their continued subordination? Since the media have been seen as important 'carriers' of dominant ideology, the increasing sophistication of the answers which have been supplied to that question has been paralleled by more complex conceptualisations of the media themselves.

For example, a belief in the idea that the dominant ideology is simply a unified set of ideas and beliefs, which a dominant class imposes upon subordinate classes from above, would lead to a view of the media as monolithic and largely unproblematic carriers of ruling-class values. This is a common enough view of the media on the Left, but it is crudely undialectical, and does not adequately explain the subtlety of and contradictions within many of the forces in play within and upon the media at any given time. During the Falklands campaign, for instance, it was tempting, and in some cases even justifiable, to denounce the media for their timorousness in uncritically reproducing the government line, and for the ease with which the government was able to manage and control information through the media for its own purposes. Yet any full account of the relationships between the state and the media during the conflict (or at any time) would need to acknowledge:

a) the genuine tensions which exist between the media and the state,

b) the divisions which exist *within* the state,

c) the divisions which exist within the media, and

d) the fact that dominant ideologies frequently appear to speak to the interests of subordinate groups.

a) Tensions between the media and the state

During the Falklands crisis there were evident divergencies of interest between the media and the state. Hence the necessity for the heavy censorship of images and stories, particularly from the South Atlantic. Hence the government's attacks upon the BBC for not being fully supportive of the war. Hence the mutual suspicion and even hostility which existed between journalists, and naval personnel and civil servants during the conflict.[11] The media may not have emerged with much credit as champions of free speech during the Falklands, but it is too cheap and simple a shot to see the media as mere lackeys of the state machine. For one thing, we do need to recognise that the credibility of the media within democratic societies rests upon their ability to demonstrate *some* independence from government, big business and powerful interest groups. Media institutions, that is, possess their *own* ideologies – their own philosophies, imperatives, conventions and practices – which will not always be entirely congruent with dominant ideologies. That is the source of any strength they possess. In the words of Richard Francis, managing director of BBC radio during the Falklands crisis, 'Whatever reputation the BBC may have does not come from being tied to the government's apron strings'.[12]

Such arguments cut very little ice with Tory MPs during the Falklands adventure. In a meeting with over a hundred Tory MPs, the BBC's Chairman, George Howard, and director-general designate, Alasdair Milne, were given a violently hostile reception, particularly in connection with a *Panorama* programme in which some Tory MPs had expressed doubts about the Government's policies. The meeting demanded Howard and Milne's resignation and the sacking of the *Panorama* production team:

'"They went for their throats," said one MP as he left the meeting. "There were blood and entrails all over the place," said another. And the former Conservative Sports Minister, Sir Hector Monroe said: "It was the ugliest meeting I have ever attended in my years as an MP".'[13]

Mrs Thatcher, not noted for her tolerance of independent criticism, shared her MPs' 'deep concern'.[14]

Ironically, many non-Tories had an equally deep concern over the media's *lack* of independence from the Government and the state, and their acceptance with apparent equanimity of the most direct forms of censorship and information control during the conflict. Much of this is attributable not to a media conspiracy, however, but to the media's role in reproducing the accounts and definitions of dominant sources (see pp. 120 and 121), and their reluctance to compromise, through criticism, their future relationships with important sources of information. As we have seen, too, there are a multiplicity of other, and frequently contradictory, influences operating upon and within media institutions. One potential influence, the audience, scarcely seemed to come into play at all during the Falklands conflict, however. There was little public outcry at the government's manipulation of the media, and few public calls for the media to carry out their proper democratic function as independent suppliers of information upon which the public could make up their own minds. One of the objectives of media education must be to ensure that this kind of situation does not occur so easily again, by building a public opinion which is concerned and well-informed about such issues, as well as supportive of the work of independently-minded broadcasters and journalists. For the sad fact is that, at the present time, we have a situation in which any journalists who seriously wish to produce challenging and informative work (on anything from the Falklands, or the North of Ireland, to the fascist tendencies within the Conservative Party) can expect hysterical blood-letting responses in the House of Commons and the tabloid press, and little overt support from the public for their pains.

b) The divisions which exist within the state

Dominant groups within society are not themselves unified but represent a multiplicity of different interests, and are continually forming and re-forming themselves into fractions and alliances which are in a constant state of movement and change. During the Falklands conflict, for example, there were significant divergencies of interest within the state, particularly:

(i) *Within the Government*, between Mrs Thatcher and her more dovish Foreign Secretary, Francis Pym. As *The Times* reported later: 'Within days of Mr. Pym's appointment, Cecil Parkinson, fellow member of the War Cabinet was walking the Commons' corridor telling everyone who would listen that Pym was no good. He even told Labour MPs Pym was being undermined from the top.'[15] There were also serious differences between Mrs Thatcher and her Secretary of State for Defence Mr Nott, as well as within backbench Conservative opinion, as we have seen.

(ii) *Between the armed services*. During the Falklands crisis there was a great deal of rivalry between the armed services. The Army, the Marines and the Navy were all concerned to gain the maximum amount of favourable publicity for their activities, and in the initial stages of the war, since there was no co-ordination of the services' PR efforts, there was always a suspicion that press briefings were being given in the interests of a particular service. This was particularly so since, given the prospect of future defence spending cuts, all of the services saw their performances in the Falklands, and the ways in which they were reported within the media as being closely tied up with their own future prospects.[16]

(iii) *Between politicians and the military*. There were major conflicts throughout the campaign between Mrs Thatcher's desire for favourable publicity (she wished to use the media to her own advantage in order to project a 'good news war'), and the military's need for operational secrecy. The Navy, for example, originally insisted that no journalists should sail with the Task Force. Mrs Thatcher's view that places must be found for journalists eventually prevailed. The most striking example of the conflict between the needs of the politicians and the military occurred over the battle for Goose Green, however. The loss of three British ships (*The Coventry*, *Atlantic Conveyor* and *Antelope*) over a period of two days meant that the Government badly needed news of a victory to restore their political credibility. Mrs Thatcher prematurely leaked news of the advance on Goose Green for purely political reasons. Out in the Falklands Colonel 'H' Jones (who was awarded a posthumous VC after the war) threatened to sue Mrs Thatcher for imparting this information to the media if any lives were lost as a result of it.[17]

(iv) *Between civil servants and professional Public Relations personnel.*
There were also major strains between civil servants (particularly
at the Ministry of Defence) and public relations specialists within
both the Ministry itself and the armed services. The PR men were
used to building 'constructive' relationships with the media of
the kind most conspicuously exemplified by the Army in the
North of Ireland, and were mortified to discover that the acting-
head of the MoD's public relations department, Ian McDonald,
had quite a different philosophy. McDonald, a professional civil
servant rather than an ex-journalist, had little sympathy with the
news demands of the media. He gave no 'off-the-record' media
briefings, and became nationally known for his terse and formal
news announcements during the crisis. To old PR hands,
McDonald's performances were amateurish, out-of-touch, and
wasted all of the opportunities which existed to project, via the
media, a more positive war effort.[18]

c) The divisions which exist within the media

Whilst the range of opinion articulated by the media frequently seems
narrow in comparison with the variety of views which exist within the
population at large, a monolithic view of the media would be as
seriously misleading as a unified concept of the state. There are
significant rivalries and divergencies of interest

(i)   *between different media* (as there were between the newspaper
and television personnel who accompanied the Task Force, for
example);

(ii) *between different organisations in the same medium.* (*The Sun* and
The Mirror carried out mutually bitter and hostile campaigns
during the conflict, whilst *The Guardian's* stance had little in
common with, say, *The Telegraph's*);

(iii) *within the same organisation* (between, for example, BBC Current
Affairs staff, who came in for a good deal of right-wing criticism
during the Falklands coverage, and BBC News staff, who toed a
much more cautious line. Even in *The Sun*, an appallingly
jingoistic leading article could sit alongside a more thoughtful
piece, by columnist John Akass, which gave by no means
unqualified support to the war.

As media teachers we should not forget that whilst it is often
necessary to make generalisations about the media, and whilst
homogeneity of media coverage is sometimes a problem, there are

dangers in failing to acknowledge the internal conflicts and often bitter differences which do exist between and within the media.

d) Dominant ideologies and subordinate groups

Finally, the idea that ruling groups *impose* a dominant ideology upon subordinate groups does less than justice to the fact that dominant ideas are often not simply *imposed*, but often appear to be *acceptable*, and even to *speak to the interests* of subordinate classes. So during the Falklands conflict, whilst the government did take important steps to manage and control public opinion, it also employed discourses around which the *general* interest could be articulated. To give one example: Mrs Thatcher was concerned to conceptualise the conflict, as indeed were many Labour politicians, as a fight for democracy against a dictatorship, a move which enabled her to mobilise a great deal of general support and to make direct comparisons with the war against Hitler and fascism. As she said on *The Jimmy Young Show* in May 1982, 'We are a democratic country . . . they are a dictatorship . . . It's just like the Channel Islands during the last war. They wouldn't easily have invited the Germans back.' Similarly, any opposition to the sending of the Task Force, or any attempts to take the Peruvian peace plans seriously would be met with a single word: appeasement. It hardly needs to be pointed out that both Labour and Tory governments had long been in the business of supplying arms to the Argentinian junta; that no criticism was made of the Chilean dictatorship during the campaign, since that country was providing safe harbours for our ships; that Mrs Thatcher has breathed scarcely a word of public criticism of President Reagan's support of undemocratic regimes (and his undermining of democratically elected governments) in Southern and Central America; or that Mrs Thatcher's own style of leadership is the most autocratic and authoritarian, and her policies the most centralised and undemocratic to have been seen in this country within living memory. In the light of this kind of evidence it is clear that words such as 'democracy' and 'dictatorship', when so freely used in the context of the Falklands conflict, functioned primarily as rallying calls to the nation *as a whole*, rather than as expressions of firmly-held principles.

What are the precise mechanisms through which this effect is achieved? How is it, exactly, that a dominant ideology can become transmuted into 'common-sensed' notions and 'natural' representations? In order to find an answer to these questions we must turn to a more detailed consideration of two key ideas in the development of theories of ideology; those of *hegemony* and *myth*.

The Italian Marxist, Antonio Gramsci's development of the concept of hegemony was intended to explain how a dominant class's leadership can come to be accepted by *consent*, as well as by force, by subordinate groups. Spontaneous consent, Gramsci argued, was mobilised in Western European bourgeois democracies through the institutions of civil society: the media, the church, the educational system, the family, and other cultural institutions. The concept of hegemony is an important one for media teachers since it defines the media (along with other civil institutions) as important sites for struggle between hegemonic and counter-hegemonic ideas. For hegemony is never won or lost for all time but has to be constantly fought for in order to be secured and maintained. For cultural workers, such as teachers, journalists and broadcasters, the concept of hegemony represents a considerable advance and offers a much more optimistic scenario for counter-hegemonic work than more mechanistic conceptualisations of cultural and civil institutions, in which they are seen as inevitably determined by society's economic base. Gramsci recognised that cultural as well as economic and political factors were instrumental in creating particular forms of consciousness. Thus, in David McLellan's words, Gramsci

'advocated a Party that was an educational institution offering a counter-culture whose aim was to gain an ascendancy in most aspects of civil society (as opposed to directly political institutions) before the attempt was made on state power ... Control of state power without hegemony in civil society was an insecure base for a socialist programme.'[19]

Hegemony, then, 'is not limited to matters of direct political control but seeks to describe a more general predominance which includes, as one of its key features, a particular way of seeing the world and human nature and relationships.'[20] That way of seeing the world is not simply the dominant class's, imposed on subordinate groups from above. It must incorporate the views and interests of subordinate groups, making whatever concessions are necessary in order to establish equilibrium and win legitimacy, without compromising the existing fundamental structures. For its part, if the working-class were ever to establish its own hegemony it would have to represent its own interests as being the interests of society as a whole. The revolutionary struggle involves the dialectical linking of both force and persuasion.

The concept of hegemony, then, is of great importance for media teachers at three different levels. First of all, it identifies both media and educational institutions, practices and theories as crucial sites for hegemonic struggle. Secondly, it provides a sophisticated conceptual tool for understanding and analysing the workings of dominant ideologies and, finally, it offers a strategic guide to the ways in which major transformations within society may be most successfully accomplished and to the crucial role of educational and media practices in bringing about such transformations.

Roland Barthes' collection of essays, *Mythologies*, first published in 1956, provided further important insights into some of the precise mechanisms through which ideological representations come to be accepted as common-sensed, and the important role played by the media in this process. Central to Barthes' thinking was the concept of *myth* which he described as a mode of representation, 'a type of speech',[21] characterised most of all by its 'naturalness'. The starting-point of Barthes' essays on different aspects of French culture (toys, tourist guides, the new Citroen, etc.)

'was usually a feeling of impatience at the sight of the "naturalness" with which newspapers, art and common sense constantly dress up a reality which, even though it is the one we live in, is undoubtedly determined by history. In short, in the account given of our contemporary circumstances I resented seeing Nature and History confused at every turn, and I wanted to track down, in the decorative display of *what-goes-without-saying*, the ideological abuse which, in my view, is hidden there.'[22]

The production of myth is conditional upon two associated repressions: of history and politics. Myth involves 'the miraculous evaporation of history' from the processes of signification. The transformation of History into Nature was, for Barthes, 'the very principle of myth'[23]:

'Myth deprives the object of which it speaks of all History. In it history evaporates. It is a kind of ideal servant: it prepares all things, brings them, lays them out, the master arrives, it silently disappears: all that is left for one to do is to enjoy this beautiful object without wondering where it comes from. Or even better it can only come from eternity: since the beginning of time, it has been made for bourgeois man ... Nothing is produced, nothing is chosen: all one has to do is to possess these new objects, from which all soiling trace of origin or choice has been removed. This miraculous evaporation of history is another form of a concept common to most bourgeois myths: the irresponsibility of man.'[24]

In denying history, Myth also denies politics: '*Myth is depoliticised speech*'.[25] What Myth 'forgets' is that reality is forged dialectically, that it is a product of human activity and struggle. This is why Barthes describes the function of Myth as being 'to empty reality; it is literally a ceaseless flowing out, a haemorrhage, or perhaps an evaporation, in short a perceptible absence.'[26] And, as history, politics and struggle flow out, during the process of representation, Nature, unchanging, and unchangeable, floods in. One of the primary tasks of media education, then, is to hold up to question the media's 'decorative display of what-goes-without-saying'. It is to challenge the media's common-sensed representations by asking whose interests they serve, by demonstrating how they neutralise contradiction, by exploring alternative representations and by developing a critical consciousness that will seek to restore the history, the politics and the struggle to the processes of representation (see pp. 204ff).

At this point we can now turn to a consideration of some of the implications of these developments in the theory of ideology for the practice of media education in schools. Before doing so, however, it should be noted that any full account of the ideological role of the media will need to take into account Althusser's work on *subjectivity* (pp. 236ff)[27] and Poulantzas's work on *masking*, *displacing*, *fragmentation* and *imaginary coherence* (pp. 213ff).[28] Above all it will need to acknowledge the general structuralist recognition that *discourse* itself is the heartland of ideology (pp. 206ff). It is perhaps in language most of all that we can see the force of Stuart Hall's words that ideology resides, not in abstract, complex and remote theories, but in 'what is most open, apparent, manifest . . .'[29]

B. Ideology in the classroom

The task of introducing the concept of ideology into the classroom is a formidable one. Some simple, but important, moves can be made, however, and the remainder of this chapter will suggest some of them.

1. First of all, it should be emphasized that simply by problematis-
    ing media representations, by refusing to accept the naturalness
    of an image, or the neutrality of a particular point-of-view, each
    student is undercutting the potency and influence of dominant
    ideologies as they are naturalised by the media. In particular, by
    encouraging the consideration of deviant, or oppositional,
    readings of media texts, the media teacher is doing a great deal to
    counteract the manipulation of public opinion through the
    media and to prevent an unhindered passage to the dissemina-

tion of dominant ideologies. In this sense media education has a vitally important democratic role to play within society, a role which is counter-hegemonic and *honourably* subversive of established authority.

2. The 'ideological' is frequently conceptualised within media education as *a level of analysis* of a text. I shall be examining some possible ways into ideological textual analysis in Section 5 below, but here it is important to stress that ideologies permeate *every* aspect of media production, distribution, exchange and consumption. Ideologies are not simply bodies of ideas. They are inscribed in concrete. For example, they are written into the conventions and practices of media production and, therefore, into the departmental structures of newspaper offices and broadcasting institutions and so, finally, into the very fabric and design of the buildings themselves.

3. Establishing the important links between, and the inter-penetration of, ideas and non-ideas, then, is a key objective within media education. Stuart Hall:

'whatever else it signals, the concept *ideology* makes a direct reference to the role of *ideas*. It also entails the proposition that ideas are not self-sufficient, that their roots lie elsewhere, that something central about ideas will be revealed if we can discover the nature of the determinancy which *non*-ideas exert over ideas.'[30]

And – we might add – which ideas exert over non-ideas.

I have shown elsewhere, for example, how at the very basic level of non-verbal communication, quite young and unsophisticated students can begin to analyse hairstyles, modes of dress, and cultural objects in terms of the choices, values and attitudes implicit within them.[31] They can begin to grasp, that is, how important ideas and values are closely woven into these taken-for-granted aspects of experience. The movement from *describing* a particular object or mode of communication to exploring the values implicit within it should be made quite consciously by students, as it is one which will be carried over to the study of the media themselves. In the primary school classroom it is possible to raise simple value questions in discussing stories and images (What is the moral of this story? In this photograph what does the photographer think is important? etc.). With older students it is important to try to develop a characteristic mode of enquiry which will move them on from the discussion of apparently trivial phenomena (game shows, comics, newspaper photographs) to a consideration of the large and significant ideas which underpin them.

Finally, it is of vital importance to ask whose interests are served by such ideas. Out of what material conditions and interests do they spring? And what are the material *consequences* of such ideas (i.e., how do they work to subvert or reinforce existing power relations within society?)? As I have argued (see Chapter One) ideologies are not simply sets of ideas, but quite literally matters of life and death, and the survival of our species. For ideas arise from, perpetuate (or challenge) and sustain (or help us change) the material conditions in which we all must live, work and die. That, in a nutshell, is why the ideological role of the media is a matter of such great importance, and the development of media education programmes a matter of such great urgency.

4. It is sometimes said that media education should encourage the ideological analysis of texts, but it is not clear what this might mean unless the precise sense in which 'ideological' is being used is made clear. If the media teacher wishes students to grasp what are perceived as the *coherent sets of beliefs* which underpin a text, then she will need to adopt one kind of approach to textual analysis. If, on the other hand, she wishes students to explore the ways in which ideologies are inscribed within particular common-sensed *discourses*, she will need to use a very different approach. There is, of course, no reason why both methods of analysis should not be used in conjunction with one another, as long as it is clear to students that two different definitions of ideology are being employed.

5. It needs to be acknowledged from the outset that for students to grapple with the major sets of beliefs which seem to underpin media texts is a difficult task. In my experience the best approach lies in having students elaborate textual meanings at *denotative* and *connotative* levels within the text before attempting to look at the text's ideological structures.

Denotation

Full denotative analysis of media texts by the group is an important first stage in analysis because

a) the visual media, in particular, are so rich in denotative meanings, and communicate to us so much information which we frequently process automatically and fail to recognise consciously as information at all, that some mapping out of the range of non-verbal channels (in particular) along which meanings are being carried is necessary within any textual analysis. To put it simplistically, if we wish to analyse a text, we must first establish what the nature of that text is. This step, of increasing general awareness of the nature of the information communicated by the text, I take to be the one referred to by Umberto Eco:

'... if you want to use television for teaching somebody something, you have first to teach somebody how to use television. In this sense television is not so different from a book. You can use books to teach but first you must teach people about books, at least about alphabet and words.'[32]

b) Even at apparently simple denotative levels of analysis, there are likely to be major discrepancies in perception between members of the group. Basic differences (and perhaps misunderstandings) will need to be ironed out before analysis can proceed to a more sophisticated level.

c) Sometimes, small and apparently insignificant details, noted by one person, can open out the ideological implications of a programme for the entire group. An example: in 1977, *Panorama*, as a contribution to Prime Minister Callaghan's Great Educational Debate, devoted an entire programme to a film by Angela Pope, *The Best Days?*, set in a London comprehensive school. The film covered a 'typical' school day, and in a key five-minute sequence a particularly disorganised and disorderly history lesson with 'an average third form' was shown in which very little seemed to be taught or learned. The teacher was ill-prepared and the class, clearly bored with the subject (nineteenth-century Prussia), largely ignored what the teacher was saying and talked amongst themselves. The scene represented was the very epitome of comprehensive education as readers of the *Daily Mail*, *Daily Telegraph* or *Daily Express* would recognise it – less a contribution to the Great Debate than a graphic demonstration of its necessity.

In looking closely at this sequence, one of the students thought she noticed something strange which no one else had observed: half-way through the lesson some writing had mysteriously appeared on what had previously been a clean blackboard behind the teacher. We checked the sequence again. The observation was correct. Indeed, *three* entire blackboards had been filled with writing by the teacher. This considerable task had apparently been accomplished in the middle of a difficult lesson with an unruly class.

Then someone else noticed something about the content of the lesson: it made no sense. The class had been given the original task of copying a map. Then, without any explanation offered within the film, we see them all copying down large chunks of writing from the board. The inconsistency was obvious. But, again, only one person had noticed it. The most likely explanation seemed to be that 'the lesson' was a fiction manufactured from the content of two lessons filmed on separate occasions. There is nothing unusual about this, of course. It is a normal and often inevitable practice in film-making. But it does undermine the status which the programme claims for the film as a serious contribution to a national debate rather than fiction. And the *degree* of compression involved is of some importance. Here we have perhaps 80 minutes of teaching encapsulated in five minutes of film. (How many football fans would ever wish to pass an opinion on a match on the basis of this amount of evidence?) The evidence presented, moreover, was clearly loaded. There was particular emphasis on the beginning and ending of 'the lesson', times when any class will be at its least settled. Since the class was copying material down from the board, there would almost certainly have been periods lacking in visual interest (i.e., when the class was working) which we do not see. The criteria (of televisuality) by which material was allowed to pass through the director's highly selective sieve are self-evident. Strict limits to the range of material available will, of course, have been set by the nature of the director's pre-shooting briefing to her cameraperson. The angle will have been established on this particular teacher and his class before the camera began to roll. Again, from the evidence available, it is quite clear what this angle was.

A great deal more could be said about this sequence, particularly its reliance on reaction shots (demonstrating how little attention is being paid to the teacher by his class) which are simply the creations of editing. I only wish to show here, however, how one hawk-eyed student, by spotting a detail (writing on a blackboard) at a simple denotative level, could unlock for everyone a number of important conceptual insights into the text.

d) A major difficulty within denotative analysis must now be confronted. We are proceeding here on the assumption that in order to analyse a media text we first need to describe it. But, of course, it is one of the major purposes of media education to demonstrate the ways in which the apparently 'factual' always involves particular ways of selecting, valuing and understanding experience. Describing and valuing are not separate, but complexly interwoven categories. Terry Eagleton has provided a simple example:

'It cannot be the case that the notion of a pure descriptive language is anything but a chimera, and an ideological chimera at that. Say you were showing someone a cathedral and you were to say "The cathedral was built in 1612", and the person said "What a strange thing to say. Why are you interested in when it was built? In my society we've got no record at all of when we built our buildings. We categorise them in terms of whether they face south-east. We've long forgotten when we built them. Why is *that* important?" What that person would be doing would be drawing your attention to the fact that what we take as a purely descriptive statement, of course operates within certain deep categories of valuation. So the distinction between fact and value is not that clear. That does not mean, on the other hand, that when we are talking descriptively about texts we are simply, in a disguised way, saying whether we like them or not.'[33]

Both our denotative reading of a text, and the text's selection and ordering of events at a denotative level, then, need to be understood from the outset as key ideological issues. For it is here, at the level of description, that the most profound choices of all are being made. We need to guard, from the very outset, then, against the seductive idea that denotation is an 'innocent' level of meaning which we can quickly dispose of before moving on to more subtle, complex and profound levels of meaning.

Connotation

It is a relatively simple matter to devise exercises which will enable quite young children to handle the concept of connotation,[34] and, indeed, analysis of texts at connotative levels of meaning are part of the stock-in-trade of most English teachers. In media, as in literary, texts, deeper themes manifest themselves as connotative 'clusters', or 'chains' of associations, nuances and suggestions through which structures of meaning (sometimes not evident to their producers) come to be revealed. Whilst in literary study the purpose of attention to connotation has traditionally been to show how the resonances of language produce in the work multi-layered complexities in meaning and structure, in media education such meanings have an *ideological* rather than a simply aesthetic purchase because of the media's continual tendency to blur the distinctions between the 'objective' and the selectively constructed, the 'real' and its representation. Connotative codes, in Stuart Hall's words, are

'the means by which the domains of social life, the segmentations of culture, power and ideology are made to signify. They refer to the "maps of meaning" into which any culture is organised and those "maps of social reality" have the whole range of social meanings, practices and usages, power and interest "written in" to them. Connotated signifiers, Barthes has reminded us, "have a close communication with culture, knowledge, history and it is through them, so to speak, that the environmental world invades the linguistic and semantic system. They are, if you like, the fragments of ideology."'.[35]

Ideological analysis

Ideological analysis – in the sense of analysis which is designed to uncover those more or less coherent sets of values and beliefs which are thought to underpin a text – consists of piecing together the text's connotative fragments. So, in *Mastermind* (BBC), for example, the single chair, the pool of light, the clipped, impersonal tones of the questioner, the cutting to ever tighter close-ups of the contestants, all contribute to dominant and oppressive associations of knowledge and learning with interrogation, humiliation and fear of failure. These associations are validated and legitimised by the formal university settings in which the show takes place, and by *their* connotative links with the importance of factual recall within the show, as well as with the frequently absurd specialisms, and predominantly middle-class backgrounds of the contestants (the odd cabbie or tube driver amongst them simply attesting to the opportunities for upward-mobility which approved knowledge can bring with it). An examination of *Mastermind's* connotative clusters, then, not only leads us directly to its major ideological themes and to its peculiarly de-humanised, hierarchical and oppressive construction of what counts as learning and intelligence. It also assures us, chillingly, that this construction has a great deal of purchase out there in the world of real and prestigious educational institutions.

Or consider television's coverage of the 1985 London Marathon.

Denotatively, coverage moves from attention to the mass to concentration upon the individual then back again to the mass. The commentator's sense of wonder at the sheer numbers participating evolves into a pleasurable roll-call of variety and difference: the young and the elderly, athletes and invalids, men and women, stars and nobodies, competitors and fun runners. From north, south, east and west they have come, these vicars, teachers and bank clerks, to jog or run in their track-suits, fancy dress or eccentric gear. The dominant connotations here – of difference, diversity, quirkiness and eccentricity – cluster together to point up a deeper, ideological unity. Behind each competitor, it is true, there is an individual story of courage, determination and the will to succeed and finish – 'to climb one's own personal mountain'. Yet the task is being undertaken not primarily out of individual pride or vanity, but in order to support a charity or neglected cause. Hence the stress by the commentators on the essential camaraderie of the occasion – on the essential unity in the midst of such eccentric variety.

But what is this unity which television constructs before our very eyes in the streets of central London? It is a powerful and appealing image of quintessential 'Britishness' (presided over by the event's sponsors, the American transnational corporation, Mars) which for all of its dottiness remains decent, tolerant of differences, humane and fundamentally at one. It is a comfortingly homogenising image, a myth which can only work, as Barthes has shown us, through the almost wilful neglect of politics (in 'real' Britain in 1985 the divisions between rich and poor, North and South, the employed and unemployed were deeper and more bitter than they had been for 50 years), and the forgetting of history (and in particular of the recently-ended coal dispute, 'real' Britain's most protracted class conflict since the end of the war).

Finally, the *Panorama* documentary *The Best Days?*, described above, presents to us in its images of indiscipline, bad teaching, pupils smoking between lessons, and noise and confusion both in and out of the classrooms, powerful representations of school which go back to such films as *The Blackboard Jungle* and *To Sir With Love*, and even to a television comedy series such as *Please, Sir*. They are representations which used to be applied in Britain to secondary modern schools, but since the 1960s we have come to recognise such images as representing the very essence of comprehensive schools – the myth of *comprehensivity* as Barthes might have termed it. Again it is a comfortingly (or uncomfortably) homogenised picture, a perfect example of what-goes-without-saying about our comprehensive educational system. Again, it can only work through the repression of history and politics. For what is at stake, in any representation of comprehensive schools, is the long and protracted struggle for a decent, non-selective state education for *all* children. Contextualise any media representation of comprehensives with that history and that struggle and you are compelled to ask a number of important questions. Why are *problems* highlighted but rarely achievements? Where does the producer of these images, or the institution which disseminates them stand in relation to that struggle? What positive and constructive criticisms are made that might help sustain comprehensive ideals?

Media analysis, then, must always attempt to push out beyond the consideration of connotative meanings towards ideological analysis. This will involve an explication of the principal assumptions and sets of ideas upon which the text is based. It will involve the restoration of those representations to their historical and political contexts, and it will entail the positing of alternative visions and representations. Finally, the ideological work of programmes like *Mastermind, The London Marathon* and *Panorama, The Best Days?* will need to be understood extra-textually, in the light both of their relationship to existing power structures, and their probable material *consequences* in perpetuating, amplifying or subverting existing power relations.[36]

6. *Ideology and discourse:* We must now turn to a consideration of how the inscription of ideology within common-sensed discourses might best be approached in the classroom. It should be noted, however, that there are no examples on record of work which has been undertaken in schools in this area. The following suggestions are therefore necessarily of a tentative and exploratory nature.

First of all it is necessary to understand that discourse theory stands traditional conceptions of language on their heads. Language, here, is not so much a labelling process, through which we assign names to a pre-existing reality. It does not simply reflect the world out there. For, as Saussure observed, 'If words stood for pre-existing concepts, they would all have exact equivalents in meaning from one language to the next; but this is not true.'[37] Rather, it is through the words (or, more accurately, discourses) which we have at our disposal, which are available to us, that we make sense of the world. Our experience of the world is not the source of language, but its *consequence*.

Since words are arbitrary signs, can we make them mean just whatever we choose? No, because language is *social:*

'Meaning is public and conventional, the result not of individual intention but of inter-individual intelligibility. In other words, meaning is socially constructed, and the social construction of the signifying system is intimately related, therefore, to the social formation itself.'[38]

There are two important points here. First of all, language, and the ways in which we experience and conceptualise the world, are intimately bound up with questions of *power*. Within any society the economically and socially powerful are those whose definitions *count*. Oppressed groups, on the other hand, are subjected, amongst other things, to the definitions of their oppressors. Secondly, the language system into which we are born pre-exists our own consciousness, and in a significant, though not absolute, sense, pre-structures the limits and possibilities of our own consciousness. As Catherine Belsey notes, 'Language in an important sense speaks us.'[39] Eagleton summarises the situation thus:

'The structuralist emphasis on the constructedness of human meaning represented a major advance. Meaning was neither a private experience nor a divinely ordained occurrence: it was the product of certain shared systems of signification. The confident bourgeois belief that the isolated individual subject was the fount and origin of all meaning took a sharp knock: language pre-dated the individual, and was much less his or her product than he or she was the product of it. Meaning was not 'natural', a question of just looking and seeing, or something eternally settled; the way you interpreted your world was a function of the languages you had at your disposal, and there was evidently nothing immutable about these. Meaning was not something which all men and women everywhere intuitively shared, and then articulated in their various tongues and scripts: what meaning you were able to articulate depended on what script or speech you shared in the first place ... Reality was not reflected by language but produced by it: it was a particular way of carving up the world which was deeply dependent on the sign-systems we had at our command, or more precisely which had us at theirs.'[40]

As ever, resistance is possible. Like ideology itself, language is not a monolithic system structuring our consciousness in a deterministic fashion, but a site of considerable struggle between competing ways of making sense of the world (i.e., between competing discourses). A condition of engaging in that struggle, however, is a recognition of the apparently 'natural' signs of language as themselves being constructed. Hence the importance within media education of the concept of *discourse*, with its emphasis upon the *use* of language to serve particular interests and particular ideological purposes.

Work on the discourses employed within a media text can develop out of work on connotations. For words with particular connotations will appear in a context which is consistent with those connotations, i.e., within a particular discourse. As Bonney and Wilson have pointed out, the words 'police' and 'cops' have the same denotations, but very different connotations, one respectful, the other derogatory. But the use of these different words will not occur in isolation :

'Each is associated with a whole range of words and phrases carrying the same opposed implications. Whereas the police restrain crowds, arrest suspects, protect citizens and detain criminals, the cops harass peaceful demonstrators, bash, push, shove, grab and threaten innocent bystanders. What we have here is a sharp distinction between two quite different ways of speaking and thinking about law enforcement.'[41]

What we have here, indeed, are two different *discourses*, two discrete ways of making sense of experience.

A brief examination of media treatment of two particularly controversial issues – the political situation in the North of Ireland and the 1984–5 coal dispute – may reveal some of the potentialities of discourse analysis within media education. For in reporting the situation in the North of Ireland, 'the words you use may betray the political path you seem to be treading', as television reporter Peter Taylor has suggested:

'At the most basic level, where is the conflict taking place? Is it in Ulster? Northern Ireland? The province? The North of Ireland? Or the Six Counties?... And once you've sorted out the names, what's actually going on there? Is it a conflict? Is it a war? A rebellion? A revolution? A criminal conspiracy? Or a liberation struggle?... Lastly, and probably most important, how do we describe those involved? Are they terrorists? Criminals? The mafia? Murderers? Guerillas? Or freedom fighters? It depends on your perception of the conflict, and who you happen to be working for at the time.'[42]

Liz Curtis, who has produced the most detailed and damning research on the media's coverage of the North of Ireland, elaborates, demonstrating how deeply inscribed within current discourses particular ideologies are. She is worth quoting at some length:

'Place-names are an immediate give-away. Northern Ireland was the name bestowed by Britain on the unit created by partition in 1920, when the border was drawn around six northeastern counties of Ireland. Republicans call it the Six Counties, while other nationalists often call it the North of Ireland: like the term Northern Ireland, this is geographically incorrect, since part of Donegal is further north than any of the British-ruled counties ... The term Ulster, the name of one of the four ancient provinces of Ireland, is frequently used by the British media and loyalist politicians to refer to the Six Counties. This usage is inaccurate, since three counties of Ulster lie in the Southern government's jurisdiction. The term is favoured by loyalists presumably because it suggests, albeit spuriously, that their present territory has a historic homogeneity ... As it did in other colonial territories, Britain put its stamp on Ireland by altering indigenous place-names. Thus Derry – Doire in Irish – was renamed Londonderry several hundred years ago after the London companies which controlled it. The British usage has never been universally accepted, and nationalists still call it Derry. British journalists generally use Londonderry, although on occasions they use both terms within the same article or programme.... While the use of place-names indicates the speaker's view of whether or not the British presence in the North is legitimate, a host of other terms reveal attitudes to the armed protagonists. Thus for British politicians and the media, the British army, the UDR (Ulster Defence Regiment) and RUC (Royal Ulster Constabulary) are the "security forces" – a reassuring term that is anathema to many nationalists – while the IRA and INLA (Irish National Liberation Army) are "terror-ists". The army "says" something happened while the IRA "claims" or "alleges" it. Victims of the army or police are "shot dead" while those of the IRA are "murdered" or "gunned down" ... The most potent words are undoubtedly "terrorist" and "terrorism". Noam Chomsky and Edward Herman have written that these words "have become semantic tools of the powerful in the Western world", and observe that they "have generally been confined to the use of violence by individuals and marginal groups", while "official violence which is far more extensive in scale and destructiveness is placed in a different category altogether" ... In the Irish context, "terrorist" and "terrorism" are used frequently in relation to the IRA and INLA, occasionally in relation to loyalist paramilitaries – who are more usually called "extremists" – and never in relation to the British army or RUC. The power of the words lies in the fact that they imply that the violence they describe is worse than violence from other sources.'[43]

Similarly, in the 1984–5 coal dispute, there were obvious divergencies between the discourses employed by the miners and the Coal Board about the dispute. For the most part the media simply reproduced the dominant Coal Board discourse. For example, they referred to the dispute throughout as 'the miners' strike' (not 'the Coal Board strike', 'MacGregor's strike', or even the more neutral 'coal dispute'), a phrase which pinned the blame for the dispute firmly on the miners. In addition, as a study by the Campaign for Press and Broadcasting Freedom suggests, though the dispute was about different possible definitions of 'uneconomic' (in relation to the closure of so-called 'uneconomic pits'), the media overwhelmingly employed the Coal Board's definition of that term:

'Instead of asking "uneconomic" in what sense and according to what kind of economic thinking? the broadcast media accepted the NCB/Government's simplistic definition of "uneconomic". Only Channel Four News made an effort to qualify the controversial term by referring to "so-called uneconomic pits" or "what the Coal Board claim to be uneconomic pits".'[44]

Finally, those miners returning to work and breaking the strike were referred to not as the 'scabs' or 'strike-breakers' of the miners' discourse, but as 'new faces', a phrase which the CPBF Study describes as 'radiantly positive'.[45] It is interesting to note, too, that Alastair Hetherington, in an article describing his research on media coverage of the dispute, also operates from the outset from within the dominant Coal Board discourse about the dispute: he refers to the dispute as 'the miners' strike', describes the activities of pickets as 'mob rule' and says 'No wonder the great police operation ... was set in motion.'[46] Discourse analysis at least holds out the hope that media teachers and their students may gain rather more critical purchase upon media coverage of the dispute than this.

The prevalence of racist and sexist discourses both within and outside of the media should also be noted. Racist discourses range from the explicit racism of much 'comedy', to the apparently unconscious attitudes which permeate programmes like *Blue Peter*,[47] and the white ethnocentricism of news and current affairs programmes. As to sexist discourses, like many men I have been alerted to their significance by the work of the women's movement over the past few years. Indeed, I now find the unconscious sexism in the language of my earlier book, *Teaching about Television*, written just eight years ago, so offensive as to be virtually unreadable.

Sexism is constantly evident in the media in the treatment and representation of women in both factual and fictional pro-grammes, in the still dominant use of patriarchal discourses, and in the institutional subordination of women within the media. The perusal of virtually any media text will testify to the continuing dominance of partriarchal discourses and practices, and reform here is long overdue. It should be noted that the Australian Broadcasting Corporation (ABC) issued specific guidelines to its producers and announcers in 1984 on the use of unconsciously sexist vocabulary. So far no such guidelines have been forthcoming within British media institutions, but some helpful suggestions for avoiding discrimination against women have been made by the National Union of Journalists (NUJ):

Instead of	*Try*
businessman	business manager, executive, boss, business chief, head of firm etc, business-woman/people
cameraman	photographer, camera operator
newsman	journalist or reporter
fireman/men	firefighter, fire service staff, fire crews
dustman	refuse collector
foreman	supervisor
ice cream man	ice cream seller
policeman/men	police officer, or (pl) just police
salesman/girl	assistant, shop worker, shop staff, representative, sales staff
steward/ess air hostess	airline staff, flight attendant
chairman	chairperson/woman, in the chair was ... who chairs the committee
best man for the job	best person/woman ...
man or mankind	humanity, human race, humans, people
manhood	adulthood
man-in-the-street	average citizen, average worker
manpower	workers, workforce, staffing

manning	staffing, jobs, job levels
manmade	synthetic, artificial, manufactured
Ford men voted...	Ford workers voted
male nurse	nurse
woman doctor	doctor
housewife	often means shopper, consumer, the cook
mothers	often means parents
girls (of over 18)	women (especially in sport)
spinster/divorcee	these words should not be used as an insult
he, his	often means he or she, or his or hers – or sentence constructions can be changed to use they or theirs
Mrs, Miss	if your publication insists on courtesy titles, at least offer women the choice of being called Ms
Mr John Smith and his wife Elsie	Elsie and John Smith
authoress	author – avoid /ess where possible
dolls, birds, ladies, Mrs Mopp	these, and puns arising from them, are not funny
pin ups	are they really news?
spokesman	official, representative

Try the double standard test – would you use this description of a man?[48]

Attending to sexist and racist discourses opens one up to some familiar criticisms: that this is a trivial issue; that it is hingeing too much on particular kinds of language-use; that sexism and racism are so deeply-rooted in our society that attention to quite small points of language may divert attention away from more serious problems of sexist and racist *behaviour*. After all, I may consciously refuse to employ racist or patriarchal discourses as far as I am able, but remain deeply prejudiced against blacks and women in my attitudes and conduct. Our analysis of the nature of discourse should indicate the importance of what is at stake, however. First of all, one should expect some surprise, and even ridicule, if one is attempting to challenge common-sense perceptions and language-uses. Secondly, the use of non-racist and non-patriarchal forms makes visible the predominant use of racist and patriarchal discourses which would otherwise remain implicit and unnoticed. It repeatedly draws attention, that is, to the facts of racism and patriarchy as *issues*. Thirdly, the co-existence within individuals of non-racist, non-patriarchal discourses and racist and sexist behaviour may be, at one level, simply hypocritical. But the existence of these contradictions does at least open up the possibilities for further change, and for the kind of critiques of individuals' behaviour which will be acceptable to them. Fourthly, it matters a great deal that the struggle to establish non-oppressive discourses should be successful, since, as we have seen, the availability of such discourses will be of crucial importance in shaping the consciousness of future generations.

Finally, it is necessary to examine some of the mechanisms through which some discourses become hegemonic, articulating not simply the interests of dominant groups but the general interest. We have already noted how, during the Falklands conflict, Mrs Thatcher employed a specific discourse about 'democracy' precisely to achieve this end. It needs to be noted here that this kind of move always involves the *appropriation* of particular concepts ('freedom', 'choice', 'the individual', etc.) from their more fully human and social meanings, and their use in a much narrower and more specific range of contexts. Nicos Poulantzas has suggested that what are involved here are processes of *masking*, *displacement*, *fragmentation* and *imaginary coherence*.

(i) *Masking:* 'One of the particular characteristics of the dominant bourgeois ideology is, in fact, that it conceals class exploitation in a specific manner, *to the extent that all trace of class domination is systematically absent from its language.*' (Original emphasis.)[49]

Hegemonic discourses, then, begin by masking the real relations of production. They also, thereby, suppress the fullest and richest potentialities of particular ideas and concepts.

(ii) *Displacement:* The masking described above is accompanied by a *displacement* of emphasis from the sphere of production to the sphere of exchange and consumption. So, for example, the phrase 'freedom of the press', if considered within the context of an exploitative, class-divided society, might be more appropriately rendered as 'the freedom of capital to indoctrinate labour'.[50] For in the sphere of production there *is* no freedom for the vast majority to set up, or even directly influence newspapers, just as in this sphere there is no democracy. The use of 'freedom' in relation to the press, then, (as with the use of 'democracy' in relation to the Falklands conflict) involves a sleight-of-hand which is achieved through the displacement of emphasis from the sphere of production to the sphere of exchange. We possess only the freedom to choose whichever newspaper (or politician) we wish. 'Consumption' in the words of Australian commentators Higgins and Moss, 'becomes a substitute for democracy. It compensates for all that is patently undemocratic in our society. Because we can choose which toothpaste to use or pizza to buy, we live under the illusion that we are free'.[51] Or, as Bonney and Wilson have suggested, the media 'construct a representation of monopoly capitalism which foregrounds the abundant variety of products (brands) available for the gratification of supposedly autonomous individuals, while entirely concealing from view the processes by which these products are produced, the undemocratic nature of decisions about what gets produced and how, and the increasing uniformity masked by the multiplication of brand names.'[52]

(iii) *Fragmentation:* Dominant discourses do more than simply mask the facts both of class exploitation and of class or collective interests. They *fragment* us, representing us, not as classes, but as what Bonney and Wilson call 'supposedly autonomous individuals', that is, as individual citizens and consumers.

(iv) However, in a final move, we are given, as individuals, *an imaginary coherence*, as we are *reconstituted* and addressed, not as classes, but as *imaginary* unities at the point of consumption: 'consumers', 'the consensus', 'public opinion', 'the nation'.

This 'paradigmatic ideological figure'[53] of Poulantzas should be helpful in enabling us to discern the essential structure of the strategies employed across a wide range of hegemonic discourses. It should reveal the impoverishment of some of the key terms appropriated by dominant discourses, and begin to restore to them their full richness and potentiality. It should demonstrate the threadbare nature of a freedom, democracy, and choice, which are confined to the market-place and are conditional upon the size of our wallets, and point up the potentialities of popular democratic control, freedom and economic justice at the point of production. And like the whole field of discourse analysis itself, it should enable our students both to understand the importance of, and begin to participate in, crucial struggles over meaning.

Chapter 7

Audience

1. Introduction

Audiences have remained, throughout the history of media education, a relatively neglected phenomenon. This is curious given that
media audiences have been, from the outset, the dominant focus of
attention for media researchers. There are two main reasons for
media education's general neglect of this important area. First of all,
it can be seen as part of media education's literary legacy, an
inheritance of literary criticism's subordination of readers to the twin
authorities of authorship (justified by the transcendence of 'genius' or
'creativity'), and the text itself (the transcendence of immanent
'meaning'). As we have seen, media education, like literary criticism,
has predominantly been based upon the beliefs that textual meanings
are produced by authors (writers/directors/producers), are inherent
within texts, and give themselves up only to experienced and sensitive
readers. Interpretation, in this view, is an ideologically innocent
activity, taking place in a social and historical vacuum, rather than a
construction reflecting or refracting the ideological positions of
readers.

The second reason why media education has tended to neglect
audiences as an area of concern is that though, in more widely-based
communications research, audiences have been of great importance,
the position allotted to them has scarcely been more dynamic than it
has been in literary-based models. In communication models,
audiences have been generally conceived of as *receivers of messages*,
and a great deal of well-funded research has been undertaken to
discover the *effects* of different kinds of communication upon their
audiences. As is well known, this research has generated few positive
results largely because of the difficulties of separating out the
influence of communications from the influence of other social
phenomena, such as the family, the peer-group, opinion leaders and
so on.

For all its interest in audiences, most empiricist communications
research has had little of interest to say about them. It has been
concerned not with *significance* but with *quantification* in its
approach to the analysis of both communication content and
audiences. What has generally been held to be of most importance is

the *number* of viewers watching a particular programme, or the *number* of interviews given to trade unionists or employers in a week's media coverage, rather than the ways in which the treatment of content might *structure audience responses* in predictable ways, or the *significance* which these experiences might have for audiences.

The development of communications research has been largely a development towards more complex understandings of media content and audience responses. So-called 'uses-and-gratifications' research, for example, was a distinct advance on earlier communication models since it posited a more sympathetic and active view of audiences. In James Halloran's words, it allowed researchers 'to get away from the habit of thinking in terms of *what media do to people* and substitute for it the idea of *what people do with the media*.'[1] Audiences were seen as actively using the media and making positive choices, based on their assessment of the likelihood of the media gratifying particular needs.

There were, however, problems with this view of media audiences. Uses and gratifications research still generally tended to be psychologically, rather than sociologically based, with an emphasis upon choices which were held to be freely made by individuals, rather than uses which were structured by considerations of race, class or gender. It was also limitingly conservative and circular:

'It represents audiences, like consumers in *lassez faire* economics, as unproblematically exercising free and rational choices in a free market, choosing the texts they like, want or need. Thus, it implies that audiences are getting what they want, that the way things are is the way they should be because the way they are is the outcome of free and rational choice. But this rests on a number of dubious assumptions and is in fact subject to the charge of being circular.'[2]

'First, it takes wants and needs, in a thoroughly empiricist way, to be unproblematically *given*. They are *there*, as part of a universal "human nature" or individual "essences". Secondly, it assumes that because people consume, and continue to consume, media products they are thereby having their (independently given) wants or needs gratified. The charge of circularity against this approach arises because of the impossibility of determining, independently of their consumption of media output, what the needs are that people have which they use the media to gratify. If we ask what these needs are, we are given a list such as: the need for diversion, for escape, for substitute company, and so on. But if we ask what evidence there is that people have such needs the answer is: the fact that they use the media to gratify them. It is hard to see how the uses and gratifications approach can break out of this circle.'[3]

As Bonney and Wilson make clear, uses and gratifications research had little to say on the ways in which wants or needs are themselves produced, and the active role played by the media in this process. It had little to say about the ways in which media content might structure audience responses in quite predictable ways, and still less about the possibilities that questions of audience might be important determinants of media content and forms. Nor did it open up many of the complex ways in which audiences work upon texts, accepting, negotiating or rejecting the rich diversity of positions offered to them by texts. Since 1980 a good deal of important research has been published on these questions. Since it has significant implications for the development of media education a brief résumé of some of its most important strands is necessary.

2. Problematising audiences: Morley, Hobson and Smythe

David Morley's study of audience responses to the television magazine programme *Nationwide*[4] was based upon the reactions of 29 socially and culturally diverse groups to the programme. Morley was concerned to examine the possible lack of 'fit' between the intentions of the producers of media 'messages', and the interpretations of their audiences. Different interpretations by different groups were not simply accounted for in terms of individual psychologies but were understood as related, in a systematic way, to sub-cultural and socio-economic differences.

'Of course, there will always be individual, private readings, but we need to investigate the extent to which these individual readings are patterned into cultural structures and clusters. What is needed here is an approach which links differential interpretations back to the socio-economic structure of society, showing how members of different groups and classes, sharing different 'cultural codes' will interpret a given message differently, not just at the personal, idiosyncratic level, but in a way 'systematically related' to their socio-economic position. In short, we need to see how the different sub-cultural structures and formations within the audience, and the sharing of different cultural codes and competencies amongst different groups and classes, "determine" the decoding of the message for different sections of the audience.'[5]

The implications of this approach to audience decoding are far-reaching, not only for media education, but for all educational interactions. For if meaning resides, not within the text itself, but in the interaction between audiences and text, then this holds true not simply in front of the television screen, but within every classroom. For teachers of all subjects, knowledge of and sensitivity to what students themselves bring to a subject will be at least as important as knowledge of and sensitivity to the subject itself. In addition, differential decodings, traditionally either repressed in many class-rooms or treated as a 'problem' to be overcome through the combined authorities of teacher, author and text, can now be given the fullest articulation as reflections or refractions of important sub-cultural differences within the group. Finally, the transformation of students, from being passive recipients of the communications of others to active meaning-makers – from objects to whom education happens, to subjects who create knowledge and make it their own – should be liberating for students and teachers alike and should help to promote the development of genuine dialogue within the classroom.

A productive and mutual openness, within dialogue, to the opinions and experiences of others, is not the same as an uncritical acceptance of them, however. For, as many critics have observed, the teacher has a right, indeed a duty, to challenge racist, sexist, ageist or similarly undesirable attitudes and experiences which may surface in the classroom.[6] But, as Connell has observed, the rights of students to criticise the certainties of the teacher, need to be just as rigorously insisted upon: 'the critical traffic cannot all be one way.'[7]

Far from positing experience as unproblematic, the whole objective of classroom dialogue here is to problematise it by 'de-naturalising' particular judgements (including the teacher's) and tracing out some of the ways in which they are systematically related to wider sub-cultural codes and formations.

Is the audience's liberation from the text absolute? Can we make texts mean whatever we wish? In one sense the answer to this must be yes. As Terry Eagleton has said, 'What, after all, is there to stop us? . . . In another sense, the idea is a simple fantasy . . . For such texts belong to language . . . and language is not, in fact, something we are free to do what we like with.'[8] (See pp. 206–7).

David Morley:

'The TV message is . . . a complex sign, in which a preferred reading has been inscribed, but which retains the potential, if decoded in a manner different from the way in which it has been encoded, of communicating a different meaning. The message is thus a structured polysemy. It is central to the argument that all meanings do not exist "equally" in the message: it has been structured in dominance, although its meaning can never be totally fixed or "closed". Further, the "preferred reading" is itself part of the message, and can be identified within its linguistic and communicative structure ... The moment of "encoding" thus exerts from the production end, an "over-determining" effect (though not a fully determined closure) in the succeeding moments in the communicative chain.'[9]

Sensitivity to the liberating possibilities of differential decoding should not blind us to the importance of discovering the dominant meaning encoded within the text and, as we have seen, a good deal of work is necessary in order to establish the dominant values of particular texts and the techniques its producers employ in order to win assent to and complicity with their ways of seeing. It is important to distinguish between 'deviant' readings which are based on a full recognition of the dominant meanings encoded within the text and those which are apparently oblivious to such meanings. It is the purpose of media education to provide students with the media competencies which will enable them to explicate the encoded text as fully as possible. What remains open is the audience's and the students' interpretation and acceptance of this text.

Adapting a basic model from Parkin[10] and Hall,[11] Morley suggests three broad frames within which a decoder may position herself in relation to media texts: *dominant* (i.e. decoding is aligned with the dominant encodings or interpretative frameworks of the message itself), *negotiated* ('decoders may take the meaning broadly as encoded; but by relating the message to some concrete, located or situational context which reflects their position and interests they may modify or partly inflect the meaning'[12]); and *oppositional* (the decoder recognises the dominant encoding, but interprets it in an oppositional way).

Parkin hypothesised that these frames formed the basis of different class-orientated 'meaning systems', but Morley, whilst working within Parkin's broad categories, is concerned to stress the complexity of real audience responses, arguing that textual decodings can no more be 'read off' from class/ethnic/gender/sub-cultural positions than meanings can be read off from textual characteristics: 'The fundamental point [is] that social position in no way directly, or unproblematically, correlates with decoding.'[13] In his own research Morley uncovered widely different decodings of *Nationwide* by groups of young apprentice engineers, shop-stewards and trade union officials, and young black students, though all groups could be designated working-class. ['The groups'] decodings of a television programme are inflected in different directions by the discourses and institutions in which they are situated. In one case, the framework derives from a tradition of main-stream working-class populism, in another from trade unions and Labour Party politics, in another, from black youth sub-cultures.'[14]

The important insight that audiences perform their own ideological operations upon texts needs to be integrated into media teaching at all levels, viz.:

a) Teachers will need to develop a sensitive and close working knowledge of the cultural competencies and sub-cultural differences which exist within their groups, so that they can predict with some accuracy the range of responses which a particular text is likely to elicit.

b) This understanding should not simply underwrite and inform the practice of teachers. It should also inform student responses, and give to students a greater awareness of the social and sub-cultural roots of their own judgements.

c) What is at stake here is rather more than personal understanding by students of the socially constructed nature of their own seemingly 'natural' responses, however. This understanding needs to be transferred to the responses of audiences to media texts generally. Teachers and students alike will need to widen their examination of media texts to include an analysis of the sense which is made of them by their audiences.

* * *

An interesting example of the way in which attention to the meanings made by audiences of media texts can produce more illuminating responses to them is provided by Dorothy Hobson's work on the much reviled soap opera, *Crossroads*. The programme is widely regarded as one of the weakest shows on British television. It is thought to be badly written, badly acted and badly produced, the *Crossroads*' team turning out three episodes each week on a remorseless conveyor-belt system. Post-production editing facilities are denied them because the company producing the show considers them too expensive to be wasted on the programme. So if actors fluff their lines or make a mistake, it is as likely as not to be left in. The show is the butt of comedians everywhere and, even within the company which produces it, enjoys very little prestige.

The problem is, of course, that *Crossroads* has huge audiences. It is this phenomenon, the vast popular appeal of a media product deemed to have little intrinsic merit (a phenomenon which has always caused profound uneasiness amongst media educators) which Dorothy Hobson's study investigates.

The heart of the study is an account of one of the most cataclysmic events in the history of British television: the decision in 1981 by a single television executive that Meg Mortimore, the central and best-loved character in the soap opera, would have to be disposed of. At one stage a competition was even mooted to decide upon the most appropriately grisly way of polishing Meg off. What Charles Denton (the executive concerned) had decided to do was to sack Noele Gordon who played the part of Meg.

The outcry was enormous. The company was inundated with mail. Its switchboards were jammed for days. Noele Gordon sold her story for a lucrative sum to a Sunday newspaper, and the whole story remained in the headlines for weeks. Overwhelmingly, those who telephoned and wrote letters were those whose views do not count for very much with television companies and advertisers; middle-aged to elderly women, and an enormous number of old-aged pensioners. Dorothy Hobson read all of their letters, sought out some of those who had written in, and then watched the show with them in their homes. She writes, movingly and affirmatively, about what those people – mainly women, and principally elderly women – got out of the programme. It is a rare glimpse of the human reality of how people, the elderly in particular, relate to the media, and it gives the lie to the kind of condescending generalisations generally made by cultural critics whenever they think of audiences as undiscriminating 'masses'. Dorothy Hobson is worth quoting in some detail:

'Perhaps the single most surprising aspect of researching and writing this book has been the awareness which it has brought to me about old people and their lives. Quite incidentally, while they wrote letters in support of the actress, they gave information about their own lives and the importance to them of some television programmes. For the letters were often not simply about television but about the way that old people experience their lives and how they feel about their role in society . . . The following are some examples:

"I think the way they have treated Noele Gordon is shocking . . . I have watched her on television for many years also *Lunch Box* and *Stars on Sunday*. I know I am old, 88 years, but I am a good judge of people. All I can say is keep going Meg we will miss you."

"I live alone and over 70 and look forward to seeing *Crossroads*. I feel she is a friend come into my home. I do hope that you can do something to save her."

"I am an OAP..."

"I am 77 and housebound..."

Why do people suddenly begin to sign their letters with their age and give social and economic status as "pensioner"? What are they trying to say about their own self-identity? There was a sense of the writers expressing in these definitions two contradictory feelings – a sense of wanting to say that they had reached a certain age and that their opinions should be taken into account, but also an expression of the feeling that they knew that their opinions would not be considered, precisely because they were now old. The responsibility for the elderly in society cannot, of course, be laid solely at the door of television companies but television can and does appear to provide one of the few pleasures and areas of contact with the world for elderly people ... Television is very important to the elderly and housebound and while the rest of society fails to alleviate the situation for many elderly people who live alone, the entertainment and sense of contact which programmes like *Crossroads* provide for its viewers are surely among the most valuable aspects of the medium. For there *is* something wrong in the lives of many people and the reassurances which they derive from fictional programmes should not be under-estimated. It may be difficult for television companies to accept this area of responsibility, but if this section of their audience is entertained by programmes which they do not themselves rate highly in professional terms, they should begin to question for whom the programmes are made.'[15]

Dorothy Hobson's conclusions have radical implications for the practice of media education:

'Television is a new form of contemporary art and communication; the possibilities for its expansion appear to be endless. If it is to progress and communicate with its audience it should free itself of the forms of criticism which are rooted in other forms of communication. Broadcasters should recognise that when they do attract a large audience they should not despise that audience nor the programmes which most appeal. A soap opera which appeals to and connects with the experiences of fifteen million people is as valid and valuable a work of art as a single play or documentary which may attract four million viewers. Neither is better nor worse than the other. They are simply different programmes and each is dependent on the understanding which the audience brings to it for its ultimate worth.'[16]

Dorothy Hobson's work is a salutary reminder of the importance of what has generally been missing both from mass-communication theories and traditional forms of media education: a sensitive exploration of the concrete responses to the media of real audiences. It is this absence which has contributed to one of media education's greatest strategic weaknesses: its generally negative and pessimistic approaches to popular media forms and their presumed effects. As we have seen, traditionally within media education, when popular texts were considered at all, they generally attracted little more than dismissive value judgements. Even today really popular texts – the television programmes most enjoyed by many school pupils (*The A Team* or *Knight Rider*, for example) are less likely to be given serious consideration by media teachers than more respectable forms such as news or documentary. There are compelling reasons for this, of course. The study of news, for example, is, these days, not only an academically respectable pursuit in its own right, with a formidable research base and fairly clearly defined methods of investigation, it is also an area in which the teacher will have the support both of numerous well-produced teaching resources and the general cultural recognition that this is an important and worthwhile area for investigation.

Teaching *The A Team* or a popular text such as *Crossroads* is an entirely different matter. *How* different has rarely been fully acknowledged. Here there is little in the way of research, and there are few teaching materials. The teacher is largely on her own. Most important of all, however, is the danger that unless she prepares her ground carefully her work is very likely to be misinterpreted. Using popular, and less culturally prestigious texts, involves more than simply teaching. It involves apprising pupils, colleagues and parents of the course's objectives, and of what it is hoped to achieve. Failure to do this could have quite foreseeable consequences: parents scandalised by misleading reports from their children or colleagues jumping to hasty and ill-informed conclusions. Small wonder, then, that media teachers confine themselves, most of the time, to safer territory.

The arguments for giving due weight to popular texts remains compelling, however. And the most compelling argument surely is that a media education which is unable to operate upon material which pupils actually watch and read, or which cannot offer pupils any insights into their own media tastes and preferences is scarcely worthy of the name.

But what is to be done with popular texts once the teacher has grasped the nettle? I have already indicated a number of ways into the analysis of popular texts, but these will count for very little unless they are accompanied by the kind of respect for the pleasures and tastes of audiences which is exemplified in Hobson's work. Implicit in that work is a damning critique of dominant attitudes to popular cultural forms and their audiences. As media teachers we need to place far more emphasis than we ever have in the past upon the pleasures and satisfactions which texts produce in audiences, to foreground pleasure both as a tool which will enable us to understand the particularity of audience responses, and as a motivating mechanism within media education itself. As Roland Barthes observed, to be a critic one also needs to be a fan, and a media education which does not enlist the enthusiasm of its participants, which is not itself engaging, diverting and pleasurable, as well as instructive, is unlikely to be of much value.

We cannot, however, simply leave matters there. We need to engage with the ideological work of popular culture. In Dorothy Hobson's *Crossroads* study, 'the experiences of the 15 million people who watch it' remain largely unproblematised, as do the needs which are gratified by the show. To return to our earlier example, acknowledging the enjoyment which many children experience in watching *The A Team* ought not to preclude a critical examination of what those pleasures are (see Section 5 below for a more detailed discussion), nor an analysis of the values implicit in the show, nor an understanding of its narrative structure, rhetorical techniques or marketing strategies; nor ought it to prohibit asking whose interests are being served by the programme. Dorothy Hobson's research does take the media teacher a long way forward. But it is necessary to go still further.

*   *   *

Ironically, the most substantial and provocative recent work of all on audiences, that of the Canadian Marxist economist, Dallas Smythe, falls firmly within the kind of 'mass society' view of the media, whose limitations we have already touched upon. Smythe's work has profound implications for the development of media education, however, since it is the most detailed and fully articulated *dialectical* account of media audiences currently available. Since Smythe's work is little known amongst media educators in Britain, an outline of his principal arguments is necessary.

The central thesis of Smythe's major work, *Dependency Road*, is that the principal products of the commercial mass media in monopoly capitalism are not programmes, newspapers or magazines, but audiences or, more precisely, *audience power*. Historically the *mass* media were 'beckoned into existence' by their ability to create the commodity of audience power, which advertisers were willing to buy. Until the 1880s the principal product of the press was news and other non-advertising content. 'Since then, the ostensibly non-advertising content of the mass-media has been produced – not as the principal product – but as the lure or free lunch with which to create an audience whose power is sold by the mass media to the advertiser.'[17]

Smythe compares audience-power directly with labour-power, but there is a significant difference. The audience does not get paid for its work. It is the media owner who produces the audience-power who gets paid. Audiences do not sell their own labour, but the media operators do:

'Are there any precedents for this particular commodity? Yes, there is a precedent, but it is an ugly one which we thought had been eliminated. Of course I refer to slavery. The slave owner provides the free lunch for the slave. The slave works but does not sell his/her labour. But someone else does – the slave owner.'[18]

For Smythe, audience power consists of much more than the delivery of audiences with particular socio-economic or gender characteristics to the advertiser, and of much more than audience loyalty to particular brands. It includes the power of audiences *to market products to themselves*. So, Smythe calculated, Canadian television audiences spent, in 1976, five times the amount spent by advertisers 'for the privilege of working without pay as audience members' through the purchasing and operating of their television receivers. Similarly,

'The full-service grocery store of 1900 is long gone with its telephone-order-filling, charge accounts, sales persons showing customers the merchandise, and delivery service. In its stead we have customers waiting on themselves with a paucity of relevant information provided by the supermarket, then waiting in line at the cash register to pay cash and transport the groceries home by their own means.'[19]

The media market *us* – the audience – not simply on the basis of our size or particularity, but also on the basis of our competence, acquired at our own expense, in self-marketing.

The mass media, then, are termed by Smythe, Consciousness Industries, and their main product is *people* who are ready 'to buy consumer goods and to pay taxes and to work in their alienating jobs in order to continue buying tomorrow.'[20] But the media also produce other forms of consciousness: 'people who are ready to support a particular policy, rather than some other policy . . . or "supporting" one or another political candidate, or supporting Israel or the Arabs.'[21] Smythe extends his argument to include not only the commercial media but public service media organisations, such as the BBC. Importantly, Smythe assigns the media not to society's super-structure (where they are inevitably placed along with educational, cultural and other ideological institutions by other Marxist critics) but to its economic base, since they are engaged in demand management, an active form of production essential to the workings of the entire economic system.'[22] (See p. 22).

Clearly we have travelled a very long way from a view of the media as essentially providers of information, entertainment and education, in which advertising plays a subordinate role. And, after Smythe, it is difficult to see advertising as a form of philanthropy which simply brings down the price of newspapers to a level which everyone can afford, or provides 'independent' broadcasting free of charge. Nor is it possible to see audiences any longer as simply the final stage of the communication process, as unproblematic receivers of 'messages'. For if the principal objective of the media is to produce particular kinds of consciousness, then questions about audiences are going to be present as important determinants at every stage of media production, from conception to completion. (See Chapter Four.)

The major weakness of *Dependency Road*, as with all mass-society theories, is that impressive though its broad historical and conceptual canvas is, the materiality of specific audience responses, and specific oppositional production practices are either not considered at all, or are treated so dismissively as to be denigrated. Nothing, it is implied, can stand in the way of the great steamroller, Consciousness Industry, any more than it could stand in the way of Althusser's Ideological State Apparatuses. The effect of such arguments is profoundly conservative. For if the battle is already lost, what point is there in struggle? The pessimism induced by this position is profoundly disabling. If newspaper stories or television programmes are seen functionally as nothing more than advertisers' 'free lunches', then does their precise content matter? Are the struggles of those who work to fulfil the liberating potentialities of the media pointless? Is media education itself a futile activity, scarcely worthy of effort, given the power of the battalions massed against it?

Though Smythe posits a dialectical view of audiences, his conception of the media is curiously monolithic, his logic positivistic. Particular effects are attributable to single causes (audience power beckons the media into existence); the media have undifferentiated effects (Consciousness Industry produces 'mind slaves'[23]). Even when speaking of subordinate racial formations in North America (Blacks,

Puerto Ricans, etc.), Smythe takes their subjection to Consciousness Industry to be total:

'The principal contradiction within their consciousness is that between *their attachment to the total message of Consciousness Industry* . . . and their desire to take a larger measure of control over their own lives . . . '[24](my emphasis.)

Media teachers, working at the interface of media text and audience response, cannot dismiss them both so summarily. Each needs to be understood, dialectically, in terms of its inner contradictions and the process of its movement and development. Each, that is, needs to be recognised as a site for struggle within which teachers, broadcasters and students can play important roles. For the media do not produce undifferentiated and direct effects, as Smythe assumes. As we have seen, audiences work upon texts in complex and different ways, just as much as texts work upon audiences. Neither audiences nor texts pre-exist the complex and contradictory networks of social and economic relations out of which each is constructed. Nor do they pre-exist their interactions with one another.

Dependency Road nevertheless opens up some rich seams for the media teacher. Smythe's view that the media are primarily involved in producing and marketing people is a platitude to those working in the media or advertising industry, but it has been slow to dawn upon us as media teachers. Important breakthroughs in student consciousness are possible, however, when they are given the opportunity to inspect the kind of journals and materials, commonplace in the industry, which treat audiences unashamedly as commodities (see pp. 79ff and 112ff).

Smythe's analysis compels the media teacher to re-assess the significance within media processes not only of audiences, but also of *advertising and public relations*. Again, this has been a central theme of this book but no-one has done more than Smythe to demonstrate the ways in which the distinctions between advertising and non-advertising material in the media are becoming increasingly difficult to make. Advertisers are increasingly putting their energies into promotional techniques which are disguised as something else (one advertising agency has even gone to the lengths of using everyday small-talk as a cover for its promotional activities by bribing taxi-drivers to give unsolicited testimonials to passengers about the quality of a particular brand of cigarette), whilst advertisements now possess many of the qualities of non-advertising material by providing information and entertainment, and telling stories (see p. 183). It is Smythe's characteristic argument that television advertisements cost so much more, and are made with so much more care than the surrounding programme material that it is they which 'contain the *concentrated* entertaining and information qualities which are spread out more thinly in the non-advertising programme content.'[25]

Finally, Smythe's thesis should encourage media teachers and pupils to assess the extent to which media *content* has become subordinate to more imperative *ideological* or *commercial* considerations. I have argued elsewhere, for example, that in its coverage of the 1984–5 coal dispute, the BBC seemed less conscious of its obligation to report events *accurately* than of its broader social 'responsibilities', in times of political and social crisis, to report events from a perspective sympathetic to the established order – in this case, the police and the Coal Board.[26] But most media are primarily *commercial* organisations. As one journalist, Brian Whitaker, has expressed it, newspapers are 'factories producing a product... Anything that needs a lot of work to get it into printable form will be the first to be rejected Apart from that, whatever happens to fill a hole in a page will be shovelled in.'[27]

As we have seen (Chapter Four), newspapers rely on comparatively few sources for their news. But Whitaker argues that many, if not most, of the columns of the average local paper are filled with 'stories' from four regular and free sources: the police, the fire brigade, the local courts and council meetings, and cites no fewer than eight trivial stories all covering fires and all 'of no conceivable interest or importance to anybody' which appeared in the *Liverpool Echo* on the same night, e.g. '*Light Blaze:* Liverpool firemen dealt with a small fire which damaged a fluorescent light fitting in the Ear, Nose and Throat Hospital...'[28]

The proliferation of non-news stories which simply fill up the space between advertisements has been recently monitored by *The Guardian*, which came up with the following examples:

> A headline in the *Bishops Stortford Gazette*, *Liz Almost Flew In*, in which Liz Taylor was reported as being within 15 minutes of landing at local Stanstead Airport, but changed her mind. The story still made the front page.

> A report on the Westcliff-based *Standard Recorder* on the Westcliff Classic Boy George lookalike contest. There were no entries.[29]

The logic of a situation in which the audience is the real commodity being sold rather than 'news' is the development of free *Advertisers* which drop all pretence of being *newspapers*, make no distinction between news stories and advertising features, exist solely on advertising revenue generated by their circulations, and are un-burdened by any obligations to their readers. The rise of data-base companies selling particular kinds of audience (with a special interest in anything from stamp-collecting to media education) to companies who may be interested in reaching them, is another facet of the same phenomenon. As we shall see, however, there is no need to go along with Smythe in regarding such developments as being entirely negative. Anti-nuclear groups, for example, have used the available space in free Advertisers to put their case in a way not normally available to them in the press, whilst a small publishing initiative like Comedia – the publishers of this book – is made possible through the effective identification of small, segmented audiences.

3. Audience positioning

I have argued that the relationship between audience and text is a dialectical one and we have observed how, as audience members, we are ultimately responsible for making sense of media texts. The remainder of this chapter will examine some of the ways in which texts *attempt to make sense of us*, by offering us positions from which we are invited to see experience in particular ways. The question, 'How are we, as audience, positioned in and by this text?', may be asked of any television programme, film or newspaper and magazine article. What does this question mean? First of all, within the visual media we, as audience members, are compelled to occupy a particular *physical* position by virtue of the positioning of the camera. Identifying and being conscious of this physical position should quickly reveal that we are also being invited to occupy a *social* space. A *social* space is also opened up for us by the text's mode of address, its setting and its format. Finally, the physical and social spaces which we are invited to occupy are linked to *ideological* positions – 'natural' ways of looking at and making sense of experience. Some examples:

a) Television news

As the news opens we are addressed by a newsreader who looks directly at the camera and delivers 'the facts'. Each viewer is given the role of direct addressee. We cut to a filmed interview. Our position changes. We are no longer directly addressed, but eavesdrop, watch and judge. The different positions assure us that some aspects of experience must be accepted (facts), whilst others (opinions) require our judgement. The highly questionable distinction within journalism between fact and opinion is sewn into the ways in which we are positioned in relation to different aspects of experience.[30]

b) *Disney Time*[31]

Radio Times describes the New Year's Day, 1985 edition of *Disney Time* as

'Comedy, adventure and music in the traditional holiday visit to the world of Walt Disney films old and new.'

The programme consists of film extracts, introduced and linked by Paul Nicholas, who is 'helped' by his own small son in a set decked out as a living room. In re-assuring contrast to his rootless but charming Jack-the-lad role in the series, *Just Good Friends*, in which he actively subverts suburban family norms, Nicholas is established, and establishes us in a family role. *Disney Time* is transmitted on Bank Holidays at tea-time, when families are represented as being gathered together in front of the TV set. As adults we are positioned specifically as parents who are prepared to forego our own preferences and tastes in order to view a children's programme. In return we can bathe in the security of a united and wholly unproblematic family circle, whose warmth is sealed and delivered by our past, present and future consumption of Disney films. The programme posits this here-and-now holiday 'family' occasion as the *essence of familiality*,[32] establishing a trans-historical continuity with our own happy childhood memories by the use of extracts from old Disney 'classics', and activating our anticipation of happy family occasions to come, when we purchase our tickets for the most recent films previewed in the show. The variety of historical positions offered to us during the programme – its retrospective and prospective movements – serves only to deny history, to assure us that the family transcends it. Just as, in spite of the cultural specificity of the programme, our knowledge of the international consumption of Disney films and artefacts assures us that the family transcends mere national and cultural boundaries. Meanwhile, in real Britain, 55% of all households consist of one or two people.[33]

c) *The Boys from the Blackstuff*

Yosser's Story. A nightclub scene in which (unemployed) Yosser Hughes meets Liverpool soccer stars Graeme Souness and Sammy Lee. Sometimes we observe events from Yosser's viewpoint. *We* feel out of place and uneasy in the general surroundings of the night club, and in the presence of the stars. As Yosser gains in confidence, however, we see him from the perspective of the footballers: an intrusive 'wierdo', who makes others and us – uneasy. We can understand why the footballers are embarrassed and drift away from him. The camera does not allow us to take a comfortable and unified position. We are not spectators viewing from a position of omniscience, of superior knowledge. Rather, the physical fragmentation of our position encourages an understanding of some of the complexities of unemployment and an awareness of the contradictions implicit within our own attitudes towards it. We are implicated both in Yosser's position and in the social embarrassment which he causes. What is denied us is a simple unitary response to the situation.

d) The radio panel programme, Any Questions?

The chairperson, by his mode of address, makes little distinction between listeners at home and the live audience, apart from an introductory filling-in of the details of the programme's location and occasional explanatory references to things which the audience at home cannot see. We, to all intents and purposes, are *there*. The programme constitutes us as an extension of the live audience. But, as I have suggested in Chapter Five, we are also, less obviously, positioned by both the *location* of the microphones, and the *balance* of sound between different microphones. For the audience at home the words of panel members possess a volume and authority which those from the body of the hall lack, and an individual panel member can easily speak over disruptions from the audience.

Norman St. John Stevas, M.P.:
'We as a society have made a commitment to moving towards and creating equal opportunity for everyone (scarcely audible cry from a member of the audience). Well, you may say nonsense, but I have been in Parliament for 20 years and I have seen people's attitudes change (more inaudible comment from the audience) and I don't require you sir to say "Nonsense" to me when I was one of the 20 Conservative MPs who refused to vote against the Race Relations Act... I was one of those MPs who supported the minority who stood out against Mr Callaghan when he took away the passports of the Asians in East Africa. So I don't require lessons about nonsense from someone from this audience. I'm entitled to say what I have done; that we are a society that believes in the ideal of equal opportunity...

John Timpson (Chairperson):
'People at home would not have heard that cry anyway, Norman

St. John Stevas, but you passed it on for them.'
                                    (Any Questions? BBC Radio 4, 16.11.84)

Sound – however natural it may seem – is just as much the end product of innumerable selection and filtering processes, just as much a construction, as visual images are. As the above extract reveals even in a live radio programme, the sounds which reach the domestic audience are highly controlled, much more so than those which are available to the live audience. For although the same sound/ authority patterns will have been set up within the hall itself, natural sounds and interruptions will impinge on the live event with much greater force. It is a long Reithean tradition in the BBC, however, that some have a greater right to be heard than others. (One of Reith's earliest reprimands to radio stations directors in 1924 ran as follows: 'In some stations I see periodically men down to speak whose status, either professionally or socially, and whose qualifications to speak seem doubtful.')[34]

The manipulation of sound is one of the subtlest, and least discernible forms of social control exercised by the media. *Any Questions?* positions us as members of a culture in which the contradictions and disagreements which separate us can be contained within, and are ultimately less important than the circle of agreed values which binds us all together. Voices which challenge this notion are rarely allowed a hearing in programmes like *Any Questions?* But if, by chance, the conventional screening devices – the careful selection of the voices we are allowed to hear – fail, the sound engineers will come, unnoticed, to the rescue. Much of the ideological work of a programme like *Any Questions?*, therefore, is achieved through the concealment of no doubt small, but nevertheless significant, differences between the positions of its live and domestic audiences, and its assurance that the programme faithfully records the world in which we live, a world, not of irreconcilable interests, but of harmony and consensus.

e) *Family Fortunes*,[35]

like many other game shows, attempts to break down the distinction between spectators and participants. We are welcomed to the show by the expansive and inclusive gesture of the host. We meet the contestants (like us, members of the public) who are organised into their 'natural' unit of the family. Families in *Family Fortunes* are white, interesting, attractive, and employed. The show invites our complicity with these assumptions, and constitutes us, too, as competitive consumers, eager to play the game alongside the contestants and admire the prizes. The contestants themselves do not behave as though they were an integral part of the show. They reveal their status as outsiders and their affinity with the studio audience by applauding throughout the proceedings. Their identification is with us, just as ours is with them. We are all spectator-participants.

In the game itself, we are invited not to display our knowledge but to guess how members of the public have answered questions. Conformity, not originality, is rewarded. The winners are those who can think most like everyone else. Or, rather, who can think most like *us*, for through the medium of public opinion we are included in the show in another role, not only as spectators and participants, but as final arbiters. Against this authority, sealed via the mediation of a beneficent technology (Mr. Babbidge, the show's computer), there can be no appeal. It renders us all subordinate. But it is, nevertheless, an authority in which we can all share. In order to do so we need to constitute ourselves as individuals-in-the-mass, to define ourselves in terms of our common assumptions, as subordinate to the dominant ideology, and to divest ourselves of minority opinions and divergent views. Participation thus becomes the highroad to a discovery of the authority of consensual norms and enables us, as individuals, to attain an imaginary unity which mirrors the imaginary coherence of our society.

I have spoken, in relation to *Any Questions?*, of the 'circle of agreed values' which is endorsed by the programme. In *Family Fortunes*, as Neil Campbell has demonstrated,[36] the circle is a literal one. The set is arranged as a semi-circle, each family being placed static and controlled, on the outside of it. The families are linked by the host, who has the freedom customarily accorded to one in his position to move between families as well as into the 'sacred' space within the circle. As in most game shows, successful contestants in *Family Fortunes* move into a different space, in order to signal their graduation or successful initiation from an earlier phase of the game. Here, representatives of the successful family move into the centre of the circle in their attempt to win a big prize. Whereas in the first part of the show all of the camera shots define that dominant circle, a circle completed by the positioning of the cameras themselves, and hence by us, as viewing audience, in the second part of the show our visual attention is centred, and much more sharply focused, upon the contestants within the sacred space of the inner circle. As Campbell suggests, what is being offered to the contestants here is 'the extra prize of visual priority.'[37]

The circle is a continuing visual and metaphoric motif throughout the show. The host's first embracing gesture to the audience includes us within the circle of the show, whilst the idea of 'the family circle', running as a strong undercurrent throughout the programme, is made manifest when the families huddle together to 'confer' over an answer. Bob Monkhouse, a former host, used the catch-phrase 'Bob's your uncle', and generally played the role of beneficent and lascivious uncle throughout the show.

So, the programme works to enclose us all within a circle, a circle of family circles, in which there is competition without conflict and rivalry without antagonism. It is the perfect model of a consumer society, freed of its inherent contradictions, in which everyone benefits, including the 'losers'. As Campbell notes, it is important that we see 'good losers, smiling people who accept second place with grace', whilst the rhetorical question : 'Have you enjoyed your day?' suggests that through the generosity of the television company even losers have at least had a break from their humdrum existence by having participated in the show.'[38]

Family Fortunes positions us, then, as audience/participants in a world which is at once one of competition and rivalry for material rewards, and one of order, harmony, consensus and equilibrium. (It is revealing that in America and Australia the show is called *Family Feuds*, an indication, perhaps, that antagonistic competitive values can be more openly espoused in those countries.) The show works to incorporate us into that world both as participants and referees and through its dominant symbolism of enclosing circularity. It represses divergencies and differences to produce a manageable public, offering to us as audience a subjectivity and a world 'without contradiction, because it is without depth, a world wide open and wallowing in the evident, it establishes a blissful clarity: things appear to mean something by themselves.'[39]

Finally, a brief note on the *sexual politics of looking*, which has been the subject of a great deal of attention over the past few years.[40] It has been argued that the media place their audiences in a position of 'dominant specularity'. As members of the audience we are 'privileged voyeurs', who look upon the activities of others from a position of safety, security and superiority. We see but we cannot be seen. We comment, but we cannot be commented upon. Some films, most notably those of Alfred Hitchcock, exploit the moral ambiguity of the voyeuristic pleasures of the audience within the structure of the films themselves. As spectators we are frequently implicated in the guilt of the characters whom, and with whom, we watch. In *Rear Window*, for example, the main character is a photographer, immobilised with a broken leg, who looks out upon a nearby apartment block. As with most media texts, we identify with a male character, and are given a masculine perspective. Here we share the photographer's role as peeping Tom. There is a moment in the film where the villain suddenly realises that he is being watched. He looks out of his window and sees the watcher. It is a chilling moment. For we, in the audience, are the recipients of his look. The roles are reversed. We become at once defenceless, suffused with guilt, and divested of our power.

Most media texts are not so explicit and reflective about their voyeurism. Yet their audiences need to be. For power relations are always inscribed within the processes of looking and being looked at. In particular, the subordination of women is both exemplified and reinforced by their frequent media representation as objects of a controlling male gaze. Of course, not all members of the audience are men, and not all men in the audience are sexist, but whatever the audience, many texts stitch us into patriarchal sexist positions as 'natural' ways of perceiving reality. Media teaching which aims to be non-sexist and non-patriarchal will need, as a first step, to make explicit, and open up to questioning, such automatic ways of seeing.

But are not men subject to the gaze of the audience too? *Selling Pictures*,[41] a teaching pack produced by the British Film Institution, contains slides of a large number of magazine covers which demonstrate very well that whereas women are generally represented as passive, smiling and alluring, and tend to look directly and frequently provocatively at us, aware that they are the focus of our attention, men are most frequently represented as involved in some kind of activity, their gaze being directed elsewhere. Goffman has analysed similar and familiar gender-orientated non-communication patterns of domination and subordination in relation to advertising.[42] 'Looking', that most natural of activities, is rarely as innocent as it appears. Particular ways of looking, reflecting dominant power-relations within society, are pre-structured within media texts (though, as always, it needs to be emphasised that they may be resisted or negotiated by audiences) and in turn come to be regarded as part, not of the dominant, but of the natural order.

Conclusion

The examination of a small number of media texts reveals the range and complexity of the positions which they construct for their audiences. Once we grasp the richness and diversity of the possible interactions between texts and audiences, then we can begin to dispense with communication models which conceptualise audiences as unproblematic recipients of messages, or as users of the media for their own gratification. Bonney and Wilson summarise:

'Being a recipient of messages is only one among many positions constructed for, and occupied by, audiences in relation to texts. By favouring that one position and ignoring others, empiricist accounts of audiences as passive give a highly misleading picture of the complex of relations that exist between texts and their audiences. Similarly, uses and gratification theorists, though representing the audience as active, over-simplify audience-text relations, seeing audiences only as users of the media for gratification, not unlike users of drugs, and ignoring the array of different, sometimes compelling, sometimes confused or contradictory, positions constructed for audiences in and by texts...'[43]

4. Subjectivity

I have attempted to stress the radical break which an emphasis upon audience-text relations makes with traditional approaches to textual study in the classroom. I have argued, too, that the comparative neglect of audiences within media education has been influenced by its literary antecedents, within which readers have been regarded as largely unproblematic. For, what reason has there been to doubt that readers are autonomous individuals, possessing a free consciousness? Indeed, the idea that we are autonomous and coherent *subjects* – literally the subjects of the actions we describe in the sentences we utter: 'I walked into the room'; 'I believe in the market economy' – is the very assumption upon which our dominant aesthetic forms are based. 'Classic realism', as Catherine Belsey has suggested, 'tends to offer as the "obvious" basis of its intelligibility the assumption that character, unified and coherent, is the source of action. Subjectivity is a major – perhaps the major – theme of classic realism.'[44]

Even here, however, the notion of 'the subject' contains a central ambiguity. For whilst on the one hand it suggests that we are free and autonomous agents, who act under no compulsion, on the other it constitutes us as possessing a fixed identity, an unalterable human nature incapable of fundamentally transforming either ourselves or the world in which we live. This paradox is powerfully conservative. It constitutes the structures within which we live as timeless and inevitable, yet also as acceptable because unimposed. Louis Althusser has formulated most precisely this central ambiguity of the notion of the 'subject'.

'In the ordinary use of the term, subject in fact means (1) a free subjectivity, a centre of initiatives, author of and responsible for its actions; (2) a subjected being, who submits to a higher authority, and is therefore stripped of all freedom except that of freely accepting his submission.'[45]

The function of ideology, for Althusser, is to *interpellate* (or hail) individuals as subjects:

'Ideology "acts" or "functions" in such a way that it "recruits" subjects among the individuals (it recruits them all) or "transforms" the individuals into subjects (it transforms them all) by that very precise operation which I have called *interpellation* or hailing, and which can be imagined along the lines of the most commonplace everyday police (or other) hailing: "Hey, you there!" Assuming that the theoretical scene I have imagined takes place in the street, the hailed individual will turn round. By this mere 180 degrees physical conversion he becomes a *subject*. Why? Because he has recognised that the hail was "really" addressed to him, and that "it was *really him* who was hailed" (and not someone else).'[46]

For Althusser this process takes place in ideology, within which individuals are *always – already subjects*. Even before its birth, a child is 'expected'. It will be born into the specific family structure which awaits it, into specific gender-related practices of rearing and education and, crucially, as we have seen, into specific discourses and discursive practices.

The relevance of these processes of interpellation (through which we attain at once both our individuality and our subjection) to the functions of the media should now be clear. For we have already noted how the media exist, most importantly, to produce not entertainment or news but *us* – that is, particular forms of consciousness – by making available a range of positions from which we (as subjects) can understand the text and make it (and ourselves) intelligible.

The implications of all of this for classroom practice have not, on the whole, been given very much consideration. In general terms, we may say that in reading media texts, students will need to be alerted to the ways in which their own consciousness is at stake. They will need to examine the ways in which they are interpellated by the text, often through a direct mode of address (e.g., by a newsreader, a comedian or a newspaper columnist) but, more frequently, implicitly through being offered subject 'positions' which (in the case of film and television) are both physical and ideological. It has been one of the purposes of this chapter to give some indication of the considerable variety and complexity of these subject positions as they are offered to us by a handful of media texts.

5. Pleasure

'Pleasure', like 'ideology', 'rhetoric', 'representation', 'audience', etc., is not a concept which has had a great deal of purchase within dominant aesthetic criticism. Indeed, 'pleasure' has been treated with much suspicion, as a category belonging more properly to the sphere of autobiography than criticism. And it is a familiar difficulty in media education that, in discussing texts, students too easily lapse into the discussion of pleasure, making immediate value-judgements and taking positions which they then feel that they must defend. It is important, as I have suggested elsewhere, for students to *withhold* judgement in order to facilitate a thorough investigation of any media text.

In view of all this, why should we take pleasure seriously? There are a number of good reasons. First of all, media education has often been (and sometimes still continues to be) such a negative enterprise that a *celebratory* approach to the subject, one which emphasises its positive and pleasurable aspects, is long overdue. Secondly, just as the negativity of many approaches to media study has finally been a disincentive to both teachers and students alike, has failed, that is, to mobilise energies and enthusiasms in any kind of sustained way, so we might hope that a media education which is itself diverting and engaging, will encourage motivation for serious work by teachers and students alike. Thirdly, it is precisely because 'pleasure' is itself one of those largely unexamined, taken-for-granted categories through which we may suspect that a dominant ideology is 'naturalised', that we should begin with our students the difficult task of problematising our pleasures. We may not be hypocrites in our pleasures but, like everything else, they may be rather less innocent than they frequently appear to be.

As soon as a group begins to engage in a dialogue about the pleasures produced by a particular text (a dialogue which, for reasons I have indicated, might best be undertaken after a good deal of preliminary investigation of the text), then one thing becomes clear. Pleasure is a highly problematic category. It is not, of course, unitary. There are different kinds of pleasure, many of which are mutually exclusive. I remember a remarkably effective introduction which a Nottinghamshire media teacher, Mike Hamlin, gave to his students on Bill Douglas's films *My Ain Folk* and *My Childhood*:

'These films won't give you many of the pleasures which you might associate with Hollywood films. They are not in colour, there's not much action, nor a great deal of excitement. They're made in a different way too – you shouldn't expect a cut every few seconds in order to keep you watching. But if you give the films a chance, I think you might find them interesting and pleasurable in very different ways.'

Of course, as teachers we are all keen to initiate students into *our* pleasures. But if this is to be successful (or tolerable to students) it needs to be a two-way process. Students should have plenty of opportunities to share their pleasures with us and with each other. This is just one of the reasons why the content of media courses should always be negotiated with students. Our ideal in media education should be to seek not the destruction of pleasure but its expansion into new and different forms of enjoyment.

There are formidable obstacles to this ideal, however, which we cannot shirk. For the fact of the matter is that some pleasures cannot be shared. Some people may be disturbed, worried or offended by the very things which others find pleasurable. There may even be elements in a text which everyone enjoys but which, on reflection, seem to be harnessed to dubious or oppressive purposes. It may be, for example, through its pleasurable patterns of identification or its dramatic qualities, that a narrative seeks to enlist our sympathies for a cause, a character or an idea that we might repudiate given the time for more mature reflection. Or, very familiarly, it might be that humour in a sitcom or an individual joke is used for racist or sexist purposes. There is a difficulty for media teachers here. For it is they, rather than their students, who are most likely to raise such issues about programmes which their students are happy to enjoy at their face value. And at their face value, of course, television comedy shows or dramatic series do not generally profess to be making statements about race, women, trade unions, the working-class, etc. Nevertheless, attitudes to such issues and groups do emerge from these programmes, often quite strikingly, and even with some degree of consistency across programmes. Indeed, many values (frequently racist, sexist or reactionary, but sometimes subversive) of a kind which could not be respectably presented within 'serious' television, can find secure niches within 'harmlessly' escapist programmes.

The problem for media teachers is the old one: they may find themselves back again in a situation where they are attacking the pleasures of their students. How can this situation best be handled? One answer is unequivocal. Laura Mulvey has advocated, in her writing, the 'destruction of pleasure as a radical weapon ... It is said that analysing pleasure or beauty, destroys it. That is the intention of this article.'[47] As teachers we cannot be so dismissive of, or antagonistic towards, the pleasures of our students. Such a strategy would, anyway, almost certainly be counter-productive. It is enough, I think, to encourage students to problematise and reflect more deeply upon their pleasures, on how they are produced and of the ideological issues at stake in them.

One non-threatening way of doing this is to look at the possible *structural* connexions between dominant beliefs and dominant modes of pleasure production. Consider, for example, the close identification with white male protagonists encouraged by most media narratives, or the use of women as objects of the controlling male gaze throughout the media. What connexions exist between these things, and patriarchal power relations and the gross subordination of women within society as a whole? Or consider the relationship of Irish jokes to Irish politics. Do some jokes justify, encourage or prepare the ground for inhumanity and persecution which are far from funny? We all, teachers and students alike, need to own up to the possibility that our media pleasures, which are actively produced for us, may be instrumental in engineering consent for forms of domination and oppression to which we are opposed. These are serious issues, but a light pedagogic touch is necessary in handling them. Problematising these issues is, in my view, the best hope we have of promoting change. But it is unlikely to be immediate and it cannot be forced. Since the initiative is, in the last resort, firmly in the lap of the students themselves, the teacher's primary objective, perhaps, should be not so much to advocate a particular view, but to promote an atmosphere of trust in which mature and serious reflection upon these important issues can take place.

Chapter 8

Futures

Introduction

The present period represents, I think, a significant watershed in the history of Media Education in this country. Over the past 50 years the important questions facing those teachers with an interest in the media have been largely *epistemological*, an emphasis which this book has itself reflected, with its concern to establish the media as a viable area for study within schools, and media education as a coherent intellectual discipline in its own right, with its own characteristic concepts, practices and modes of enquiry. Over the next 20 years or so, however, much more attention will need to be paid to *strategic* questions, that is, to questions of legitimation, circulation and dissemination, as well as co-operation, co-ordination and interaction. This is not to assert that media educators now have most of the epistemological answers and no longer need to develop their subject, but it is to suggest that any radical developments within the field are more likely to emerge from an increasing awareness by media educators that media education is too important to be simply hived off into its own separate curriculum slot – vital though it is to establish and defend that slot. Media education, I would want to argue, should not be confined to the province of media teachers. We need to think of it as a specialist subject in its own right, certainly, but also as an element which will need to *inform the teaching of all subjects*. Perhaps most importantly of all, media education should be thought of as a *lifelong* process, within which many agencies, institutions and individuals will have important roles to play. This chapter will examine some of the ways in which more 'holistic' or 'ecological' approaches to media education – approaches which emphasise the importance of *partnership* between those agencies with a legitimate interest in the field, both inside and outside of the school, might begin. This will be considered under the two general headings of Media Education Across the Curriculum, and more general 'holistic' approaches to integrating different agencies into the field.

A. Media education across the curriculum

There are important reasons why media teachers should encourage the development of media education and media literacy skills in the teaching of all subjects:

1. Media materials are being increasingly used in a routine way in the teaching of all subjects, as more of their ostensible content finds its way on to videotape and film. It seems likely that the media will be used, as they have within schools in the past, predominantly as 'transparent' carriers of information, unless media teachers intervene. It is obviously of some importance that they should do so, if only because their own teaching is unlikely to be effective if it is being actively counteracted elsewhere in the school. One aspect of this issue is particularly relevant at the present time. Hit by severe financial cutbacks, many schools are finding it difficult to provide as wide a range of educational materials as they did in the past, and are beginning to rely, increasingly, upon glossily packaged and presented film, video and other materials produced by multi-national corporations, government departments and other well-financed institutions and agencies. It is a matter of some importance that such material should not be consumed innocently, but read critically. In particular, the basic media literacy technique of relating media messages to the political, social and economic interests of those who are producing them, needs to be encouraged as a matter of course by teachers of all subjects.[1]

2. Media Education across the curriculum needs to go beyond problematising media materials, however. For the media are constantly working over much of the manifest *content* of school subjects. Students do not turn up to our classes with blank minds ready to be filled with knowledge. Rather, they bring to every topic (as we all do) all kinds of prejudices, misconceptions, ideas, and stereotypes, many of which they have picked up from the media. Effective teaching will need to take this into account, and might well begin with a consideration of media representations of the topic at hand. Certainly teachers of all subjects will find it valuable to have an informed interest in, and up-to-date knowledge of media treatment of the topics they cover.

3. Apart from the content of different subject areas, the media frequently make statements about the *nature of academic disciplines themselves*. As we shall see, any science or history

teacher who wishes her students to challenge the notion of her subject as a largely undisputed body of ideas, theories and facts, will need to counteract the messages about her subject disseminated by news programmes, drama series, and even advertisements. The issues raised here in a vestigial form are already firmly on the agenda of many subject specialists, and there are both a growing body of literature and examples of institutional practice which point to highly practical ways in which links between media educators and other subject specialists may be forged. The hard lessons of the general failure of Language Across the Curriculum policies need to be learned, however. In particular, the enterprise is unlikely to succeed if it is seen by subject departments as a form of territorial encroach-ment. It is enough, perhaps, to begin by opening the channels of communication and initiating dialogue with subject specialists so that they may assess for themselves the relevance to their own subjects of critical media reading skills. Some of the most interesting work already undertaken in a number of curriculum areas, as well as possibilities for future development, may be briefly summarised.

Geography

To argue for the importance of media literacy in the study of geography may seem, in one sense, perverse. For if one of media education's fundamental aims is to reveal the constructed nature of the seemingly spontaneous and natural, then geography's domain *is* 'the natural' – the landscapes and environment in which men and women live and work. There are, however, three compelling reasons why media literacy should be high on the list of teacher objectives in any geography course.

First of all, geography is a subject in which visual images have a particularly prominent place. It is, *par excellence*, the subject of mediated, second-hand experiences, dealing primarily with regions of the country or of the world which cannot be brought directly into the classroom. Hence, the use of visual images which, in the words of one geographer, 'offer a short cut to the understanding of ideas or features that would otherwise require lengthy explanation' and 'evoke powerful and long-lasting images of what places are like.'[2] At this level the kind of questions raised in this book on sources, selection, captioning, agenda-setting, etc., are eminently applicable to the analyses of photographs and films which are all too often handled transparently by the geography teacher. One of the most imaginative degree courses in geography taught in Britain (at Oxford

Polytechnic), for example, has as its first objective that 'students should be able to apply to a film a similar level of critical evaluation that they would expect to apply to a book.'[3] Jenkins and Youngs, who devised the course, constructed a pre-course investigation which revealed the limited extent to which even quite sophisticated students were aware of the issues at stake in the course. Students were asked to write down words and ideas which they associated with the phrase 'Documentary Film'.

'Students' responses indicated a strong view that documentary films were "objective" and had a factual commentary. A later question asked: "With reference to any documentary film you have seen, indicate how certain film techniques were used by those who produced the film to convey meaning to the audience." Overall, the students' response to this question indicated a very superficial awareness of these issues... '[4]

In an honest and by no means entirely favourable evaluation of their course, Jenkins and Youngs nevertheless note that it was rated very highly by students for interest, and that at the end of it students were well able to analyse film and television critically. One student commented: 'It's changed the way I not only look at television and film, but also the way I read books and articles...' Further, students also perceived a strong connection between visual literacy and geography as a discipline, and were able to move from the study of film and television to an understanding of the selective nature of geographic *writing* and analysis.[5]

The kind of questions raised by media educators go beyond problematising geographical *materials*, however. They reach to the very *substance* of the subject. It is not just that films and photographs of rural or urban landscapes are inevitably selective and contain a point of view. For, from our knowledge of audiences, we know that the very landscape itself, when we look at it, will mirror our values. What we see will be systematically related to broader philosophic ideas and ideologies. Here is the American geographer, D. W. Meinig:

'Take a small but varied company to any convenient viewing place overlooking some portion of city and countryside and have each, in turn, describe the "landscape" (that "stretch of country as seen from a single point", as the dictionary defines it), to detail what it is composed of and say something about the "meaning" of what can be seen. It will soon be apparent that even though we gather together and look in the same direction at the same instant, we will not – we cannot – see the same landscape. We may certainly agree that we will see many of the same elements – houses, roads, trees, hills – in terms of such denotations as number, form, dimension, and colour, but such facts take on meaning only through association; they must be fitted together according to some coherent body of ideas. Thus we confront the central problem: any landscape is composed not only of what lies before our eyes but what lies within our heads.'[6]

Meinig enumerates 'ten versions of the same scene', ten organising ideas which are frequently used to make sense of landscapes, e.g., Landscape as Nature (Romanticism); Landscape as Habitat (Environmentalism); Landscape as Artefact (Technocracy); Landscape as Wealth (Capitalism), etc. Landscapes are not simply 'given'. They carry meanings for us which have been actively *produced* in ways in which students and teachers alike need to understand.

And here the argument turns full circle. For some of the most potent sources of our ideas about our environment are the media. Different environments and geographical regions are, indeed, so thoroughly worked over by the media, in images so familiar and natural to us that geography teachers need to acknowledge that whenever they teach about a particular region or country they are competing with images, often fragmented, but sometimes remarkably coherent, which already exist inside the heads of their students. Indeed, research by Virginia Nightingale has shown that television was as likely to be cited by school children as a source of information about other countries as parents or school.[7] 'In relation to particular important countries (the USA and USSR) it was cited almost exclusively.'[8] Further, 'the reality of the TV world was believed to be a true representation of the USA,'[9] a staggering thought when one realises that this 'reality' is often that of *Charlie's Angels* or *Starsky and Hutch*. Nightingale noted that

'Television's information about other countries was as likely to be embedded in entertainment formats as in news/documentary ones. Entertainment experiences noticeably fostered a sense of familiarity, sympathy and excitement with the USA. Entertainment genres (War and Spy films) perpetuated distrust and dislike towards Germany and the USSR, and reinforced the more critical and political news perspectives about them ... Predictably, *television news* provided the children with information about a larger number of countries than entertainment formats. Most such information was consciously articulated as "bad news" – disasters, earthquakes, fighting. It provided another distinguishing criterion between countries: the Safe and the Unsafe. Preoccupation with making judgements about safety and danger once again eclipsed the potential for political and social understanding of the current affairs of the countries discussed (Iran, Afghanistan, Kampuchea, Zimbabwe and Uganda).'[10]

Clearly there are exciting potentialities here for the study within geography of what have been characterised as 'image regions'. Image regions, according to Youngs, 'constitute often popular and non-rationalised images of, for example, climate, social systems, terrain, social attitudes and mores. They are the naive images that we rely on to explain things rapidly to ourselves.'[11] J. W. Watson has written on 'the role of illusion' and 'image geography' in his study of the geography of North America,[12] and Youngs in an extended case-study has considered the American Ante-Bellum South as 'a state of mind' rather than 'a condition of land'.[13] Youngs considers the influence of the Waverley novels of Sir Walter Scott, the work of Harriet Beecher Stowe, the novel and film of Margaret Mitchell's *Gone With the Wind*, as well as more recent romantic fiction in establishing the south as:

'the remote and romantic world of [the] plantation... gallant and debonaire young men ride home... to find waiting for them supernaturally beautiful heroines in farthingales. The flirtations and courtships, the duels and dances, which fill the idle days of these charming men and women seem always to be set against a scene of manorial splendour dominated by a mansion with a glistening white portico overlooking green lawns sloping down to a placid river. In the cottonfields the darkies, too numerous to be counted, sing contentedly at their work.'[14]

Youngs compares these images with the actuality of the ante-bellum South in which the leading crop was corn, not cotton, smallholdings were far more numerous than plantations, 75% of whites did not own slaves, southern hospitality was 'much over-rated', a typical planter's house was 'just a box'[15] and the planters themselves not aristocrats but farmer labourers and small farmers. Clearly there is scope here for similar work in schools, in which media images are compared with geographical realities. How do the images of Dallas in *Dallas*, Denver in *Dynasty* or Miami in *Miami Vice* compare with the socio-economic realities of those cities?

More generalised images of urban and rural environments frequently appear in television advertisements, soap-operas, films, coffee-table books, posters and other media. Often functioning as 'natural' backdrops to their ostensible subjects, such images crystallise enormously powerful ideological values. The country here is generally a place to be consumed, admired, visited and idealised, an object of affectionate nostalgia and the repository of innocent pastoral values, quaint customs, traditional crafts, and an essentially British stability and order. Schlesinger, Murdock and Elliott have noted a characteristic use of landscape in dramatic series dealing with 'terrorism', such as *The Professionals*. Terrorists are generally stereotyped as 'foreigners' and

'often played off against idealised images of "Englishness". Landscape is particularly important here. In a number of the programmes we looked at, terrorists were shown disrupting quintessentially English settings such as vicarages in rolling parklands, the Kent orchard country, and elegant eighteenth century buildings and squares.'[16]

As we have seen, media education involves the study of structured absences, and what are persistently absent from rural iconography are problems of rural poverty, exploitation, unemployment and poor communications. As Howard Newby has suggested,[17] mythical beliefs about the splendidly bucolic life of agricultural workers have greatly damaged their chances of improvements in wages, and working and living conditions.

In a perceptive case-study of six films on the *Regions of Britain* distributed by Shell UK[18] – the kind of material frequently used by teachers of geography – Youngs and Jenkins have demonstrated how the films present precisely this kind of idealised, unproblematic and distorted view of the British countryside.[19] The films are essentially travelogues of picturesque areas such as the *Cotswolds*, the *Peak District*, and the *North-West Highlands*. They are available free of charge and are almost certainly used principally as 'transparent' sources of information by those who show them. Indeed, I can remember being given memory tests on very similar films to these in my own school days.

As we have seen, one of the cornerstones of media literacy lies in the ability to relate media content to the interests of the sources who produce it. And here, that most basic question of all – who is producing this material and for what purposes? – is the key to unlocking the ideological significance of the films. Why *should* Shell UK make films about the British countryside? Simply raising that question leads, in my experience, to very productive thinking by students, along a number of inter-related lines. The first is the recognition that Shell UK's corporate image is inextricably bound up with the British countryside, and students will be able to cite many manifestations (maps, *County Guides*, advertisements, etc.) of this corporate strategy. The second is that the image of the countryside which is appropriated by Shell has remarkable similarities with that disseminated by manufacturers of brown bread, cheese, pickle and other 'traditional' factory foods. It is an image which is mythic, Arcadian, and entirely mystificatory. Yet there is an important distinction to be made between Shell's links with the countryside, and those of other products. For, in the case of Shell, the product is conspicuous by its absence. It is simply Shell's *name* which we associate with ruralism.

A moment's thought will reveal why this is the case. Attention to what Shell actually *produces* immediately blows the myth apart. For students do not need to be told that oil companies are actually pollutors of the environment on an international scale. Nor do they need reminding that Shell is a trans-national corporation which owes no allegiance to a particular country. Its loyalties are to its shareholders and it will move its interests to wherever profits are greatest, with little concern for the mutilated communities and landscapes which it leaves behind.

Shell films, like all other 'educational' materials produced by corporate interests or arms of the state, should be read as advertisements. Youngs and Jenkins's systematic analysis of the *Regions of Britain* films has much in common with the kind of approach to media texts suggested in this book. They also suggest a number of practical activities which demonstrate just how much the kind of exercises used by media teachers are relevant to progressive geography teaching. Geography departments, for example, are frequently the richest repositories of visual material in the entire school, and Youngs and Jenkins, whilst drawing attention to the existence of materials like *Teachers' Protest*, also suggest that geography teachers 'use those old field-trip slides. Get pupils to use the same slides to tell different stories.'[20] They have also devised a simulation in which groups of pupils are required to produce storyboards, scripts or film treatments about an area such as The Peak District from different points of view (e.g., as Agricultural Workers, representatives of The English Tourist Board, a group of local teenagers, a trans-national corporation, The Forestry Commission, etc.).

It should also be noted that both the images and texts of geographical text-books themselves frequently perpetuate the kind of myths which a functional media literacy would need to challenge, particularly in their Eurocentric and all too frequently racist depiction of developing countries. Three major studies in the mid-1970s of images of Africa, Asia and the Middle-East in American text-books[21] revealed the disturbing but probably unsurprising facts that most text-books perpetuated stereotypes, were badly researched, made moral judgements under the guise of providing factual information, assumed economic and technological change was always good, and failed to convey other societies as they feel from the inside. A recent study by Hicks has confirmed the truth of these findings for British text-books. Hicks argues that the nature of 'Third World' images in text-books can only be understood in the light of our imperialist past, a past with which geography has been indissolubly linked as a discipline:

'... explorers such as Stanley noted the link between geography and the role of the British Empire. Climate was seen as an important factor in explaining racial inferiority, and determinism firmly underpinned imperialist attitudes.'[22]

Hicks summarises the principal ethnocentric and racist assumptions about the 'Third World' in British geography text-books thus:

'1. Poverty is due to inbuilt obstacles and/or chance.

2. Do the right things and "take-off" to development occurs.

3. There are too many hungry people in the [third] world.

4. Peasant farmers need education and everyone needs help.

5. Colonialism didn't happen, except for the benefits.

6. Minorities don't exist, or need our help in coping.'[23]

Hicks notes those questions about the 'Third World' which are not discussed – what we have called the texts' 'structured absences':

'Are people poor because there are too many of them or are there many because there is widespread poverty?... Should we be examining questions of "wealth control" as well as birth control?... Why are there no text-books that deal with the role of the multinational agribusiness corporations in world food politics? Why is it only the poor that go hungry?... What about Aboriginal land rights and multinational mining companies? Living conditions on tea plantations? Life in Soweto? Why are such struggles conveniently ignored?'[24]

One reason is that other images are simply more easily available. In a small-scale study of geography text-books written for the 16+ age-group, David Wright demonstrated that 84% of the photographs depicting South Africa were provided by the South African Government Information Service and allied bodies:

'In every book the pictures of South Africa consisted of five elements:

1. magnificent scenery (e.g., Table Mountain; Drakensberg; rugged coastline; flowers in Karoo);

2. impressive skyscrapers (e.g., Johannesburg; Cape Town; Durban);

3. huge mines (e.g., Rand goldmines; Kimberley diamonds);

4. prosperous farmland (e.g., Cape vineyards; Natal sugar; Veld sheep);

5. picturesquely dressed Africans by their kraals (e.g., Eastern Cape; Natal).

The picture is almost entirely "rose-tinted", and it is virtually identical to the image of South Africa promoted by the South African Tourist Corporation.'[25]

Absent from the images were any depictions of the life and livelihood of the great majority of South Africans, of the townships in which they live or the apartheid under which they suffer. Wright concludes that the blame for the prevalence of a rose-tinted view of South Africa does not lie only with the South African Government, but also with the authors and publishers of text-books who disseminate and perpetuate such partial images so uncritically.

More recently Wright has pointed to the sexism of many geographical images. In half of the text-books analysed the ratio of photographs of men to photographs of women was 5:1. And, of course, girls will find little to aspire to in these images:

'There is an almost total lack of photographs of girls and women showing any individual initiative or doing a job that involves skill, training or intelligence.'[26]

It is evident in all of these cases that a functional media literacy could be invaluable in raising important questions about the taken-for-granted visual illustrations which are used in all classrooms, and in encouraging teachers and students to treat school books and images not as transparent carriers of knowledge, but as culturally loaded texts which need to be actively deconstructed and critically read.

Finally, it should be noted that mainstream broadcasting does occasionally carry major series which are of direct interest to geographers. Two notable recent examples are Yorkshire TV's series on China, *The Heart of the Dragon*, and David Attenborough's 12-programme series, *The Living Planet*. An excellent booklet accompanying *The Heart of the Dragon*[27] has been produced for Yorkshire TV by Alan Jenkins, raising questions of visual representation and selection in the programmes, and suggesting a wide range of photoplay and simulation exercises. *The Living Planet*, which attracted an average of over ten million viewers for each episode, has already been used by some teachers in their geography courses.[28] An interview with Attenborough on the series was carried out by two geographers, Jacquelin Burgess and David Unwin, for the *Journal of Geography in Higher Education*.[29] Fascinatingly, the issues raised by the interview parallel in a remarkable way some of the key questions explored in this book: the determinants of the series; the narrative format; audience pleasure; programme economics; 'setting up' situations and 'cheating'; the use of music, and the distortion and manufacture of sound. It is becoming very clear that questions of representation have as important a role to play in the development of a critical geographical education as they have in relation to the specialist study of the media themselves.

Science

'I have taken three sciences to "O" level (i.e., 16 years old) and at no time have the workings of the car, radio, TV, vacuum cleaner, tape-recorder or fridge ever been explained to me ... Nor, during any of my science lessons, have I heard anything about the moon landings or the exploration of the universe. The food crisis, the population explosion and the complete field of agriculture have all gone completely unmentioned ... The great success of the TV science documentaries and the increasing membership of many amateur scientific societies suggests an opposite trend to that seen in the school laboratory. It's not unusual to find kids discussing with animation last night's *Horizon* during school break and then disrupting their physics lesson with equal enthusiasm ... '

(Extracts from an essay by a British Schoolboy)[30]

'Science' is the site of a number of important ideological conflicts. Since the subject was first introduced into schools there have been those who have argued for a 'science of everyday life' in which the aim of the teacher should be 'to make children observant and reflective; to make them think and reason about the objects around them.'[31] Others have argued that science should be 'a training of the mind to rival the classics ... to work towards a higher level relating abstract thought and observation ... The child therefore had to learn scientific language and did not use that of the home. The theory was that the skills of observation and reasoning would transfer from the discipline to any other context.'[32] As a generalisation, one might say that the 'science of everyday life' approach has informed most science teaching in the early years of schooling, especially through its integration into environmental education. As science begins to be taught as a discipline in its own right, however, there is an increasing tendency to regard it as a specialist 'discipline of the mind'. Hence the paradox noted at the beginning of this section by the school student. For the remoteness of much school science from the realities of the students' own environment is thrown into sharp relief by the popularity of scientific subjects and issues within popular culture. Apart from the whole genre of science-fiction, there are constant references to science and technology in newspapers, films, magazines and novels. Television, in both news and entertainment programmes, constantly packages scientific issues and information in 'the language of the home' to make them more generally accessible. There is at least a case for arguing that some of this material might profitably be integrated into the school science curriculum. This could both encourage student motivation and point up the relevance of school science by drawing connexions between scientific issues raised by the media, and the scientific principles underlying them, which are the province of the school. Indeed, in a recent study, Neil Ryder has shown how a short television news story of the emergency at the Three Mile Island Nuclear Reactor could be used very constructively with school students in precisely this way.[33]

Yet it is necessary to go much further. For it is of little value if the media, in providing material for a socially relevant science curriculum, are assumed to be simple purveyors of experience. This 'experience' itself needs to be subjected to critical analysis, both as science *and* as media. What will this involve?

First of all, I think, an awareness of the competing and conflicting aims, objectives and philosophies available within science. As with other subjects in schools, science is too often presented as an undisputed body of ideas, observations, theories and facts. As Karl Popper suggested many years ago:

'A young scientist who hopes to make discoveries is badly advised if his teacher tells him, "Go round and observe," and he is well advised if his teacher tells him: "Try to learn what people are discussing nowadays in science. Find out where difficulties arise and take an interest in disagreements."'[34]

A major area of disagreement lies in the central purposes and functions of science itself. Is science objective and impartial? Is it ideologically loaded? Is it based on facts and proven theories? Is it linked inextricably with progress? Is it politically neutral? Has it been deflected from its true purposes by the state and dominant economic interests? As Gardner and Young have suggested:

'Television could play an important role in the critical evaluation of the issues raised by science. This means opening up the process of origination of new knowledge and scrutinising the goals and purposes built in to research areas, machines, products and procedures. Science and technology (literally) embody choices and priorities selected from the manifold ways of ordering and using natural processes. In that sense, agenda-setting and research policy determine what knowledge and priorities will be pursued. Television is extremely important in this process since it has become the principal agenda-setting medium in our society as far as the general public is concerned.'[35]

The appeal here is to television producers to open up the medium to these issues, and to move away from what Gardner and Young consider to be a dangerously one-dimensional view of science as it is currently presented by television. But their appeal applies equally powerfully to teachers, particularly, though not of course exclusively, when they use popular television material. As to the dominant representational codes in television science programmes, Gardner and Young have commented perceptively:

'The usual mode of presentation of a topic in science is narrative, linear, expository and didactic. The course of the programme alternates between voice-over and "talking head". A talking head is television's way of saying "this is brought directly to you without distortion or mediation." In the case of science programmes this form of presentation is usually reinforced by racks of test tubes or an impressive piece of apparatus directly behind the talking head, a white lab coat or other apparel, and the knowledge that we are being addressed by "the top man [sic] in the field" or the "rising star". The talking head is either directly addressing the camera or speaking across camera to an unseen interviewer whose questions have been edited out. This is in striking contrast with interviews on programmes where it is accepted that the issue is controversial and open, to some minimal degree at least, to public scrutiny, doubt, debate, etc. . . . In those programmes we see and hear the interviewer and cut back and forth from interviewer to various protagonists, speaking directly to one another, being challenged and arguing on camera. When scientists disagree on television, one talking head is followed by another, and they are almost never in direct conversation, much less in debate. Similarly, the telling of the story does not convey direct conflict but rather the solving of a mystery, the fitting together of pieces of a puzzle. Stark disagreement is an interruption in the plot line. Science and its telling are synonymous with progress and convey a sense of authority and the advancing edge of objectivity. By these devices and conventions, among others, a special status for scientific knowledge is assured. It is positivist in that it privileges scientific knowledge above other forms of inquiry and in that it separates facts from their contexts of meaning and represents them as above the battle of competing interest groups and classes.

When voice-over is employed, the characteristic tone is moderate, assured, reasoned. It is appropriate to a "community" which is presented as neutral, objective, normally harmonious, disinterested and working for the good of humankind. Humour, irony, paradox and rhetorical questioning are rare, as are invitations to the viewer to dissent, criticise or respond.'[36]

Television programmes about science which are introduced into the classroom, then, need to be 'read' both as science and as media, both as content and as representation. We do not necessarily have to assent to Gardner and Young's particular interpretation to agree that neither content nor representation can be neutral. They express particular ideological orientations, and exclude others. Finally, it should be added that the creative use of video and audio media by children to *present* ideas and areas of controversy within science has been developed by a number of science teachers. Directed at an audience of younger children or members of the public, this kind of work offers an imaginative alternative to the presentation of scientific data in written form, and can encourage students to develop alternatives to the media's dominant paradigms for presenting science.

English

Teachers of English have had a long-standing interest in Media Education, and I have already attempted to chart in some detail (Chapter Three) the shifting relationships which have existed between English teaching and the media over the past 50 years. Generalising from this history one can say that English teachers have not, on the whole, been conspicuously successful in developing approaches which have led to a greater understanding of the media in their own right. Rather, the media have been seen, first as *threats* to language and literature through their debasement of cultural standards, and then as *ersatz forms* of literature which could be conceptualised, evaluated, and often simply dismissed, through the application of categories and values having their roots in literature. All of this work functioned in what looked like elitist ways to assert the primacy and authority of high-culture media texts, and ultimately of literature itself.

Media education, when undertaken by English teachers, tended to be a largely evaluative and negative undertaking for which neither teachers nor students showed any sustained appetite. It led to the importation into the study of the media of a whole range of categories and concepts derived from the study of literature: discrimination, authorship, character, value; and placed into sharp relief literary criticism's lacunae (ideology, economics, audience, politics, culture, history). In their exclusive concentration on media texts, English teachers fatally neglected the contexts within which those texts were produced, distributed and consumed. They were able to give little account of the media as consciousness industries. One of the important consequences of the historical failure of 'English' to provide any adequate conceptual basis for making sense of the media was to place many English teachers outside of the most progressive developments taking place within the field from the early 1970s onwards.

Not that this was how it appeared to them at the time. For what looked like the increasing colonisation of media study by social scientists frequently seemed to bring with it little more than an increase in impenetrable jargon, and a regrettable absence of close textual reading. But this response was to underplay both the extent to which the most important work in developing critical approaches to the study of the media was *inter-disciplinary*, and the important contributions made by many with backgrounds in literary studies to this endeavour. On the whole, most progress was made by those who regarded the media as being too important to be recuperable to this or that subject area, who had the confidence to stand outside of their own discipline, assess its strengths and weaknesses, and recognise the powerful contributions which could be made to an understanding of the media by other specialisms. Within English this has produced, since around 1980, an interesting reversal. For whilst any further moves to recuperate media study to an English whose eternal verities remain largely unquestioned would have little credibility, literature itself is becoming increasingly seen as simply one signifying practice amongst many, and as amenable to the kind of critical approaches outlined in this book as any other symbolic form.[37]

So the re-birth of interest in the media by (particularly younger) English teachers has been a very different phenomenon from its predecessors. Far from the field being regarded as one in which modern media are put firmly in their place by the mature and confident judgements of those educated in an older and far wider tradition, media studies is increasingly being seen by many English teachers as providing a long-awaited injection of critical and radical thinking into a field in which the liberal-humanist tradition has long since ceased to have either energy or much in the way of intellectual credibility.

The role which English teachers can play within media education, then, is an important one. They can restore to the discipline a much needed experience and facility in textual analysis, though, to be sure, this will be, in certain crucial respects, a very different kind of activity from their normal stock-in-trade. They will need to *unlearn*, that is, many of their most cherished assumptions and approaches, and unload a great deal of the critical baggage acquired during their literary training. They will also need, as I have suggested, to step outside of their own discipline and explore the contributions which other subject areas have made to media studies. Above all, they must regard the media as significant and important areas of study in their own right, and worthy of serious consideration on their own terms, rather than as subordinate to and recuperable by English. If they can achieve this and, in addition, restore to the discipline a clarity of language and thought which has too frequently eluded it in the past decade, then English teachers will have an important and honourable role to play in the future of media education.

History

We are now fast approaching the time when skills in 'reading the media' will be part of the established repertoire of all students and teachers of history. For the most detailed and evocative evidence is becoming increasingly available to historians through the media of photography, film, newspapers, radio and television. These media lend themselves to imaginative use in the classroom. One teacher, Robert Unwin, has suggested problem-solving approaches to the use of comics and photographs, asking pupils to crop photographs in order to present different points-of-view, or to place a selection of photographs of the same person in the correct historical sequence. He has also applied this kind of approach to much neglected earlier visual forms, such as tapestries, engravings and portraits.[38] Apart from their importance as *sources* of historical material, however, the media can also function as *modes of presentation* within the teaching of history, through the imaginative use of newspaper, radio and television simulations in the reporting and assessment of historical events and evidence.

The general theoretical framework for studying the media which has been described in this book may be applied, quite appropriately, to historical evidence carried by the media. Indeed, in its questioning of the general status of visual evidence, and its foregrounding of questions of determinants, ideology, sources, rhetoric and audience, it may even provide a rather sharper focus to the study of historical documents than is normally found in most schools and colleges. The important question of the precise validity or 'truth' of visual evidence (see Chapter Five) will be of particular significance to the historian, and in that respect future historians (and history teachers) will need to acquire highly developed media literacy skills.

But if media evidence is conceptualised as a construction, doesn't this compromise the validity of television, film and newspapers as historical evidence? Not at all. It should, rather, sharpen awareness of the selective and partial nature of *all* historical documentation. And it should show the door to any transcendental notion of historical 'truth'. The increasing importance of media evidence in history teaching, that is, should ensure our understanding that historical 'truth' is not unitary or one-dimensional, and that we must settle for, at best, honest representations, and for most of the time, simply representations which will need to be interpreted in relation to the interests of their sources. And, of course, it should be stressed that media representations can often provide unique evidence of lesser 'truths' about atmosphere and mood, and can provide the kind of personal and particular detail which is beyond the scope of other forms of documentation. John F. Kennedy spoke of television

'giving people a chance to look at their candidate close-up and close to the bone. For the first time since the Greek city-states practised their form of democracy, it brings us within reach of that ideal where every voter has the chance to measure the candidate himself.'[39]

That same privilege is now vouchsafed to the historian and the widespread availability of media evidence does mark a significant step forward in our attempts to understand the past. It brings in its wake, of course, such phenomena as the manufacture and polishing of political personalities and information *for* the media, and the convergence of politics and advertising. The distinction between highly managed and manipulated 'official' information, and the views and perspectives of ordinary citizens which generally remain hidden from history, is an especially important one for the history teacher who wishes to use media sources. For the media have frequently been censored and appropriated by governments for their own purposes during times of crisis. And those are precisely the times in which historians tend to have a special interest. 'The first casualty when war comes is truth' as Senator Hiram Johnson put it, famously, in 1917,[40] and studying the media at such times may be to engage in nothing more than the study of lies, distortions and propaganda. It is within this context that the availability (through the recent proliferation of mass-produced cameras) of photographs, home movies, and amateur films can have a special value to the historian. For this kind of material, in spite of its technical limitations, can have far greater veracity than any amount of official footage. It can provide an alternative, personal and experiential dimension to the great events of the day and assure students that, however unambiguously official history often seems to present its accounts, there are always other views. It is evident that the potentialities and problems of handling media evidence will require the development of quite new skills of interpretation by the historian, and it is important that these should be defined and introduced into school systems as a matter of some urgency.

It should be stressed that this kind of work can take place just as effectively with primary school pupils as with pre-university students. Fines and Verrier, for example, have provided detailed accounts of work in which younger children have produced and assessed documentation upon events written from different perspectives. Here are some of the activities of the historian which children were expected to undertake:

1. recognise that contemporaries are likely to have held different views about a personality, group of event(s) in history than might people examining them today;

2. recognise clearly the standpoint and attitudes of an observer;

3. reconstruct the situation in which the observation was made;

4. evaluate the reported observation on the bases of the motivation and the purpose of the report;

5. search out all available evidence;

6. process similar evidence in like fashion;

7. distinguish clearly between different points of view in the evidences;

8. compare evidences to see whether they confirm one another;

9. steadily build up a picture of the subject that is both coherent and credible in the light of the evidence;

10. produce a convincing and satisfying account which is as fair as possible to all the sources.[41]

Many of these activities have clear parallels with the objectives of a media literacy programme, and the kind of activities which I have suggested in this book are simply logical extensions into media evidence of some of the most promising and innovative approaches developed within history teaching over the past decade.

History teachers might also wish to consider what kind of critical purchase students might gain upon the constant stream of words and images from and about the past presented by the media. Hollywood films, television costume dramas, nostalgic advertisements and historical documentaries are just a few of the wide range of sources of historical images presented by the media. The first step might be for students to recognise that such images represent a *use* of the past for today's purposes. The focus of attention, that is, should not be exclusively upon the past, upon, say, the accuracy of the representation, still less its transparency as 'past experience'. Rather, a particular text should be seen as an ideological 'working' of the past for the purposes of the present. Students need to ask why this particular subject has been chosen, why it is being treated in this way, what 'lessons' are being drawn from it, and with whose point of view we are being encouraged to identify. This is to draw attention, through the use of easily accessible and understandable material, not to history, but to the *writing* or *portrayal* of history, that is to questions of historiography. It is to draw attention to the existence of different schools of thought about history and to the existence of important disputes between historians about the functions and purposes of history. Colin McArthur has shown, in an important study, how the portrayal of history on British television derives from a liberal historiography which has the following features:

'a belief in the uniqueness of the event; a belief in the free-will and moral responsibility of individuals; a belief in the role of historical accident... a strong reliance on the role and testimony of individual (particularly "great") men and women; a strong concern with the nation-state both in its political and military dimensions; a belief in progress and in "chronological monism" '[42]

Bennet *et al.* have observed some of the structured absences of tele-history:

'the history of imperialism (as opposed to colonial history) or the history of the labour movement... feminist history... also received scant attention. Even historical dramas with little commitment to historical accuracy – the royal soap operas in particular – carry a particular construction of British history pivoting around the personalities and activities of monarchs.'[43]

The determinations of *television as an institution* upon the representation of history might also be raised, even with quite young children: the emphasis upon sequential narrative, the importance of 'character', the necessity to entertain and the reluctance to portray abstract ideas, the need for 'action' and the stress upon all of those other professional common-sensed notions of what constitutes 'good television'.[44]

At this point, the close connection between the dominant practices of the media and of historiography, and the remarkable coherence of their effects should be apparent. Both are grounded in empiricism, in the presentation of unproblematic facts which 'produce their own explanation, leaving out of account the predispositions of the observer categorising them as "facts" in the first place.'[45] As we have seen (p. 30), to raise questions about the way in which the world is represented by the media is inevitably to challenge the dominant ways in which the world is represented within the school curriculum. For 'realism... informs most educational practice and a great deal of educational theory.'[46] Reading the media and reconstituting academic disciplines, then, are part of the same project. In Brecht's words:

'Realism is an issue not only for literature: it is a major political, philosophical and practical issue and must be handled and explained as such – as a matter of general human interest.'[47]

B. Holistic approaches to media education

In arguing for more integrated approaches to Media Education, I will briefly consider four areas (amongst many) in which co-operation seems both possible and advisable:

1. Interaction between media educators and parents.

2. Interaction between media educators and media personnel.

3. Interaction in the training function: in the training of media personnel, and the training of teachers.

4. The development of Media Centres: institutions with a specific remit to encourage interaction and integration.

1. Interaction between educators and parents

We need to begin by stressing that *some* interaction between teachers and parents is an inevitable part of any Media Education programme. This is because Media Education is a form of curriculum development which will not only be new to most parents, but one which will be especially open to misinterpretation and misunderstanding. For example, the introduction of popular television programmes into the classroom may be regarded by some parents with suspicion and even hostility. Moreover, Media Education constitutes an area in which the school curriculum is likely to impinge upon domestic habits of media consumption.

The media teacher who can generate parental understanding and support, who can take parents into her confidence about her curriculum objectives, and who can work co-operatively with parents and parental groups will find that she has important allies in her task of developing a critical understanding of the media amongst her pupils. A number of approaches to working with parents may be briefly suggested:

Media workshops

Such workshops could hope to –

(i)   raise consciousness amongst parents of the work undertaken in the classroom by the media teacher;

(ii) encourage parents to analyse the media and discuss media issues at their own level of sophistication;

(iii) suggest concrete ways in which parents could interact with their children. A great many of the exercises suggested both in this book and in *Teaching About Television* could easily be adapted for informal use by parents with their children. First of all, any kind of discussion about what is on the screen is likely to be of some value in encouraging children to articulate their perceptions and feelings. My own preference in watching TV in a family situation is not to *tell* children things, although this might occasionally serve a useful purpose. But prediction games can be fun ('What's going to happen? Do you think he'll get killed? How will this end?') and they don't need to divert attention away from the screen. Running dialogues on the issues and values raised by what is happening on *Dynasty* or *The News* or *Knight Rider* can be mutually illuminating and pleasurable for parents and children alike. Unlike reading, television viewing can be, at its best, a stimulating and essentially *communal* activity in which children should be encouraged to play a full part. Indeed, recent evidence on the use of television by ethnic minority children and their families has revealed that many children of Asian origin use the medium to teach their mothers, in particular, about aspects of European culture and language with which they may be unfamiliar.[48] This is a particularly striking example of the kind of role reversal which frequently takes place when adults and children talk about the medium.

Viewing logs
Encouraging parents and children to keep a formal record – say for a week – of the child's television viewing (hours of watching, types of programmes, programme preferences, etc.) or newspaper reading, can facilitate discussion, encourage the analysis of problems and lead to a positive action programme for both teachers and parents. Both certainly need to know precisely what children's patterns of media consumption are if they are to engage in either formal or informal media education.

Information resources
Specialist media teachers can help provide parental groups with information they may need to investigate a problem in an enlightened way. This may involve the provision of accessible digests of research in areas of interest, making available sources of hard information about the media, or providing details of media organisations (and individuals within them) who are receptive to public feedback.

Working within the community
The most effective co-operation is likely to develop not by asking parents to come into educational institutions after work, but by taking workshops, exhibitions and displays into local community bases, such as libraries and community centres.

Reaching wider parental and public groups
Media educators should be particularly adept at using local and national media to their own advantage. Many media teachers will have developed their own contacts within the media, and these can be used to advantage in the coverage of positive developments within media education which can reach a wider audience of parents.[49]

2. Inter-action between media teachers and media personnel

There are few developments which could have as important an impact upon the future success and quality of media education than fruitful collaboration between media teachers, and journalists and broadcasters. Media professionals, after all, have an up-to-date experience and knowledge of the day-to-day workings of the media which teachers lack, and they are able to illuminate media practices, and the ways in which particular texts were produced, with a specificity of detail beyond the scope of educators. In my own media teaching, for example, some of the very best experiences have been provided for the pupils and students by journalists and broadcasters, and I shall try to indicate in this section some very simple steps which media teachers can take in order to develop mutually beneficial collaborative relationships with media professionals.

Unfortunately, contacts between teachers and media workers, indeed between the educational and media *systems*, have frequently been characterised by a high degree of mutual hostility and distrust. When teachers and media professionals do get together they need to be aware that they are entering a veritable minefield of possible confusions and misunderstandings. Some analysis of these difficulties and of the divides which separate the two parties is evidently necessary if the ground is to be cleared for future co-operation and progress.

First of all, that long legacy of negative and unconstructive attitudes, particularly of the educational system towards the media, needs to be owned up to. Too many teachers, to this day, continue to ignore the media in their teaching, or see them as a threat to the cultural values of which they alone are the true guardians. In these circumstances it is hardly surprising that many in the media see teachers as being out of touch with the real world, dull, censorious, and providing an education which is largely irrelevant to the needs of children and adolescents. Nor is it surprising that those who presume to teach *about the media* are likely to be viewed with particular suspicion. This suspicion is heightened by the legitimate worries which many journalists and broadcasters have about the nature of media education. In my own experience the anger and hostility towards media education which sometimes rises to the surface amongst media professionals can generally be traced to one of a number of possible misunderstandings about the nature of the subject.

The first misunderstanding is that media education is a form of *moral protectionism*, with media teachers as moral guardians, whose duty it is to protect children from excesses of sex and violence in the media. This misunderstanding seems to have been the basis of the media's reaction to the DES document *Popular Television and Schoolchildren*.[50] Lurking behind this misunderstanding seems to be the fear that media teachers may constitute part of a censorship lobby which wishes to control and limit the freedom of journalists and broadcasters.

The second misunderstanding is that media education is a movement designed to improve children's media tastes. That is, it is a generally worthy, improving and patronising movement. Journalists, particularly, are often very much opposed to this kind of thing. The worst media sin, after all, is to lecture or attempt to improve your audience. The media provide what the public wants; media education is seen, on this view, as giving its customers what is good for them.

The third view of media education is one which sees it as being an entirely negative and critical activity, rather than one which is in any sense concerned to explore the pleasures which students take from the media. Representatives of media institutions are frequently reluctant to extend a co-operative hand to an enterprise which seems intent upon making their institutions the butts of a continuous stream of frequently uninformed criticism. Clearly there is room for a great deal of debate on this issue, but many media teachers would readily acknowledge that whilst developing in students a critical under-standing of the media is of fundamental importance, media education ought to be a celebratory and pleasurable activity too, and that this aspect of the subject is one which has been all too frequently neglected in the past. For their part, media professionals will need to understand that any apparent imperviousness to constructive debate, any refusal to take well-documented criticism from outside on board, is always likely to make it appear that the media are the exclusive preserve of an elite, rather than bastions of a democratic society.

The fourth common misunderstanding amongst media pro-fessionals is the idea that media education, particularly within tertiary education, is a form of vocational training. I have discovered, through the experience of being mistaken for a teacher of journalism, that neither they nor their work are held in very high esteem by practising journalists.

Underpinning many of the doubts which media professionals have about media education – doubts with which I have myself a great deal of sympathy – there lies both a justifiable scepticism about the qualifications and experience of media teachers, and a concern at the quality and accuracy of what is passed on to young people about the media, very often on the basis of very slender knowledge of the constraints and conditions under which journalists and broadcasters work. Media teachers, in my experience, are only too ready to acknowledge the limitations of their own background and training in the media. That is why they invariably welcome as much informed help as media practitioners are able to give them. Media teachers are largely motivated by a conviction of the importance of students' understanding the media, as well as by their own interest in the field, and they attempt to keep themselves as up-to-date as they are able with issues and developments in the media. Most media teachers (myself included) would claim no more specialist knowledge than that, and most of us are constantly looking out for contacts with practitioners in order to make our own work more disciplined and professional. We need the help of broadcasters and journalists if we are to achieve that.

I wish to turn now to two major obstacles facing media

practitioners who wish to co-operate with schools. First of all, any intervention which looks like a form of public relations is likely to be resisted by media teachers. Perhaps the least satisfactory form of input to a media studies course is a formal talk given to a passive group of students, extolling the noble role of the media in serving the public, and delivered by the editor of a local newspaper or a high-ranking member of a broadcasting organisation. Such occasions can be fruitful if students have been properly briefed on the kinds of issues which a promotional talk is most likely to avoid. But in my experience the cause of education has generally been better served by *working* journalists and broadcasters who can talk engagingly about particular texts which they have produced, and who can cast a critically informed eye upon their own practices. The local chapel of the NUJ (National Union of Journalists) can be a useful source of contacts for teachers wishing to develop this kind of collaboration. Journalists have also been prominent in the campaign for Press and Broadcasting Freedom, another useful source of local contacts for teachers.[51]

'Educational' material disseminated by media institutions and personnel *can* be of value as long as the teacher and her students remain aware of the interests inscribed within it. There is, for example, both in Britain and throughout Europe and the USA, a concerted effort being made by newspapers, worried about falling circulations and the fact that many of the school population (their readers of the near future) never see a newspaper, to introduce *Newspapers in Education* schemes.[52] Generally such schemes promote an entirely uncritical use of newspapers. They are concerned to stress the liveliness, attractiveness and relevance of newspapers within the study of school subjects, as an adjunct to text-books, and there is much to be said for these arguments. What is left out of the account is the reliability and quality of the information which newspapers supply. If there are good reasons for expanding the use of newspapers throughout the school curriculum, then there are even better ones for ensuring that this development is accompanied by a commensurate expansion in media literacy schemes across the curriculum. Newspapers in Education programmes too readily promote the idea that the very *use* of the media in the classroom itself constitutes a form of media education.

The second major barrier between media practitioners and media teachers is one which has already surfaced in this book: the very different ways in which the two groups are likely to conceptualise the media themselves. As we have seen, the two most frequent metaphors used by practitioners about the media, those of the mirror and the window, assume relatively unproblematic relationships between the media and the external world. The media either reflect reality or provide a transparent view of it. This view, I have argued, is precisely what media teachers would most strenuously wish to challenge. These fundamentally different premises underlie most of the serious, and frequently rancorous, disagreements and debates which take place between educators and media practitioners. Can there be any compromise between these apparently incompatible ways of understanding the media? Certainly the effort is worth making on both sides if it will produce a genuinely higher quality of media education in our schools, and students and pupils who are better informed about the media.

For our part, we might, as media teachers, reconsider our argument that the media *manufacture* 'reality', and that media representations are entirely concocted in newspaper offices or television studios. I have attempted in this book to move slightly away from this position and to acknowledge the authenticity of much visual evidence, the value and acceptability (indeed, inevitability) of many media practices, and even to argue that we all take a good deal of media evidence on trust, and are justified in doing so. We have seen, too, how the meanings which are assigned to events are frequently not manufactured by the media at all, but are *reproduced* by the media from other sources – sources which may, however, have produced them with the media in mind.

Clearly, notions of media manufacture are less than adequate in dealing with any of these cases. But so, too, are simple notions of reflection, as this book has continually demonstrated. Media professionals can surely acknowledge the extent to which they are inevitably involved in processes of *representation*, own up to the nature of their own mediating practices, and begin to examine some of the values implicit within them without necessarily believing that their integrity is being compromised.

It is, then, around such concepts as *reproduction* and *representation* that teachers and practitioners might begin to find some common ground for dialogue. We need, too, to think through these concepts dialectically, in ways which will acknowledge the mutually re-inforcing influences and effects which the media and the world outside of the media have upon each other. That, at least, might provide a more constructive framework for debate, and help us to abandon more simplistic and less helpful notions of manufacture and reflection.

3. Interaction in the training of teachers and media personnel

I have already argued that a critical understanding of media processes should be an important part of the training of all teachers, whatever their subjects, and that broadcasters, journalists and other media workers can play an important part in this training. Similarly, trainee media workers need to grasp the wider significance of the representations they produce, and to understand the complex ways in which they may be read and used by audiences. Whilst there are some institutions in which the professional training of photographers, journalists and broadcasters is seen as a *critical* as well as a practical activity, in many it is not. There is a strong case for urging that the training of media personnel include media *education* as well as media production if only because, as professionals, they may ultimately be employed in institutions which are indifferent to such concerns.

4. Media centres

This chapter has provided a handful of examples of the kinds of productive interchanges possible between agencies and individuals with a stake in the development of media education. Little or no mention has been made of the constructive roles which could be played by many other groups, such as media researchers, community groups, and the public at large. Clearly there is a case to be made for the development of quite new kinds of institutions – Media Centres – which would have a specific remit to encourage the kinds of co-operation outlined here. Such centres might ideally

(i) be based within a specific community, rather than within an existing 'educational' institution;

(ii) replace the current piece-meal approach to media education by acting as regional focal points for the discussion of media issues, the development of lifelong media education programmes and the integration of those agencies with an involvement in or concern about the media;

(iii) develop a resources base for professionals and public, which would include video-tapes and equipment, films and film equipment, media books, teaching materials, periodicals, re-search papers, etc;

(iv) organise seminars and lecture programmes for a wide range of participants. These should be principally, though not ex-clusively, public events, and some might be linked to accredited school, college and University courses;

(v) provide training and facilities for the production of community-based newspapers, video and radio, and provide help with the problems of producing, distributing and circulating information for community-based groups and individuals;

(vi) draw into media education much-needed additional funding
from central government, local authorities, research foundations, arts associations and television and newspaper companies.

Such developments lie ahead in the, perhaps not too distant, future.
Meanwhile, media teachers who are still struggling to establish a
place upon the timetable can be assured that it is they, and not those
who oppose them, who represent our best educational future, a future
in which all who are concerned to realise the full social and
democratic potentialities of the media must co-operate to ensure that
people everywhere are liberated rather than enslaved by the new
information order.

Notes

Chapter 1: Why?

1. L. Masterman, *Teaching About Television*, Macmillan, 1980, p. 197, n. 19.
2. Jeremy Tunstall, *The Media in Britain*, Constable, 1983, p. 135.
3. Stuart Hall, 'Culture, the media, and the "ideological effect"', in J. Curran *et al.* (Eds.), *Mass Communication and Society*, Arnold, 1977, pp. 340–1.
4. Humphrey McQueen, *Australia's Media Monopolies*, Visa, Melbourne, 1977, pp. 10–11.
5. Dallas Smythe, *Dependency Road: Communications, Capitalism, Consciousness and Canada*, Ablex, New Jersey, 1981, pp. 13–14.
6. *Ibid*, p. 20.
7. Roland Barthes, 'Introduction to the Structural Analysis of Narratives', in S. Heath (Ed.), *Image-Music-Text*, Fontana, 1977, p. 89.
8. Smythe, *op. cit.*, p. 20.
9. Hall, *op. cit.*, p. 341.
10. Roland Barthes, *Mythologies*, Cape, 1972. The quotations which follow are from the Preface.
11. Michael Cockerell, Peter Hennessy and David Walker, *Sources close to the Prime Minister*, Macmillan, 1984, p. 148.
12. See, for example, Cockerell, Hennessy and Walker, *op. cit.*, 143 ff; Robert Harris, *Gotcha!*, Faber and Faber, 1983; and The Glasgow University Media Group, *War and Peace News*, Open University Press, 1985.
13. *Learning to Be: The World of Education Today and Tomorrow*, UNESCO/Paris, Harrap/London, 1972, pp. 151–2.
14. Harris, *op. cit.*, p. 151
15. Cockerell *et al.*, *op. cit.*, p. 57.
16. Liz Curtis, *Ireland: The Propaganda War*, Pluto Press, 1984, p. 253.
17. Tunstall, *op. cit.*, p. 7.
18. Cockerell *et al.*, *op. cit.*, p. 34. Chapter Three contains an account of the workings of the system of Lobby journalism. See also J. Tunstall, *The Westminster Lobby Correspondents*, RKP, 1970.
19. *The Guardian*, September 10th, 1984.
20. S. Kelley, Jnr., *Professional Public Relations and Political Power*, John Hopkins, Baltimore, 1956, p. 10.
21. *Ibid*, p. 230.
22. See, for example, The London Media Project, *Get It On*, Pluto Press, 1984, and D. MacShane *Using the Media*, Pluto Press, 1979.
23. Tunstall, *op. cit.*, p. 147.
24. Cockerell *et al.*, *op. cit.*, p. 189.
25. *Ibid*, Chapter 9. See pp. 118–9 for details of Bernard Ingham's row with BBC assistant director-general, Alan Protheroe.
26. See 'Advertising for a Change', *Marxism Today*, January, 1985, for an interview with Johnny Wright of Wright and Partners, and Richard Paterson, 'Fragments of Neil', in L. Masterman (Ed.), *Television Mythologies*, Comedia, 1985, for an analysis of the media image of Neil Kinnock.
27. J. Wills, Appendix to I. Lister, G. Allen *et al.*, *Report of the Political Research Unit*, University of York, undated.
28. J. Wills, *Television and Political Education*, unpublished MA thesis, University of York, 1977, p. 3.
29. See L. Masterman, *Teaching About Television*, *op. cit.*, p. 77. This issue is discussed in some detail in Tunstall, *op. cit.*, pp. 161–5.
30. DES, *English from 5 to 16*, DES, 1984.

31. I am grateful to American media educator, Ron Curtis, for this felicitous slogan.
32. See Ian Connell, 'Fabulous Powers: Blaming the Media', in L. Masterman (Ed.), *Television Mythologies, op. cit.*, p. 88ff.
33. For detailed analyses of this phenomenon see the work of Herbert I. Schiller, particularly *Who Knows: Information in the Age of the Fortune 500*, Ablex, 1981, Chapter Three, *Information and The Crisis Economy*, Ablex, 1984, Chapter Three, and *Electronic Information Flows: New Basis for Global Domination*, Paper presented to the International Television Studies Conference July 11–13, 1984, at the London Institute of Education. The British Film Institute hope to make many of the papers from this conference available in the near future.
34. Schiller, *Electronic Information Flows, op. cit.*, p. 3.
35. Schiller, *Who Knows, op. cit.*, p. 55.
36. Schiller, *Electronic Information Flows, op. cit.*, p. 10.
37. 'Computers changing the teacher's role – Williams', *The Times Educational Supplement*, 26.10.84, p. 5.

Chapter Two: How?
1. Masterman, *op. cit.*, pp. 3–4.
2. J. Bruner, *The Process of Education*, Harvard, 1960, pp. 12–13.
3. The idea may have come originally from Magritte's *L'usage de la parole*, in which the words *Ceci n'est pas une pipe* appear under a drawing of a pipe. This is reproduced in Chapters 1 and 2 of Bill Nichols, *Ideology and the Image*, Indiana University Press, Bloomington, 1981.
4. D. Smythe, *Dependency Road*, Ablex, New Jersey, 1981, p. 13.
5. *Ibid.* On reproduction, see L. Althusser, 'Ideology and Ideological State Apparatuses', *Lenin and Philosophy and other essays*, New Left Books, 1971. ('As Marx said, every child knows that a social formation which did not reproduce the conditions of production at the same time as it produced would not last a year.' (p. 123).)
6. F. R. Leavis, 'How to teach Reading', in *Education and the University*, Chatto and Windus, 1943, p. 126.
7. See Masterman, *op. cit.*, Chapter 8 and 'Screening the Media', *The Guardian*, 27.1.81. for a more detailed discussion of the place of practical work within Media Education.
8. M. Alvarado and Bob Ferguson, 'The Curriculum, Media Studies and Discursivity, *Screen*, Vol. 24, No. 3, May/June, 1983, pp. 20–1, n. 3. The quotation used, which has been slightly shortened in the *Screen* article, is taken from an original paper by Alvarado and Ferguson on which the *Screen* article is based.
9. Freire's classic text is *Pedagogy of the Oppressed*, Penguin, 1972.
10. See P. Freire, *Pedagogy in Process*, Seabury, N.Y., 1978, p. 101.
11. *Ibid*, p. 115.
12. See P. Freire, *Pedagogy of the Oppressed, op. cit.*, Chapter Two, for Freire's critique of banking education. This critique is discussed in relation to television education in Masterman, *Teaching About Television*, Chapter 2.
13. See the work of Klaus Riegel for early and innovative discussions on dialectical thinking, especially K. F. Riegel, *Foundations of Dialectic Psychology*, Academic Press, 1979. For more recent developments see Paula Allman, 'Dialectic Operations, our logical potential', *Aspects*, No. 26, Spring, 1984.
14. See, for example, Manuel Alvarado, 'Television Studies and Pedagogy' and Bob Ferguson, 'Practical Work and Pedagogy', both in *Screen Education*, No. 38, Spring, 1981. For responses to those articles see Len Masterman, 'TV Pedagogy', *Screen Education*, No. 40, Autumn/Winter, 1981–2, and Andrew Bethell, 'Eyeopeners', *Screen Education*, No. 41, Winter/Spring, 1982. For a general critique of progressive pedagogies see V. Walkerdine, 'It's Only Natural: Re-thinking child-centred Pedagogy', in A. M. Wolfe and J. Donald (Eds.), *Is There*

Anyone Here From Education?, Pluto Press, 1983.

15. See, especially, Antonio Gramsci, *The Prison Notebooks*, Lawrence and Wishart, 1971, Chapter 2. For a commentary on Gramsci's philosophy of schooling, see Harold Entwistle, *Antonio Gramsci: Conservative Schooling for Radical Politics*, RKP, 1979.
16. Discussed in Entwistle, *op. cit.*, pp. 78ff.
17. Ferguson, *op. cit.*, and Maureen Stone, *The Education of the Black Child in Britain*, Fontana, 1981.
18. DES, *Primary Education in England*, HMSO, 1978, para. 3.20..
19. DES, *Aspects of Secondary Education in England*, HMSO, 1979, pp. 83 and 94.
20. Henry A. Giroux, *Ideology, Culture and the Process of Schooling*, The Falmer Press, 1981, p. 127.
21. For a more detailed account of the minutiae of classroom organisation and pupil assessment in media education, see Len Masterman, *op. cit.*, Chapter 2.

Chapter 3: How not to...
1. F. R. Leavis and D. Thompson, *Culture and Environment*, Chatto and Windus, 1933.
2. G. Pearson, *Hooligan*, Macmillan, 1983, p. 33.
3. Leavis and Thompson, *op. cit.*, p. 1.
4. *Ibid*, pp. 3–5.
5. *Ibid*, pp. 111, 121 and 143.
6. The most comprehensive study of Thompson's work and influence has been undertaken by Brian Doyle, *Some Uses of English: Denys Thompson and the Development of English in Secondary Schools*, Centre for Contemporary Cultural Studies, University of Birmingham, 1981. For background on the formation of NATE, see N. Martin (Ed.), *NATE – The First Twenty-One Years*, NATE, (49 Broomgrove Road, Sheffield S10 2NA), 1984.
7. D. Thompson, 'Introduction' to D. Thompson (Ed.), *Discrimination and Popular Culture*, Penguin, 1964, p. 20.
8. K. Windschuttle, *The Media*, Penguin, Australia, 1983, pp. 152–3.
9. Q. D. Leavis, 'The Discipline of Letters', *Scrutiny XII*, 1, Winter, 1943, p. 18ff.
10. Cited in F. Mulhern, *The Moment of 'Scrutiny'*, Verso, 1981, p. 199.
11. *Ibid*, p. 32, from F. R. Leavis, *'Scrutiny': A Retrospect*, Cambridge, 1963, pp. 1–2.
12. Terry Eagleton, *Literary Theory*, Blackwell, 1983, p. 31.
13. *Ibid*, p. 36.
14. Leavis and Thompson, *op. cit.*, p. 82.
15. F. Mulhern, seminar on *F. R. Leavis and the Moment of 'Scrutiny'*, Nottingham University, School of Education, Autumn, 1983.
16. D. Thompson, 'Advertising God', *Scrutiny*, 1, 3, December, 1932.
17. Mulhern, *The Moment of 'Scrutiny'*, *op. cit.*, Chapter One.
18. M. Arnold, *Culture and Anarchy*, in G. Sutherland, *Matthew Arnold on Education*, Penguin, 1973, p. 204.
19. *Ibid*, p. 183.
20. *Ibid*, p. 199. The most detailed critique of this aspect of *Culture and Anarchy* has been provided by Raymond Williams, 'A Hundred Years of Culture and Anarchy', *Problems in Materialism and Culture*, Verso, 1980.
21. See Eagleton, *Literary Theory*, *op. cit.*, p. 27.
22. Board of Education, *The Teaching of English in England*, (The Newbolt Report), 1921, HMSO, para. 233. Newbolt, who chaired the committee, was the same Sir Henry Newbolt who wrote the line 'Play up! play up! and play the game!'
23. *Ibid*, para. 234.
24. G. Sampson, *English for the English*, Cambridge, 1921. This passage – from the preface – was added in 1926. Doyle, *op. cit.*, p. 53 notes that Denys Thompson 'edited an edition of Sampson's book which was published in 1970 but does not include the 1926 preface.'

25. Mulhern, *The Moment of 'Scrutiny'*, *op. cit.*, pp. 330–331.

26. F. R. Leavis, 'Mass Civilisation and Minority Culture', *Education and the University*, Chatto and Windus, 1943, p. 144.

27. NUT, *Verbatim Report of Conference on 'Popular Culture and Personal Responsibility'*, NUT, 1960.

28. Peter Black, *The Mirror in the Corner*, Hutchinson, 1972, p. 111.

29. J. Tunstall, *op. cit.*, p. 39.

30. *Ibid.*

31. *Report of the Committee on Broadcasting* (The Pilkington Report), HMSO, 1962.

32. Through its proposal that facilities be given to the BBC to provide BBC 2 and its impact upon the Television Act, 1964, which strengthened the ITA (later the IBA) at the expense of the companies and led to the rejigging and revoking of some of the franchises by the Authority in 1967.

33. R. Williams, NUT *Verbatim Report*, *op. cit.*, p. 18.

34. *Half Our Future* (The Newsom Report), HMSO, 1963, paras. 475–6.

35. L. Masterman, *Teaching About Television*, *op. cit.*, pp. 15–16.

36. S. Hall and P. Whannel, *The Popular Arts*, Hutchinson, 1964, p. 15.

37. *Ibid*, p. 109.

38. *Ibid*, p. 207.

39. *Ibid*, pp. 39 and 50.

40. *Ibid*, pp. 257ff.

41. *Ibid*, pp. 127–30.

42. R. Hoggart, 'Culture – Dead and Alive', *Speaking to Each Other, Vol. One: About Society*, Chatto and Windus, 1970, pp. 131–2. The original article appeared in *The Observer*, 14 May, 1961.

43. David Holbrook, 'Quite Useful Neutrals', *The Use of English*, Vol. 17, No. 3, Spring, 1966.

44. Graham Murdock and Guy Phelps, *Mass Media and the Secondary School*, Macmillan, 1973, p. 33.

45. *Ibid*, p. 46.

46. B. Firth, *Mass Media in the Classroom*, Macmillan, 1968, p. 98.

47. N. Tucker, *Understanding the Mass Media*, Cambridge University Press, 1966, p. 83.

48. *Ibid*, p. 121.

49. Firth, *op. cit.*, p. 68.

50. *Ibid.*

51. Tucker, *op. cit.*, pp. 136–7.

52. R. Wellek, 'Literary Criticism and Philosophy', *Scrutiny*, vol. 4, March, 1937, p. 376.

53. F. R. Leavis, 'Literary Criticism and Philosophy: A Reply', *Scrutiny*, VI, 1, June, 1937, pp. 60–1.

54. Mulhern, *op. cit.*, p. 175.

55. UNESCO, *Teachers and Out of School Education*, unattributed and undated UNESCO paper, Paris, circa 1983.

56. The Communication Studies Advanced level GCE syllabus is set by the Associated Examining Board, Wellington House, Aldershot, Hants. GU11 1BQ. For two conflicting views of the syllabus, see Jim Cook and David Lusted, 'A Product of a Set of Confusions', *The Media Reporter*, Vol. 2, No. 2, 1978, and G. Burton, 'Having it both ways', *The Media Reporter*, Vol. 2, No. 3, 1978.

57. C. Lorac and M. Weiss, *Communication and Social Skills*, Wheaton, 1981.

58. Associated Examining Board, *Expanded Notes for the Guidance of Teachers of AEB GCE A Level Communication Studies*, AEB, 1977.

59. This brief account owes a great deal to the more detailed work by James Halloran, Graham Murdock and Robin McCron at Leicester University. See, especially, J. D. Halloran, 'Mass Communication: Symptom or Cause of Violence?', *International Social Science Journal*, v. XXX, n. 4, 1978, and G.

Murdock and R. McCron, 'The Television and Delinquency Debate', *Screen Education*, Spring, 1979, No. 30.

60. Bonney and Wilson, *op. cit.*, pp. 15 and 28. Bonney and Wilson offer an excellent and more detailed critique of the communication model than I have had space for here.

Chapter Four: Determinants

1. Even within film studies, the area where most work has been done, and most resources are available on teaching about institutions, a recent bibliographical guide could find little evidence that this kind of work was being undertaken within schools. See David Lusted (Ed.), *Guide to Film Studies in Secondary and Further Education*, British Film Institute, 1983, p. 75.
2. BFI Education, *Selling Pictures*, The British Film Institute, 1983.
3. BFI, 'The Companies You Keep', *Selling Pictures*, p. 1, *ibid.*
4. *Ibid.*, p. 5.
5. For a sophisticated yet accessible example of this kind of approach, see Richard Paterson, 'The Production Context of *Coronation Street*', in R. Dyer, C. Geraghty. et al., *Coronation Street*, British Film Institute, Television Monograph No. 13, BFI, 1981, pp. 53ff.
6. Jeremy Tunstall, *The Media In Britain*, Constable, 1983.
7. D. Morley and B. Whitaker (Eds.), *The Press, Radio and Television*, Comedia, 1983.
8. BBC, *Annual Report and Handbook*, BBC. IBA, *Television and Radio*, annually, IBA.
9. *Report of the Committee on the Future of Broadcasting*, (The Annan Report), HMSO, 1977.
10. *Royal Commission on the Press*, 1974–7, HMSO, 1977.
11. A. Smith (Ed.), *British Broadcasting* and *The British Press since the War*, both published by David and Charles, 1974.
12. *Benn's Press Directory*, published annually by Benn Business Information Services Ltd.
13. *Broadcast*, Knightway House, 20 Soho Square, London W1Y 6DT. *Campaign*, 22 Lancaster Gate, London W2 3LY. *Mediaworld*, 52/53 Poland Street, London W1V 3DF. *UK Press Gazette*, Bouverie Publishing Co. Ltd., Rooms 244–249, Temple Chambers, Temple Avenue, London EC4Y 0DT. *Marketing*, Marketing Publications, 22 Lancaster Gate, London W2 3LY. *Marketing Week*, 60 Kingly Street, London W1R 5LH.
14. *BRAD*, (British Rate and Data), available monthly from 76 Oxford Street, London W1N 9AD. JICNARS, *National Readership Surveys*, 44 Belgravia Square, London SW1X 8QS.
15. Available from Sales Department, CRAC Publications, Hobsons Ltd., Bateman Street, Cambridge, CB27 1LZ.
16. Available from the Advertising Standards Authority, Brook House, 2–16, Torrington Place, London WC1E 7HN.
17. *Viewpoint*, BLA Business Publications, 2 Duncan Terrace, London N1 8BZ.
18. The Broadcasting Complaints Commission, 20 Albert Embankment, London SE1 7TL. BARB, Knighton House, 56 Mortimer Street, London W1N 8AN.
19. See Michael Leapman, *Barefaced Cheek*, Hodder & Stoughton, 1983.
20. Tony Benn, *Arguments for Democracy*, Cape, 1981, p. 105.
21. J. Whale, *The Politics of the Media*, Fontana, 1977, pp. 84–5.
22. Audit Bureau of Circulations (ABC) figures, August, 1985.
23. See J. Curran and J. Seaton, *Power without Responsibility*, Methuen, 1985, Chapter 10, for a discussion of ownership concentration and proprietor power in the press.
24. Graham Murdock and Peter Golding, 'Capitalism, Communication & Class Relations', in J. Curran, M. Gurevitch and J. Woollacott (Eds.), *Mass Communication and Society*, Arnold and O.U. Press, 1977, p. 30.

25. Cited by Tom Baistow, 'An Express that is running into the Sidings', *The Guardian*, 13/11/1982.
26. Murdock and Golding, *op. cit.*, p. 30.
27. *Ibid*, p. 26.
28. H . McQueen, *Australia's Media Monopolies*, Visa, 1977, p. 39.
29. *Who Owns Whom*, Duns and Bradstreet, Annually. The Press Council, *The Press and the People*, the annual report of the Press Council.
30. Hugh Cudlipp, *The Prerogative of the Harlot*, The Bodley Head, 1980.
31. Michael Leapman, *Barefaced Cheek*, Hodder & Stoughton, 1983.
32. Raymond Williams, *Communications*, Penguin, 1962, pp. 117ff.
33. *Ibid*. See also The Annan Report, *op. cit.*, Chapter 6; Nicholas Garnham, 'Public Service versus the Market', *Screen*, Vol. 24, No. 1, Jan./Feb. 1983; L. Masterman, 'The Battle of Orgreave' in L. Masterman (Ed.), *Television Mythologies*, Comedia, 1985; Ian Connell, 'Auntie shows her Age', *Marxism Today*, May, 1985; Stuart Hood, 'Auntie shows Her Age', *Marxism Today*, June 1985.
34. Ed Buscombe, 'Disembodied Voices and Familiar Faces', in L. Masterman (Ed.), *op. cit.*
35. Stuart Hood, *A Survey of Television*, Heinemann, 1967, Chapter 2. Morley and Whitaker, *op. cit.*
36. Tom Burns, *The BBC: Public Institution and Private World*, Macmillan, 1977.
37. The British Film Institute, *Granada: The First Twenty-five Years*, BFI dossier Number 9, BFI, 1981.
38. Geoffrey Robertson, 'Law for the Press', in James Curran (Ed.), *The British Press: A Manifesto*, Macmillan, 1978, p. 225.
39. *The Times*, 27.3.84.
40. *Ibid*.
41. The Official Secrets Act is discussed in more detail in Robertson, *op. cit.*, pp. 207–8; Whitaker, *op. cit.*, pp. 66ff; and Cockerell *et al.*, *op. cit.*, pp. 15ff and 129–30.
42. L. Curtis, *op. cit.*, pp. 165–172. In 1979 a *Panorama* team spent about 15 minutes filming armed IRA men as they stopped traffic and sealed off the small Irish village of Carrickmore. This brought the wrath of all the political parties down upon the BBC and the untransmitted film was handed over to the police by the BBC under the Prevention of Terrorism Act. The film was never transmitted.
43. Cited by Curtis, *op. cit.*, p. 149.
44. *Ibid*, p. 143.
45. *New Statesman*, 31.12.1971, pp. 911–12 and cited by Curtis, *op. cit.*, p. 14. The effect of the Prevention of Terrorism Act upon reporting in the North of Ireland is detailed in Curtis, *op. cit.*, pp. 171–2 and 250–1.
46. The law of libel is discussed in detail by Robertson, *op. cit.*, pp. 216ff and Whitaker, *op. cit.*, p 73ff.
47. Whitaker, *op. cit.*, p. 78.
48. Robertson, *op. cit.*, p. 214.
49. Cockerell *et al.*, *op. cit.*, p. 15.
50. Ibid, p. 11.
51. Robertson, *op. cit.*, p. 205.
52. P. Schlesinger, G. Murdock and P. Elliott, *Televising Terrorism*, Comedia, 1983, p. 111.
53. *Ibid*.
54. *Ibid*, p. 113.
55. S. Hood, *A Survey of Television*, *op. cit.*, p. 19.
56. *Ibid*, p. 20.
57. See Whitaker, *op. cit.*, p. 69ff, and Annabelle May and Kathryn Rowan (Eds.), *Inside Information: British Government and the Media*, Constable, 1982, Chapter 5.

58. Antony Easthope, 'A Strategy for Television News?', *Free Press*, (Bulletin of the Campaign for Press and Broadcasting Freedom), Jan./Feb., 1984, No. 21.
59. *Ibid.*
60. The Glasgow University Media Group, *War and Peace News*, *op. cit.*, pp. 13ff.
61. See, for example, the initiatives of Sir Robert Mark when he was Commissioner of the Metropolitan Police, Schlesinger *et al.*, *op. cit.*, pp. 114ff.
62. Schlesinger *et al.*, *op. cit.*, pp. 119ff.
63. S. Hood, *On Television*, Pluto Press, 1980, pp. 46–7. BBC Governors and IBA Members are listed in the BBC and IBA Annual Handbooks. For further information on their backgrounds, see *Who's Who*.
64. The Annan Report, *op. cit.*, pp. 54–5.
65. See S. Hood, 'Auntie shows her Age', *op. cit.*
66. S. Hood, *On Television*, *op. cit.*, pp. 28–9.
67. A. Easthope, *op. cit.*
68. Anthony Smith, 'Internal Pressures in Broadcasting', *New Outlook*, No. 4, 1972, pp. 4–5, quoted in Burns, *op. cit.*, p. 195.
69. E. McCann, 'The British Press and Northern Ireland', in S. Cohen and J. Young (Eds.), *The Manufacture of News*, Constable, 1973, p. 260.
70. Geoffrey Robertson, *People Against the Press*, Quartet, 1983.
71. The Press Council, *The Press and the People*, annually.
72. Broadcasting Complaints Commission, *Report of the Broadcasting Complaints Commission, 1984–85*, B.C.C., 1985.
73. G. Murdock, 'Authorship and Organisation', *Screen Education*, Summer, 1980, No. 35, p. 30.
74. M. Alvarado and E. Buscombe, *Hazell: The Making of a TV Series*, BFI/Latimer, 1978, p. 141.
75. *Did You See...?*, BBC 2, 10.2.1985.
76. Leslie Halliwell, cited in G. Lealand, *American Television Programmes on British Screens*, Broadcasting Research Unit, 1984, p. 22.
77. See A. Mattelart, X. Delcourt and M. Mattelart, *International Media Markets*, Comedia, 1984.
78. J. von Sooster, 'After the Goldrush', *Broadcast*, 11.1.85.
79. The 'internationalisation' of image-markets has been paralleled by the growth of international 'co-productions'. See A. Mattelart *et al.*, *op. cit.*, pp. 78ff.
80. Daniel J. Boorstin, *The Image*, Pelican, 1963, Chapters 1 and 2.
81. J. Curran, 'Advertising and the Press', in J. Curran (Ed.), *The British Press: A Manifesto*, *op. cit.*, p. 240. See, also, Table 11.2, pp. 236–7, for breakdown of the growth of advertising – sponsored features, 1946–76.
82. *Ibid*, p. 235.
83. Cited by J. Curran, 'The press as an agency of social control: an historical perspective', in G. Boyce, J. Curran and P. Wingate (Eds.), *Newspaper History: from the 17th century to the present day*, Sage/Constable, 1978, p. 69. The quotation is from Cyril Freer, *The Inner Side of Advertising: a practical handbook for advertisers*, Library Press, 1921, p. 203.
84. Curran, 'Advertising and the Press', *op. cit.*, pp. 246 and 248.
85. *Ibid*, p. 253ff.
86. See L. Masterman and P. Kiddey, *Understanding Breakfast Television*, M. K. Media Press, 1983, p. 15. The source is a TVAM promotional videotape aimed at advertisers.
87. *Ibid.*
88. D. Smythe, *Dependency Road*, *op. cit.*, p. 15.
89. Source: TVAM promotional video.
90. Charles Wintour, *Pressures on the Press*, Deutsche, 1972, pp. 35–6, cited by Curran, 'Advertising and the Press', *op. cit.*, p. 229.
91. John Whale, *The Politics of the Media*, Fontana, 1977, p. 85.
92. *Ibid*, pp. 81, 82 and 84.

93. See Dorothy Hobson's study of the *Crossroads'* audience, *Crossroads, the Drama of a Soap Opera*, Methuen, 1982.
94. G. Murdock, 'Authorship and Organisation', *op. cit.*, p. 25.
95. S. Hood, *On Television*, *op. cit.*, p. 35. Hood has provided the most lucid and incisive account currently available on programme makers and controllers. See *On Television*, Chapters 3 and 4.
96. G. W. Brandt (Ed.), *British Television Drama*, Cambridge University Press, 1981.
97. H. J. Gans, *Deciding What's News*, Vintage, 1980, p. 289.
98. S. Chibnall, *Law and Order News*, Tavistock, 1977, p. 172.
99. Gans, *op. cit.*, n. 3., p. 360.
100. For a fuller account of television coverage of the Orgreave picket line, see L. Masterman, 'The Battle of Orgreave', in L. Masterman (Ed.), *Television Mythologies*, *op. cit.*
101. Whitaker, *op. cit.*, p. 32.
102. Ian Baker, 'The Media as an Institution', in P. Edgar (Ed.), *The News in Focus*, Macmillan, Melbourne, 1980, pp. 180–1.
103. Curtis, *op. cit.*, p. 246.
104. See Chibnall, *op. cit.*, p. 178ff, and John Whale, *The Half Shut Eye*, Macmillan, 1969, p. 141ff.
105. Whitaker, *op. cit.*, pp. 38–9.
106. S. Hall *et al.*, *op. cit.*, pp. 58–9.
107. Whitaker, *op. cit.*, p. 31–2.

Chapter 5: Rhetoric

1. It is necessary to use both of the terms 'illusionism' and 'realism' in order to distinguish between those occasions when the media purport to present their audiences with unmediated reality, as in a piece of TV news film or coverage of a sporting event (illusionism), and those occasions when it is clear to audiences that they are reading sets of conventions (as in a play or film) signifying 'the real' (realism). It should be noted, however, that in the discussion below Brecht's reference to illusionism alludes to what I have called realism. This is because Brecht wished to retain a more dialectical sense of realism through which, in spite of his anti-illusionism (in his sense) and his use of techniques to break the flow of the narrative and invite the participation of the audience, he could nevertheless represent important truths. Brecht therefore remained committed to realism in spite of his anti-illusionism. For a résumé of the meanings of 'realism', see Raymond Williams, *Keywords*, Fontana, 1976, and The Open University Popular Culture Course, Unit 15, *Reading and Realism*, The Open University Press, 1981.

It should also be noted that an Australian teacher, John Docker, has argued that far from being dominated by realism, television owes a great deal to popular theatrical forms such as 'melodrama, romance, vaudeville, farce, adult pantomime, musical comedy, fantasy, magic, Shakespearean adaptations and the unrealist like.' It would, perhaps, be more accurate to say that whilst television content has been dependent on these traditional forms, its mode of presentation remains, generally, an illusionist one. See John Docker, 'In Defence of Popular Culture', *Arena* 60, 1982, pp. 65–6, cited by K. Windschuttle, *The Media*, Penguin, Australia, 1984, p. 160.
2. Terry Eagleton, *Marxism and Literary Criticism*, Methuen, 1976, pp. 64–5.
3. D. L. Altheide, *Creating Reality: How TV News distorts Events*, Sage, 1976, p. 184.
4. R. Barthes, 'Introduction to the Structural Analysis of Narratives', in *Image-Music-Text*, Ed. S. Heath, Fontana, 1977, p. 89.
5. Joe McGinniss, *The Selling of the President*, Penguin, 1970, p. 78.
6. Marisa Horsford, *Poems*, Your own stuff press, Nottingham, 1981.
7. See, for example, Paul Merrison's excellent video-tape, *Media Kids OK?* available

from the Centre for Educational Technology, Knighton Fields, Herrick Road, Leicester.

8. See Appendix A.
9. Claud Cockburn, *I, Claud*, Penguin, 1967, p. 147.
10. Altheide, *op. cit.*, p. 76 ff.
11. Jerry Mander, *Four Arguments for the Elimination of Television*, Morrow Quill, New York, 1978, pp. 303, 305 and 310.
12. H. M. Enzensberger, 'Constituents of a theory of the media', *New Left Review*, No. 64, November/December 1970, p. 20.
13. J. Tunstall, *op. cit.*, p. 162. See also BBC, *News Broadcasting and the Public in 1970*, BBC, 1971, for research on the public's views of television news.
14. R. Barthes, 'The Rhetoric of the Image', *Image-Music-Text, op. cit.*, p. 44.
15. John Berger and Jean Mohr, *Another Way of Telling*, Writers and Readers, 1982, pp. 92, 93 and 96.
16. Frank Webster, *The New Photography*, John Calder, 1980, p. 155.
17. See L. Masterman, 'The Battle of Orgreave', L. Masterman (Ed.) *Television Mythologies*, *op. cit.*, for a detailed analysis of television coverage of this event.
18. Berger and Mohr, *op. cit.*, pp. 89, 91 and 92.
19. R. Barthes, 'The Rhetoric of the Image', *op. cit.*, p. 38 ff.
20. L. Masterman, *Teaching About Television*, *op. cit.*, Ch. 3.
21. Cited by Susan Sontag, *On Photography*, Penguin, 1979, p. 192.
22. J. P. Golay, *Introduction to the Language of Image and Sound*, BFI Advisory Document, BFI, 1973, p. 5.
23. Cited in H. Evans, *Pictures on a Page*, Heinemann, 1978, Introduction.
24. Andrew Bethell, *Eyeopeners Two*, Cambridge University Press, 1981, pp. 5–6.
25. M. Simons and A. Bethell, *Choosing the News*, ILEA English Centre, Sutherland Street, SW1V 4L11, 1979.
26. H. Evans, *op. cit.*, cropping exercises are presented on pp. 190, 193–4 and 196–231. A layout exercise is given on pp. 249–50.
27. *Ibid*, Introduction.
28. L. Masterman, *Teaching about Television*, *op. cit.*, p. 152.
29. *We Bring You Live Pictures*, BBC 2, 26 March, 1984.
30. *Ibid*.
31. Unfortunately *Protest for Peace* has now been withdrawn from general distribution.
32. All of these quotations are cited by Tom Levin, "The Acoustic Dimension", *Screen*, Vol. 25, No. 3, May–June, 1984. This edition of *Screen* is specifically devoted to soundtrack, particularly in the cinema.
33. In 1979 one in every three households in Britain were without a telephone. Office of Population, Censuses, and Surveys Monitor, *General Household Survey, 1979*, 1980.
34. H. Gans, *op. cit.*, p. 140.
35. Philip Knightley, *The First Casualty*, Quartet, 1982, p. 381.
36. Daniel J. Boorstin, *The Image*, Pelican, 1963, Chapters 1 and 2.
37. See Howard Tumber, *Television and the Riots*, BFI, 1982, p. 7 ff, and P. Schlesinger, G. Murdock and P. Elliott, *Televising Terrorism*, Comedia, 1983, Chapter 5.
38. Cited in J. Bakewell and N. Garnham, *The New Priesthood*, Allen Lane, 1970, p. 173.
39. H. M. Enzensberger, 'Constituents of a theory of the media', *New Left Review*, No. 64, November/December, 1970, p. 20.
40. When an interview is shot with a single camera, the film generally covers only the responses of the interviewee. The responses of the interviewer ('noddies') are shot separately at the end of the interview and cut into the film later. By cutting away to the interviewer during a filmed interview, the director is able to cover over any edits in the words and images of the interviewee, and thus present an edited and

constructed event as a seamlesssly continuous one.

41. H. Evans, *op. cit.*, Introduction.
42. Ian Baker, 'Looking Inside the Media as an Institution: Studies of the News-Gathering Process', P. Edgar (Ed.), *The News in Focus*, Macmillan, Melbourne, 1980, p. 175.
43. *Ibid*, p. 177.
44. Bakewell and Garnham, *op. cit.*
45. F. Wiseman, 'Pride, Patience and Prejudice', *The Guardian*, 17 March, 1981.
46. C. Williams (Ed.), *Realism and the Cinema: A Reader*, Routledge and Kegan Paul in association with the British Film Institute, 1980, p. 220.
47. Studies of the role of these publications have been made by Colin McArthur, 'Setting the Scene: *Radio Times* and *TV Times*', E. Buscombe, (Ed.), *Football on Television*, British Film Institute Television Monograph No. 4, 1975; and by John O. Thompson, 'TV Magazines: Workers' Profiles' in L. Masterman (Ed.), *Television Mythologies*, Comedia, 1985. For examples of the use of *Radio Times* and *TV Times* materials in teaching about televised sport, see L. Masterman, *Teaching About Television*, *op. cit.*, pp. 112–114.
48. S. Hall *et al.*, *Policing the Crisis*, Macmillan, 1978, pp. 54–5.
49. For a detailed discussion on these techniques, see C. Brunsdon and D. Morley, *Everyday Television: Nationwide*, British Film Institute Television Monograph No. 10, BFI, 1978, Chapter 3.
50. Cited by Schlesinger, Murdock and Elliott, *op. cit.*, p. 55.
51. TUC, *A Cause for Concern*, TUC, 1979, p. 30. 'Winter of industrial mis-reporting' is Dennis MacShane's phrase, 'There's a new bitterness . . . 'The *Media Reporter*, Vol. 13, No. 3, 1979.
52. This extract is reproduced from C. S. Higgins and P. D. Moss, *Sounds Real*, University of Queensland Press, 1982, p. 138.
53. S. Hood, *On Television*, Pluto Press, 1981, pp. 3–4.
54. *Ibid*, p. 5.
55. Glasgow University Media Group, *Bad News*, *op. cit.*, p. 26.
56. Precisely this point was raised as early as 1953 in relation to the Budget broadcasts of that year, when Mr Butler, the Chancellor of the Exchequer, broadcast from 11 Downing Street, whilst Mr Gaitskell, the Shadow Chancellor, was interviewed the following evening from the television studios in Lime Grove. See G. W. Goldie, *Facing the Nation*, The Bodley Head, 1977, pp. 130–1.
57. R. Williams, *Television: Technology and Cultural Form*, Fontana, 1974, p. 59.
58. L. Masterman, *Teaching About Television*, *op. cit.*, p. 68 ff.
59. Discussed by Roland Barthes, 'Structural Analysis of Narratives', S. Heath (Ed.), *Image, Music, Text, op. cit.*, p. 105 ff.
60. Terry Eagleton has suggested, very usefully, that Freud's famous description of the *fort-da* game can provide a simple model for analysing even the most complex narratives:

'Watching his grandson playing in his pram one day, Freud observed him throwing a toy out of the pram and exclaiming fort! (gone away), then hauling it in again on a string to the cry of da! (here). This, the famous forta-da game, Freud interpreted in *Beyond the Pleasure Principle* (1920) as the infant's symbolic mastery of its mother's absence; but it can also be read as the first glimmerings of narrative. Fort-da is perhaps the shortest story we can imagine: an object is lost, and then recovered. But even the most complex narratives can be read as variants on this model: the pattern of classical narrative is that an original settlement is disrupted and ultimately restored. From this view-point, narrative is a source of consolation: lost objects are the cause of anxiety to us, symbolizing certain deeper unconscious losses (of birth, the faeces, the mother), and it is always pleasurable to find them put securely back in place . . . Something must be lost or absent in any narrative for it to unfold: if everything stayed in place there would be no story to tell. This loss is distressing, but exciting as well: desire is stimulated by what we cannot quite possess, and this is one source of narrative satisfaction. If we could never possess it, however, our excitation might become intolerable and turn into unpleasure; so we must know that the object will be finally restored to us, that Tom Jones will return to Paradise Hall and Hercule Poirot will track down the murderer. Our excitation is gratifyingly released: our energies have been cunningly "bound" by the suspenses and repetitions of the narrative only as a preparation for their pleasurable expenditure. We have been able to tolerate the disappearance of the object because our unsettling suspense was all the time shot through by the secret knowledge that it would finally come home. Fort has meaning only in relation to da.' *(Literary Theory, op. cit., pp. 185–6)*

61. Much of the work described here may be directly applied to the teaching of literature. An excellent resource for English teachers is the compilation *Changing Stories*, published by the ILEA English Centre, in which students are encouraged to read critically and change the story lines of a number of traditional folk tales and fairy stories. See B. Mellor with J. Hemming and J. Leggett, *Changing Stories*, ILEA English Centre, 1984.

62. For other examples of this phenomenon see L. Masterman, *Teaching About Television, op. cit.*, Chapter 6, 'Football on Television'.

63. S. Heath and G. Skirrow, 'Television: A World in Action', *Screen*, Vol. 18, No. 2, Summer 1977, p. 58.

64. A. Smith, 'The long road to objectivity and back: the kinds of truth we get in journalism', G. Boyce, J. Curran and P. Wingate (Eds.), *Newspaper History*, Constable, p. 168.

65. See Keith Waterhouse, *Daily Mirror Style*, Mirror Books, 1981, for a detailed though now somewhat dated account of *The Mirror's* stylistic features.

66. B. E. Phillips, 'Novelty without Change', *Journal of Communication*, Autumn 1976, cited by Higgins and Moss, *op. cit.*, p. 85.

67. Gill Davies, 'Teaching about Narrative', *Screen Education* 29, Winter 1978/79, p. 70.

68. Colin MacCabe, 'Realism and the Cinema: Notes on some Brechtian Theses', *Screen* Vol. 15, No. 2. Also in T. Bennett, S. Boyd-Bowman *et al.* (Eds.), *Popular Television and Film*, BFI and The Open University Press, 1981, p. 217.

69. Colin MacCabe, 'Days of Hope – a Response to Colin McArthur', *Screen*, Vol. 17, No. 1, Spring 1976, and in T. Bennett *et al.* (Eds.), *op. cit.*, p. 310.

70. R. Barthes, 'Introduction to the Structural Analysis of Narratives', *op. cit.*, p. 79.

71. Quoted in J. Wolff, 'Bill Brand, Trevor Griffiths and the debate about political theatre', *Red Letters*, No. 8, 1978. See also The Open University *Popular Culture*, Block 4, Unit 15, 'Reading and Realism', pp. 95–6, Open University Press, 1981. The whole unit is a useful introduction to current debates about realism.

72. T. Eagleton, *Literary Theory, op. cit.*, pp. 103 ff, 135 ff, and 185 ff.

73. Jim Cook, 'Narrative, Comedy, Character and Performance', *Television Sitcom*, BFI Dossier 17, BFI, 1982, p. 13 ff.

74. Terry Lovell, 'A Genre of Social Disruption', *Ibid*, p. 19 ff.

75. Marion Jordan, 'Realism and Convention'; Richard Paterson and John Stewart, 'Street Life', both in *Coronation Street*, BFI Television Monograph No. 13, BFI, 1981.

76. S. Heath and G. Skirrow, *op. cit.*

77. C. Bazalgette and R. Paterson, 'Real Entertainment: The Iranian Embassy Siege', *Screen Education*, No. 37, Winter, 1980/81.

78. J. Langer, 'The Structure and Ideology of the "Other News" on Television', P. Edgar (Ed.), *op. cit.*, p. 13 ff.

79. R. Silverstone, *The Message of Television*, Heinemann, 1981.

80. D. Lusted (Ed.), *op. cit.*

81. S. Neale, *Genre*, BFI, 1980.

82. BFI Education, *Narrative* (teaching pack), BFI, 1981.
83. Open University, *op. cit.*
84. T. Bennett *et al.*, (Eds.), *op. cit.*
85. D. Hebdige and G. Hurd, 'Reading and Realism', *Screen Education* 28, Autumn, 1978.
86. V. Propp, The Morphology of the Folktale, Texas University Press, 1973. R. Barthes, *Introduction to the Structural Analysis of Narratives, op. cit.*, and *S/Z*, Cape, 1975. G. Genette, *Narrative Discourse*, Blackwell, 1980.

Chapter 6: Ideology
 1. R. Williams, *Keywords*, Fontana, 1976, p. 126.
 2. Stuart Hall, 'Culture, the Media, and the "Ideological Effect"', J. Curran, M. Gurevitch and J. Woollacott (Eds.), *Mass Communication and Society*, Edward Arnold, 1977, p. 325.
 3. Cited in Williams, *op. cit.*, p. 126. Williams's historical analysis of ideology should be consulted as one of the most accessible and concise analyses of the concept.
 4. *Ibid*, p. 127.
 5. Marx and Engels, *The German Ideology*, cited by Williams, *op. cit.*, p. 127.
 6. Williams, *op. cit.*, p. 128.
 7. T. O'Sullivan, J. Hartley, D. Saunders and J. Fiske, *Key Concepts in Communication*, Methuen, 1983, p. 109.
 8. See Williams, *op. cit.*, p. 129.
 9. In *Letter to the Federation of the North*, cited by Williams, *op. cit.*, p. 129.
10. *Ibid.*
11. See The Glasgow University Media Group, *War and Peace News, op. cit.*; R. Harris, *op. cit.*, and Cockerell *et al.*, *op. cit.*, Chapter 8.
12. Cited in Cockerell *et al.*, *op. cit.*, p. 159.
13. *Ibid*
14. *Ibid*, p, 158.
15. Cited in Cockerell *et al.*, *op. cit.*, p. 154.
16. The Glasgow Media Group, *War and Peace News, op. cit.*, p. 23.
17. Cockerell *et al.*, pp. 166–7.
18. The Glasgow Media Group, *War and Peace News, op. cit.*, pp. 18 and 23.
19. D. McLellan, *Marxism after Marx*, Macmillan, 1979, p. 187. See, also, Antonio Gramsci, *Prison Notebooks* (Eds. Q. Hoare and G. Nowell-Smith), Lawrence and Wishart, 1971, pp. 57 ff and 245 ff.
20. R. Williams, *Keywords, op. cit.*, p. 118.
21. R. Barthes, *Mythologies, op. cit.*, p. 109.
22. *Ibid*, p. 11.
23. *Ibid*, p. 129.
24. *Ibid*, p. 151.
25. *Ibid*, p. 143.
26. *Ibid.*
27. L. Althusser, *op. cit.*
28. N. Poulantzas, *Political Power and Social Classes*, New Left Books, and Sheed and Ward, 1965.
29. S. Hall, 'Culture, the Media and the "Ideological" Effect', *op. cit.*, p. 325.
30. S. Hall, 'The Hinterland of Science: Ideology and "the Sociology of Knowldge"', Centre for Contemporary Cultural Studies, *On Ideology*, Hutchinson, 1978, pp. 10–11.
31. L. Masterman, *Teaching about Television, op. cit.*, Chapter 3.
32. U. Eco, 'Can Television Teach?', *Screen Education*, No. 31, 1979, p. 15.
33. T. Eagleton, Seminar on *Marxism and Structuralism*, Nottingham University, June, 1982.
34. L. Masterman, *op. cit.*, p. 56 ff.

35. S. Hall, *Encoding and Decoding in the Television Discourse*, Centre for Contemporary Cultural Studies, University of Birmingham, 1973.
36. For further examples of ideological analyses of particular television programmes see Masterman (Ed.), *Mythologies, op. cit.*, and Masterman, *Teaching About Television, op. cit.*, pp. 62 ff, 65 ff, 166 ff, 170 ff and 172 ff.
37. F. de Saussure, *Course in General Linguistics*, Fontana, 1974, p. 116.
38. C. Belsey, *Critical Practice*, Methuen, New Accents, 1980, p. 42.
39. *Ibid*, p. 44.
40. T. Eagleton, *Literary Theory*, Blackwell, 1983, pp. 107–8.
41. Bonney and Wilson, *op. cit.*, p. 5.
42. P. Taylor, cited in L. Curtis, *op. cit.*, pp. 133–4.
43. *Ibid*, pp. 134–5.
44. D. Jones, J. Petley *et al.*, *Media Hit the Pits*, Campaign for Press and Broadcasting Freedom, 1985, p. 24.
45. *Ibid.*
46. A. Hetherington, *op. cit.*
47. See Bob Ferguson, 'Black Blue Peter', in L. Masterman (Ed.), *op. cit.*, p. 34.
48. NUJ, *Equality Style Guide*, published by NUJ Equality Council, Acorn House, 314/320 Grays Inn Road, London WC1.
49. N. Poulantzas, *Political Power and Social Classes*, Verso, 1978, p. 214.
50. The phrase is James Curran's, 'The press as an agency of social control: an historical perspective', in Boyce *et al.*, *op. cit.*, p. 60.
51. Higgins and Moss, *op. cit.*, p. 51.
52. Bonney and Wilson, *op. cit.*, p. 194. Bonney and Wilson are here referring to advertisements, but their remarks apply with equal force to the ideological operations of the media as a whole.
53. S. Hall, 'Culture, Media and the Ideological Effect', *op. cit.*, p. 337.

Chapter 7: Audience

1. James D. Halloran (Ed.), *The Effects of Television*, Panther, 1970.
2. See P. Elliott, 'Uses and Gratifications Research: A Critique and a Sociological Alternative' in J. Blumler and E. Katz (Eds.), *The Uses of Mass Communications*, Sage, 1974.
3. Bill Bonney and Helen Wilson, *Australia's Commercial Media*, Macmillan, Melbourne, 1983, pp. 19–20.
4. David Morley, *The 'Nationwide' Audience*, Television Monograph No. 11, The British Film Institute, London, 1980.
5. *Ibid*, p. 14–15.
6. See, for example, Manuel Alvarado, 'Television Studies and Pedagogy', *Screen Education*, No. 38, Spring, 1981, and Judith Williamson 'How Does Girl Number Twenty Understand Ideology?', *Screen Education*, No. 40, Autumn/Winter, 1981/2.
7. Ian Connell, 'Progressive Pedagogy', *Screen*, Vol. 24, No. 3, May/June, 1983, pp. 53–4.
8. T. Eagleton, *Literary Theory*, *op. cit.*, p. 87.
9. D. Morley, *op. cit.*, pp. 10–12.
10. F. Parkin, *Class Inequality and Political Order*, MacGibbon and Kee, 1971.
11. Stuart Hall, *Encoding and decoding in the Television Discourse*, stencilled occasional paper, Centre for Contemporary Cultural Studies, University of Birmingham, 1973.
12. D. Morley, 'Cultural Transformations: the politics of resistance', H. Davis and P. Walton (Eds.), *Language, Image, Media*, Blackwell, 1983, pp. 109–110.
13. *Ibid.*, p. 117.
14. *Ibid.*

15. Dorothy Hobson, *Crossroads: The Drama of a Soap Opera*, Methuen, 1982, pp. 147–9.
16. *Ibid*, p. 171.
17. Dallas Smythe, 'Capitalism, Advertising and the Consciousness Industry'. An interview with Henry Mayer, *Media Information Australia*, No. 31, February, 1984, p. 22.
18. *Ibid*.
19. *Ibid*, p. 23.
20. Dallas Smythe, *Dependency Road: Communications, Capitalism, Consciousness and Canada*, Ablex, New Jersey, 1981, p. 13.
21. *Ibid*, p. 14.
22. *Ibid*, pp. 13; 24–25; 49–51; 272–3.
23. Smythe, 'Capitalism, Advertising and the Consciousness Industry', *op. cit.*, p. 24.
24. Smythe, *Dependency Road*, *op. cit.*, p. 283.
25. *Ibid*, p. 15.
26. L. Masterman, 'The Battle of Orgreave', in L. Masterman (Ed.), *Television Mythologies*, *op. cit.*
27. B. Whitaker, *op. cit.*, pp. 24–5.
28. *Ibid*, p. 26.
29. These stories were collected by Alan Rushbridger, 'Diary', *The Guardian*, 22 and 23 August, 1984.
30. This example is adapted from Bonney and Wilson, *op. cit.*, p. 22.
31. It was Cary Bazalgette's analysis of *Disney Time* which led me to look closely at this particular programme. This analysis leans heavily on her more detailed account. See C. Bazalgette, 'All in Fun: Su Pollard on *Disney Time*', in L. Masterman (Ed.), *Television Mythologies*, *op. cit.*
32. See Roland Barthes, *Mythologies*, *op. cit.*, pp. 120–1 and 130 for the necessity of 'barbarous but unavoidable neologisms'.
33. Central Statistical Office, *Social Trends 1985*, Chart 2.6, p. 33, HMSO, 1985. The number of one-person households has virtually doubled from 12% in 1961 to 23% in 1983.
34. Cited by N. Garnham, *Structures of Television*, BFI Television Monograph No. 1, BFI, 1973, p. 8.
35. The following notes on *Family Fortunes* owe a great deal to an original unpublished paper by Neil Campbell, one of my own PGCE students at Nottingham University in 1981–2: N. Campbell, The Ideology of the Quiz Show: the closed Circle of Family Fortunes. I have also found useful Bill Lewis, 'TV Games: People as Performers', in L. Masterman (Ed.), *Television Mythologies*, *op. cit.*
36. Campbell, *op. cit.*
37. *Ibid*.
38. *Ibid*.
39. Barthes, *Mythologies*, *op. cit.*, p. 143.
40. See, especially, Laura Mulvey, 'Visual Pleasure and Narrative Cinema', *Screen*, Autumn, 1975, Vol. 16, no. 3, and the special double issue of *Screen*, Vol. 23, Nos. 3–4, September/October, 1982, on 'Sex and Spectatorship'.
41. The British Film Institute, *Selling Pictures*, Image Project Unit 2, BFI, 1983.
42. E. Goffman, *Gender Advertisements*, Macmillan, 1979.
43. Bonney and Wilson, *op. cit.*, pp. 21–2.
44. Catherine Belsey, *Critical Practice*, Methuen, 1980, p. 73. The brevity of my own account greatly over-simplifies a great deal of complex work on subjectivity. Belsey's own résumé of this work is recommended to teachers wishing to read further, as is Louis Althusser's classic essay 'Ideology and ideological state apparatuses', *Lenin and Philosophy* and other essays, New Left Books, 1971.
45. Althusser, *op. cit.*, p. 169.

46. *Ibid*, pp. 162–3.
47. Laura Mulvey, 'Visual Pleasure and Narrative Cinema', *op. cit.*

Chapter 8: Futures
1. See P. Wiegand, *A Biased View*, University of London Institute of Education, 1982, and D. Wright, *Distorting the Picture*, *The Times Educational Supplement*, 6.11.81., p. 20.
2. P. Wiegand, *op. cit.*, p. 26.
3. A. Jenkins and M. Youngs, 'Geographical Education and Film: An Experimental Course', *Journal of Geography in Higher Education*, Vol. 7, No. 1, 1983.
4. *Ibid*.
5. *Ibid*.
6. D. W. Meinig, 'The Beholding Eye: Ten Versions of the same scene', in D. W. Meinig (Ed.), *The Interpretation of Ordinary Landscapes*, Oxford University Press, New York, 1979, pp. 33–34.
7. Virginia Nightingale, *International Imagery: A Study of British Children's Explanations of other Countries.* Unpublished paper available from the author at Kuring-gai College of Advanced Education, Sydney, Australia, p. 5. See also V. Nightingale, 'Images of Foreigners: The British Report', in *Young TV Viewers and their Images of Foreigners*, Siftung Prix Jeunesse, Munich, 1982.
8. V. Nightingale, *International Imagery, op. cit.*, p. 5.
9. *Ibid*, p. 4.
10. *Ibid*, pp. 6 and 5.
11. M. J. Youngs, *The Ante-Bellum South as an Image Region*, Discussion Paper in *Geography*, No. 12, Oxford Polytechnic, Oxford, 1980.
12. J. W. Watson, 'The Role of Illusion in N. American Geography', *Canadian Geographer*, 13 (1), 10–27; 1970/71; J. W. Watson and T. O'Riordan (Eds.), *The American Environment: Perceptions and Policies*, John Wiley, London, 1976.
13. M. J. Youngs, *op. cit.*, p. 6. The phrases are J. W. Watson's in Watson and O'Riordan, *op. cit.*, p. 19.
14. C. H. Bohner, *John Pendleton Kennedy, Gentleman from Baltimore*, Baltimore, The John Hopkins Press, 1961, p. 73, cited by Youngs, *op. cit.*, p. 1.
15. W. J. Cash, *The Mind of the South*, Thames and Hudson, London, 1971, pp. 15–16. Cited by Youngs, *op. cit.*, p. 37.
16. Schlesinger, Murdock and Elliott, *op. cit.*, p. 84.
17. H. Newby, 'A One-Eyed Look at the Country', *New Society*, Vol. 53, 1980, pp. 324–5.
18. The films are available from Shell Film Library, 25 The Burroughs, Hendon, London NW4 4AT (01-202-7803).
19. M. Youngs and A. Jenkins, 'Shell-Shocked: Critical Film Analysis and Teaching Strategies', *Geography*, January, 1984.
20. *Ibid*, p. 51.
21. S. J. Hall, *Africa in U.S. Educational Materials*, Afro-American Institute, New York, 1976. *Asia in American Textbooks*, Asia Society, New York, 1976; W. J. Griswold, *The Image of the Middle East in Secondary School Textbooks*, Middle East Studies Association of N. America Inc., New York, 1975.
22. D. Hicks, *Images of the World: An Introduction to Bias in Teaching Materials*, Occasional paper No. 2, Centre for Multi-Cultural Education, Institute of Education, London University, London, 1980, p. 7.
23. *Ibid*, p. 16.
24. *Ibid*, pp. 14–16.
25. David Wright, 'Distorting the Picture', *The Times Educational Supplement*, 6.11.81, pp. 20–21.
26. David Wright, 'The reluctant convert', *The Times Educational Supplement*, 29.3.85, p. 44.

27. A. Jenkins, *Modern China. The Heart of the Dragon*, Yorkshire Television, Spring, 1985.

28. See Jacquelin Burgess and David Unwin, *Exploring the Living Planet with David Attenborough*, Journal of Geography in Higher Education, Vol. 8, No. 2, 1984, p. 111.

29. *Ibid.*

30. *New Scientist*, 3.iii.1977, p. 525, cited by N. Ryder, *Science, Television and the Adolescent*, Independent Broadcasting Authority, 1982, p. 173.

31. R. Dawes, a 19th century pioneer of the Science curriculum, cited by D. Layton, *Science for the People*, Allen and Unwin, 1973, p. 42.

32. The view of another 19th century scientist, J. Henslow, paraphrased by N. Ryder, *op. cit.*, p. 305.

33. N. Ryder, *op. cit.* Ryder's study additionally raises a great many other issues and is exempt from the criticism which follows.

34. K. R. Popper, 'A Rational Theory of Tradition', in *Conjectures and Refutations*, Routledge and Kegan Paul, London, 1974, cited in Ryder, *op. cit.*, p. 169.

35. C. Gardner and R. Young, 'Science on TV: A Critique', in T. Bennet *et al.* (Eds.), *Popular Television and Film*, The British Film Institute and The Open University Press, 1981, p. 177.

36. *Ibid*, pp. 177–8.

37. For the most accessible accounts of current debates on the status of literature see T. Eagleton, *Literary Theory*, *op. cit.* and P. Widdowson (Ed.), *Re-Reading English*, Methuen, 1982.

38. R. Unwin, *The Visual Dimension in the Study and Teaching of History*, Teaching History Series, No. 49, The Historical Association, London, 1981.

39. Cited by J. Whale, *The Half Shut Eye*, Macmillan, London, 1969, p. 42.

40. Cited by P. Knightley, *The First Casualty*, Quartet, London, 1978. Preface.

41. John Fines and Raymond Verrier, *The Drama of History*, New University Education, 1974, p. 84.

42. C. McArthur, *Television and History*, Television Monograph No. 8, The British Film Institute, 1978, p. 9. Against 'chronological monism' McArthur sets 'the notion of differential temporality in one historical period and the posing of conceptual relationships among events in diverse historical periods (e.g., the English Revolution of 1649, the French Revolution of 1789 and the Russian Revolution of 1917).'

43. Bennet *et al*, *op. cit.*, pp. 285–6.

44. See S. Hall, 'Television and Culture' in *Sight and Sound*, Autumn, 1976, London, pp. 246–252, for an analysis of professional notions of 'good television'.

45. McArthur, *op. cit.*, p. 7.

46. Alvarado and Ferguson, *op. cit.*, p. 20.

47. Cited by McArthur, *op. cit.*, p. 27.

48. See Marsha Jones and Jo Dungey, *Ethnic Minorities and Television*, Centre for Mass Communication Research, University of Leicester, 1983, Chapter 5.

49. I am greatly indebted to conversations with Dr. Dorothy Singer of Yale University for these specific suggestions. Many of the ideas discussed in the second part of this chapter emerged out of a UNESCO Conference on Media Education held in Marseilles in March, 1983.

50. See David Lusted, 'Feeding the Panic and Breaking the Cycle', *Screen*, Vol. 24, No. 6, November–December, 1983 (especially p. 87) for an analysis of press reactions to the DES Report.

51. See pp. 101–2.

52. See, for example, *Looking at Newspapers* and *Newspapers in Education*, both produced free by The Newspaper Society (the association of publishers of the regional and local press), Whitefriars House, Carmelite Street, London EC4Y 0BL.

ANNOTATED BIBLIOGRAPHY
(* denotes work of particular interest to media teachers)

Altheide, D.L.
Creating Reality — How TV News distorts events, Sage 1976.
> Important American study of televised news. Particularly good on news 'angles' and the narrative sequencing of events within news programmes. Excellent final section on how to watch the news 'defensively'.

*Althusser, L.
'Ideology and Ideological State Apparatuses' in *Lenin and Philosophy and other essays*, New Left Books, 1971.
> Important essay on how the reproduction of the relations and conditions of production is assured by the State. The notion of Ideological State Apparatuses provides a powerful conceptual tool for teachers wishing to demonstrate parallels between the functions and practices of schools and the media.

Alvarado, M. and Buscombe, E.
Hazell: The Making of a TV Series, BFI/Latimer, 1978.
> Detailed account of the production of a popular television series, and one of the few available sources for teachers wishing to examine 'TV as industry'. One of the best programmes from the series, 'Hazell Meets the First Eleven' may be hired from the BFI, and should be used in conjunction with the book.

Alvarado, M. and Ferguson, R.
'The Curriculum, Media Studies and Discursivity', *Screen* Vol. 24 No. 3, May/June 1983.
> An important article arguing that teaching about the media involves a radical critique of all school subjects, which like the media, tend to be conceptualised as forms of 'realism' rather than as symbolic systems.

Alvarado, M. and Stewart, J.
Made for Television: Euston Films Limited, Methuen/BFI, 1985
> Analysis of the production methods, interviews with the personnel, and critical assessments of the programmes of Euston Films, makers of *Minder*, *The Sweeney*, *Fox*, *Out* etc.

Aubrey, C. (Ed.)
Nukespeak: the Media and the Bomb, Comedia, 1982
> Collection of essays of variable quality and from a variety of perspectives on the media and the Bomb. Very good contributions from Paul Chilton on nuclear language (Nukespeak) and Richard Keeble on how to change media distortion. Keeble's piece contains a run-down on strategies, contacts, resources, literature and programmes of action which is directly relevant to media teachers.

Aubrey, C., Landry, C. and Morley, D.
Here is the Other News — Challenges to the Local Commercial Press, Minority Press Group, 1980.
> The history of the local radical press since 1970, with an examination of the problems it faces over economics and distribution.

Bakewell, J. and Garnham, N.
The New Priesthood, Allen Lane, 1970
> Potted but illuminating interviews with producers, writers and executives in television. Enjoyable reading. Sections on News, Documentary, Current Affairs, Drama and Light Entertainment.

Barthes, R.
Camera Lucida, Hill and Wang, N.Y., 1981.
> Barthes' extraordinarily moving and perceptive account of the fascination of photographs. Excellent insights into the specificity of photography, the personal meanings of photographs, and their ideological functions and effects.

Barthes, R.
The Eiffel Tower and other Mythologies, Hill and Wang, N.Y., 1979.
  A recently published collection of contemporary myths. The title essay is the most impressive and developed piece in this collection.
Barthes, R.
Image-Music-Text, Fontana/Collins, 1977.
  Collection of essays containing three key texts, 'The Rhetoric of the Image', a semiological analysis of an advertisement photograph with an important discussion of different levels of analysis of visual material; 'Introduction to the Structural Analysis of Narratives', a difficult but influential contribution to the literature on narrative structure; and 'The Photographic Message', a useful starting point for the analysis of press photographs.
*Barthes, R.
Mythologies, Cape, 1972
  A key work. Contains analytical vignettes on different aspects of popular culture (Strip-tease, Wrestling, Toys, etc.), together with a longer theoretical essay, *Myth Today* which has been (and continues to be) widely influential.
Beharrell, P. and Philo, G. (eds.)
Trade Unions and the Media, Macmillan, 1977.
  Essays covering a good deal of the *Bad News* territory. Most interesting, because most original are two short studies of media coverage of students and farmworkers.
Belsey, Catherine.
Critical Practice, Methuen, New Accents, 1980.
  Along with Eagleton's *Literary Theory: An Introduction*, this is the best and most accessible introduction to recent developments in critical theory.
Bennett, T., Martin, G., Mercer, C. and Woollacott, J.
Culture, Ideology and Social Process, Basford and the Open University, 1981.
  One of a number of excellent Open University readers, this time supporting the *Popular Culture* course. Contains essays exemplifying 'culturalist' and 'structuralist' approaches, and there is a section devoted to Gramsci and hegemony. Recommended.
Bennett, T., Boyd-Bowman, S. et al,
Popular Television and Film, The British Film Institute, and the Open University, 1981.
  An Open University Reader for their *Popular Culture* course, usefully collecting together some of the most influential articles on *Genre*, *Television* (Current Affairs, Football, Science), *Film and Pleasure*, and *History, Politics and Narrative* (The *Days of Hope* debate).
*Berger, J.
'From today art is dead', *Times Educational Supplement*, 1 December 1972.
  Clarion call for a new approach to visual education. An important and seminal article.
*Berger, J.
Ways of Seeing, BBC and Penguin, 1972
  An influential work, providing a political perspective on the history and genres of fine art, and making thematic, ideological and iconic connexions between them and popular culture.
Berger, J. and Mohr, J.
Another Way of Telling, Writers and Readers, 1982.
  Important essay by Berger on the nature of photographic communication (following Barthes and Sontag), and a photo-essay by Jean Mohr. Suitable for sixth form students and above, as well as teachers.
Berman, E.
'Preface' to *Basic Video in Community Work*, Inter-action Advisory Service Handbook No. 5, Inter-action Imprint, 1975.
  Sensible and restrained account of the value and limitations of video in community work.

Best, G., Dennis, J. and Draper, P.
Mass Media and the National Health Service, Unit for the Study of Health Policy, 1977.

> Impressive report on coverage of health issues and the Health Service in the media. Looks at the dominant images and interpretative frameworks for reporting (e.g. health is equated with the consumption of more and more health services, and with the development of modern scientific medicine) and contains case-studies of reporting on particular issues.

*Bethell, A.
Eye Openers (One and Two), Cambridge University Press, 1981.

> Two excellent booklets for secondary school pupils in which they are required to manipulate and interrogate photographs and their meanings. *Eye-openers One* examines optical illusions and problems of seeing, visual codings, photography and personal identity, and visual narrative. *Eye-openers Two* looks at news photographs, documentaries, and advertising images. The suggested exercises should be both illuminating and appropriate for secondary school pupils. Recommended.

Bethell, A.
Viewpoint 2, Thames Television, (undated).

> Imaginatively produced booklet to accompany the *Viewpoint 2* Television series. Contains discussion exercises on media coverage of Youth, Race, Workers and Welfare. Recommended.

Bibby, A. Denford, C. and Cross, J.
Local Television: Piped Dreams? Redwing, 1979.

> Excellent critical analysis of community television by three workers from community video stations. Much of the analysis is applicable to educational video.

Birkett, J. and Twitchin, R.
Understanding Television, Thames Television, 1983.

> Attractively produced booklet to accompany Thames' *Understanding Television* series. Includes very useful classroom activities on contsructing meaning through manipulating images and commentary, as well as sections on television production, television philosophy and policy, the television audience, and Dutch television. Recommended.

Birt, J.
'Can television news break the understanding barrier?', *The Times*, 22 February 1975.

Birt, J., and Jay P.
'Television journalism: the child of an unhappy marriage between newspapers and film', *The Times*, 30 September 1975.

Birt, J. and Jay, P.
'The radical changes needed to remedy TV's bias against understanding', *The Times*, 1 October 1975.

Birt, J. and Jay, P.
'How television news can hold the mass audience', *The Times*, 2 September 1976.

Birt, J. and Jay, P.
'Why television news is in danger of becoming an anti-social force', *The Times*, 3 September 1976.

> Influential series of articles in The Times, criticising the distinction between television news and current affairs and arguing that television news is a hybrid form which needs to break away from its historical antecedents, newspaper journalism and film, and develop its own forms which would enable it to treat subjects in the depth, and with the expertise they deserve. The present determinants of television news forms lead to shallowness and superficiality of treatment which constitute a 'bias against understanding'.

Black, P.
The Biggest Aspidistra in the World, BBC, 1972.

> A publication to celebate the BBC's 50th anniversary. Contains a potted personal (and entertaining) history of BBC TV programmes.

Black, P.
The Mirror in the Corner, Hutchinson, 1972
  Generalised history of the BBC and ITV up to the early 1970's with particular emphasis upon the political events leading up to the advent of ITV. Clear on events, superficial on ideas and arguments.

Blanchard, S. and Morley, D.
What's This Channel For? Comedia, 1982.
  Collection of papers written before Channel Four went on air, expressing the hopes of critics, feminists, blacks, young people, etc., for genuine alternative practices to be given encouragement by the new channel.

Blumler, J.G., Gurevitch, M. and Ives, J.
The Challenge of Election Broadcasting, Leeds University Press, 1978.
  An examination of how television covered the two election campaigns of 1974, written by a research team from Leeds University. Attempts to come up with solutions to problems that will be acceptable to the political parties, the broadcasters and the audience. Covers party political broadcasts, news bulletins at election time and the dangers of providing *too much* election coverage and alienating the viewers.

*Bonney, Bill and Wilson, Helen.
Australia's Commercial Media, Macmillan, Melbourne, 1983
  Though dealing with Australian media, this is the best available book on media teaching in Higher Education.

Boorstin, D.J.
The Image, Pelican, 1963.
  Classic early American study of 'pseudo-events' and personalities, created specifically for the media. The trends outlined continue unabated in today's media.

Boston, R. (ed).
The Press We Deserve, RKP, 1970.
  Critical essays on the press by Raymond Williams, Tom Baistow, D.A.N. Jones and others. There are specific chapters on women's journalism, sport, financial journalism and reviewing.

Boyce, G., Curran, J. and Wingate, P. (eds).
Newspaper History: from the 17th century to the present day.
  An invaluable collection of historical perspectives on the press with sections on Structure, Ownership and Control, the Organisation and Occupation of Journalism, and Press, Politics and Society. Recommended.

Boyd-Barrett, O.
The International News Agencies, Constable, 1980.
  Important study of an influential, but much-neglected field, the role, and workings of international news agencies. This full-length study examines their ownership, markets and finances, as well as their internal structures. Each of the 'big four' agencies (AP, AFP, Reuters and UPI) is described and analysed.

Brandt, G.W. (ed).
British Television Drama, Cambridge University Press, 1981.
  Critical studies of television dramatists (Jim Allen, Trevor Griffiths, Alan Plater, etc.) by diverse hands. Not wihout value, but inevitably weakened by its concentration upon authorship, and its neglect of the economic and institutional contexts within which television drama is actually produced.

Briggs, A.
The History of Broadcasting in the United Kingdom.
Vol. I The Birth of Broadcasting OUP 1961
Vol. II The Golden Age of Wireless OUP 1965
Vol. III The War of Words OUP 1970
Vol. IV Sound and Vision OUP 1979
  Actually, much more a history of the BBC rather than broadcasting, with most of the 'facts' painstakingly pieced together from official and semi-official

documentation (with all of the problems and weaknesses this implies). More useful as a source of information than of ideological insights.

BBC.

Audience Research Findings, BBC.

Annual reviews are available of these findings which cover audience size and reactions, and detailed case studies on particular series or aspects of broadcasting. An invaluable source of data.

BBC.

Handbook, BBC annually.

Invaluable yearly handbook of facts and information about the Beeb's activities.

The British Film Institute.

Television Monographs, BFI.

1. *Structures of Television* by Nicholas Garnham.
2. *Light Entertainment* by Richard Dyer.
3. *Television and the February 1974 General Election* by Trevor Pateman.
4. *Football on Television* edited by Ed. Buscombe.
5. *Television News* by Richard Collins.
6. *Television Documentary Usage* by Dai Vaughan.
7. *Broadcasting and Accountability* by Caroline Heller.
8. *Television and History* by Colin McArthur.
9. *Television: Ideology and Exchange* edited by John Caughie.
10. *Everyday Television: Nationwide* by Charlotte Brunsdon and David Morley.
11. *The Nationwide Audience* by David Morley.
12. *WDR and the Arbeiter Film* by Richard Collins and Vincent Porter.
13. *Coronation Street* by Richard Dyer et al.

Important sources for teachers. The series represents one of the few attempts at extended analysis on different aspects of television available in Britain. Details of the most important monographs are given under their authors.

The British Film Institute.

Media Education Conference, 1981, BFI and University of London, Goldsmiths' College, 1982.

A report of the second national Media Education Conference held at Goldsmiths' College, London in 1981. Contains a conference report by Connell and O'Shaughnessy, and papers on Media Education in the 1970's by David Lusted, and Media Education in the 80's by Len Masterman.

The British Film Institute and Society for Education in Film and Television.

Report of 1976 Conference on Film and Television Studies in Secondary Education, BFI, 1976.

The report offers a useful survey of progress in and attitudes towards film, television and media studies in the mid-seventies.

The British Film Institute.

Teaching Coronation Street, BFI, 1983.

A teachers' guide to classwork on the soap opera which should be used in conjunction with the *Coronation Street* monograph (by R. Dyer et al), and slides and tapes from the series available from the British Film Institute. Imaginatively compiled, it contains interesting exercises for the classroom, and well-chosen support material. Recommended.

The British Film Institute Dossier No. 9.

Granada: the First 25 Years, BFI, 1981.

Extremely useful collection of documents, articles and information about the history of the television company. Contains chapters on The First Night, the First Election Broadcasts, Television in 1959, Sidney Bernstein, *Coronation Street*, and Current Affairs and Documentary.

The British Film Institute Dossier No. 15.

Tonight, BFI, 1982.

Contains a short history of the famous BBC current affairs programme and an

extract from Goldie relating to the programme.
The British Film Institute Dossier No. 17.
Television Sitcom, BFI, 1982.
> Very useful collection of papers in an area where the literature is particularly thin. Contains detailed analyses of *Yes Minister*, *Hi-De-Hi*, and discussions of ideology, sexual stereotyping, etc.
The British Film Institute Dossier No. 19.
Drama — Documentary, BFI, 1983.
> Excellent collection of materials on the genre relating to the controversies aroused by particular programmes (*Cathy Come Home*, *Law and Order*, etc.), and outlining the principal areas of debate. Also contains a check-list of British drama-documentaries since 1946, and a useful bibliography.
*Brunsdon, C. and Morley, D.
Everyday Television: Nationwide, BFI, 1978. Television Monograph No. 10.
> Excellent and accessible analysis of the *Nationwide* programme exploring its main ideological themes, and drawing attention to the mediating functions of anchorpersons. Very useful for teachers.
Burgin, V.
Thinking Photography, Macmillan, 1982.
> A collection of essays which attempts to develop a materialist analysis of photography with contributions from Eco, Benjamin and Burgin himself. Looks at the production of meaning of photographs within social institutions and within the unconscious.
Burns, T.
The BBC: Public Institution and Private World, Macmillan, 1977.
> A long-awaited organisational study of the BBC by a sociologist. Based on two sets of interviews in the early 1960's, and early 1970's, and therefore somewhat dated by the time of publication. Many of the attitudes expressed still no doubt exist, however, and the book is important both as background reading and for its direct insights into the organisational politics of news, current affairs, sport and light entertainment.
Buscombe, E. ed.
Football on Television, BFI Monograph No. 5, 1975.
> The most detailed study available of a televised sporting event, the 1974 World Cup.
Buscombe, E.
Television Studies in Schools and Colleges, IBA Report in *Screen Education* No. 12, Autumn 1974.
> An early exploration of issues and practice in Television Studies. Sections on 'Why study television?' and 'What should one teach about television?' are followed by descriptions of seven different television courses and a 'model' course.
Butler, D.E.
The British General Election of 1955, Macmillan, 1955.
Butler, D.E. and Kavanagh, D.
The British General Election of February 1974, Macmillan, 1974; and *The British General Election of October 1974*, Macmillan, 1975.
Butler, D.E. and King, A.
The British General Election of 1959, Macmillan, 1960; *The British General Election of 1964*, Macmillan, 1965; and *The British General Election of 1966*, Macmillan, 1966.
Butler, D.E.. and Pinto-Duschinsky M.
The British General Election of 1970, Macmillan, 1971
> Butler et al's seven studies of British elections since 1955. Each contains a chapter on broadcast coverage.
Butler, D.E. and Stokes, D.
Political Change in Britain, Penguin, 1971.
> Contains chapter on the impact of the media on political change.

Camerawork No. 14 1979
    Issue of *Camerawork* devoted to 'Reporting on Northern Ireland', with excellent
    photographs and articles on media coverage of events in the six counties.
Campaign for Free Speech on Ireland.
The British Media and Ireland, CFSI.
    Important polemical pamphlet on media censorship on Ireland with contributions
    from Schlesinger, Elliott, Arden and D'Arcy and others.
CPBF
Are you in the Picture? Campaign for Press and Broadcasting Freedom, 1983.
    Short booklet attacking the attempt of broadcasting institutions to impose
    consensus views. Looks briefly at the ways working people, blacks, women,
    Northern Ireland, and nuclear disarmament are handled by the media.
Carpenter, E.
Oh, What a Blow that Phantom Gave Me! Paladin, 1976.
    Extraordinary collection of media anecdotes and illuminations by an
    anthropologist (and former colleague of McLuhan) who demonstrates how print
    and the electronic media 'swallow cultures'.
Carroll, D.
General and Communication Studies: Don't You Believe It! Macmillan, 1981.
    A lively text-book for Further Education Students in the Macmillan Technician
    Series. Contains exercises on Mass Communication, Political Literacy, and
    Ideology.
Caughie, J. ed.
Television: Ideology and Exchange, BFI 1978: Television Monograph No. 9.
    Seven disparate but extremely useful essays from foreign sources. 'Underlying the
    collection is the assumption that television does function as an Ideological
    Apparatus'

Chadman, E., Chester, G. and Pivot, A.
Rolling Our Own, Minority Press Group, 1981.
    Looks at the activities of women in publishing — as printers, writers and
    distributors — and gives useful advice to women working in these fields. A useful
    source for studies of women and the media.
Chibnall, S.
Law and Order News, Tavistock, 1977.
    Excellent study of crime-reporting in the British press, with insights into how news
    is manufactured and managed by the police and the army. Contains chapter on
    press coverage in Northern Ireland and a useful summary of the research on news
    values.
Cleverley, G.
The Fleet Street Disaster, Constable, 1976.
    Sub-titled 'British national newspapers as a case-study in mismanagement', this is a
    rare account — and indictment — of the management of the national newspaper
    industry. Excellent detail and discussion on all aspects of the economics of
    newspapers — profits, advertising, circulation and salaries — though the precise
    data itself is inevitably dated.
*Cockerell, M., Hennessy, P. and Walker, D.
Sources Close to the Prime Minister, Macmillan, 1984.
    Superb inside account of political news manipulation written by three working
    journalists. Excellent analyses of the Lobby system, the Conservative's 1983
    election campaign, media coverage of the Falklands conflict, the role of the Prime
    Minister's Press Secretary, and the State's news management machinery.
    Compulsive and essential reading, since it points the way towards promising future
    developments within media education.
Cohen, P. and Gardner, C. (eds).
It Ain't Half Racist, Mum, Comedia and Carm, 1982.
    Published in conjunction with the Campaign Against Racism in the Media (Carm),

this collection of short pieces by concerned media workers looks at different aspects of racism in the media, and proposes strategies for counter-action.

*Cohen, S. and Young, J.
The Manufacture of News, Constable, 1973. Revised and extended, 1981.
A collection of important, and often indispensable texts on the news media's treatment of deviancy and social problems. Cross-media in content, and an important in-service text for media teachers.

*Colledge, C.
Classroom Photography, Ilford (14–22 Tottenham Court Road, London W1P 0AH).
An excellently produced, yet simple guide to making photographs in the classroom without a camera or darkroom. Invaluable for Primary and lower Secondary School teachers since it suggests ways in which this kind of work might be integrated into the Primary School curriculum (particularly in Science). Strongly recommended.

Collins, R.
Television News, BFI Monograph No. 5, BFI, 1976.
A useful study of some of the assumptions and practices of British televised news. Covers news values, economics, and style.

Conrad, P.
Television: The Medium and Its Manners, RKP, 1982.
Reflections on aspects of television with examples from British and US Television. Contains chapters on game shows, news programmes, ads, soap opera, etc.

Cook, J. and Hillier, J.
'Film and Television Education in Great Britain', *Screen Education* No. 18, 1976.
Survey of developments in media teaching up to the mid 70's.

Cooke, B.
Writing Comedy for Television, Methuen, 1983.
A book aimed at would-be writers of TV comedy scripts but very useful for teachers and students who wish to analyse television humour. Excellent on the different techniques available for getting a laugh. Covers sitcoms, sketches, 'quickies', and stand-up comedy.

Corner, J. and Hawthorn, J. (eds).
Communication Studies: An Introductory Reader, Arnold, 1980.
An introductory reader to the field for students. Contains a short section on Mass Communication.

*Coward, Rosalind
Female Desire, Paladin, 1984.
Excellent collection of essays on cultural representations of women and female sexuality. Covers a wide range of media topics from agony aunts to ideal homes, horoscopes to the Royals. Very readable and highly recommended.

CSE Communication Group.
Hunt on Cable TV: Chaos or Coherence? The Campaign for Press and Broadcasting Freedom, 1982.
A critical look at the Hunt Report on cable television. Argues that it is not enough for communications 'policy' to be settled by market forces, and that the labour movement needs to develop alternative community-based strategies for cable.

Cudlipp, H.
The Prerogative of the Harlot, The Bodley Head, 1980.
Fascinating and horrifying study of the personal vendettas, and megalomania of five press barons — Hearst, Northcliffe, Rothermere, Luce, and Beaverbrook. A handy source for those wishing to put questions of media ownership and control into a recent historical context.

Culler, J.
Barthes, Fontana, 1983.
Short study of Barthes, in the 'Modern Masters' series, as literary historian, critic, structuralist, hedonist, mythologist, etc.

*Curran, J. (ed).

The British Press: A Manifesto, Macmillan, 1978.
Important and sustained critique of the British Press which examines in detail questions of ownership and control, media 'professionalism', the role of advertisers, news management, government control on what can be published, and the lack of pluralism in the press. Looks at future developments in newspaper technology, and proposes a variety of solutions for Press reform. Particularly important contributions from Raymond Williams, Stuart Hall, James Curran, and Golding and Murdock.

Curran, J., Gurevitch M. and Woollacott, J. (eds).
Mass Communication and Society, Arnold, 1977.
Excellent reader for the Open University course on *Mass Communication and Society*. Contains overview articles designed to summarise discussion and research. Particularly valuable are the contributions of Stuart Hall on the media and ideology, James Curran on the history of the press, and Murdock and Golding on ownership and control.

*Curran, J. and Seaton, J.
Power without Responsibility, Fontana, 1981. New edition, 1985.
A useful text largely on the history of the press and broadcasting set within a political context. Also contains sections on theories of the media, and suggestions for reform.

*Curtis, Liz.
Ireland: the Propaganda War, Pluto, 1984.
An intelligent, thorough and accessible survey of the shocking recent history of the British media's coverage of the North of Ireland. The book carefully documents numerous examples of distortion, censorship and the fabrication and fantasising of events. The book is especially revealing on the media's willingness to reproduce as facts, material from the Army, the RUC and the Northern Ireland Office's propaganda machines. Essential reading for all media teachers and older students. The book provides compelling reasons for giving media coverage of the North of Ireland an important place in any media studies curriculum.

Davis, H. and Walton, P.
Language, Image, Media, Blackwell, 1983.
Essays on the 'languages' of the press, advertising, photography, and broadcasting.

Day, R.
Day By Day, Kimber, 1975.
Somewhat self-indulgent book in which Day 'interviews' himself to celebrate his twentieth year on the TV screen. Superficial treatment of most of the issues it raises.

Day, R.
Television: A Personal Report, Hutchinson, 1961.
First-hand account of the development of television news, with some interesting insights on interviewing.

*DES.
*Popular TV and Schoolchildren, DES, 1983.
Important recognition by the DES that media studies should be encouraged in schools. Indeed 'specialist courses in media studies are not enough: all teachers should be involved in examining and discussing television programmes with young people'. The report itself is not particularly impressive — simply the reflections of fifteen teachers on the picture of the adult world presented to young people by mainstream television.

Dorfman, A.
The Empire's Old Clothes, Pluto Press, 1983.
Important analysis of popular comics and magazines and their concealed social and political messages. Examines such figures and institutions as Babar the Elephant, Donald Duck, the Lone Ranger and *Reader's Digest*. 'By asking readers to take another long — and mischievous — look at these cultural products, I am in fact

challenging them to look at their own selves and their society with eyes newer than their clothing'.

Dorfman, A. and Mattelart, A.
How to Read Donald Duck, International General, 1975.
A detailed study of Donald Duck comics and how they embody capitalist-imperialist ideology.

Dougall, R.
In and Out of the Box, Collins and Harvill, 1973.
Best-selling and readable autobiography of the long-serving BBC newsreader. Documents the changes in styles of news presentation since the 1930's.

Downing, J.
The Media Machine, Pluto Press, 1980.
Interesting Marxist analysis which interleaves chapters on class exploitation in work, racism and sexism, with chapters on how these issues are handled (and exacerbated) by the media. Highlights the distinctions between media construction and oppressive realities.

Dyer, G.
Advertising as Communication, Methuen, 1982.
A useful text for older students as well as teachers, covering history, effects, content analysis, and semiotics in relation to advertising.

Dyer, R. et al.
Coronation Street, Television Monograph No. 13, BFI.
A first-rate study of the long-running soap opera with excellent contributions by Richard Paterson on the institutional and organisational contexts of the show, Terry Lovell on ideology and Christine Geraghty on narrative.

Dyer, R.
Light Entertainment, BFI Television Monograph No. 2, B.F.I., 1973.
The starting point for any teacher wishing to work in the area of pop and variety shows. The monograph does not examine 'light entertainment' as it is normally thought of within the BBC (i.e. comedy shows, quiz programmes etc. are not included).

Dyer, R.
Stars, BFI, 1982.
Essentially a film studies book (containing analyses of Brando, Wayne, Monroe, etc.) but the findings are just as relevant to the study of other media. Examines stars as social phenomena, as images, and as signs. Excellent on the ideological implications of the star system.

*Eagleton, T.
Literary Theory: An Introduction, Backwell, 1983.
Brilliantly incisive and occasionally very funny survey of modern literary theory. Important reading for media teachers since it gives essential background to many of the most recent critical approaches to the media.

Eco, U.
'Can Television Teach?', *Screen Education* No. 31, Summer 1979.
Valuable contribution to the case for television study in schools. Eco argues that the television teacher needs to know the social origin and cultural level of students in order to understand their differential decodings of the same television images. Also contains a critique of the first *Viewpoint* series.

Edgar, D. et al.
Ah! Mischief. The Writer and Television, Faber and Faber, 1982.
Reflections of varying quality about play-writing for television — and their own work in it — by Edgar, Griffiths, Schuman, Hare et al.

Ellis, J.
Visible Fictions, RKP, 1982.
Examines the differences between cinema and broadcast TV in their social roles, their forms of institutional organisation, and their aesthetic procedures.

Enzensberger, H.M.

'Constituents of a Theory of the Media', *New Left Review* 64 November–December 1970.

A seminal paper which moves beyond still current theories of the media (including 'manipulative' theories) towards the necessary constituents of any socialist media strategy. 'Marxists have not understood the consciousness industry and have not been aware of its socialist possibilities.'

Evans, H.

Editing and Design, Heinemann.

A major five-volume work on journalistic techniques. Many are of value to both teachers and students.

Book One: Newsman's English, 1972.

How to write good, clear, concise and vivid English. Helpful discussion on how to analyse new stories and write them effectively, with lots of examples from a variety of sources. Contains editing exercises which have possibilities for imaginative classroom use.

Book Two: Handling Newspaper Text, 1974.

Covers readability, sub-headings, text-breakers, etc. and contains a lengthy case-study exercise on a running story.

Book Three: News Headlines, 1974.

A whole volume devoted to Headlines — how to write them, how to compress ideas, mistakes to avoid etc. Contains comparative examinations of headline types, and a headline thesaurus. Contains a wealth of material which could be put to imaginative use in the classroom.

*Book Four: Pictures on a Page, 1978.

An essential classroom source of material on mediation in photography. Illustrates not simply how photographs select and filter 'reality' but also how they can be edited, cropped and manipulated to convey different meanings. Crammed with visual puzzles, problems and conundrums. A key work.

Book Five: Newspaper Design, 1973.

A detailed examination of newspaper layout illustrated with a host of examples., Chapters on the Front Page, Page Layout, The Tabloid Newspaper etc.

Evans, H.

Good Times, Bad Times, Wiedenfeld and Nicholson, 1983.

Controversial account of Evans' editorial reign at Times Newspapers. Interesting coverage of important cases concerning press freedom and public rights, including the Thalidomide story and the publication of the Crossman diaries, but the book is principally of interest for the details it gives of Rupert Murdoch's takeover of *The Times*, his subsequent breaking of promises on editorial freedom, and his transfer of the titles of Times Newspapers to his own multi-national corporation, News International.

Facetti, G. and Fletcher, A.

Identity Kits: A Pictorial Survey of Visual Signals, Studio Vista, 1971.

A profusely illustrated guide to signs and signals, and an invaluable pupil introduction to the field of semiology.

Firth, B.

Mass Media in the Classroom, Macmillan, 1968.

A handbook for teachers containing chapters on Newspapers, Magazines, Television, Advertising and Film. There is a sympathetic introduction which summarises the main arguments within Media Education up to the mid-1960's. Suggestions for classroom activity lack very much in the way of any theoretical framework, and there is no indication of pupil response to the ideas suggested.

Fisher, J.

Funny Way to be a Hero, Paladin, 1976.

Excellent study of stand-up comedians with invaluable lengthy extracts from their old music-hall routines. Many of the comedians included (Max Bygraves, Ken

Dodd, Frankie Howerd, Morecombe and Wise) are now established broadcasting stars. A first-class source for work on comedy.

Fiske, J.
Introduction to Communication Studies, Methuen, 1982.
A useful guide to the main models, theories and concepts used in the study of communication. There is some emphasis on semiotics and there are chapters on empirical methods, and ideology and meanings.

Fiske, J. and Hartley, J.
Reading Television (New Accents Series), Methuen, 1978.
Semiotics-based approach to television. Somewhat idiosyncratic (it argues that TV serves a 'bardic' function), the book nevertheless contains useful analyses of popular television programmes (*Match of the Day*, *The Generation Game*, *The Sweeney*, etc.)

Formations.
Of Pleasure, RKP, 1983.
First of the *Formations* series. Fourteen contributions on the theme of pleasure. Good contributions from Bennett on Blackpool Pleasure Beach, and Eagleton on a single line from Yeats. No overall theoretical framework; readers are left to make the connections themselves — if they can.

*Galtung, J. and Ruge, M.
'The Structure of Foreign News', *Journal of International Peace Research* No. 1, 1965. Reprinted in Tunstall (1970). A lengthy extract is also available in Cohen and Young, op. cit.
Classic early essay on news values which remains influential, and is possibly still the best starting-point for analysing news in the secondary school classroom and above. Amongst the criteria of news-value discussed are frequency, ethnocentricity, inheritance, elitism, negativity, etc.

Gans, H.J.
Deciding What's News, Hutchinson, 1982.
Valuable sociological study of US news media (CBS and NBC Television News and *Newsweek* and *Time* Magazines), with a thorough treatment of most of the issues surrounding news. Less critical than most British studies, but contains a useful concluding section recommending a more multi-perspective approach to the production of news. Needs to be treated with some caution by British readers since, whilst many of Gans' findings are applicable to the British media, others — especially many of those relating to the press — are not.

Gardner, C. (ed.)
Media, Politics and Culture, Macmillan, 1979.
Uneven collection of essays offering a socialist perspective on the media. Valuable contributions from Raymond Williams on the Growth and Role of the Mass Media, and Gillian Skirrow on Education and Television.

Garnham, N.
Structures of Television, BFI Monograph No. 1 BFI, 1973 (revised 1978).
An examination of the ideological assumptions behind the organisational structures of British television, and the relationship between broadcasting institutions and the state.

Gauthier, G.
The Semiology of the Image, BFI Advisory Document, 1976.
An important paper which proposes a semiological approach to the study of images in the classroom. This may not be a realistic approach in most secondary schools, but Gauthier's paper does offer readers many fruitful ideas on teaching about images. Slides accompanying the paper may be bought or hired from the British Film Institute.

Gieber, W.
'Across the desk: a study of 16 telegraph editors', *Journalism Quarterly* Vol. 33, 1956.
Gieber, W.

'How the 'gatekeepers' view civil liberties news', *Journalism Quarterly*, 1960.
Gieber, W. and Johnson, W.
'The city hall beat: a study of reporters and source roles', *Journalism Quarterly* 38, 1961.
> Three early studies of 'gatekeeping', one of the most influential models of news management and control in the 1960's.

*Glasgow University Media Group.
War and Peace News. Open University Press, 1985.
> Excellent analyses of broadcast coverage of the Falklands crisis and the peace movement.

*Glasgow University Media Group.
Bad News, RKP 1976; *More Bad News*, RKP 1980; *Really Bad News*, Writers & Readers, 1982.
> Very important series of research studies on television news broadcasts with particular emphasis upon the coverage of industrial relations. Produced compelling evidence of anti-trade-union bias. The first two volumes contain a great deal of data. *Really Bad News* is probably the best starting-point for teachers and students — it is cheaper, more accessible, and summarises many of the most important findings of the earlier volumes.

*Goffman, E.
Gender Advertisements, Macmillan, 1979.
> Profusely illustrated analysis of representations of gender in advertisements. Particularly good on relating non-verbal communication patterns in ads (touch, facial expressions, height and size, clothing) to patterns of domination and subordination in sexual relations.

Golay, J.P.
Introduction to the Language of Image and Sound, paper available from the British Film Institute, BFI, 1973.
> Seminal paper on visual literacy, integrating practical and analytical work. Especially valuable for its suggestions for work with primary and lower secondary pupils, an age-group generally ignored in discussions about media studies.

Goldie, G.W.
Facing the Nation: Television and Politics 1936–76, The Bodley Head, 1977.
> Clearly written account of the development of political television at the BBC between 1936 and 1976 by an influential BBC Head of Department. Illustrates, through a host of anecdotes and examples, the principles governing election and party political broadcasts, political interviews, and TV appearances by politicians. Whilst ostensibly asserting the independence of the BBC, the book actually demonstrates the routine ways in which the BBC is subjected to covert political pressure and generally reacts to such pressure by exercising excessive caution.

Golding, P.
The Mass Media, Longman, 1974.
> General sociological account in the 'Aspects of Modern Sociology' series. Chapters on history, structures and organisation, the media and the social system, etc.

Golding, P. and Middleton, S.
Images of Welfare, Martin Robertson, 1982.
> A study of the images of welfare and poverty that appear in the media. Examines the history of social policies for the poor, and the assumptions and imagery that have framed these policies, particularly in the press, before looking at images of the welfare state portrayed by the media today. Also includes a survey on public attitudes to poverty and welfare.

Golding, P. and Murdock, G.
'Privatising Pleasure', *Marxism Today*, October 1983.
> Important short account of patterns of ownership and control in the new telecommunication industries —telecommunications, computing and television. 'Many people, perhaps most, will find themselves with few real choices, worse

basic services, less chance of having their views and interests fairly represented, and virtually no chance of helping to shape future policy', as a result of the wholesale privatisation of the new communications industries.

Greenberg, S. and Smith, G.

Rejoice!, Campaign for Press and Broadcasting Freedom, 1983.

Excellent account of the relationships between the media and the Government during the Falklands War and a salutory reminder of the need to defend media independence during times of crisis and war.

Groombridge, B.

Television and the People, Penguin, 1972.

Argues for the importance of television's potential role in helping to create and maintain a more participatory democracy. Contains a useful chapter on Information as Spectacle, which examines the barriers to the authenticity of the information and news presented by television.

Gurevitch, M., Bennett, T. et al.

Culture, Society and the Media, Methuen, 1982.

A much revised reader for the Open University's course on *Mass Communications and Society*. Eleven essays covering media theories, ideology, ownership and control, race, etc. A very useful collection.

*Hall, S.

'*Culture, the Media and the Ideological Effect*', in Curran, Gurevitch and Woollacott (eds) (1977).

Important and careful analysis of how 'the media serve ceaselessly to perform the critical ideological work of 'classifying out the world' within the discourses of the dominant ideologies'. Excellent on locating Gramsci's and Althusser's contribution to our understanding of the ideological work of the media. Valuable too in its analysis of the principle media functions of a) constructing social knowledge b) assigning preferred meanings to this knowledge and c) organising fragmented and pluralistic views into a consensus.

*Hall, S.

'The Determinations of News Photographs, *Working Papers in Cultural Studies* No. 3, Autumn 1972, Birmingham University Reproduced, in Cohen and Young.

Excellent analysis of the function of photographs in newspapers. Required reading for teachers.

Hall, S.

Encoding and Decoding in the Television Discourse, Paper available from the Centre for Contemporary Cultural Studies, Birmingham University, 1973.

Television seen as 'a form of systematically distorted communication' through the 'lack of fit' between the frameworks of knowledge employed by encoder-producers and decoder-receivers. The paper challenges the predominantly behaviourist approach of most mass-media research by positing a model involving four possible decoding modes: the dominant, the professional, the negotiated (containing adaptive or oppositional elements), and the oppositional. The notion of differential decoding has important implications for classroom practice in media education.

Hall, S.

'The Hinterland of Science: Ideology and the "Sociology of Knowledge"', in Centre for Contemporary Cultural Studies, *On Ideology*, Hutchinson, 1978.

Traces the complex evolution of the concept of ideology in philosophy and sociology from the French Revolution onwards. Historically used as a concept by those who wished to 'unmask the historicity of ideas'. 'Whatever else it signals, *Ideology* makes a direct reference to the role of *ideas*. It also entails the proposition that ideas are not self-sufficient, that their roots lie elsewhere, that something central about ideas will be revealed if we can discover the nature of the determinancy which *non*-ideas exert over ideas'.

*Hall, S.

'Television and Culture', *Sight and Sound* Vol. 45, No. 4, Autumn 1976.

Examines the 'deeply manipulative' nature of television particularly in relation to programmes which appear to be transmitting 'raw' events. The second part of the article contains a useful commentary upon Benjamin's essay, *The Work of Art in the Age of Mechanical Reproduction*.

*Hall, S.
'A World at One with Itself' *New Society* 18th June 1970.
Argues that the consensus assumptions of news programmes mystifies rather than clarifies 'real events in the real world'. A key article. Reprinted in Cohen and Young op. cit.

*Hall, S., Critcher, C. et al.
Policing the Crisis, Macmillan, 1978.
A major work which begins with a detailed case-study of media coverage of a 'mugging' trial, and opens out to consider media constructions of race, and law and order, and the role of the media in helping to create a major ideological move to the right during the 1970's. Contains an excellent chapter on the social production of news, which argues that the media are in a position of structured subordination to their major news sources and *reproduce* dominant definitions and interpretations of events which have their origins elsewhere. Also examines the 'fit' between dominant ideas ('consensual values') and professional media ideologies.

Hall, S., Hobson, D., Lowe, A. and Willis, P.
Culture, Media, Language, Centre for Contemporary Cultural Studies, and Hutchinson, 1980.
Some excellent contributions to media studies in this collection, paticularly from Hall on encoding/decoding, Hobson on Housewives and the Media, and Connell on news.

*Hall, S. and Whannel, P.
The Popular Arts, Hutchinson, 1964.
The classic text on media education in the 1960's. An excellent handbook for teachers in that decade, containing many interesting analyses of films and popular literature, as well as popular musical forms such as the Blues. Made a major step forward in arguing that discrimination ought to be exercised, not *against* mass-media products, but *between* them, since many popular cultural products are worthy of consideration as art, and are capable of being evaulated by quite traditional aesthetic criteria. Television is treated somewhat negatively, and is not given the weight that its importance and influence deserve.

Halloran, J.D., Murdock, G. and Elliott, P.
Demonstrations and Communications: A Case Study, Penguin, 1970.
Excellent case-study on newspaper and television coverage of a 1968 anti-Vietnam march and demonstration. Events tended to be fitted into a preconceived formula by the media, and the formula itself provided the media's frame of reference in subsequent news stories.

Harris, P.
Reporting Southern Africa, UNESCO, 1981.
An account of the role of international news agencies in reporting on Southern Africa, as well as of the government control of news and the harassment of journalists.

Harris, R.
Gotcha!, The Media, the Government, and the Falkands Crisis, Faber and Faber, 1983.
Readable, sinister, and at times hilarious account of the exploits, activities and battles of the journalists who covered the Falkland crisis. Excellent detail on the secrecy of the military and the Civil Service, their manipulation of public opinion, their intimidation of broadcasters, and their manufacture of misformation.

Harrison, S.
Poor Men's Guardians, Lawrence and Wishart, 1974.
Interesting historical account of the struggles for a radical and working-class press

from the 18th Century to 1974. Argues for the development of a genuine democracy of the written and spoken word in all the media, against current monopolies.

Hartley, J.
Understanding News, Methuen, 1982.

Intended as a guide for students in Sixth Forms and Higher Education, this study in the *Studies in Communication* series adopts a semiological stance to its subject, and covers a great deal of ground very effectively (Hartley is excellent on news values, the coverage of dissent, news narratives, and news as entertainment and fiction. All of these topics are embraced as part of the book's central concern to explicate the nature of news as ideology.). The book fails to achieve one of the avowed aims of the series, however, 'to introduce readers to the most important results of contemporary research'. There is no adequate summary of, or guidance to, the voluminous literature on news, or the views of contending theorists. For this reason the book is perhaps best considered as an original contribution to the literature on news rather than as an adequate guide to existing work.

Hartmann, P. and Husband, C.
Racism and the Mass Media, Davis-Poynter, 1974.

Research report concentrating principally upon the press's contribution to the state of race relations in Britain. Television is briefly examined in chapters on 'The News Media' and 'The Entertainment Media'.

Harvey, S.
May 1968 and Film Culture, British Film Institute, 1978.

Clearly written and intelligent account of developments in Film Culture since 1968 with excellent chapters on 'Notions of Cultural Production' and 'Ideology and the Impression of Reality' which are directly relevant to issues facing media theory and practice. Interesting too on the potentialities and possibilities of radical readings of media texts.

*Heath, S. and Skirrow, G.
'Television: A World in Action', *Screen* Vol. 18, No. 2, Summer 1977.

A key essay, A detailed analysis of a typical film from the *World in Action* series, which focuses upon the nature of television as a 'specific signifying practice'. 'What is missing so often in analyses of television programmes is any reference to the fact of television itself, and to the ideological operations developed in that fact; there is a generality of ideology in the institution, 'before' the production of a particular ideological position'.

Higgins, A.P.
Talking about Television, British Film Institute, 1966.

One of the few sources which reveals pupil responses to the medium, but pupil discussion rarely moves beyond low-level chat, and the teaching lacks even an ill-defined conceptual framework.

*Higgins, C.S. and Moss, P.D.
Sounds Real. University of Queensland Press, 1982.

This Australian book is the only full-length critical study of radio currently available. Contains many interesting analyses of transcripts from phone-ins, advertisements and news programmes. Especially useful on the dramatic and narrative forms of radio.

Himmelweit, H.T., Oppenheim, A.N. and Vince, P.
Television and the Child, Oxford University Press, 1958.

Classic empirical study on the effect of television on 10–11 and 13–14 year olds. Though statistically out of date, the study is still valuable for its sensible and unhysterical generalisations on children's viewing habits, and its critique of television westerns and crime series.

Hirsch, F. and Gordon, D.
Newspaper Money, Hutchinson, 1975.

Short readable book on newspaper economics looking at marketing, readership, sales, and costs.

*Hobson, D.
Crossroads: The Drama of A Soap Opera, Methuen, 1981.
A sympathetic study of *Crossroads* and its audience. Excellent on the values and pleasures transmitted to its audience — and particularly to large numbers of elderly people — by a programme generally derided by the press and other programme makers. Illuminates the gulf between those who control broadcasting and many of those who watch it.

Hoch, P.
The Newspaper Game, Calder and Boyars, 1974.
Newspapers as businesses 'oriented to serving the advertising and other brainwashing needs of the rest of capitalist business' in order to create the conditions for its reproduction.

Hoggart, R.
Speaking to Each Other Vol. One: About Society, Chatto and Windus, 1970.
Collection of occasional articles by the author of *The Uses of Literacy*, including a number on the media. (*The Uses of Television*; *Television as the Archetype of Mass Communications*; *The Daily Mirror and its Readers*; *the BBC and Society*; *the Pilkington Report* etc.)

Hoggart, R.
The Uses of Literacy, Penguin, 1958.
It would be difficult to over-estimate the significance of this book, the first sympathetic and detailed study of post-war working-class culture and the beginning of the movement to establish media and cultural studies as legitimate fields for serious enquiry. The book is still a useful source of ideas and insights on many aspects of popular culture.

Hoggart, R. (ed.)
Your Sunday Paper, University of London Press, 1967.
Inevitably rather dated now, this collection of essays on different aspects of Sunday newspapers is still a useful source of ideas for classroom analysis. See especially Stuart Hall on gossip columns and 'personalisation', and Raymond Williams on 'criticism'.

Hollins, T.
Beyond Broadcasting: Into the Cable Age, BFI, 1984.
Full account of developments in cable both in Britain and abroad.

Hood, S.
The Mass Media (Studies in Contemporary Europe), Macmillan, 1972.
Clear survey of patterns of ownership and control of the broadcasting media and the press in Europe since the war. Needs to be brought up to date on recent changes in ownership, but still a valuable source for teachers wishing to develop work on the media as industries.

*Hood, S.
On Television, Pluto Press, 1980.
Excellent introduction to television from a radical perspective. Chapters on The Screen, The Audiences, The Programme-Makers, The Controllers, The Fourth Channel, New Technology etc. Recommended for older students, and as background reading for teachers.

Hood, S.
Radio and Television David and Charles, 1975.
Delightfully subversive tongue-in-cheek contribution to a series on 'The Professions', which makes clear the conventional nature of most television and of the people who work in it. Very sound on the general ideological tendencies of comedy, sports programmes, soap-operas and documentaries. Ideal back-ground text for fifth and sixth formers.

Hood, S.
A Survey of Television, Heinemann, 1967.
Still a first-rate introduction to many aspects of the medium by a seasoned

profesional. Differences between Charter and Act, and video and film are spelled out, and there are insights into problems of programme planning, and the roles of producer, director, engineers and others involved in the process of making television programmes.

Howkins, J.
New Technologies, New Policies? BFI, 1982.

Short research report on the social and economic implications of the explosion in video technology. Chapters on satellite, cable, interactive and textual systems, and cassettes and discs. Written early in 1982 the study has already been overtaken by more recent developments in many fields, but the historical background it gives remains of value.

Hunt, A.
The Language of Television, Eyre Methuen, 1981.

A book with a number of important strands. The first part argues (not entirely convincingly) that some television comedy shows demolish the kind of 'official reality' which is the stock-in-trade of 'serious' television. The second reports on three imaginative video-projects of the kind for which Hunt has become justifiably well-known. The third is an important exploration of the role television might play in any genuinely popular education.

Husband, C. (ed.)
White Media and Black Britain, Arrow, 1975.

Essays by activists, journalists and academics on how the British media represent a white view of the world in which black voices are distorted or ignored.

The Independent Broadcasting Authority.
Television and Radio, Published Annually.

The IBA's annual guide to independent television and independent local radio. Useful source of current information.

Inglis, F.
The Name of the Game, Heinemann, 1977.

Explores the contrary pulls of 'mass expression and mass manipulation' in sport. Contains a chapter on sport and the media, mainly devoted to an alanysis of newspaper journalism.

Inter-Action.
Basic Video in Community Work, Inter-Action Advisory Service Handbook No. 5, Inter-Action, 1975.

Excellent introductory guide to using video with a sensible introduction by Ed. Berman: 'Video is in danger of becoming the wonder-drug of community work. Today's wonder drug is tomorow's pedestrian pill. Improvements in people's lives are hardly wrought by opiates ... Calling upon the equipment when it is appropriate rather than looking for things to do to fill up time is the better approach to using the medium.' Also contains down-to-earth and precise advice on the functions video can usefully perform in community work and (by extension) in schools and colleges.

*International Commission for the Study of Communication Problems.
Many Voices, One World, (The MacBride Report), UNESCO, 1980.

Important international study of 'the totality of communication problems in modern societies'. Raises questions of human rights in relation to communication — 'the right of individuals and nations to communicate and exchange messages' — and examines one-way flows of information, concentration of media ownership, cultural dominance, the power of transnational corporations, censorship, and technological changes in relation to their adverse effects on the right to communicate.

James, C.
Visions before Midnight, Cape, 1977; *The Crystal Bucket*, Cape, 1981; *Glued to the Box*, Cape, 1983.

Three highly readable collections of pieces from James's *Observer* television column. Good jokes and witty observations, but weak on theoretical perspectives. Where a point of view does emerge it is invariably reactionary. On the whole the pieces exemplify the author's belief that television criticism should reflect the medium's ephemerality.

Jenkins, S.
Newspapers, The Power and the Money, Faber and Faber, 1979.
> A short analysis of what is wrong with the newspaper industry, paying specific attention to owners — both the old press barons and the new (Thomson, Murdoch and Matthews) — and to the printing unions.

*Jones, D., Petley,J., Power, M. and Wood L.
Media Hits the Pits, Campaign for Press and Broadcasting Freedom, 1985.
> An extremely useful booklet which presents some of the principal issues arising out of the media's coverage of the 1984/5 coal dispute.

Jones, G., Connell, I. and Meadows, J.
The Presentation of Science by the Media, Primary Communications Research Centre, University of Leiester, 1978.
> Research study on how interpretations of science are constructed by newspapers, radio and television. Looks at major scientific themes in the media, the major sources of information, the processes to selecting scientific material, and, particularly, the intermediaries who present science to the public.

*Jones, K.
Graded Simulations, (3 volumes), Blackwell, 1985.
> The long-awaited publication of Kenneth Jones' classic simulations at a reasonable price. Volume One, which contains *Front Page* and *Radio Covingham* should be known by all media teachers.

Jones, M. and Dungay, J.
Ethnic Minorities and TV, Centre for Mass Communications Research, University of Leicester, 1983.
> Detailed and important research study on the attitudes of immigrant communities to television programmes with special reference to Light Entertainment and Drama.

Jones, M.
Mass Media Education, Education for Communication and Mass Communication Research, Centre for Mass Communication Research, University of Leicester, 1984.
> Report commissioned by UNESCO looking at some of the models used for studying the media and communication systems in different parts of the world.

King, J. and Stott, M. (eds).
Is This Your Life? Virago, 1977.
> Study of images of women in the media. Separate chapters on Newspaper, Radio, TV, Women's Magazines, Films, Popular Fiction and Comics.

Knightley, P.
The First Casualty, Quartet, 1982.
> Extremely readable series of case studies on how journalists have reported wars from the Crimean War onwards. The catalogue of censorship, lies, suppression, invention and distortion is disquieting, illuminating, and highly relevant to an understanding of the role of journalists in time of crisis today.

Lambert, S.
Channel Four: Television with a Difference? BFI, 1982.
> Detailed historical account of the origins of Channel Four together with details of the aims, objectives, organisation and finance of the new channel.

Lealand,G.
American Television Programmes on British Screens Broadcasting Research Unit, 1984.
> Very interesting research study containing information about American programmes on British television, and a survey of opinions on their quality and interest. Also looks at possible future developments in this area and contains case-

studies on the amount of American material on television in a number of other countries (Japan, Italy, Brazil, New Zealand etc.)

Leapman, M.

Barefaced Cheek, Hodder and Stoughton, 1983.

A well-researched and scathing biography of Rupert Murdoch. Simultaneous insights into the unacceptable faces of both capitalism and the media. An invaluable source for work on ownership and control.

Leavis, F.R. and Thompson, D.

Culture and Environment, Chatto and Windus, 1948.

First published in the 1930's, this practical handbook had an enormous influence as a clarion call to educational resistance against the corrupting influence of the media. 'Pupils must be taught to discriminate and resist' the low level satisfaction and cheap emotional responses encouraged by the media. More positively, the book contains many examples of exercises from newspapers, magazines and advertisements, and was instrumental in making the discussion of popular texts in the classroom an acceptable and intellectually respectable activity for many teachers. In this sense the book paved the way for later work by teachers who possessed a more sympathetic attitude to the media. *Culture and Environment*'s moralistic and negative attitude to the mass media, nevertheless, continues to have much educational influence today.

Lewin, K.

'Psychological Ecology (1943)' in *Field Theory in Social Science*, Harper 1951.

An article of some historic interest, since it is the original source of the 'gatekeeper' model of news selection. Kurt Lewin's article, however, describes not news production, but the purchasing habits of housewives. His explanation of how food reached the family table suggested that 'food moves step by step through a channel . . . Entering or not entering a channel . . . is effected by a gatekeeper'. Lewin argued that this model held good, not only for food, but for the travelling of a news item through particular communication channels — a suggestion developed over a decade later by D.M. White.

Lewis, P.M. (ed.).

Radio Drama, Longman, 1981.

A collection of interesting essays on the much neglected field of radio drama (covering *The Archers* and *Mrs. Dale's Diary*, as well as more high-brow work). The contribution by Graham Murdock on sociological perspectives on radio drama is particularly useful.

Lewis, P.M.

Whose Media? Consumers' Association, 1978.

A consumers' guide to broadcasting, giving factual information on how broadcasting is organised, looking as possible ways of organising broadcasting in the future in the wake of Annan, and finally providing guidance on how to use the media.

Local Radio Workshop.

Nothing Local About It, Comedia, 1983.

Excellent analysis of one week of local broadcasting in London, showing the lack of *local* radio output and analysing the reasons for this. Contains data on music, news, magazines, and phone-in outputs, and suggests ways of making local radio more responsive and accountable to local needs.

London Community Video Workers Collective.

Directory of Video Tapes, Islington Community Press, 1979.

Very useful directory of a wide range of video tapes available from the collective. Gives a variety of community, political and educational subject entries from Adult Education to Youth Drama, plus details of how to hire the tapes.

*Lowndes, D.

'The Unesco Survey and the British Situation', *Screen Education* No. 18, Spring 1976.

Because the enormous resources of the consciousness industries far outstrip those of education, 'liberal' teaching approaches to the media are now in fact repressive. Media studies should include a totalising conceptual framework which would expose the implicit and explicit beliefs pumped out by the mass media, and of which the concept of ideology would be a central part. Lowndes goes on to discuss the few texts available for developing in teachers a radical theoretical background to media studies. An important article.

Lowndes, D., Horrox, A. and Skirrow, G.
Viewpoint, Thames Television, 1976
   Useful ideas and references on media teaching are contained in this teacher's handbook to accompany the television series.

Luckham, B. (ed.).
Audio-Visual Literacy, proceedings of the Sixth Symposium on Broadcasting Policy, University of Manchester, 1975.
   An attempt to clarify the concept of audio-visual literacy with reference to *Dr. Who* and *Star Trek*. Apart from contributions by Buscombe and Hood an extremely weak collection with little insight offered into either of the programmes chosen and even less into the nature of audio-visual literacy.

Lunatic Ideas.
School Without Walls and the Corner House Bookshop, 1978.
   How newspapers dealt with the subject of education, young people and schools during the summer of 1977. Contains a great deal of documentation, and will be quite accessible to many pupils.

Lusted, D.
Television Genre Study. The British Film Institute, 1979.
   Helpful BFI paper describing a Further Education course on Television Detective series.

*Lusted, D. and Drummond, P. (eds).
T.V. and Schooling. BFI, 1985.
   Collection of essays developing issues raised by the DES Report *Popular T.V. and Schoolchildren*.

*McMahon, B. and Quin, R.
Exploring Images, Bookland, W. Australia, 1984.
   Attractive and profusely illustrated book for students enabling them to analyse pictures and decode images. Recommended.

*MacShane, D.
Using the Media, Pluto Press, 1979.
   A handbook for workers and community activists on how to deal with the press, television and radio, and how to use these media to advantage. However, the book is also an invaluable guide for school/college groups considering activities with professional media involvement. Usefully brings together notes on conventions and codings, and guidance on how to work within (or change) them. It thus demonstrates the ways in which a critical media education course might go hand-in-hand with practical involvement. Covers such issues as how to write press releases, do's and don'ts for interviews, how to make contact with media professionals etc. Strongly recommended.

Magee, B.
The Television Interviewer, Macdonald 1966.
   Analysis of the craft of television interviewing by a practitioner. Also includes an account of the making of a typical current affairs programme (*This Week*). Apart from containing helpful techniques for carrying out, or analysing interviews, the book contains useful insights into research for interviews, and on the art of marrying commentary with visuals.

Margagh, J.
The Abuse of Power, Allen, 1978.
   Interesting historical account of the relationship between the Press and twelve

Prime Ministers (from Lloyd George to James Callaghan).

*Masterman, L. (ed.).
Television Mythologies, Comedia, 1985.
Short essays on a wide range of television programmes (e.g. *Breakfast Time*, *That's Life*, *Top of the Pops*, *One Man and His Dog*, *The A Team*, etc.) as well as such topics as advertisements, continuity announcers, television previewing and criticism etc. Intended as a tribute to Roland Barthes' original *Mythologies*, the collection should be of interest to media teachers, and older students.

Masterman, L.
Media Education in the 1980's, Journal of Educational Television, Vol. 9 No. 1, 1983.
An attempt to map out a conceptual framework for future media study in schools and colleges on the basis of recent work in media research.

*Masterman, L.
Teaching About Television, Macmillan, 1980.
Tries to demonstrate how television can be studied in a disciplined way in schools. Contains guidance for classroom practice, and argues for television to be taught within a 'progressive' pedagogy. Contains chapters on 'tele-literacy', news, sport and practical video work.

Masterman, L.
'Television and the English Teacher' in *New Directions in English Teaching*, edited by Anthony Adams, The Falmer Press, 1982.
Charts the shifting relationship between English teachers and television from the late 50's onwards, and argues that English teachers will need to unlearn a good deal of their literary training, and acquire new skills if they are to teach about television effectively.

Masterman, L. (ed.).
Television Studies: Four Approaches, British Film Institute Educational Advisory Document, BFI, 1979.
Accounts of how different aspects of television (Sport, Interviewing, Documentary, Visual Coding) were taught with students. One account relates to schools, the rest describe work done in Higher Education.

*Masterman, L. and Kiddey, P.
Understanding Breakfast Television, MK Media Press, 1983.
A study Unit on Breakfast TV for teachers and students. Already overtaken by major changes in the policies and the personnel associated with Breakfast TV, the study should nevertheless be of some value in providing 'historical' documentation on the origins of early morning television in Britain, and the importance of advertisers in determining the nature of this particular TV product. Contains simulations and exercises for classroom use.

Mattelart, A. et al.
International Image Markets, Comedia, 1984.
An examination of international trends in image production and consumption which explores imbalances in international communication flows and the impact of international markets on media products.

Mattelart, A.
Multinational Corporations and the Control of Culture, Harvester, 1979.
Examines the role of the new technologies in securing the dominance of transnational corporations over media, culture and the leisure industries.

McArthur, C.M.
Television and History, British Film Institute, 1978, Television Monograph No. 8.
Usefully points to the ways in which the presentation of the past, both in fictionalised and factual television programmes, is dominated by a bourgeois conception of history and of television forms. Both the general theoretical stance and the discussion of particular programmes (*Upstairs, Downstairs*; *Days of Hope* etc.) should be of considerable interest to teachers.

May, A. and Rowan, K.
Inside Information: British Government and the Media, Hutchinson, 1982.
> Very useful collection of extracts and papers illustrating the theory and practice of information control within the British system of government. There are sections on *The Law and The Press*, and *Broadcasting and The State*, and case studies of key areas of confrontation such as Northern Ireland, Nuclear power policy, the Concorde Project. Useful background resource for work on media determinants.

McKeown, N.
Case Studies and Projects in Communication, Methuen, 1982.
> An imaginative approach to communication studies, using case-studies and projects as the basis for introducing principles and theories of communication. Aimed at students.

McLoone, M. and MacMahon, J. (eds).
Television and Irish Society RTE/IFI, 1984.
> Excellent collection of essays celebrating 21 years of Irish television. Good on drama and serials, and the representation of women and the urban working class.

McLuhan, M.
Understanding Media, Routledge and Kegan Paul, 1964.
> McLuhan's unique interpretation of the history of communication, with separate chapters on each medium.

McQuail, D.
Sociology of Mass Communications, Penguin, 1972.
> A sociological reader on the media with sections on Mass Media and Mass Society, The Audience, Organisations, Structural Analysis and Policy Issues. Especially useful are the contributions of Enzensberger, (op. cit.) and Nordenstreng on news.

McQuail, D. and Windahl, S.
Communication Models, Longman, 1981.
> Schematic presentation of the principal models available for the study of mass-communications. Of some value as a reference book; deadly if used as a student text-book.

McRobbie, A. (ed.).
4 on Four, Birmingham Film Workshop and West Midlands Arts, 1982.
> Transcripts of four public debates on Channel 4 covering the Campaign for Welsh Language Broadcasting; the employment and representation of women on television; independent film; and news and current affairs. The debates took place in Autumn 1981, a year before Channel Four opened, and contributors include Stuart Hood, Ian Connell, Helen Baehr, Charlotte Brunsdon, Rhodri Williams and Alan Fountain.

Miliband, R.
The State in Capitalist Society Quartet, 1973.
> Includes a section on the mass media which gives a crisp Marxist analysis of them as a 'crucial element in the legitimation of capitalist society'.

Minority Press Group.
Where is the Other News?, Minority Press Group, 1980.
> An important and interesting study of the neglected field of distribution. Looks at the publishing, wholesaling and retailing of magazines, and at the ways in which controversial ideas are excluded by the biggest publishing companies and retailers. Contains a useful directory of radical magazines.

*Morley, D.
The 'Nationwide' Audience, BFI Television Monograph No. 11, 1980.
> An important study of audience reponses to *Nationwide*. Provides a usefully critical account of traditional models of audience research, and then charts the responses of twenty-eight different groups to the programme. The responses are varied, interesting, sometimes fascinating, but need to be treated with some caution, since all were made within specifically educational rather than domestic contexts.

*Morley, D. and Whitaker, B.

The Press, Radio, and Television: An Introduction to the Media, Comedia, 1983.
An excellent general introduction to the media, usable by Advanced Level Students and above. Covers ownership of the press, structures of control in television, legal and organisational constraints in radio, and the impact of technological change in different media. Recommended.

Mulhern, F.
The Moment of 'Scrutiny', Verso, 1981.
The most comprehensive analysis available of the influential Cambridge literary quarterly, *Scrutiny*, and of the 'cultural current' which we know as Leavisism.

Munro, C.
Television, Censorship and the Law, Saxon House, 1979.
Study of censorship in British television, and of the legal constraints, and internal and external pressures on TV production.

*Murdock, G. and Phelps, G.
Mass Media and the Secondary School, Schools Council Research Studies, Macmillan, 1973.
Important research study examining differences in teacher and pupil perceptions of the mass media. Raises a large number of questions about the nature of an effective media education, pinpointing the negativity of many teachers' attitudes to the media as a principal stumbling-block to progress. Very perceptive on student/pupil responses to pop music.

*Murphy, B.
The World Wired Up: Unscrambling the New Communications Puzzle, Comedia, 1983.
Very well researched short book on the global politics of Satellite TV and the multinationals' involvement in it. Excellent insights into how things look to people inside the multi-national corporations. Recommended.

Murphy, D.
The Silent Watchdog, Constable, 1976.
Why local newspapers do so little to challenge corruption in local government. Looks at the variety of factors producing bland and superficial journalism, and at the contradiction between a 'free press' and the practices of a capitalist industry.

*Murray, J.F. (ed.).
Television Studies in Scottish Schools, Scottish Council for Educational Technology, 1980.
An excellent discussion document designed to encourage teachers to think seriously about initiating Television Studies courses in schools. Contains contributions from practising teachers, based on very interesting work in the secondary school.

National Association for Multi-Cultural Education.
Multi-Cultural Education Vol. 9 No. 2, Spring 1981.
A special double issue of *Multi-Cultural Education* devoted to *Race and The Media*, with contributions from Pines on Blacks in Films, Bazalgette et al on the BFI pack, *Images and Blacks — the American Experience*, Ferguson on teaching about myth, Gardner on *Black Employment in the Media* etc., together with relevant book reviews. Recommended.

Neale, S.
Genre, BFI, 1980.
Contains a useful appendix on film extract material available for teaching about film narrative.

Nicholls, Bill.
Ideology and the Image, Indiana University Press, 1981.
A useful text for Higher Education students exploring questions of ideology and social representation principally in relation to the cinema.

Nightingale, V.
'Images of Foreigners: The British Report' in *Young TV Viewers and Their Images of*

Foreigners, Siftung Prix Jeunesse, Munich, 1982.
Part of an international study on Images of Foreigners on Television, carried out by
the Prix Jeunesse Foundation. The British study provides fascinating material on
Images of the USA, USSR, Germany, France and Australia which exist in the
heads of British children. Good starting point for work on stereotypes.
NUT.

Popular Culture and Personal Responsibility, NUT, 1960.
Verbatim Report of the important and influential 1960 conference with major
contributions from R.A. Butler, Raymond Williams, Jack Longland, Arnold
Wesker, Roy Shaw and many others. Indicative of the wave of concern felt by
responsible middleclass opinion about the products of commercial television.
The Open University.

Mass Communication and Society, A third level Social Sciences course of fifteen
units. The Open University Press, 1977.

Block One The media: contexts of study.
Unit 1   Issues in the study of mass communication and society by Michael
              Gurevitch and Carrie Roberts.
Unit 2   Mass communication as a social force in history by James Curran.
Block Two The study of culture.
Unit 3   The media and social theory: mass-society theories and conceptions of
              class by Tony Bennett.
Unit 4   Popular culture and high culture by John Hartley and Terence Hawkes.
Unit 5   Mass communication in cross-cultural contexts: the case of the Third
              World by Oliver Boyd-Barrett.
Unit 6   Messages and meanings by Janet Woollacott.
Block Three The audience.
Unit 7   Mass-media effects: a sociological approach by James Halloran.
Unit 8   The political effects of mass communication by Jay Blumler.
Unit 9   Projects: (a) The Open University as a media system. (b) Black music.
Block Four Media organisations.
Unit 10   Patterns of ownership; questions of control by Graham Murdock.
Unit 11   Organisations and occupations by Margaret Gallagher.
Unit 12   Hollywood: a case study by Janet Woollacott.
Block Five Media and society.
Unit 13   The media as definers of social reality by Tony Bennett.
Unit 14   How the media report race by Peter Braham.
Unit 15   The power of the media by Peter Braham.
The Open University.

Popular Culture, A second level course of thirty-two units. The Open University
Press, 1981.

Block 1 Popular culture: themes and issues.
1/2   Christmas: a case study.
3   Popular culture: history and theory.

Block 2 The historical development of popular culture in Britain.
4   The emergence of an urban popular culture.
5   The music hall.
6   Popular culture in late nineteenth and early twentieth century Lancashire.
7   British cinema in the 1930's.
8   Radio in World War II.
Block 3 Popular culture and everyday life.
9   Approaches to the study of everyday life.
10   Leisure activities: home and neighbourhood.
11   Holidays.
12   Interpreting television.
Block 4 Form and meaning.
13   Readers, viewers and texts.

14   Meaning, image and ideology.
15   Reading and realism.
16   'Reading' popular music.
17   Pleasure.
Block 5   Politics, ideology and popular culture.
18   Popular culture and hegemony in post-war Britain.
19/20   Pop culture, pop music and post-war youth.
21   James Bond as popular hero.
22   Television police series and law and order.
23   Class, sex and the family in situation comedy.
Block 6   Science, technology and popular culture.
24   The rock music industry.
25   The image and mass reproduction.
26   The popular image of science and scientists.
27   Science fiction.
Block 7   The state and popular culture.
28   Culture and the state.
29   Language, literacy and schooling.
30   Male school counterculture.
31/32   Conclusion.

Orwell, G.
'Boys Weeklies' in *Inside the Whale*, Penguin, 1962.
> Classic discussion of pre-war comics. Still usable with today's pupils.

O'Sullivan, T., Hartley, J., Saunders, D. and Fiske, J.
Key Concepts in Communication, Methuen, 1983.
> A handy and accessible reference text for media teachers and students.

Partridge, S.
Not the BBC/IBA: The case for community radio, Comedia, 1982.
> Examines the case for community radio, and gives down-to-earth advice for those wishing to develop or particpate in community radio networks.

Pateman, T.
Television and the February 1974 General Election, British Film Institute Television Monograph No. 3, BFI, 1974.
> Study of the first 1974 election, written specifically with the teacher in mind, though not classroom orientated. The appendices are longer than the text itself and perhaps more valuable. They include transcripts of two contrasting Robin Day interviews.

Photography Workshop.
Photography/Politics: One, Photography Workshop (undated).
> Radical photographic 'annual' by the producers of *Camerawork*. Sections on Against the Dominant Ideology, Left Photography Between the Wars, and Left Photography Today. Profusely illustrated.

Robertson, G.
People Against the Press, Quartet, 1983.
> Devastating critique of the Press Council.

Rogers, R. (ed.)
Television and the Family, UK Association for the International Year of the Child, and the University of London Department of Extra-Mural Studies, 1980.
> A collection of papers from a conference on television and children. Examines 'what we know' about television and the family, and makes some suggestions on how interaction between television and the family can be improved.

Ryder, N.
Science, Television and the Adolescent, Independent Broadcasting Authority Report, 1982.
> Lengthy report on adolescents' responses to a four minute TV News Story on the Three Mile Island nuclear reactor emergency. Points up the irrelevance of much science teaching to the world in which adolescents live, and demonstrates how the media can be effectively 'read' and integrated into school science subjects.

*Schiller, H.I.
Communication and Cultural Dominance, International Arts and Science Press, White Plains, New York, 1976; *Who Knows? Information in the Age of the Fortune 500*, Ablex, N. Jersey, 1981; *Information and the Crisis Economy*, Ablex, 1984; *Electronic Information Flows: New Basis for Global Domination*, paper presented to the National Television Studies Conference, July 11–13, 1984 at the London Institute of Education, BFI, 1984.

> Schiller's work should be more widely known amongst media teachers than it currently appears to be. His is perhaps the most urgent and important voice in the field of communications policy coming out of the United States at the moment. Schiller argues that current emphases upon the spread of communications technology, the privatisation of information, and the doctrine of the 'free flow' of information have powerful ideological importance in spreading capitalist values and structures throughout the world. They are crucially important weapons of American dominance. Schiller argues that these trends are going largely unchallenged, and urges the development of national communications policies to counteract the pervasive influence of transnational capitalist conglomerates.

Schlesinger, P., Murdock, G. and Elliott, P.
Televising 'Terrorism', Comedia, 1983.

> Important survey of coverage of terrorism in factual and fictional television programmes. Very good on the relationship between the media and the State, and on the divergencies in perspective between different television forms.

*Schlesinger, P.
Putting 'Reality' Together, Constable, 1978.

> Detailed, intelligent and clearly written sociological study of BBC News. Contains a chapter on *The Reporting of Northern Ireland*. The best study currently available in the well researched field of broadcast news. Essential reading.

*Scottish Council for Education Technology and the Scottish Film Council.
Media Education in Scotland, SCET and SFC, 1979.

> Excellent discussion document outlining the theoretical basis of Media Studies in schools and colleges, and outlining curricular aims in the Primary School, early secondary, later secondary, Further Education and Community Education, and Teacher Education, with additional sections on Resources and Resource Organisation, and Assessment. Recommended for any teacher about to set up a Media Studies syllabus at whatever educational level.

Screen and *Screen Education*.
SEFT, 29 Old Compton Street, London, W1V 5PN.

> These two quarterlies, published by the Society for Education in Film and Television (SEFT), recently merged into *Screen*, now published bi-monthly. The former *Screen* was principally devoted to theoretical articles on film; *Screen Education* was aimed specifically at media teachers. Below is a summary of the editions of the magazines most relevant to media education.

Screen Education No. 12 Autumn 1974.

> Special number on TV Studies.

No. 14 Spring 1975.

> Issue devoted to Media Studies — Methods and Approaches.

No. 18 Spring 1976.

> Issue on UNESCO Survey on Media Education in Europe.

No. 19 Summer 1976.

> Reflections on the past work of SEFT and the BFI Educational Advisory Services. Articles on quiz shows and football.

No. 20 Autumn 1976.

> Special issue on *The Sweeney*.

No. 21. Winter 1976/77.

> Issue on Practical Work in TV/Media Studies.

No. 22 Spring 1977.

> Issue on Popular Culture and Education.

No. 34 Spring 1980.
Issue on Popular Culture and Cultural Studies.
No. 35 Summer 1980.
Issue on Television Drama.
No. 36 Autumn 1980.
Issue on The Politics of Representation.
No. 37 Winter 1980/81.
Contains two excellent papers on Media coverage of the Iranian Embassy Siege by Schlesinger, and Bazalgette and Paterson.
No. 38 Spring 1981.
Issue on Media Pedagogies.
No. 40 Autumn/Winter 1981/2.
Articles on representations of law and disorder, and on media pedagogy.
No. 41 Winter/Spring 1982.
Papers on Quiz Shows and Popular Culture.
Screen

Vol. 19 No. 4 Winter 1978/9	Papers on the World Cup and sit-com.
Vol. 20 Nos. 3/4 Winter 1979/80	Stuart Hood and Brecht on Radio. John Wyver on Channel 4.
Vol. 21 No. 3 1980	John Caughie on Documentary Drama
Vol. 21 No. 4 1980/81	Papers on Channel Four and British TV Today.
Vol. 22 No. 2 1981	Papers on documentary and comedy.
Vol. 22 No. 4 1981	TV Issue.

Screen (incorporating Screen Education)

Vol. 23 No. 1 May/June 1982	Papers on classic serials, *The History Man*, and photo-history.
Vol. 24 No. 1 Jan/Feb 1983	Issue on *Reflections on Television*.
Vol. 24 No. 3 May/June 1983	Issue on *Teaching Film, and TV*.
Vol. 24 No. 4/5 July–Oct 83	Papers on Channel 4, the Single Play, and *Brookside*.
Vol. 24 No. 6 Nov–Dec 1983	Excellent article by David Lusted on Press reactions to DES document *Popular TV and Schoolchildren*. Ian Connell on Commercial Broadcasting and the British Left.
Vol. 25 No. 1 Jan–Feb 1984	Articles on TV melodrama, soaps and serials.
Vol. 25 No. 2 March–April 1984	Issue on *Watching Television*.
Vol. 25 No. 3 May–June 1984	Issue on *Sound*.
Vol. 25 Nos. 4–5 July–Oct 1984	Double issue on various aspects of film and TV.
Vol. 25 No. 6 Nov–Dec 1984	Issue on Independent Film.
Vol. 26 No. 1 June–Feb 1985	On British Cinema.
Vol. 26 No. 2 March–April 1985	On TV and video.

Sendall, B.
Independent Television in Britain, Vol. 1:*Origin and Foundation 1946–62*; Vol. 2: *Expansion and Change, 1958–68*. Macmillan, 1982.
First two volumes of a lengthy history of Independent Television.
Seymour-Ure, C.
The Political Impact of Mass Media, Constable, 1974.
Well written study of the political effects of the mass media. Principally concerned with newspapers and including some excellent case studies (on Enoch Powell, Private Eye etc.) — good examples of the kind of original work which students might try for themselves — and a general survey of mass media coverage of general elections from 1945–70.

Seymour-Ure, C.
The Press, Politics and The Public, Methuen, 1968.
>An early academic study of the Press with sections on readership, political and legal restraints, and Lobby Correspondents and the Press Gallery.

Shubik, I.
Play For Today: The Evolution of Television Drama, David-Poynter, 1975.
>An account of the development of television drama with useful insights (not all of them intentional) into the dominant role of the producer.

Silverstone, R.
The Message of Television, Heinemann, 1981.
>Detailed analysis of the drama series, *Intimate Strangers*, in terms of myth and narrative structure. The analysis is preceded by a consideration of the most influential theories of myth and narrative.

Smith, A.
British Broadcasting, David and Charles, 1974.
>Valuable source of important documents in the history of broadcasting, including Acts of Parliament, codes of practice and key statements by broadcasters and politicians.

Smith, A. (ed.).
The British Press Since the War, David and Charles, 1974.
>Invaluable collection of source materials on the British Press since the war. Covers finance and ownership in Fleet Street, the Press and the Law, the Principles and Practice of the Press, and Newspapers and Workers' Participation.

Smith, A.
The Geopolitics of Information, Faber and Faber, 1980.
>Gives the historical background and the contemporary arguments on the North-South 'cultural domination' debate. Covers unequal news flow, the swamping of traditional cultures, Third World media stereotyping, and the difficulties of control.

Smith, A.
The Newspaper, Thames and Hudson, 1979.
>Glossy international history of newspapers, profusely illustrated.

Smith, A.
The Politics of Information, Macmillan, 1978.
>Collection of short papers on a wide range of issues and topics relating to broadcasting and the press. Useful contributions on Television Coverage of the 1974 election, Television coverage of Northern Ireland, and News Values.

Smith, A.
The Shadow in the Cave, Quartet, 1976.
>Lengthy study of broadcasting structures in Britain, USA, France, Japan and Holland. Chapter Three deals with news presentations.

Smith, A.
Telecommunications and the Press, Post Office Corporation, 1977.
>Short research report commissioned by the Post Office explaining the impact of telecommunications upon print. The main recommendation is 'that the new means should not be used to shore up . . . otherwise decaying structures, though it should not either be used deliberately to destabilize healthy print media'.

Smith, A. (ed.).
Television and Political Life, Macmillan, 1979.
>Six essays by different authors on the relationship between political broadcasters and the state in six countries. Smith himself makes the British contribution.

Smith, A.C.H.
Paper Voices:The Popular Press and Social Change 1935–65, Chatto and Windus, 1974.
>Detailed study of the *Daily Express* and *Daily Mirror* up to 1965.

*Smythe, D.
Dependency Road, Ablex, 1981.

Still little known in Britain, this is one of the few seminal books to have been written on the media over the past few years. Though chiefly a study of Canada's cultural dependency on American mass communications, *Dependency Road* is excellent on the media as Consciousness Industry, the audience as commodity, the centrality of advertising within modern media, media imperialism and media economics.

Sontag, S.
On Photography, Penguin, 1979.

Essays demonstrating how the authority of photography in increasing understanding and conveying truth is spurious.

*Spiegl, F.
Keep Taking the Tabloids, Pan, 1983.

Funny and comprehensive anatomy of tabloid clichés and language. A useful stimulus for classroom work.

Startline.
The Published material of the Schools Council Moral Education 8–13 Project, Longmans/Schools Council, 1978.

The Startline materials contain large numbers of excellent photographs and posters, designed 'to increase children's awareness of the verbal and non-verbal aspects of behaviour' and 'to heighten their perception and sensitivity to other people's needs, attitudes and feelings'. Although intended for 8–13 year old pupils, the materials represent a rich resource for studying non-verbal communication at any educational level. The suggested activities and games relating to the material are imaginative and appealing.

Stearn, G.E. (ed.).
McLuhan Hot and Cold, Penguin, 1968.

A 'critical symposium' on McLuhan's work with interesting contributions from Tom Wolfe, Raymond Williams, George Steiner and Susan Sontag.

Swallow, N.
Factual Television, Focal Press, 1966.

Straightforward professional account of television news, documentary, current affairs, magazine programmes, etc. by a producer. Raises a number of issues, but there is little incisive critical discussion.

Taylor, A.J.P.
Beaverbrook, Hamish Hamilton, 1972.

Definitive and monumental biography of Beaverbrook. Long, but readable, and historically impressive.

*Taylor, R.L.
Art, an Emeny of the People, Harvester, 1978.

Brilliant polemic against culture — 'a confidence trick practised on the masses' — and the concept of 'art', whether bourgeois or revolutionary proletarian. Argues that art ('an invention of the aristocracy') has been tied to the development of the bourgeoisie and that it is not a value which is objectively determinable. Contains an excellent discussion of the concept of revolutionary proletarian art, and ends with an analysis of the movement to include jazz within the category of art.

Thomas, H.
With an Independent Air, Wiedenfeld and Nicholson, 1977.

First-hand account of the development of commercial television by one of its top executives. Engagingly written, but with little questioning of the triviality of much of the output he describes.

Thompson, D. (ed.).
Discrimination and Popular Culture, Penguin, 1964.

Influential collection of essays commissioned as a result of the important NUT Conference on *Popular Culture and Personal Responsibility* in 1960. The essays attempt, not entirely successfully, to discrimninate between the trivial and the worthwhile within popular culture, generally through applying fairly traditional criteria of evaluation. The collection is now largely of historic interest, though the attitudes and arguments they embody still linger on.

Thompson, J.O. (ed.).
Monty Python: Complete and Utter Theory of the Grotesque, BFI, 1982.

A 'dossier' containing interviews with members of the *Python* team, reviews of their work, and extracts on the grotesque.

Tinker, J.
The Television Barons, Quartet, 1980.

Inside stories about Grade, Bernstein, Frost, et al. Interesting, gossipy but with little analysis.

Took, B.
Laughter in the Air, Robson/BBC, 1976.

'An informal history of British Radio Comedy' from 1922 to the present day, which contains extracts from the scripts of numerous shows. Useful background reading for pupils studying broadcast comedy.

Tracey, M.
The Production of Political Television Routledge, 1978.

A study of the determinants of political television is followed by a pot-pourri of case studies on the General Strike and the BBC, the retiring of Sir Hugh Greene, the *Yesterday's Men* affair, and ATV's coverage of the 1974 General Election.

TUC — *How to Handle the Media*, TUC 1979.
TUC — *A Cause for Concern*, TUC, 1979.
TUC — *Behind the Headlines*, TUC, 1980.

Three useful booklets produced by the TUC as a result of their concern with media coverage of trade unionists and industrial relations. *How to Handle the Media* is a guide for trade unionists, *A Cause for Concern* examines media coverage of industrial disputes, and *Behind the Headlines* puts the basic case for Trade Union dissatisfaction with the media, stressing particularly the lack of pluralism and accountability in media ownership and control.

Troyna, B.
Public Awareness and the Media: A Study of Reporting on Race, Commission for Racial Equality, 1981.

Research study on the reporting of racial issues in the press from 1976–8, and on local radio in Leicester and Manchester, together with an assessment of their effects upon social attitudes.

Tucker, N.
Understanding the Mass Media, Cambridge University Press, 1966.

'A practical approach' to media teaching, this is another book stimulated by the 1960 NUT Conference. Contains chapters on the Press, Advertising, Film, Television, and Magazines and Music. Sensitively written, but operating within the discriminatory paradigm prevalent in the 1960's.

Tulloch, J. and Alvarado, M.
Dr. Who: The Unfolding Text, Macmillan, 1983.

Detailed study of the long-running series based on interviews with artists, and production staff involved with the series since 1963. Examines *Dr. Who* as 'a very complex and dense text', and as commodity.

Tumber, H.
Television and the Riots, BFI, 1982.

Short research report on television coverage of the urban riots in Britain in the summer of 1981. Argues that there is no convincing evidence that TV produced a 'copy-cat' effect which incited further violence by projecting images of the riots.

Tunstall, J.
Journalists at Work , Constable, 1971.

Sociological study of specialist correspondents — aviation, football, fashion, education etc. — based on interviews and questionnaires on career structures, political affiliations, domestic backgrounds, relationships with competitors etc.

Tunstall, J.
The Media are American, Constable, 1977.

Wide ranging historical survey of the international flow of communications. Rejects any simple notions of 'media imperialism'.

*Tunstall, J.
The Media in Britain, Constable, 1983.
> A very useful source of information on the British media. Surprisingly weak in its discussion of issues, however.

Tunstall, J. (ed.).
Media Sociology: A Reader, Constable, 1970.
> Curiously dated collection of essays. The best contributions are by Burns, and Galtung and Ruge.

Tunstall, J.
The Westminster Lobby Correspondents, RKP, 1970.
> Sociological study of Lobby correspondents — their relationships with each other, their employers, and their news sources; their working conditions; political opinions etc. Interesting on the competing demands, within the job, of publicity and secrecy.

*UNESCO
Media Education, UNESCO, 1984.
> Collection of essays on developments in media education around the world.

Unwin, R.
The Visual Dimension in the Study and Teaching of History, The Historical Association, 1981.
> Stresses the importance of understanding visual evidence in history. Advocates the study of photographs, cartoons, paintings, caricatures, and visual 'strips' (such as the Bayeux Tapestry) in history and demonstrates the importance of all students acquiring visual literacy in making sense of these media across the curriculum.

Vaughan, D.
Television Documentary Usage, British Film Institute Television Monograph No. 6, BFI, 1976.
> Written by someone who has worked extensively within the medium, 'this monograph is more an autobiography than a work of research'. Difficult going at times but some useful material on the working assumptions of documentary practice and on the pervasiveness of 'mannerism' — the attempt by film to approximate to the condition of verbal prose.'

Waites, B., Bennett, T. and Martin, G. (eds).
Popular Culture: Past and Present, Croom Helm and The Open University Press, 1982.
> Open University reader on historical approaches to different aspects of popular culture (cinema, football, broadcasting, science fiction, motor-bike culture etc.).

Walker, M.
Powers of the Press, Quartet, 1982.
> A study of twelve 'great newspapers' (including *The Times*), their histories, finances, policies and ways of working. Ends with a case-study of how each newspaper covered events in Iran from 1971 to the fall of the Shah.

*Waterhouse, K.
Daily Mirror Style, Mirror Books, 1981.
> A critical — often appreciative — examination of the *Daily Mirror*'s 'way with words'. Sections on cliché, cross-headings, narrative structures, adjectives etc. Invaluable for any critical work on tabloids.

*Webster, F.
The New Photography, John Calder, 1980.
> Argues, with numerous examples, that training in photography needs to go beyond traditional technicist approaches and acknowledge the social and political role of photography. An excellent introduction for students to complex ideas in visual communication including the most accessible introduction to semiology currently available. Recommended.

*Webster, F.
Dangers of Information Technology and Responsibilities of Education, Faculty of Modern Studies Occasional Papers No. 2, Oxford Polytechnic, 1985.

Accessible and devastating critique of the uncritical acceptance of Information Technology by the British educational system. Highly recommended.

Wedell, E.G.

Broadcasting and Public Policy, Michael Joseph, 1968.

Inevitably dated examination of the relationship of broadcasting to public policy. Looks at how the broadcasting media operate, how their institutional forms influence the programmes they produce, and the kinds of choices open to the public. Still of some value for its information on the role of controllers and producers.

Wesker, A.

Journey into Journalism, Writers and Readers, 1977.

A personal account of life and work at *The Sunday Times*. Useful as background reading.

Whale, J.

The Half Shut Eye, Macmillan, 1969.

Anecdotes on television coverage of politics in Britain and the USA in the 1960's. Some insights into news, interviews, political constraints upon broadcasting, and the coverage of elections and party conferences. Little is provided in the way of any theoretical framework.

Whale, J.

Journalism and Government, Macmillan, 1972.

General 'inside' account from a journalist on how journalists work, and particularly on their relationship with politicians.

Whale, J.

The Politics of the Media, Fontana, 1977.

An insufferably patronising study of the media. Argues the case for consumer sovereignty — the media are as they are because 'most people's minds are lazy, capricious, shy of abstract ideas mildly prurient and soon bored'. The influence of advertising is 'trivial'; 'the press is predominantly conservative in tone because its readers are'; 'Businessmen . . . still seem to like owning newspapers . . . the spirit of public service never wholly dies' etc. The book offers as insights — there is no real analysis — every conceivable establishment myth about the press, broadcasting and the nature of the audience.

Whannel, G.

Blowing the Whistle, Pluto Press, 1983.

A rare study of socialist perspectives on sport. Provides alternative ways of understanding sport from the dominant paradigms projected by the media, and there are useful discussions on such issues as sponsorship, finance, and politics in sport, which have a direct relevance to the presentation of sport in the media.

White, D.M.

'The Gatekeeper': A Case-Study in the selection of News', *Journalism Quarterly* Vol. 27, 1950.

Influential American study of the news choices of a newspaper's telegraph editor. Shows how subjective, how much based on the gatekeeper's attitudes and experiences, the communication of news really is.

*Whitaker, B.

News Limited, Minority Press Group, 1981.

Not as widely known as it ought to be, *News Limited* is a short but trenchant critique of the newspaper industry by a practising radical journalist. Excellent on the working practices of journalists, the management of news by sources, and news values. Also presents a number of case studies of alternative journalistic practice from the *Liverpool Free Press*.

Widdowson, P. (ed.).

Re-Reading English, Methuen, 1982.

An important collection of essays by English specialists on the crisis in English Studies. Relevant to media studies since many of the debates about nature of English Studies, and literary criticism in particular, have their origins in recent developments in the fields of media and cultural studies.

Wiegand, P.
A Biased View, University of London Institute of Education, 1982.
> Excellent short paper on how photographs can be a source of bias in geography. Points the way to the development of a media education within geography.

*Williams, C. (ed.).
Realism and the Cinema: A Reader (BFI Readers in Film Studies), RKP and BFI, 1980.
> An indispensable collection of key texts on realism, which is relevant to the student of television as well as the cinema. The extracts are linked by a contextualising and critical commentary and cover the historical development of realist positions, a detailed critical case-study of the work of Flaherty, questions of style and ideology, and the ways in which specific film techniques have been associated with particular kinds of realism. The collection as a whole clarifies and gives a historical perspective on some of the most important political and aesthetic questions of the day in relation to film and TV.

Williams, R.
Communications, Penguin, 1962. Revised 1968.
> Inevitably dated in the information it presents, *Communications* nevertheless contains useful material on newspaper content, discussion of a number of media controversies (high and low culture; the media and violence; media paternalism), and a final chapter on proposals for media reform which are still worth noting.

Williams, R.
The Country and the City, Chatto and Windus, 1973.
> Scholarly study of the myths surrounding the countryside and the city in literature and society. The ideologies and values discussed continue to have great relevance to the symbolic resonances which urban and rural landscapes possess within popular culture.

*Williams, R.
Keywords, Fontana, 1976.
> An essential source. Culture, Art, Media, Mediation, Ideology, Hegemony, Standards, Taste, Sensibility and Image are just a few of the words whose derivations, development and modern meanings are explored in depth.

Williams, R.
The Long Revolution, Pelican, 1965.
> Contains important historical accounts of *The Growth of the Popular Press* and *The Growth of the Reading Public*.

Williams, R.
Television: Technology and Cultural Form, Fontana, 1974.
> Examines technology and social change, the characteristic 'forms' of television and the concept of 'planned flow' ('The defining characteristic of broadcasting') with an original and useful analysis of television in terms of its flow rather than its discrete programme units.

Williamson, J.
Decoding Advertisements, Marion Boyars, 1978.
> Important and intelligently written analysis of a large number of advertisements using semiological, Freudian, and post-Freudian psychological approaches to uncover their ideological work.

Wills, J.D.
Television and Political Education, unpublished MA thesis, University of York, 1977.
> Examines how television might be used in schools and colleges to increase the political awareness of young people. Contains interesting small-scale surveys of students' reactions to news and political programmes.

Wilmut, R.
From Fringe to Flying Circus, Eyre Methuen, 1980.
> Interesting history of one strand of British comedy, covering twenty years from

Beyond the Fringe to *Monty Python* via *TW3*, *The Goodies* and other shows. Includes script extracts and interviews with the personalities involved.

Wilson, H.H.
Pressure Group, Secker and Warburg, 1961.
    Detailed account of the campaign to introduce commercial television. Very good on the relation of the Conservative Party to external commercial pressures.

Windschuttle, K.
The Media, Penguin, Australia, 1984.
    A comprehensive critical survey of the media, and very useful for British teachers and Higher Education students, even though it deals principally with Australian media. Good on the political economy of the media, the book's besetting weakness is its tendency to crudely over-simplify theories with which it disagrees.

Winship, J.
'A Woman's World: *Woman* — an ideology of Feminity', in Women's Study Group, *Women Take Issue*, Hutchinson, and the Centre for Contemporary Cultural Studies, University of Birmingham, 1978.
    Excellent ideological analysis of *Woman* magazine.

Winston, B.
The Image of the Media, Davis-Poynter, 1973.
    A slim volume which summarises the principal issues and arguments in sociological and cultural studies of the media and then turns to information theory as 'the only approach which really talks the same language as the new media'.

Wintour, C.
Pressures on the Press, Deutsch, 1972.
    'An editor looks at Fleet Street'. Insider's account of legal, advertising, trade-union, and other pressures on newspapers. Anecdotal and readable, but as with most books produced by journalists, there is little understanding or apparent interest in the ideological role of the press.

Worsely, T.C.
Television: the Ephemeral Art, Alan Ross, 1970.
    Reviews from the 1960's, with a particular emphasis upon drama productions, by the television critic of the *Financial Times*.

Wright, A.
Local Radio and Local Democracy, IBA Fellowship Report, 1980.
    A rare study of the contribution of local radio to the political education of its listeners. Contains chapters on news, phone-ins, and coverage of election, and local politics.

Wykes, J. and Mottershead, C. (eds).
Teaching Television in the School and College Curriculum, ILEA, 1978.
    Report on the teaching of television in London schools and colleges. A brief introduction on 'Why teach about TV' is followed by a bibliography and a selection of syllabuses and papers from teachers, and finally some notes on equipment.

OFFICIAL PUBLICATIONS RELEVANT TO MEDIA EDUCATION

a) The Press

Royal Commission on the Press 1947–49. HMSO 1949.

Royal Commission on the Press 1961–62. HMSO 1962.

Royal Commission on the Press 1974–77. HMSO 1977. Cmnd. 6810

The 1974–77 Commission also published the following Research Reports and Working Papers:

Research Reports

1. *Industrial Relations in the National Newspaper Industry* presented by ACAS, 1977. Cmnd. 6680.

2. *Industrial Relations in the Provincial Newspaper and Periodical Industries* presented by ACAS, 1977. Cmnd. 6810–2.

3. *Attitudes to the Press*, 1977. Cmnd. 6810–3.

4. *Analysis of Newspaper Content* by D. McQuail, 1977.

5. *Concentration of Ownership in the Provincial Press* by N. Hartley, P. Gudgeon and R. Crafts, 1977. Cmnd. 6810–5.

6. *Periodicals and the Alternative Press*, 1977. Cmnd. 6810–6.

Working Papers

1. *New Technology and the Press* by Rex Winsbury, 1975.
   A study of the experience of the new technology in the USA.

2. *A Review of Sociological Writing on the Press* by D. McQuail, 1976.

3. *Studies on the Press* by O. Boyd-Barratt, C. Seymour-Ure, and J. Tunstall, 1977.
   Contains important material on foreign news, and science and medicine reporting, relationships between the party system and the national press, readers' letters to the press, editorial sovereignty, and industrial relations. An invaluable source.

4. *The Women's Periodical Press in Britain, 1946–76*, by Cynthia L. White, 1977.
   Useful paper on women's fiction periodicals, fashion periodicals, and general service and entertainment magazines since 1946.

b) Reports on Broadcasting in the UK

Sykes 1923

Crawford 1926

Selsdon 1935

Ullswater 1936

Beveridge	Contains a minority report advocating commercial broadcasting, 1951.
Pilkington	*Report of the Committee on Broadcasting* HMSO, 1962. Report articulating and clarifying many of the doubts felt in the early sixties about the effect of commercial broadcasting upon the general culture.
*Annan	*Report of the Committee on the Future of Broadcasting* HMSO, 1977. Obligatory reading. Its twenty-nine chapters raise almost all of the arguments and issues in current debates about broadcasting. Unfortunately, its price will put it out of the reach of most students and teachers.

c) Recent Official Publications on the New Technology

Acard (Advisory Council for Applied Research and Development), *Information Technology* HMSO, 1980.

Home Office, *Direct Broadcasting by Satellite*, HMSO, 1981.
Cabinet Office/Information Technology Advisory Panel, *Report on Cable Systems*, London, HMSO, February 1982.
Department of Industry, *The Future of Telecommunications in Britain*, London, HMSO Cmnd. 8610, July 1982.
The Report of the Inquiry into Cable Expansion and Broadcasting Policy, (Report of the Hunt Committee), London, HMSO, October 1982. Cmnd. 8679.
Home Office/Department of Industry, *The Development of Cable Systems and Services*, London, HMSO, April 1983. Cmnd. 8866.

d) *Educational Reports Making Reference to the Media and/or Media Education.*
Report on Secondary Education (The Spens Report), HMSO 1938 pp. 222–3.
An early expression of concern over the effects of the media upon pupils.
15 to 18 (The Crowther Report), HMSO, 1959, Vol. 1 paras. 510 and 66.
The first official call for an 'inoculative' media education to provide a 'counter-balancing assistance' to media influence.
Half Our Future (The Newsom Report), HMSO 1964, paras. 475–6.
An influential statement on the importance of media study which legitimised the Film Studies movement of the following decade, but may unwittingly have held back the development of television study.
A Language for Life (The Bullock Report), HMSO 1975, esp. chapter 2, para. 8 and chapter 22 para. 14.
Demonstrates the significance of television viewing in the child's experience and urges teachers to use this experience constructively in educating their pupils.
DES, *Popular TV and Schoolchildren*, DES, 1983. See bibliographic entry under DES.

APPENDIX A

RESOURCES FOR MEDIA EDUCATION

1 Bibliographical, research, and reference resources
2 Simulations
3 Photoplay materials
4 Teaching packs
5 Teacher training resource
6 Regional resource banks
7 Regional networks, groups and contacts
8 Journals and Magazines
9 Organisations with an interest in Media Education

1. BIBLIOGRAPHICAL, RESEARCH AND REFERENCE RESOURCES

a) Bibliographies

The following sources contain bibliographical material on media education and related areas:

Cooke, L. (ed.), *Media Studies Bibliography*, BFI, 1984.

A very useful guide, conveniently arranged by subject.

Lusted, D. (ed.) *Guide to Film Studies in Secondary and Further Education*, BFI, 1983.

An exemplary bibliographical guide to film studies.

British Film Institute, *Television Studies: A Select Booklist*, BFI, 1982.

Masterman, L. *Teaching About Television*, Macmillan, 1980.

Two detailed, but now somewhat dated TV Studies bibliographies.

The Bookshop at the Triangle Catalogue, Aston University, Gosta Green, Birmingham B4 7ET. (021-359-3979 extension 5359)

The most comprehensive annotated catalogue of media books and periodicals currently available. Free from the above address.

In Scotland the best selection of media books is held by the First of May Bookshop which also issues a free annotated catalogue (43 Candlemaker Row, Edinburgh EH1 2QB. Tel: 031-225-2612).

Women and the Media: A recommended reading list on Women and the Media is available from Women's Media Action, c/o A Woman's Place, Hungerford House, Victoria Embankment, London WC2 (please enclose SAE).

The Advertising Association's Information Centre issue a reading list on *Women in Advertising* (Abford House, 15 Wilton Road, London SW1V 1NJ, Tel: 01-828-2771).

The B.F.I. Education Catalogue published annually, is available free from the BFI. It contains information on all BFI Education materials, publications, slide packs and forthcoming courses and conferences. (81, Dean St. LONDON W1.)

Teaching Media Studies, (eds K. Cowle and E. Dick), The Scottish Film Council, 1984 (revised in 1985) is an excellent introductory guide to resources and methods in media education. From The Scottish Film Council, Dowanhill, 74 Victoria Crescent Road, Glasgow (Tel: 041-334-9314).

Film, TV and Video Material

A Catalogue of available visual material may be obtained from: BFI Film and Video Library, 81 Dean Street, London W1 Tel: 01-437-4355.

A list of films made by Regional Arts Associations (Regional Film Directory) is available from: West Midlands Arts, Brunswick Terrace, Stafford ST16 1BZ

b) Research Resources

Communication Research Trends: An excellent quarterly digest of recent research on different aspects of the media. Contains focussing articles, reviews of major work and lists of contacts and work in progress. Recommended as a way of keeping up-to-date with recent developments in the media. Subscriptions are £4.00 per year. Details from the Centre for the Study of Communication and Culture, 221 Goldhurst Terrace, London NW6 3EP.

Vol. 1	No 1: The Ethics of Mass Communication
(1980)	No 2: The New International Information Order
	No 3: Broadcasting Policy and Media Reform
	No 4: Bias in the News
Vol. 2	No 1: The Telematic Society
(1981)	No 2: Censorship in the Media
	No 3: Television's Influence on Cultures
	No 4: The Language of Film and Television
Vol. 3	No 1: The Challenge of Cable Television
((1982)	No 2: New Approaches to Media Education
	No 3: Critical Views of Advertising
	No 4: Secrecy, Privacy and the Right to Information
Vol. 4	No 1: Concentration of Media Ownership
(1983)	No 2: Satellites for Development, Broadcasting and Information
	No 3: Improving Children's Television
	No 4: Book Publishing in a Changing Environment
Vol. 5	No 1: Youth and Rock Music

(1984)   No 2: Communication, Technology and Culture
          No 3: Television Viewing and Family Communication
          No 4: TV as Story Telling
Vol. 6   No 1: Journalism, the Press and New Technology
(1985)

Register of Research on Mass Media and Mass Communication
A register of current media research published annually by the Centre for Mass Communication Research, University of Leicester, 104 Regent Rd, Leicester.

Social Trends, published annually by HMSO, provides up-to-date statistical information on TV viewing and radio listening, attendance at theatres and cinemas, and the reading of newspapers and magazines by social class. Issued by the Central Statistical Office.

Two periodicals are especially useful for keeping abreast of current research:
Media, Culture and Society is an invaluable source for current work on the political implications of the new technology, whilst *Media Information Australia*, though generally orientated towards Australia's media, contains excellent digests of recent books and articles, and up-to-date briefings on all aspects of the media.

Finally, a number of trade statistical and research resources (JICNARS, BRAD etc.) are listed in Chapter 4 (pp. 79–80).

c) Reference Resources
See Chapter 4 (pp. 78ff).
To these may be added
Keywords by Raymond William (see bibliography)
Key Concepts in Communication by T. O'Sullivan, J. Hartley, D. Saunders and J. Fiske (see bibliography).
BFI Film and Television Yearbook, excellent annual directory of information, resources and contacts on all aspects of film and TV.

2. SIMULATIONS

(a) Front Page:
A simulation by Kenneth Jones in which students work as sub-editorial teams for a local newspaper. Their task is to select the most important stories from those they are given (as material in an in-tray exercise), and produce appropriate headlines for them. Suitable for all ages from Primary school pupils to adults. In *Graded Simulations*. Volume One, Blackwell, 1984.

(b) Radio Covingham:
Classic simulation by Kenneth Jones in which students produce their own radio news-magazine programme from material provided in an in-tray exercise. *Radio Covingham* itself should be regarded as a basic model which

the teacher should adapt, perhaps using entirely new material, for use with her own students. In *Graded Simulations*, Volume One.

(c) Teachers' Protest:
Now somewhat dated, but still excellent material for producing a whole range of documentary-based simulations. Produced by Michael Simons, Cary Bazalgette and Andrew Bethell. Distributed by the Society for Education in Film and Television (SEFT) for the ILEA English Centre. Available from SEFT, 29 Old Compton Street, London W1V 5PL.

(d) Choosing the News:
Designing the front page of a newspaper and cropping photographs. Devised by Andrew Bethell and Michael Simons. Produced by the ILEA English Centre; distributed by SEFT (address above).

(e) The Football Game:
Editing, anchorage and montage exercises permitting multiple points of view about a football game and its surrounding activities. Includes forty transparencies of a Celtic-Aberdeen game, video material and twenty accompanying sets of the same photographs printed on separate sheets for use by individual groups. From the Scottish Film Council, 74 Victoria Crescent Road, Dowanhill, Glasgow.

(f) The Brand X Game:
The Brand X Game involves the construction of a press advert. Students select their product and target audience, and utilising the extensive photographic material and guidance information in the pack, produce the advert. Self-analysis is an integral part of the exercise. Complete with Teacher's Notes. From the Scottish Film Council (address above).

(g) The Baxters' Project:
How is a television advertising campaign put together and how does it work? This multi-media teaching unit takes a well known Scottish product (soup) and illustrates the demands of the client, the responses of the advertising agency, and the final results. The pack comprises video, tape/slide, photographic and print material.

(h) Television Specificity, Television News and Programme Planning Simulation are three original simulations described in my own *Teaching About Television* (see Bibliography).

(i) Crisis in Sandagua:
Simulation for upper secondary and adult groups dealing with British press coverage of Third World news. Includes ideas for preparatory and follow up work. From Development Education Project, 801 Wilmslow Road, Manchester M20 8RG.

(j) Making the News:
A teaching pack on news produced by the Save the Children Fund and designed to encourage an understanding of developing countries in general, and Bangladesh in particular. Includes two simulations and a game which can be adapted for use with top primary pupils and upwards. Available free from The Save the Children Fund, Mary Datchelor House, 17 Grove Lane, Camberwell, London SE5 8RD.

3. PHOTOPLAY MATERIALS

There are now quite a wide variety of photographic packs available for work on narrative and montage:

The Visit:
An exercise in which students create suspense through the sequencing of single images. Produced by Andrew Bethell for the ILEA English Centre, and distributed by SEFT.

The Station:
Montage exercise requiring students to create a particular mood. Produced by the ILEA English Centre and distributed by SEFT.

Gone Fishing:
Students construct a story, play, comic strip or report from a series of photographs. Available from the ILEA English Centre, Sutherland Street, Ebury Bridge, London SW1.

The Fairground:
Students are asked to construct narratives from different perspectives using photographs. Available from the ILEA English Centre.

The Market:
A simple framing and cropping exercise. From a single photograph students frame different detail in order to tell a story. From the ILEA English Centre. Distributed by SEFT.

4. TEACHING PACKS

(a) Starters: Teaching Television Title Sequences:
Produced by Roy Twitchin and Julian Birkett this excellent pack consists of analyses of seven title sequences from a variety of television programmes with student worksheets and accompanying slides. A videotape of the seven sequences can be hired from the British Film Institute, who also distribute the pack.

(b) Talking Pictures:
By Mike Clarke and Peter Baker, Mary Glasgow Publications, 1981. Tape-slide material containing a good deal of useful material which can be adapted for school students of all ages.

(c) Reading Pictures:
A pack from the BFI consisting of three graded exercises on image analysis. This is the first unit of the BFI Image Project, and could be used with top primary and lower secondary school pupils although it is intended for slightly older students. Consists of slides, photosheets, a student worksheet and a teacher booklet. Available from BFI.

(d) Selling Pictures:
The second unit of the BFI Image Project. This one examines the important issues of marketing images, and stereotyping. Consists of a booklet, *The Companies You Keep*, (which looks at questions of media ownership and control, and also contains some excellent material on the work of advertising agencies), a useful poster of women's magazine covers, and accompanying slides, photographs and teaching notes. Aimed at older secondary students and available from BFI.

(e) Teaching Coronation Street:
BFI pack taking up issues raised in the BFI Television Monograph on *Coronation Street* (ed. R. Dyer). Very good on the construction of narrative and character. Suitable for older secondary school students and above. Contains slides and teacher's notes. Six episodes of *Coronation Street* are available from the BFI Film and Video Library.

(f) Swallow Your Leader:
Produced by Cary Bazelgette for the ILEA English Centre. Documentary pack consisting of slides, student information sheets, teacher's notes and sound-track extracts. Distributed by SEFT.

(g) Teaching TV News:
Very useful pack on beginning TV news analysis. Contains videotape and slide material, exercises for students and teacher's notes. Produced by and available from BFI Education Dept.

(h) Clwyd Media Materials:
A series of pupil booklets and accompanying materials for GCSE courses in Media, and third year secondary 'Media Within English' modules. Booklets are available on The Press, The News, *Coronation Street*, Early Cinema, The Western, Video in the Classroom, Hitchcock, Teenage Magazines, Film Narrative, etc. Available from Chris Points and Linda McIver, Clwyd Media Studies Unit, Centre for Educational Technology, Civic Centre, Mold, Clwyd. (Tel: 0352 55105).

(i) Understanding Breakfast Television: By Len Masterman and Paul Kiddey.
Resources and ideas for teaching about Breakfast TV. Useful on the origins of Breakfast TV in Britain and on the influence of advertisers. From MK Media Press, May Cottage, Toad Lane, Elston, Newark, Notts. Price £2.25.

(j) Hazell Meets The First Eleven:
Study unit on one of the best programmes from the *Hazell* series (Thames). A videotape of the programme is available for hire from the BFI Film & Video Library. The Unit consists of a large number of slides, teaching notes and other documentation on the series. From the British Film Institute. Inevitably now somewhat dated.

(k) The Semiology of the Image: By Guy Gauthier, 1976.
Worth mentioning as one of the first available packs exploring the semiology of the image. Needs adapting for use with school students. Most of the images are taken from non-British sources (principally France and the USA). Available from SEFT.

(l) King's Royal:
How one episode of a BBC Scotland Television Drama is produced with a comparison between the book and the teleplay, interviews with cast and crew, student projects and teacher's notes. Price £3.00 plus a blank 30 minutes VHS video tape. From the Scottish Film Council.

(m) Front Page News, ILEA English Centre, (Sutherland Street, Ebury Bridge, London SW1).
Excellent teacher and student booklets by Michael Simons, Jane Leggett et al designed to encourage the study of newspapers in the classroom. The student booklet in particular is very attractively laid out and contains some fascinating material. Recommended.

(n) Teaching TV Sitcom, BFI Education.
Very useful booklet, with slides, and videotape. Includes ideas for classroom activities, as well as analyses of particular sitcom episodes, and a good deal of resource material.

(o) The Stars: Teachers' Study Guide 1 by Richard Dyer, BFI.
A teaching handbook for star study based on Dyer's earlier book on *Stars* (see bibliography). It contains a substantial section on the content of star study, and a detailed resource list including examples of course materials and syllabuses.

(p) Star Dossier One: Marilyn Monroe compiled by Richard Dyer, BFI.
A fascinating compilation of slides and print materials on Monroe with an expert guide to the materials by Dyer.

(q) Picture Stories by Yvonne Davies, edited by Cary Bazalgette.
A variety of simple exercises and photographs for studying images in primary schools. Notable as one of the few available resources specifically designed for the primary school. Produced and distributed by BFI.

(r) Ilford Manual on Classroom Photography:
An excellently produced resource full of ideas for working with 'light sensitive materials', particularly in the primary school classroom. Available from Ilford Classroom Manual, P.O. Box 21, Southall, Middlesex UB2 4AB (£8.50).

5. TEACHER TRAINING RESOURCE

Media Kids O.K.? by Paul Merrison.
Excellent videotape and accompanying notes showing how much of the simulation and other teaching material currently available was successfully adapted for use in the primary school. Also contains many other original ideas for practical work. The emphasis is upon developing critical awareness through practical activities. An extremely useful resource for teacher training and INSET work. Available from the Centre for Educational Technology, Knighton Fields, Herrick Road, Leicester.

6. REGIONAL RESOURCE BANKS

Resource banks of teaching materials and information on Media Education are available for consultation at the following centres:

Berkshire:	South Hill Park Arts Centre
	Bracknell
	Berkshire (0344 427272)
Birmingham:	Dawlish Road Teachers' Centre
	Selly Oak
	Birmingham
	B29 6BW (021 4728108)
Dover:	Kent Educational TV Centre
	Barton Road
	Dover (0304 202827)
Leicester:	Leicestershire Media Education Project
	Centre for Educational Technology
	Herrick Road
	Leicester (0533 706906)
Northampton:	Arts Centre
	College of Further Education
	Booth Lane South
	Northampton
	NN3 3RF (0604 403322)
Nottingham:	Resources Centre
	School of Education
	University of Nottingham
	University Park
	Nottingham
	NG7 2RD (0602 506101)
Sheffield:	Melbourne House Teachers' Centre
	5 Melbourne Avenue
	Sheffield (0742 663163)

7. REGIONAL NETWORKS, GROUPS AND CONTACTS:

At the time of writing (mid-1985), a de-centralised federal structure of regional development groups for media education has already been established in Scotland, and is beginning to emerge in England, Wales and Ireland. Contacts for further information:

Avon Media Teachers
Andy Freeman
The Ridings High School
Winterbourne
Bristol
BS17 1JL

Bedfordshire MEI (Media
  Education Initiative)
Nick Jemmett
Hastingbury School
Hill Rise
Kempston
Bedford

Berkshire
Dave Stewart
Film & Video Education
  Officer
South Hill Arts Centre
Bracknell
Berks

Bradford
Dave Richards
National Museum of
  Photography
Princes View
Bradford
BD5 0TR

Humberside
Paul Kelley
75 Mill Road
Cleethorpes
DN35 8JB

*Kent Media Studies
  Association*
John Hole
Kent Educational TV
  Centre
Barton Road
Dover, Kent

*Leicester Media
  Education Project*
Mike Clarke
Leicestershire Centre for
  Educational Technology
Herrick Road
Leicester
LE2 6DJ

*Media Education
  Initiatives — Merseyside*
Adrian Bailey
25 Lucerne Street
Aigburth
Liverpool
L17 8XT

Norfolk MEI
Kingsley Canham
Cinema City
St Andrews Street
Norwich
NR2 4A9

*North East Communi-
  cations Teachers'
  Association*
Frank Turns
TVEI Resource Centre
Thorny Close School
Telford Road
Sunderland
SR3 4EN

*Media Education
  Initiative (North West)*
Tim Wall
Accrington & Rossendale
  College
Sandy Lane
Accrington
Lancs
BB5 2AW

Northamptonshire
Martin Ayres
Film Education Officer
Arts Centre
College of FE
Booth Lane South
Northampton
NN3 3RF

Nottingham
Len Masterman
School of Education
University of Nottingham
University Park
Nottingham
NG7 2RD

Oxfordshire
Lynne Fradlund
Oxford Film Workshop
The Stables
North Place
Headington
Oxford

Sheffield
Christine Grant
Earl Marshall Campus
Earl Marshall Road
Sheffield
S4 8LA

South West MEI
Richard Hopper
South Devon College
Newton Road
Torquay
Devon

Suffolk MEI
Christine Beckingham
11 Rozlyne Close
Oulton Road
Lowestoft
Suffolk

Surrey MEI
Margaret Taylor
Magna Carta School
Thorpe Road
Staines
Surrey

Wales

South Wales
Tim O'Sullivan
Dept. of Behavioural and
    Communication Studies
Polytechnic of Wales
Pontypridd
Mid Glamorgan
CF37 1DL

North Wales
Chris Points and Linda
    McIver
Clwyd Centre for
    Educational Technology
County Civic Centre
Mold
Clwyd
CH7 1YA

Ireland
Martin McLoone
Education Officer
Irish Film Institute
65 Harcourt Street
Dublin 2

Northern Ireland
John Hill
New University of Ulster
Coleraine
Co. Derry
Northern Ireland
BT52 1SA

Scotland

East Strathclyde
(*all Strathclyde except
    Ayr division*)
Brian MacLean
Cathkin High School
Whitlawburn
Cambuslang
Glasgow
G72 8YS

S.E. Scotland (*Lothian
    Region/The Borders*)
Julie Watt
Communications Studies
    Department
Stevenson College of FE
Bankhead Avenue
Edinburgh
EH11 4DE

Tayside
Keith Thomson
Art Department
Perth Academy
Perth
PH1 1NJ

Ayrshire
Alastair MacDonald
Greenwood Teachers'
    Centre
Dreghorn
Irvine

Grampian Region
Carol Niven
Kemnay Academy
Bremner Way
Kemnay
Inverurie
Aberdeenshire

Highland Region
Alex Gilkson
Culloden Academy
Culloden
Inverness

Fife
Dick Connor
Balwearie High School
Balwearie
Kirkcaldy
Fife
KY2 2LY

Central Scotland
Dan Macleod
Department of Film & TV
    Studies
Stirling University
Stirling

Dumfries & Galloway

Steve Megson
Kirkcudbright Academy
Kirkcudbright
DG6 4JN

8. JOURNALS AND MAGAZINES

The Media Education Journal
Twice yearly from
The Scottish Curriculum
Development Centre
Moray House College of Education
Holyrood Road
Edinburgh
EH8 8AQ

Founded in 1984 the Journal of the Association of Media Education in Scotland has quickly established itself as the best classroom-orientated publication available to media teachers in Britain. Essential reading.

published by Comedia

Media, Culture and Society
School of Communication
Polytechnic of Central London
18–22 Riding House Street
London
W1P 7PD

Recent issues have also established this journal as important reading for media teachers, particularly in the area of information technology, and developments in cable and satellite.

Screen
(incorporating *Screen Education*)
SEFT
29 Old Compton Street
London
W1V 5PL

Bi-monthly theoretical film and TV journal. Worth looking at, but *Screen* has always experienced difficulty in relating its concern with theoretical issues to the realities of educational practices, and remains, at the present time, very remote from the world of most media teachers.

The English Magazine
ILEA English Centre
Sutherland Street
Ebury Bridge
London
SW1

Excellent magazine for English teachers. Well abreast of most recent and interesting developments in English. Frequently carries articles on media education.

OVERSEAS JOURNALS

Metro
PO Box 222
Carlton South
Victoria 3053
Australia

The most polished and professionally produced Media Education Journal currently available. The journal of the Australian Association of Teachers of Media (ATOM). Recommended.

Media Information Australia
Research and Information
Australian Film & TV School
13–15 Lyonpark Road
North Ryde
NSW 2113
Australia

Excellent research-based yet accessible Australian quarterly on the media. A unique publication, a mine of information and excellent value for money. Strongly recommended for British libraries and media resource centres.

Critical Arts
c/o Dept of Journalism & Media
  Studies
Rhodes University
PO Box 94
Grahamstown 6140
South Africa

First class Media Studies journal
ploughing a lone progressive furrow
in South Africa.

*The Australian Journal of Screen
  Theory*
School of Drama
University of New South Wales
PO Box 1
Kensington
NSW
Australia

Theoretical journal on film and
television. Australian equivalent of
Screen.

OTHER PUBLICATIONS WITH AN INTEREST IN MEDIA AND MEDIA EDUCATION

Block
Related Studies Office
Middlesex Polytechnic
Cat Hill
East Barnet
Herts

Fine Arts and visual culture journal.

Camerawork
121 Roman Rd
London 2X 0QN

Alternative photography journal.

English in Education
49 Broomgrove Rd
Sheffield
S1O 2NA

Journal of the National Association
for the Teaching of English. Carries
occasional media education articles.

Free Press
CPBF
9 Poland Street
London
W1V 3DG

Bulletin of the campaign for Press &
Broadcasting Freedom.

Journal of Educational Television
c/o 80 Micklegate
York
YO1 1JZ

Mainly concerned with Educational
Television, but has an interest in TV
and Media Studies. Journal of the
Educational Television Association.

*Journal of Geography in Higher
  Education*
Geography Section
Faculty of Modern Studies

Is developing a strong interest in the
development of media literacy skills
in Geography.

Oxford Polytechnic
Headington
Oxford
OX3 0BP

The Media Reporter
Brennan Publications
148 Birchener Way
Allestree
Derby

Quarterly journal covering mainly journalism, but with a lively interest in media education.

Schooling and Culture
Cultural Studies Department
ILEA Cockpit Arts Workshop
Annexe
Princeton Street
London
WC1

Thematically-based arts education quarterly which frequently deals with the media.

Teaching English
Scottish Curriculum Development
   Centre
Moray House College of Education
Holyrood Road
Edinburgh
EH8 8AQ

Journal of English teachers in Scotland. Strong interest in media education.

TLK (2Teaching London Kids)
40 Hamilton Road
London
SW19

Excellent progressive educational magazine. Well informed on developments in media education.

Women's Media Action
c/o A Woman's Place
Hungerford House
Victoria Embankment
London
WC2

Bi-monthly magazine of the Women's Media Action Group.

NEWSLETTER

Initiatives
SEFT
29 Old Compton St
London
W1V 5PL

SEFT's termly national newsletter. Invaluable source of information on conferences, meetings and events. Carries articles and book reviews. Recommended.

TRADE JOURNALS

Admap
44 Earlham St
London
WC2 9LA

The best source of current ideas and thinking in the fields of advertising and marketing. Containing substantial articles and papers from conferences. Monthly.

Airwaves
IBA
70 Brompton Rd
London
SW3

Quarterly journal of the IBA. Articles on broadcasting policy and research. Freely available to schools.

Broadcast
Knightway House
20 Soho Square
London
W1V 6DT

The broadcasting industry's weekly magazine. Invaluable source of recent information and gossip.

Campaign
22 Lancaster Gate
London
W2 3LY

The advertising industry's weekly magazine. Useful articles on current campaigns.

Marketing
Marketing Publications Ltd
22 Lancaster Gate
London
W2 3LY

Weekly magazine of news and opinion on marketing with a section on media topics.

Marketing Week
60 Kingly St
London
W1R 5LH

Weekly magazine of marketing. Informative on media issues.

Media Week
Wilmington House
Church Hill
Wilmington
Dartford
Kent
DA2 7EF

Bright and breezy weekly magazine with useful feature articles and an up-to-date data section.

Mediaworld
52/53 Poland St
London W1V 3DF

Excellent monthly media magazine, particularly good on market analyses. A mine of information and ideas. Recommended.

UK Press Gazette
Bouverie Publishing Co. Ltd
244-249 Temple Chambers
Temple Avenue
London EC4 0DT

'Journalism's newspaper', published weekly. Invaluable resource for press studies.

9. Organisations with an interest in media education

Education Department
The British Film Institute
81 Dean St
LONDON W1

The Association for Media Education
in Scotland (AMES)
(see p. 331 for list of AMES Regional
development groups).

The Scottish Film Council
Dowanhill
74 Victoria Crescent Rd
GLASGOW
G12 9JN

The Irish Film Institute
65 Harcourt St
DUBLIN 2

The Society for Education in Film
and Television (SEFT)
29 Old Compton St
LONDON W1V 5PL

APPENDIX B: BRITISH PRESS CONGLOMERATES[1]

The following tables are reproduced from *Power without Responsibility* by James Curran and Jean Seaton, Methuen, 1985. Chapter Seven of this book has an excellent discussion on *The press in the age of conglomerates.*

Main British press interests	Selected other media interests	Selected non-media interests
Pergamon (Maxwell)		
Daily Mirror *Sunday Mirror* *Sunday People* *Daily Record* *Sunday Mail* (Total circulation: 11.7 million)	Central Independent TV Rediffusion Cablevision Pergamon Press International Learning Systems British Printing and Communications Corporation	E.J. Arnold (furniture) Hollis Plastics Paulton Investments Jet Ferry International (Panama) Mares Australes (Chile)
News Corporation (Murdoch)		
Sun *News of the World* *The Times* *Sunday Times* *Times Educational Supplement* (Total circulation: 10.2 million)	Satellite TV Collins (Fontana) News Group Productions (New York) Channel Ten-10 (Sydney) *Daily Sun* (Brisbane)	Ansett Transport (Australia) Santos (Natural Gas — Australia) News-Eagle (Offshore oil — Australia) Snodland Fibres Whitefriars Investment

Fleet Holdings (Matthews)	*Daily Express* *Sunday Express* *Daily Star* *The Standard* Morgan-Grampian Magazines (Total circulation: 7.1 million)	TV-AM Asian Business Press (Singapore) Specialist Publications (Hong Kong) Capital Radio	JBS Properties M G Insurance Lefpalm Ltd David McKay Inc. (USA) (Trafalgar House)[2]
Reed Group[3]	IPC Magazines IPC Business Press Berrows Newspapers (Total circulation: approx. 12 million)[4]	Fleetway Publications (USA) Hamlyn Books Anglia TV A & W Publishers Inc. (USA) Européenne de Publications SA (France)	Crown Paints Maybank/Krever International (Bahamas) Reed Finance (South Africa) Reed Consolidated Industries (Australia) Consolidated Industries Holdings (Zimbabwe)
Associated Newspapers (Rothermere)	*Daily Mail* *Mail on Sunday* *Weekend* Northcliffe Newspapers Associated South Eastern Newspapers (Total circulation: 5.3 million)	London Broadcasting Company Herald-Sun TV (Australia) Plymouth Sound Wyndham Theatres Harmsworth House Pub. (USA)	Blackfriars Oil (North Sea) Bouverie Investments (Canada) Burton Reproduction GmbH (W. Germany) Transport Group Holdings Jetlink Ferries
International Thomson Organization (Thomson)[5]	Thomson Regional Newspapers *Scotsman* Northwood Publications Whitehorn Press Standbrook Publications Illustrated Newspapers (Total circulation:	Thomas Nelson Michael Joseph Radio Forth Thomson Publications (South Africa) Thomson Communications (Denmark)	Thomson North Sea Thomson Holidays Rym SA (Tunisia) Britannia Airways International Thomson Organisation — Canada (parent company)

Pearson Longman (Cowdray)	Westminster Press group *Financial Times* *The Economist* *Northern Echo* *(Total circulation: 1.8 million)*	Longman Penguin Goldcrest Films Yorkshire TV Viking (USA) Morie Channel	Midhurst Corporation (USA) Whitehall Mining (Canada) Lazard Bros Royal Doulton Tableware Camco Inc. (USA)
British Electric Traction[3]	Argus Newspapers Illustrated Publications Model and Allied Publications Industrial Newspapers Electrical Press *(Total circulation: 1.4 million)*	Capital Radio Thames Television Reditune GmbH (W. Germany) Communication Channels Inc. (USA)	Eddison Plant BET Investments (property) United Freight Holdings (Australia) United Passenger Transport (South Africa) Almana-Boulton (Qatar)
Lonrho (Rowland)	*Observer* George Outram and Co. Scottish and Universal Newspapers *(Total circulation: 1.3 million)*	Radio Clyde Border TV Radio Ltd (Zambia) Times Newspapers (Zambia) Gramma Records (Zimbabwe)	Whyte and Mackay Distillers Firsteel Group Consolidated Holdings (Kenya) Construction Associated (Zimbabwe) HCC Investments (South Africa)

Sources: Who Owns Whom 1983; Company Reports; Audit Bureau of Circulation (1983); Press Council; Independent Broadcasting Authority.

Notes: [1]All circulation figures exclude freesheets and controlled circulation magazines. [2]Now an associated company, formerly the conglomerate parent company. [3]No dominant shareholder. [4]Excluding circulation of trade, technical and professional publications. [5]Not including North American chain of TV, radio and press interests.

APPENDIX C

UNESCO Declaration on Media Education

This declaration was issued unanimously by the representatives of 19 nations at UNESCO's 1982 International Symposium on Media Education at Grunwald, Federal Republic of Germany. It is reproduced here since media teachers may well find it useful to quote or cite in preparing rationales, justifications or explanatory documents relating to media education.

'We live in a world where media are omnipresent: an increasing number of people spend a great deal of time watching television, reading newspapers and magazines, playing records and listening to the radio. In some countries, for example, children already spend more time watching television that they do attending school.

'Rather than condemn or endorse the undoubted power of the media, we need to accept their significant impact and penetration throughout the world as an established fact, and also appreciate their importance as an element of culture in today's world. The role of communication and media in the process of development should not be underestimated, nor the function of media as instruments for the citizen's active participation in society. Political and educational systems need to recognise their obligations to promote in their citizens a critical understanding of the phenomena of communication.

'Regrettably most informal and non-formal educational systems do little to promote media education or education for communication. Too often the gap between the educational experience they offer and the real world in which people live is disturbingly wide. But if the arguments for media education as a preparation for responsible citizenship are formidable now, in the very near future with the development of communication technology such as satellite broadcasting, two-way cable systems, television data systems, video cassette and disc materials, they ought to be irresistible, given the increasing degree of choice in media consumption resulting from these developments.

'Responsible educators will not ignore these developments, but will work alongside their students in understanding them and making sense of such consequences as the rapid development of two-way communication and the ensuing individualisation and access to information.

'This is not to underestimate the impact on cultural identity of the flow of information and ideas between cultures by the mass media.

'The school and the family share the responsibility of preparing the young person for living in a world of powerful images, words and sounds. Children and adults need to be literate in all three of these symbolic systems, and this will require some reassessment of educational priorities.

Such a reassessment might well result in an integrated approach to the teaching of language and communication.

'Media education will be most effective when parents, teachers, media personnel and decision-makers all acknowledge they have a role to play in developing greater critical awareness among listeners, viewers and readers. The greater integration of educational and communications systems would undoubtedly be an important step towards more effective education.

'We therefore call upon the competent authorities to:
1. initiate and support comprehensive media education programs — from pre-school to university level, and in adult education — the purpose of which is to develop the knowledge, skills and attitudes which will encourage the growth of critical awareness and, consequently, of greater competence among the users of electronic and print media. Ideally, such programs should include the analysis of media products, the use of media as means of creative expression, and effective use of and participation in available media channels;
2. develop training courses for teachers and intermediaries both to increase their knowledge and understanding of the media and train them in appropriate teaching methods, which would take into account the already considerable but fragmented acquaintance with media already possessed by many students;
3. stimulate research and development activities for the benefit of media education, from such domains as psychology, sociology, and communication science;
4. support and strengthen the actions undertaken or envisaged by U.N.E.S.C.O. and which aim at encouraging international cooperation in media education.'

Grunwald, Federal Republic of Germany, 22 January 1982

Other titles from Comedia

No. 29 **WHAT A WAY TO RUN A RAILROAD** – An analysis of radical failure by Charles Landry, David Morley, Russell Southwood and Patricia Wright.
£2.50

No. 28 **FOURTH RATE ESTATE** — An anatomy of Fleet Street by Tom Baistow
£3.95 paper, £10.50 hardback

No. 27 **THE YEARS OF THE WEEK** by Patricia Cockburn
£6.95 paper only

No. 26 **TEACHING THE MEDIA** by Len Masterman
£5.95 paper, £12.00 hardback

No. 25 **MAKING SENSE OF THE MEDIA** — A 10-part media studies course by Holly Goulden, John Hartley and Tim O'Sullivan
£25 paper only

No. 24 **TELEVISION MYTHOLOGIES — Stars, Shows and Signs** edited by Len Masterman
£3.95 paperback, £10.50 hardback

No. 23 **COMMUNITY, ART AND THE STATE — a different prescription** by Owen Kelly
£3.95 paperback, £10.50 hardback

No. 22 **READING BY NUMBERS — contemporary publishing and popular fiction** by Ken Worpole
£3.95 paperback, £10.50 hardback

No. 21 **INTERNATIONAL IMAGE MARKETS — in search of an alternative perspective** by Armand Mattelart, Michele Mattelart and Xavier Delcourt
£4.95 paperback, £12.00 hardback

No. 20 **SHUT UP AND LISTEN: Women and local radio — a view from the inside** by Helen Baehr and Michele Ryan
£1.95 paperback only

No. 19 **THE BRITISH MEDIA: A guide for 'O' and 'A' level students** by Moyra Grant
£1.25 paperback only

No. 18   **PRESS, RADIO AND TELEVISION — An introduction to the media**
edited by David Morley and Brian Whitaker
£1.80 paperback only
Published jointly with the Workers Educational Association

No. 17   **NINETEEN EIGHTY-FOUR in 1984: Autonomy, Control and
Communication** edited by Crispin Aubrey and Paul Chilton
£3.95 paperback, £10.50 hardback

No. 16   **TELEVISING 'TERRORISM': Political violence in Popular culture** by
Philip Schlesinger, Graham Murdock and Philip Elliott
£4.95 paperback, £12.00 hardback

No. 15   **CAPITAL: Local Radio and Private Profit** by Local Radio Workshop
£3.95 paperback, £10.50 hardback

No. 14   **NOTHING LOCAL ABOUT IT: London's local radio** by Local Radio
Workshop
£3.95 paperback, £10.50 hardback

No. 13   **MICROCHIPS WITH EVERYTHING: The consequences of information
technology** edited by Paul Sieghart
£3.95 paperback, £9.50 hardback
Published jointly with the Institute of Contemporary Arts

No. 12   **THE WORLD WIRED UP — Unscrambling the new communications
puzzle** by Brian Murphy
£3.50 paperback, £9.50 hardback

No. 11   **WHAT'S THIS CHANNEL FO(U)R? An alternative report** edited by
Simon Blanchard and David Morley
£3.50 paperback, £9.50 hardback

No. 10   **IT AIN'T HALF RACIST, MUM — Fighting racism in the media** edited
by Phil Cohen
£2.95 paperback, £7.50 hardback
Published jointly with the Campaign Against Racism in the Media

No. 9   **NUKESPEAK — The media and the bomb** edited by Crispin Aubrey
£2.50 paperback, £7.50 hardback

No. 8   **NOT THE BBC/IBA — The case for community radio** by Simon
Partridge
£1.95 paperback, £5.00 hardback

No. 7   **CHANGING THE WORLD — The printing industry in transition** by
Alan Marshall
£3.50 paperback, £9.50 hardback

No. 6　**THE REPUBLIC OF LETTERS — WORKING-class writing and local publishing** edited by David Morley and Ken Worpole
£3.95 paperback, £8.50 hardback

No. 5　**NEWS LTD — Why you can't read all about it** by Brian Whitaker
£3.95 paperback, £9.50 hardback

No. 4　**ROLLING OUR OWN — Women as printers, publishers and distributors** by Eileen Cadman, Gail Chester, Agnes Pivot
£2.25 paperback only

No. 3　**THE OTHER SECRET SERVICE — Press distribution and press censorship** by Liz Cooper, Charles Landry and Dave Berry
£1.20, paperback only

No. 2　**WHERE IS THE OTHER NEWS — The news trade and the radical press** by Dave Berry, Liz Cooper and Charles Landry
£2.75 paperback only

No. 1　**HERE IS THE OTHER NEWS — Challenges to the local commercial press** by Crispin Aubrey, Charles Landry and David Morley
£2.75 paperback only